How employable will you be when you graduate from your business and management degree? How can you ensure that your time as a student is spent developing skills essential to the business world? Will you be poised to take on the job market with confidence and land your dream job?

This study guide bridges the gap between your degree and your future career by connecting your study skills to the professional ones you'll need. Designed to be a companion throughout your degree, this easy-to-use reference work simultaneously develops your employability whilst also helping you to succeed at university. Throughout your studies it will keep you focused on your future career by:

- teaching 'bridging skills' that enable you to apply your learning to professional practice
- showing how study skills such as diagnostics, planning and management, critical reading and knowledge transformation are used in the workplace
- demonstrating why 'thinking skills' such as critical thinking and reflection, developing arguments, problem solving, decision making, creative thinking and ethical thinking are vital to employers
- helping you to understand, early in your degree, what employers are looking for so that you can develop 'career readiness' as you study and gain work experience
- guiding you in developing a unique, evidence-based CV and using self-knowledge to make the right career choice.

Studying for your Future Employability provides a range of scenarios and activities to demonstrate the links between study skills and professional skills, along with techniques familiar in the workplace. With IT skills embedded throughout, this is the perfect study skills textbook to accompany business and management students who want to make their time in education count.

Sheila Tyler is a developmental psychologist specialising in management learning. She chaired the internationally taught Professional Certificate in Management at The Open University and was instrumental in developing problem-based and online collaborative learning. Publications include *The Manager's Good Study Guide*. She is now a learning design consultant.

'At the outset of a course of study its successful completion can take precedence over everything else; study skills an additional "nice to have" and a new or better job a long term aim. This book very successfully illustrates, through engaging and well-constructed scenarios, how those skills that facilitate successful study morph seamlessly into those skills that enable students to get employment and develop successfully within it. It encourages and supports readers to extract knowledge, skills and learning from all they do; to learn how to apply it to new situations and to become expert at learning and continuing to learn - skills that are vital in a changing and complex work environment.'

Sue Parr, *Director of Professional and Executive Programmes, WMG, University of Warwick*

'Dr Tyler has provided students with a comprehensive set of tools and resources to help make sense of higher education. Her guidance is written in a no-nonsense, easy to understand style with plenty of helpful examples which readers should be able to relate to. Overall, a practical and valuable guide to effectively managing business study and preparing for future careers.'

Dr Sharon Slade, *Senior Lecturer, The Open University Business School*

'*Studying for your Future Employability: A Business Student's Guide* by Sheila Tyler is a critical and informative guide for students. The book is engaging and imaginative in its approach. The inspiring guide is beautifully crafted and yet practical and resourceful. Above all it is a must read for those aspiring for business success and personal development.'

Kiran Trehan, *Professor of Leadership and Enterprise Development, University of Birmingham*

STUDYING FOR YOUR FUTURE EMPLOYABILITY

A business student's guide

Sheila Tyler

Routledge
Taylor & Francis Group

LONDON AND NEW YORK

First published 2017
by Routledge
2 Park Square, Milton Park, Abingdon, Oxon OX14 4RN

and by Routledge
711 Third Avenue, New York, NY 10017

Routledge is an imprint of the Taylor & Francis Group, an informa business

British Library Cataloguing in Publication Data
A catalogue record for this book is available from the British Library

Library of Congress Cataloguing in Publication Data
A catalog record for this book has been requested

ISBN: 978-1-138-83353-1 (hbk)
ISBN: 978-1-138-83354-8 (pbk)
ISBN: 978-1-315-73545-0 (ebk)

Typeset in Bembo
by Out of House Publishing

Printed and bound in Great Britain by
TJ International Ltd, Padstow, Cornwall

Contents

FIGURES

Tables

ACKNOWLEDGEMENTS

I am indebted to Professor Pam Shakespeare who critically read drafts of this book and made invaluable suggestions, drawing on her deep knowledge of practice-based open learning. I am also grateful to Funmi Mapelujo for her kind help and support. Thanks are due, too, to all my former students and colleagues at The Open University and IBM who taught me how to teach and for providing me with the inspiration and encouragement to experiment. Writing is intense work and it helps to have playful diversions, for which I thank my wonderful little grandchildren Serafino, Ewan, Viola and Matthew.

CHAPTER ONE

Your journey to success

Can a book change your life? No, *you* change your life. A self-help book simply helps you to change the ways you think and act till they become habits. It takes practice. If you're prepared to do that, then reading this book *will* change your life. How?

Higher education is supposed to change you, to help you to see with 'new eyes' and equip you for your life ahead. But whether it does, and how much, depends on some critical factors. You can harbour self-limiting beliefs about yourself and what learning is. You can skim over learning like skating on ice, treating education as an uncomplicated handing-down of knowledge from accepted authorities. Alternatively, you can challenge self-limiting beliefs and develop enabling ones. You can come to understand knowledge as open to question, to be interpreted and made your own. Through self-awareness and reflection you can master learning how to learn. You can equip yourself for independent lifelong learning. Your can change your view of yourself and the world. Then you are not the same person you were.

Study skills help you make these life-changing gains. They are much more than just a collection of study tools and techniques to be forgotten when you graduate. Study skills are valuable in all aspects of your life and to employers because they are *transferable*. They can be generalised to contexts other than those in which they were learned as the examples in Box 1.1 show.

Box 1.1 From study to work

Consider the skills involved in writing an assignment: they include information literacy (finding, sifting and evaluating sources of information), critiquing and weighing up evidence, developing and structuring your argument for your audience and then presenting your work appropriately. If you put yourself in the shoes of a project manager you can see how these skills can be transferred to the manager's job of gathering relevant information for a project proposal, making sense of it, deciding whether it contains flaws and determining its fitness for purpose and how it can be used to make a persuasive case to present to senior staff.

Now consider problem-solving. Given a case study or business scenario, you need to identify the problem, analyse possible causes, develop and evaluate options, make decisions and plan the implementation of the solution. Throughout, you apply your knowledge, question assumptions and think logically, critically and creatively. What do you need to do to solve a problem in the workplace? Exactly the same. You would probably be expected to implement your solution, too, as well as monitor progress and gain feedback. But when you study you also do this. You implement solutions, monitor progress and gain feedback every time you prepare and complete an assignment. Your time at university is brim full of opportunities to gain transferable study skills that enhance your employability and your value to employers.

It is easy to see how study skills are transferable to the workplace. Also known as core, key or general skills, transferable skills contribute to your *employability* and are the foundation on which many professional, work-focused skills are built. There are multiple perspectives on employability; no single theory exists and there are no measures of it (Williams et al., 2015). A view that influences many perspectives, however, is that of Peter Knight, a founder of discourse on higher education and employability: employability is 'skilful practice' that makes individuals more likely to gain employment and to be successful in their chosen occupations. Transferable skills make a substantial contribution that results from *interplay* between the skills and

- your self-concepts and personal qualities
- your engagement with and approach to learning
- your understanding of what you are studying
- your ability to reflect on your learning to understand *how* you learn
- your understanding of how to transfer your knowledge, skills and practices to contexts other than those in which you learned them.

Study skills, then, involve all of a person. For example, you learn the skill of identifying and questioning assumptions and find that you've made assumptions about yourself; you revise your self-belief to a less self-limiting one. You learn the skills of working with others and, in doing so, become more appreciative and confident. Because there are few study skills that are *not* transferable, transferable skills are referred to as study skills from this point in this book.

Knight's definition of employability (Yorke and Knight, 2006) embraces achievements, transferable skills, self-beliefs, personal qualities and personal knowledge of how to learn, acquired by self-awareness of, and reflection on, one's own learning processes. It also embraces 'the ability to operate in situations of complexity and ambiguity' (Yorke, 2006). Other perspectives emphasise the developmental nature of employability: a learning journey in which you become employable as you learn. You develop your personal attributes and capabilities, gain confidence and better understanding of yourself as you acquire subject knowledge and apply it in the wider context of university and the outside world. While, potentially, you could tick off the acquisition of study skills on a checklist, in practice such an activity is only indicative.

It should come as no surprise, then, that many transferable skills and elements of employability cannot be taught. They are learned through the doing of studying in a state of mindful awareness. So whose responsibility is it to ensure your acquisition of such skills and your employability? Is it a responsibility shared between you and your university? How hard is it for universities to provide students with appropriate opportunities? Read on before you respond: it may change your opinion.

Historically, only a tiny minority of UK school-leavers attended university. Students came predominantly from sociocultural backgrounds that had already equipped them for academic and career success. They were reared and educated in the liberal arts traditions that emphasised the development of the intellect through modern and ancient language-learning, history, literature and the arts, politics, economics, philosophy, grammar, logic, critique and the conventions of debate and argument. They possessed what's known as personal, social and cultural 'capital'. They knew how to network and to present themselves. They got the top jobs, even though up to the mid-twentieth century many types of work such as teaching, nursing, journalism, banking and finance, and many public service jobs didn't require a university degree. Policy changes in the 1960s and an increase in the number of universities didn't change the picture much. Fewer than 6 per cent of school leavers attended and the additional places were largely taken by the same kind of student; study skills, if provided at all, were reserved for failing students. Two decades later, only 15 per cent of school leavers entered university, fewer than in other advanced industrial nations. This helped neither the need for a more-skilled workforce nor greater participation in higher education by students from lower socio-economic backgrounds.

By the early 1990s the 'massification' of higher education was underway, part-funded by students themselves. Participation increased to around 40 per cent of 18–19-year-old school leavers in 2016. However, this rapid expansion and the increase in so-called 'non-traditional' students presented universities with a dilemma. No longer could – or can – they assume that all students possess the 'social and cultural capital' to fully benefit from higher education and gain the capabilities that employers want. At the same time, employers have berated universities for failing to produce graduates with the 'right' skills, capabilities and attitudes. Changes to Western and global economies mean that employers want more, too: they want more-advanced skills and new know-how.

It's tough meeting the needs of students and the demands of employers, however. Many universities have responded by introducing compulsory study skills courses. Teaching study skills outside the 'real' content and context of coursework is rarely an unqualified success, however. Why? Not least because study skills need to be gained and practised by students in the heat of dealing with unfamiliar and sometimes difficult content under time pressure. Ever conscious of what 'counts' (assignment grades), students easily justify their neglect of the most important transferable skills that take time and effort, such as reflection.

Embedding study skills in courses is attractive – and a number of universities try to do this – but this is no guarantee of success. In degree programmes comprising a menu of modules it's hard to provide a full range of opportunities, especially for study skills that require continuity of effort and practice. Assessment regimes can overemphasise some skills at the expense of other, hard-to-assess ones. Further, it's not easy for universities to arrange work experience for students or get them to create achievement portfolios that don't count towards their degree, say Yorke and Knight (2006).

Employers themselves are subject to external conditions including continuing globalisation, technological advances and shifting consumer demands (UKCES, 2014) that require them to change to survive: they may not be able to predict the skills needed a decade from now. And, despite the view of employers that business and management graduates lack an adequate range of skills – or fail to use them – many organisations find it difficult to provide training (Department for Business Innovation and Skills' Leadership and Management Network Group, 2012). According to the department (Pollard et al., 2015), employers want proven analytical and problem-solving skills, the ability to work with others, oral and written communications skills, business awareness and leadership, along with personal attitudes, values and qualities such as passion for work and business, motivation, adaptability and flexibility. Unfortunately for employers, and perhaps for universities, high academic grades don't necessarily reflect the possession of these competences. Without doubt, students focus on grades and not enough on learning, as they follow the more tangible academic rewards.

Where does this leave students and employability? According to Tomlinson (2012), 'The problem of managing one's future employability is therefore seen largely as being up to the individual graduate.' In other words, for the most part it's down to you. The result is a race among undergraduates to gain advantage over one other. Astute students raise their game to acquire, and demonstrate that they have, what employers want. They scrutinise employers' needs and prepare themselves, poised for the best jobs. The transition to work is risky, however, so their preparation is careful. Investments of time and effort are made in order to stand out from the crowd of new graduates. They understand the need for learning skills for continued professional development and to avoid unemployment and continual job change. They take individual responsibility for their learning and development.

How will you prepare yourself, acquiring good grades and important employability skills? This book shows you how to do this while you study. As a business and management student you are lucky: there is a unique relationship between the content of what you study and the world of work. This helps you to recognise the relationship between study skills and employability and to readily identify opportunities to learn and use them as you study. But you'll have to practise: they need to become habits.

You may also want to step outside your studies and seek voluntary work, short work placements or vacation internships with the specific aim of enhancing and honing your skills. Paid work, too, can do so much more than just funding your degree. Such experiences familiarise you with the labour market and with organisations, what they do, why they do it and how: you become 'business aware'. You can also bring your experiences to bear on your academic learning, enhancing your understanding and ability to question.

You probably realise, now, why understanding and practising study skills *in context* is what produces the best results. But there is one more skill that you need to know about, and it's one rarely mentioned: the skill of transfer.

The problem of transfer has vexed psychologists for decades. When you learn something, how does it get transferred from the context of learning to a different context? To gain some idea of the problem, consider numeracy. It's no use if you learn to solve algebraic equations in the classroom but can't work out long it will take your river taxis to get from A to B and back again given the speed of the current which aids the taxis in one direction and works against them in the other. What about understanding financial statements and making budgetary decisions based on them, or calculating return on investment? Knowledge isn't fully developed until it's at your finger tips. That's *knowing*. Everyone has had experience of learning something in one context and then having to start again when it's required in another context later on. Fingertip knowledge is crucial to efficient functioning.

To turn study skills into those that truly contribute to your employability you need to use every opportunity to transfer them and use them in as many different contexts as possible. The skills become habitual behaviours that you know when to use – or, at least, you do when you stop to reflect. When you can do this you have employability credentials, or competence – the term that employers often use. They are the basis of professional skills because you can apply them in different contexts and so can build on them. For every different context in which you apply a skill, whether while studying or in your professional work, you improve and extend your knowledge and hone the skill.

Your approach to learning can aid or hinder learning transfer. Simply memorising and reproducing information won't help. What *will* make a difference is the effort to understand, deconstruct, critique and reinterpret information and transform it into your *own* knowledge. Your self-awareness of *how* you learn (rather than *what*) and knowledge transfer are key to how you, your knowledge, your employability and your professional skills develop and improve over time and job changes; indeed, over a lifetime. Engagement with these skills helps you to gain the most from your degree studies.

This book shows you how the skills you need for study are used in the workplace, and vice versa: how those you need at work can help you to improve your study practices. It does so through scenarios and activities designed to introduce you to skills and to test your understanding of them. As a bonus, the text and activities include management tools and techniques commonly used in workplaces. This interweaving of study skills and professional skills along with workplace tools and techniques should leave you in no doubt about the nature of employability.

How to use this book

Use this book *as* you study. Familiarise yourself with the content first, then use the parts that are relevant to your study activities. Most sections are designed as stand-alones so you can look them up without reading the whole book or a whole chapter. Margin notes suggest other sections that may be relevant. If you need to read one section before another, this is indicated in the text.

There are two chapters that are best read as a whole: Chapter 3, *How you learn* and Chapter 9, *Your career in business and management*. Chapter 9 emphasises the need to begin to prepare for your career early on in your first year of study. Early preparation helps you to monitor your skills-acquisition progress and remedy important gaps over the course of your studies so that you improve your employability.

It takes time to develop study skills and employability and it takes determination when there are so many demands on your attention. But acquiring skills is essential to knowledge gain and employability. You owe it to yourself to make the necessary efforts: that way, you realise your full potential. The rest of your life depends on it.

Terminology

The book uses the term 'study skills' to embrace learning techniques and transferable skills. Activities, scenarios and examples are designed to demonstrate transferability. For ease of reading, the book cites few authors; rather it is an interpretation of many sources, it presents refined views, consensus perspectives and the distilled knowledge of the author. Cited works are often classic or authoritative sources that have stood the test of time and have yet to be bettered or, as academic convention demands, are the original sources of ideas on which others have built.

Chapter summary

❖ Higher education can change you as a person in positive ways but whether it does depends on factors such as your beliefs about yourself, learning and knowledge acquisition.

❖ Study skills are more than techniques; they embrace the whole person and include self-awareness and reflection. These help you to master learning how to learn in order to make changes.

❖ Study skills are transferable and contribute to employability: they are the foundations of workplace skills. This book uses the terms study skills because they have few aspects that are not transferable to the workplace.

❖ There are many perspectives on employability – and no measure of it. Some researchers emphasise the ability to perform in complex and uncertain situations while others focus on the developmental nature of employability: you become employable as you learn, developing personal attributes, capabilities and self-understanding.

❖ Study skills must be acquired by *doing*; in one sense employability is the skilful practice of study skills. You become an expert, lifelong learner.

❖ Responsibility for gaining study skills and developing employability reside with the individual – you.

❖ In the past, universities did not have to teach study skills but the demographics of undergraduates have changed. At the same time, employers demand more of new graduates because organisations have to survive in a changing world.

❖ It is difficult for universities to teach study skills and students often make efforts only in what 'counts' towards their degree.

❖ To contribute to employability, skills need to be used in contexts other than those in which they are learned. Opportunities for transfer of skills and knowledge may seem to be limited when you are studying but you can practise transfer in various ways.

❖ The vital element is that you *engage* with study skills to improve your learning, develop yourself and increase your employability.

References

Department for Business Innovation and Skills Leadership and Management Network Group (2012) *Leadership and management in the UK – the key to sustainable growth. A summary of the evidence for the value of investing in leadership and management*, Department for Business Innovation and Skills, London, The Stationery Office.

Pollard, E., Hirsh, W., Williams, M., Buzzeo, J. and Marvell, R. (2015) *Understanding employers' graduate recruitment and selection practices*, Department for Business Innovation and Skills Research Paper No. 231, London, The Stationery Office.

Tomlinson, M. (2012) 'Graduate employability: a review of conceptual and empirical themes', *Higher Education Policy*, vol. 25, no. 4, pp. 407–431 [Online]. DOI: 10.1057/hep.2011.26 (Accessed 15 April 2016).

UK Commission for Employment and Skills (UKCES) (2014) *Employer skills survey 2013: UK results* (January) Evidence Report 81, London, The Stationery Office.

Williams, S., Dodd, L.J., Steele, C. and Randall, R. (2015) 'A systematic review of current understandings of employability', *Journal of Education and Work* [Online]. DOI: 10.1080/13639080.2015.1102210 (Accessed 15 April 2016).

Yorke, M. and Knight, P.T. (2006) 'Embedding employability into the curriculum', *Learning and Employability*, Series 1 No. 3. The Higher Education Academy [Online]. DOI: 10.1108/17561391111106016 (Accessed 5 March 2016).

Yorke, M. (2006) 'Employability in higher education: what it is – what it is not', *Learning and Employability*, Series 1 York, The Higher Education Academy [Online]. Available at www.heacademy.ac.uk/assets/documents/tla/employability/id116_employability_ in_higher_education_336.pdf (Accessed 5 March 2016).

CHAPTER TWO

Planning and managing your studies

Joe works for a large retailer in the highly competitive food sector. He's working on one of the organisation's many projects designed to make it more efficient. As always, resources are limited and the deadline is demanding. He's confident that he and the other team members will deliver on time, however. The project design went through several draft phases before the final specification and seems well thought out. It takes account of cost, scheduling of tasks, who does what and when, monitoring and reviewing progress, and how the success of the project will be assessed.

Joe often finds that several project activities he is responsible for run in parallel but he prioritises them so he can give his full attention to one task at a time. Some prioritised activities don't seem very significant, but he knows the order in which the tasks need to be done. To an outsider, yesterday morning's job of locating and downloading data from a central database might not have looked urgent and important but Joe knew that he'd need time to understand the figures and their implications before he used them today. In his calendar, he'd blocked out the uninterrupted time he needed to engage with the data in addition to entering the task and the deadline.

He plans and diaries less important tasks, or those that are not urgent right now, for 'quiet' days when he knows the workflow will be slower. He sets aside a little time each day to prioritise: in addition to project tasks he needs to fit in others if he can. Today, for example, he received a request from a senior manager asking if he 'could find just a moment' to supply some information for a presentation. The request isn't straightforward and Joe will need more details.

Joe always notes how long each project activity takes him and compares it against the project schedule to see whether a task has taken more, or less, than the allocated time. He needs to do this for the project manager, but he's found it very useful for his own work. While every project is different, individual tasks can be similar, and it helps him to manage his workload better. He has regular discussions with the project manager and the project team to review progress. If things aren't going to plan, changes are made to put the project back on track. Minor changes can make a surprisingly big difference. One thing he's learned is that complex projects hardly ever go to plan, but invariably there's a solution.

Reflecting on his time at university Joe recalls:

> *I clung to methods and study habits that had got me through my later school years; I was afraid to take risks and experiment, even though it was a 'safe' learning environment and we were encouraged to try more effective ways of doing things. Now I realise that every course I studied was a 'project'. It would have been so useful to have understood that at the time and learned planning and workload management skills properly. I guess I just didn't see the bigger picture – the relationship between study skills and professional skills, and how they help you to be more efficient and effective.*

It is clear that Joe is not a student. So why does he feature here in a book on study skills? It's to illustrate effective planning and workload management (and self-management) skills – skills which Joe recognises only now as founded on the study skills he learned at university. Joe is giving you the benefit of what he wishes he knew then: how the study skills you need *now* are the foundation for the professional skills you will need *later*. The Chinese proverb *A journey of a thousand miles begins with a single step* means that every long and potentially difficult journey has a starting point. This is your first step on your journey to succeeding at university and becoming an effective business and management professional.

This chapter is designed to help you acquire planning and management skills for study that will form the basis for professional skills. The relationship between how you study at university and how effective you will be as a professional is a strong one. Our starting point, however, is more personal.

Dealing with concerns

Almost all students starting a degree programme have concerns of some kind – even the most able learners. Unresolved concerns affect your academic performance so it's wise to recognise them and deal with them swiftly. Every new university student is unique: your particular circumstances and prior experiences are different from those of other students. Consider this list of common, performance-affecting anxieties.

I'm concerned that that my academic ability may not be sufficient. The relationship between academic performance at school and at university is not as strong as you'd imagine. For mature students, the link can be very weak indeed. School study is different in many ways from higher education study, which requires a high level of independence and critical thinking. Important factors in university success include good study skills and study habits along with the motivation to learn.

In general, low confidence in academic ability has a negative effect on performance at university, although the reasons are unclear. It may be that, for students who lack academic confidence, low grades serve to confirm their self-beliefs, while more confident students are motivated to learn from feedback. Low academic confidence can also lead to perfectionism. In such cases, students set themselves exacting standards. A good rule of thumb is: *Don't aim for perfection; aim to get it done.*

You are likely to have the ability to succeed at university. Students who drop out of university are most likely to do so for other reasons such as adjustment difficulties, lack of commitment, financial hardship, health problems and low self-confidence. If you know your academic self-confidence is low, try to develop new ways of thinking about yourself. Identify negative self-beliefs and replace them with positive ones. The past is the past; you and your university should be interested in your *potential*.

I'm not very motivated when it I sit down to study; I'm concerned about my commitment. Motivation to study is an important factor in succeeding at university. Students who lack it are often procrastinators: they put off study sessions and when they are studying they are easily distracted. Being organised and acquiring good study habits are vital. Use incentives and rewards to motivate yourself initially, if you need to. You will know that your motivation and commitment have improved when you feel a sense of satisfaction and achievement when you complete a study activity. To boost your study motivation and commitment in general try:

- joining in social activities that help you to feel you 'belong'
- participating in a small study group (members are good at motivating one another)
- telling others about your study plans (it helps you to keep to them)
- ensuring the social support of your family and friends (kind words of support and encouragement *do* help).

I don't really have any career in mind and I'm concerned that I might lose interest in studying. Students with 'career orientation' have a longer-term goal, so gaining a university degree is simply an essential step towards it. There are many students for whom this isn't so but it doesn't affect their progress through a degree programme. Provided you've chosen an academic discipline in which you are interested, not having a career goal doesn't matter as much as engaging with your studies. When you engage with your studies you develop yourself and the way you think. Education itself is *supposed* to be life-changing. This is an important goal in its own right.

It's never too soon to think about what you will do when you graduate so visit your university's careers advice service early. You can access additional help via reputable websites such as the UK Government's National Careers Service. Your ideas and aspirations may change but you can ensure that all your decisions are informed. A number of organisations and sectors offer work placements, part-time employment and internships during vacations. Developing a career goal can help you to find a compelling reason for studying.

I'm concerned about how much time it will take to study a course and pass it. Universities normally state the average number of hours needed to study a course and sometimes for each week or for each unit of study. Some students will take more time and others less than the average. However, study time doesn't equate well to academic performance and grades. This is because students who spend longer studying often do so for lack of study skills. Aim to acquire them to ensure that your study time is effective.

If you are a full-time student who works part-time, then also consider limiting your work hours. Working for more than 10–15 hours a week (estimates vary) has a negative impact on academic performance. If you need to work, then focus on improving your time-management skills. Part-time students who work full-time should have fewer concerns: academic success is likely to be equal to that of full-time students who don't work (McKenzie and Schweitzer, 2001). The reasons are not established but part-time students who work full-time may benefit from clear career goals, high motivation and good time-management skills developed at work.

I'm a mature student and I'm concerned about my ability to remember information. Many mature students express this concern, even when 'mature' can mean any age above 21 in the UK. The world's oldest students graduated when they were over 90. Reassuringly, research into aging reveals:

- productivity is highest when people are about 40 years old
- work quality can remain high for decades
- age doesn't diminish creativity: it can be at its highest in later life
- declines in memory are seen at 60 and over but are not inevitable – 'deep' processing of information maintains and improves memory and cognitive function.

See How do you go about your learning? in Chapter 3

No mature student should be concerned about diminishing cognitive ability or changes in memory. If you put effort into understanding what you are learning you may forget the surface detail but you're more likely recall the concepts.

I'm studying through the medium of English but English isn't my first language. I'm worried that my language skills will affect my academic performance. English is becoming the language of global choice in higher education. One result is that UK universities attract students from all over the world. There are advantages for all students. Such diversity offers cross-cultural exchange of ideas and the potential for international networking and professional work. Your English language skills will improve naturally but there are actions you can take to speed up the process.

- Seek help from your university. Many universities provide language support services. Make use of these as soon as you can.
- Integrate socially. Socialise with students from different cultures and language groups: it's too easy (and comfortable) to spend your free time with students whose first language you share.
- Allow for additional study time. Studying through the medium of a second (or third or fourth) language takes longer. An international study of non-UK IBM managers who studied part-time found that, despite their fluency in English, they took *on average* 25 per cent longer to study than did first-language English speakers (Tyler, 2001). Allow for extra study time and accept it as usual.

Studying seems to take me longer than it does other students. Few students learn at the same speed and even individual speed is variable depending on what is being learned. If your study skills are poor or it's some years since you studied, your learning speed will be quite slow at first. Assuming you fully intend to improve your study skills, this does not matter much. Understanding what you study is more important. Equally, developing your study skills and allowing time for experimentation help you to improve your study efficiency and effectiveness. Thus, learning can be slower initially before you speed up and achieve more in less time.

Seek advice on key readings and tasks with the aim of accomplishing those while you enhance your skills. As you improve, challenge and extend yourself by elevating your study goals. Don't settle for being a 'minimalist'.

I'm worried about assessment. It's rare for students *not* to be concerned about assessment – the amount, type and standards required. The next section of this chapter deals with the topic and Chapter 5 is devoted to assessment. The more information you have about assessment, the more effective your planning and scheduling; the more assignments you do, the less concern you should have. A certain level of 'text anxiety' is necessary, though. It optimises performance. The trick is to prevent anxiety levels from becoming too high, impairing your performance.

> **ACTIVITY 2.1** Now consider your own concerns. Identify them as fully as possible, provide reasons for your concerns and then decide on the ways in which you can reduce or overcome them.

You probably found that it was easy to identify your concerns and less so to find reasons for them and know how to deal with them. It's often hard to justify concerns when the cause may be uncertainty, which itself can lead to worries and anxiety. One solution is to monitor your concerns after a few weeks to see which ones remain, if any: many have a tendency to disappear because they are unfounded or your perspective on them has changed or because information has replaced uncertainty. Those that may require solutions often involve time and this can be a problem if you fund your studies by working. You'll need to think creatively about solutions and seek whatever help is offered by your university. Your fellow students are another source of help and support.

Assessment

The moment has arrived. Emma sent her first report on staffing issues in branch offices to her line manager, Mia, last week and now they are about to discuss it. Emma, new in her role as area manager, is quite pleased with the report but will Mia be happy with it too? Mia *manages by objectives*. Instead of being concerned about how Emma organises her work, Mia expects her to deliver outputs that meet the objectives and are on time – usually in the form of reports, which will be followed by a meeting while Emma is still new to the job. Mia begins by asking Emma about her preparation of the report. By the end of the meeting, Emma recognises that while the report was well presented and covered key staffing issues, it was too descriptive and lacked suggested solutions. On her way home, Emma realises that the report reflects her work processes: she needs to understand causal factors and to do that she needs to explore issues more fully with the staff involved.

We and our work are assessed continually. Imagine that Emma simply filed her reports month after month and received no feedback. She would learn very little. We are subject to a range of forms of assessment from job interviews to annual appraisals. We are also assessed informally day by day as we go about our work, when we give a presentation, chair a meeting or lead a team. We learn from the informal and formal feedback we receive, whether this is a simple 'Well done' or a colleague's contribution to our annual appraisal suggesting we might participate more in meetings. When we recognise where improvements need to be made we are in a position to make them.

Studying for a degree is no different. Without feedback from any study assignment you did you would find improvement of your performance very difficult. Academic assessment seems different because it is more regulated: the learning of each student on a course must be assessed in the same way using the same criteria. Any examination is undertaken by all students on the same day. This is because assessment must be normative and fair to students. Assessment is higher education's way of *managing (student learning) by objectives*.

Constructive feedback

Effective educators provide constructive feedback on many assignments so that the process of assessment feels more like encouragement, support and coaching.

Constructive feedback on longer assignments such as essays and reports often takes the form of margin comments ('You could have discussed theory Z here'; 'Why is this so?' 'Good point!') and a short summary. The classic style, used by The Open University, UK, for such summaries is to begin with a positive statement about the work followed by three or four areas that could have been improved on, then end with words of encouragement. It is discouraging for students if teachers set out an exhaustive list of improvements. Rather, good educators do the following:

- correct errors and misunderstandings
- diagnose any problems with the work (for example, the structure of your text)
- comment on your thinking and learning skills or on process (for example, you may have arrived at a conclusion without providing enough supporting evidence or ignored contrary evidence).

This kind of feedback helps you to gain a better grade next time. Be sure to ask about any comments you don't understand. Even if an assignment is poor, the feedback should serve to encourage you and indicate what you can do to address any issues next time. In short, effective feedback is a constructive dialogue between you and your teacher.

Formative assessment

Not all assignments are marked in this way and not all of them 'count' towards your degree. It's a good idea to find out how each course you are taking is assessed. Formative assignments are usually 'low stakes', for example, a short PowerPoint presentation: they earn few or no marks. The primary role of formative assessment (the term used to refer to all formative assignments) is to monitor learning. It ensures that students are acquiring the understanding and skills they are supposed to and are achieving particular course learning objectives (these state what students are expected to be able to do as a result of studying the course). Often, the objectives that are 'tested' formatively are those that are *hard to learn and hard to assess* using conventional 'reading and writing' methods. For example, a learning objective may be 'effective teamwork online' or 'to be able to use basic IT tools'.

> **ACTIVITY 2.2** It's useful to consider things from a different perspective than your own. If you were a university educator, how might you assess the objectives of effective online teamwork and use of IT skills?

To assess how well students had met the online teamwork objective, you probably decided on having students work on a task in a virtual team. Working out how to assess how well each student performed as a team member might have been tricky. Observation of regular and constructive participation and contribution to the task output would take far too long. But participation (what each student contributed and how often) might be 'measured', as might the team's output and/ or individual reflections on the team's performance.

For the IT skills objective, you probably had a number of ideas including a PowerPoint presentation, which could be assessed by the educator observing the presentation and judging it on the use of PowerPoint, the clarity of the information presented and so on.

Types of formative assessment

Formative assessment can include the following assignment types.

1. Presentations
2. Summaries of lectures
3. Outlines or plans of work that will be assessed in other ways later
4. Group or team work of various types, such as working on problems or case studies
5. Reviews of academic journal articles
6. A briefing note for a group discussion
7. A financial statement drawn from a set of figures
8. A problem or problem scenario for group discussion
9. A poster
10. Role play
11. Entries in a reflective learning diary or blog
12. Contributions to a problem-solving wiki activity
13. Multiple-choice tests (tick-box answers to questions)
14. Peer-marked work (you and another student mark each other's work).

ACTIVITY 2.3 Consider what each of the above assignment types might 'test'. You'll need to consider how much each one depends on knowledge, understanding and using knowledge as well as skills, such as communication and working with others. You'll also need to think about whether each type of assignment helps students to learn something in the process of carrying it out.

It's probably clear to you that many of the assignment types are designed to develop understanding but in different ways, many of them relevant to the workplace. Being able to summarise knowledge as in Assignments 2 and 6 is an important skill that requires and demonstrates understanding. The brevity of summaries and briefing notes means you have to prioritise information and place it in a logical order, usually for the benefit of others (although it benefits you, too). Assignments 1 and 9 involve communicating knowledge to others using visual techniques and creative thinking. Assignment 1 also involves verbal communication. Assignment 3 involves planning, a skill that requires logical thinking. Assignments 4, 5, 8 and 12 involve critical thinking, with 4, 8 and 12 also involving teamwork skills.

Assignments 7 and 10 involve transfer of knowledge, while 10 also involves perspective-taking. Assignment 7 may do, too, if you need to 'read' the financial statement from the perspective of different stakeholders (those who have an interest in an organisation, including front-line staff, shareholders and suppliers). Assignment 11 requires critical reflection, a vital and fundamental skill.

It's likely that the most difficult assignment to untangle was No. 14, the peer-marked work. It is a quick and powerful way of improving academic performance. It's not the marks that count, but the learning that goes on when students are exposed to each other's work. You may also have wondered about Assignment 13, multiple-choice tests, too. They can be used to quickly check knowledge and have value if feedback is instant and they are used in conjunction with other types of assessment. In all but Assignment 13, which is more of a diagnostic test, you learn by going through the process of producing the output.

Formative assignments are often mandatory: although each may earn few marks, there is a requirement to submit them. The list of examples is far from exhaustive, so expect to find novel forms. While formative assessment may be 'low stakes', it will give you a taste of the variety of 'assessment' you may expect in a job later.

Summative assessment

Summative assessment refers to all summative assignments and is 'high stakes'. The role of these summative assignments is to measure student learning at key stages of a course or at the end of one. Examinations are in this category and may be held at the end of a course, a year or a degree programme. Summative assessment can include:

- essays and reports
- projects
- examinations
- a portfolio of work.

A portfolio can be a collection of low-stakes assignments but a final piece of work may require students to make connections and perhaps apply their knowledge to a case study or scenario.

A course may award, for example, 50 per cent of marks in total to a number of low-stakes assignments and 50 per cent to one, summative assessment.

However you are assessed and whatever the marks breakdown, assignments will be aligned to the learning objectives of a course. These learning objectives often include not only the knowledge and skills you will gain from studying the course but more general skills that undergraduates are expected to learn. These include, for example, information literacy, IT competency and various types of thinking. Good educators set out learning objectives for courses and provide

See *Understanding assignment requirements* in Chapter 5

the criteria on which each assignment is be judged. You may be provided with checklists and guidance to help you achieve good grades. Your teachers want you to succeed on their courses as much as you want to.

Getting ready to study: a place to work

Next time you board a crowded commuter train, notice what people are doing. Many will be using their digital devices to read and respond to messages, read documents and make occasional phone calls. You probably won't find any of them trying to compile a report, a financial budget or a project plan. The promise of digital technology was that we could carry out our work, study and social activities wherever we were. But if you've ever tried to work on a crowded train or in a busy café, you'll know this promise has been only partially fulfilled.

While 'anywhere' technology allows us to make use of 'down' time, such as travel, a physical place to work that's comfortable with everything to hand is essential for most people even if they study or work at a distance and use digital technology. Many students are provided with study space in their on-campus accommodation. But if your circumstances are different, identify a suitable work space and arrange it for *efficient* study. If what you need is to hand and well organised, you won't waste time looking for it. Arrange the space for *effective* study, too: it's best *not* to use the bed for reading tasks as it's the easiest way to fall asleep!

Effective study needs your full attention so protect your work space from interruption and distractions: if you allow interruption or seek distraction, study will seem never-ending and you will be constantly hurrying to catch up.

Distractions It's wise to study without the distractions of music – and telephone, email/social media/the internet, radio and TV. As computers usually offer all of these functions, ask yourself whether you need your computer for *every* study session. Alternatively, exercise rigorous self-discipline (with rigorous self-monitoring).

Interruptions Reduce interruptions by closing the door to your study space and letting others know when you are working. Switch off your phone or don't respond to calls, texts or email. Have 'out of office' responses switched on when you're studying. Make advance arrangements for meeting up and working with other students.

When you want a change of scene, the university library is ideal if you need to read academic journal articles, for example. It's also a good place to study between lectures if you live off-campus, and it may be a suitable place if your student accommodation is noisy. Workplaces often have 'hot desks' that anyone can use. 'Hot desk' workers learn to be highly organised because they must leave the hot desk as they found it. Similar habits are vital if you study in more than one location or don't have access to one, permanent study space. Whatever your situation, being organised and managing your study environment helps to develop good study habits. When you sit down you expect to work.

Planning your studies

Developing your study strategy

Just as every business needs a strategy so, too, does every student. So what is a strategy? A strategy is a high-level plan: it sets out how the available resources will be used to achieve a goal. When you are a student it's wise to do this before planning individual study sessions for which you need study *tactics*. Tactics are 'on-the-ground' plans.

First you need to identify your overall goal, such as:

- to gain a degree in business and management.

You may want to refine the goal, for example,

- to gain a particular degree class and maximise my employability as I study.

Then you devise a strategy – your approach to obtaining these goals, such as:

- spend sufficient time studying
- learn skills that will enhance my learning.

You then develop objectives – specific and measurable actions or steps – to achieve your strategy, focusing more precisely on *what* you will do and when. (The term 'tactic,' is often used for achieving a single objective.)

Your main resources are those provided by your university and, importantly

- you
- your time
- your ability to finance your studies.

A good starting point to developing a strategy is a technique common in business and management – a force-field analysis, a framework devised by the social psychologist, Kurt Lewin (1890–1947) in the USA. It's in common use now to help people assess who or what is helping to achieve a goal and who or what is producing restraints or barriers. It's then possible to investigate further to see if the positive factors – the driving forces – can be strengthened and whether the negative factors – restraining forces – can be reduced.

ACTIVITY 2.4 First define your goal. Then consider the factors that motivate you or assist you to achieve it – driving forces – and those that can block or hinder movement towards it – restraining forces. Driving forces may include your desire to secure a well-paid job when you graduate, your parents' aspirations for you, your confidence in your own ability based on previous academic success. Restraining forces might be your time, your anxieties about studying, your desire to socialise or to make the most of team sport opportunities. Identify all the potentially restraining and driving forces that you can think of.

Then use a diagram like the one shown in Figure 2.1, with your goal in the middle, the driving forces on the left and restraining forces on the right. Make arrows thicker to show the strength of particular forces and longer to show their duration. Your anxieties might be acute but new for example, whereas your parents' aspirations for you may be resolute and enduring. Alternatively, give each arrow a number (use low numbers to indicate low strength). These conventions are used to assess whether, overall, the drivers are stronger than the restraining forces and roughly by how much, or vice versa. (It's not the number of factors that matters but how powerful each is.)

When you have completed the diagram, consider the 'balance' between the drivers and the restraining forces. One way of thinking about this is to use the concept of weighing scales. If the restraining forces are few and the drivers strong, then you have no significant barrier to address. Often, however, restraining forces are stronger than the drivers. If this is the case, consider carefully each driver and each restraining force individually. Each will have one or more causes or contributory factors.

A tool used frequently by business and management professionals to identify causes or contributory factors is a fishbone diagram (see Figure 2.2). Each 'bone' of the fish skeleton is a contributory or causal factor.

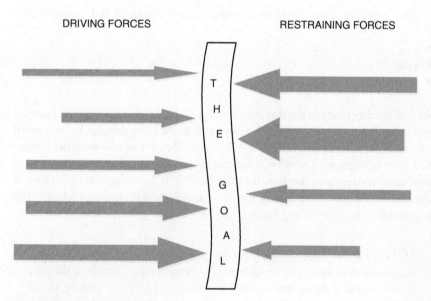

Figure 2.1 Force-field diagram

Based on an original conception by Lewin, 1947

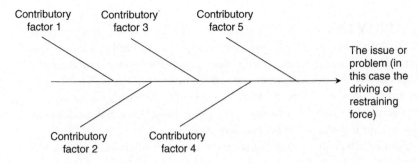

Figure 2.2 Fishbone diagram

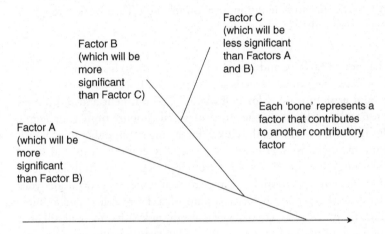

Figure 2.3 Adding to a fishbone diagram

If, for example, one restraining force is lack of time, you might consider all the demands on your time, including non-study activities. Students living away from home for the first time are likely to underestimate these time demands. They may now have to shop, cook and clean for themselves on a regular basis as well as doing their own laundry. Some main causes may have secondary causes and these in turn may be caused by something else. In such cases, secondary 'bones' are added to the primary ones, as in Figure 2.3. 'Bones' can be added to these secondary ones too. Consider this example.

For Ellie, a cause of, or contributory factor to, insufficient time is that she is the star player in her home region's badminton team. The 100-kilometre return trip for weekly practice and matches will be time-consuming and costly (the primary cause) but she is reluctant to withdraw because of pressure from the other players (a secondary cause), some of whom have aspirations to become professional players. Being the star player also boosts her general self-esteem and acts as an incentive to use her time in this way (another causal or contributory factor).

ACTIVITY 2.5 Investigate any significant restraining forces you identified in Activity 2.4 using a fishbone diagram. Consider carefully each causal or contributory factor. Then develop some possible solutions. For example, Ellie decides she can save time and money by joining her university badminton club which would satisfy her sporting interest and be equally confidence-building. Her home town team, she believes, will understand her reasons if she explains her problem clearly.

Aim to reduce the strength of restraints or to turn them into drivers. For example, while reducing your social activities you could convert some into incentives for periods of effective study. If you join university clubs and societies to continue some non-study interests, being with other students can boost your commitment and motivation to study. Then work through the drivers to see if they can be strengthened.

The activity is not an easy one and you may want to return to it several times. You are looking for creative and constructive solutions. 'Yes but ...' is not a solution and you should explore reasons for inflexibility. Commitment and motivation can be increased by seeking a higher level of social support from your family and friends. This might also have the effect of reducing a restraining force which can be significant for a number of students – family commitments and social demands. Let family and friends know that you need to prioritise study activities.

If financial concerns are a restraining force or contribute to one, consider your income and expected expenditure. Create a simple Excel spreadsheet and a simple budget. Alternatively, use a free app that will make the task easier. You will still need numeracy skills, however. See Box 2.1 to find out how you can improve them.

Box 2.1 What if your numeracy skills aren't good?

Your university will almost certainly be able to help you with numeracy. It's not unusual to find students who haven't mastered or have forgotten basic arithmetic. Your university may also be able to help you to understand and manage your finances. Many websites offer self-help or free short courses on numeracy; some also offer help with understanding and managing finance. Choose a respected provider such as a university or government-funded one. The Open University, UK, offers free, short courses that can be studied online through *OpenLearn*. Durations range from three to 30 hours in bite-size sessions. If your numeracy skills are poor, the BBC has a maths website for adults, *Skillswise*, that takes you stepwise through the basics. Make time now or in vacations to refresh your knowledge: not only will numeracy and understanding finance help you in your business and management studies, they will be of use in all aspects of your life now and later.

Sometimes it's helpful to use a multiple cause diagram if, on reflection, you find there are a number of causes of a problem or hindrances that are not linked

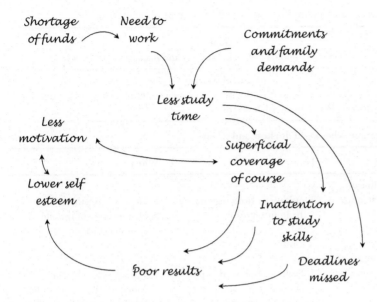

Shortage of funds

Need to work

Commitments and family demands

Less study time

Less motivation

Lower self esteem

Superficial coverage of course

Inattention to study skills

Poor results

Deadlines missed

Figure 2.4 Simple multiple cause diagram

together in a simple linear fashion and that may reinforce one another. Figure 2.4 shows an example in which the problem of feelings of low motivation and self-esteem can be traced back to financial difficulties and family commitments and demands. Use the multiple cause diagram if it seems helpful and return to the force-field analysis when you have a clearer idea of what the key issues are.

You should now have sufficient information to develop a general strategy for your studies, one that sets out how you will organise and use your resources to meet your goal. To complete the task, develop a general statement that describes your strategy together with a set of actions and an implementation plan that describes precisely how you will reorganise your resources.

ACTIVITY 2.6 Use the headings in Table 2.1 to set out your goal (identified in Activity 2.4) and your general strategy, which you should derive from the results of your work on Activities 2.4 and 2.5. Then list the actions you need to take and when you will carry them out. Table 2.1 has already been completed using the example of Ellie. You can review and develop your goals and general strategy at any time and add more actions as they become clearer to you. Keep your completed version of Table 2.1 where you can see it.

Now you carry out the actions. Some will not be arduous and not all need to be done immediately. You need self-discipline, however. Provide incentives for yourself if you find it hard to begin with. When you practise self-discipline, it becomes a habit.

Table 2.1 Goal, strategy, initial actions and implementation plan

	Goal	
	Gain at least a second-class honours degree in business and management	

	General strategy	
	Create more time by managing outside interests, increase commitment and motivation for study and reduce moderate financial concerns	

Implementation: what I will do, how and when

What	How	When
1. Reduce time on outside interests	1. Withdraw from regional badminton team 2. Join university badminton club	1. Next visit (October 6) 2. First meeting of the club this semester (October 2)
2. Improve financial situation	1. Seek vacation work – possibly summer schools support work on campus. 2. Learn to cook. 3. Limit weekly expenditure on socialising to (amount).	1. Visit careers office on Monday; ask friends and family to watch for local advertisements 2. Find at least one friend who can (and who's willing to!) teach me 3. Start now. Find best app for smartphone and monitor weekly spending
3. Improve commitment and motivation to study	1. Talk to family about taking more interest in my study and reducing pressure to attend all family events 2. Find a 'study buddy' about the same level as me 3. See what's available at the Freshers' Fair that might help	1. Start with the next phone call! 2. Ask at every opportunity if anyone suitable on my courses is willing to meet up regularly 3. Go to Freshers' Fair on Tuesday
4.[...]		

Practical preparations for study

Planning your time

Getting your degree is your overarching goal. Implementing your study strategy should result in making it achievable. But you will still need to organise your study time. Systematic time and workload planning and managing your plan don't come naturally.

Colin plans his time somewhat vaguely: he needs to spend as much time as he can in the library today and tomorrow. At lunchtime, though, he got talking with friends. He justified this to himself because they talked about the last lecture which some of them found confusing. It was 3pm before he reached the library and then he remembered he needed to buy his mother a birthday card. He might as well do his shopping at the same time, he thought. He tried to catch up with an evening visit to the library but he spent most of the time on one of the library's computers keeping up with his school friends. At the end of the day, most of his library work is still ahead of him, although thanks to his long lunch he is less confused about the lecture.

Sian, a mature student with two pre-school-age children, is studying part-time on a course that requires 12 hours' study a week. When she enrolled for the course, she thought the study hours would be relatively easy to fit in. Her day is structured around the children's needs and she's reasonably organised domestically. But try as she might, there never seems to be time during the day. Study time is confined to the evenings after she's put the children to bed and cleared up the house. Often she doesn't start studying till 9pm. Usually she manages to study for an hour before her eyes start to close. She wonders how she'll find time to prepare her first assignment.

You may recognise some elements in these scenarios or have different difficulties with time. If planning and time management are new to you, or if you find it difficult to know where to begin, then carry out Activity 2.7.

ACTIVITY 2.7 For one week, log everything you do and how long it takes. Include sleeping, eating, shopping, cooking, organising your room, laundering your clothes, and socialising in all its guises from planned get-togethers to unplanned chats in the communal kitchen and use of social media. For mature students who work or have childcare responsibilities the list will include different and probably more items. A pencil-and-paper approach is probably best, using a free, downloadable chart that covers one week. Choose one that divides time into short periods, such as 30 minutes, from Monday till Sunday. When you have completed your log, analyse how you spend your time. Self-knowledge will help you to identify time-wasting activities and help you to work out how to budget your time.

The next logical step is to plan your time for each course, then create more-detailed plans for each week and ultimately for each day, just as you would for a project. Before you can divide up larger tasks into manageable pieces, however, you'll need information about each course you will be studying in the current semester. You need to know:

- how many hours' study are required on average
- how the course is assessed
- a description of what's required for each assignment

- the length of each assignment (if it is a written one)
- how many marks each assignment will contribute to your overall grade
- whether an assignment relates to a study activity, such as group work which may restrict your flexibility for preparation
- likely preparation time if guidance is given
- the deadline for each assignment
- any end-of-semester examinations
- the form of any examination (some examinations have material you see beforehand).

Most universities provide such information, often online. The workload may be initially disconcerting but ultimately it helps you to feel a sense of control.

ACTIVITY 2.8 Find out this information now. Then set out the important dates for each course on a chart or study planner. A printed academic year planner is useful because you can pin it up where you study and see your commitments at a glance. The planner can be created digitally provided it's possible to view at least one complete semester on one screen and it can be printed. Free study planner apps for smart phones, tablets and computers are available online but check they can provide a whole-semester view.

When you have marked all the key dates for each course, add:

- your main personal, family and social commitments
- holidays.

This is your basic plan. Now, tentatively block out periods of time for reading, assignment and seminar preparation, exam revision and your other study and non-study activities. These should include any part-time or voluntary work commitments and any significant domestic activities. Use the average weekly study time for courses and allow an additional two hours a week for organising your studies if the average time doesn't include this. You will need to check email, message boards or forums, locate recommended reading material in the library, keep your study materials (and space) organised and continue to plan your activities. Getting to and from lectures and the library may amount to several hours a week, too.

When you block out study time, ensure these are *regular, uninterrupted periods of study*. Finally, leave a little *contingency* time, that is, time for overruns and unexpected events.

Mostly likely, the first thing you have noticed is how little of your time is not occupied. Secondly, you are likely to see some awkward clashes such as assignment deadlines for different courses on the same dates or an obligation just before a deadline. Resolving such clashes often means working ahead, to complete an assignment before the deadline or working on two assignments in parallel, starting both earlier. An assignment based on a learning activity at a fixed time leaves you with some 'juggling of commitments' to do. Then you must weigh up where your time and efforts are best placed in terms of your learning and study outcomes. In general, it's sensible to prioritise assignments that 'count' more to your overall course grade and degree. When planning revision for exams 'little and often' is most effective. Leave a day between completing your revision and the exam to review your learning. Last-minute cramming has a negative effect on long-term memory retention.

See Prioritising in this chapter

If this is the first time you have set out all your commitments and activities at once, your planner may look daunting. But the important thing is that you have a basic master plan to work to. Keep your planner where you can see it and check it at a glance, particularly when other commitments and invitations arise (don't over-commit when you have choices). You can modify your planner at any time. Return to it after you have carried out the other activities in this chapter and improve it as you gain experience.

Annotating and amending your planner

Annotate your planner, but without cluttering it (you will need more detailed study session plans and often weekly and daily *To do* lists). As you become more knowledgeable about how long tasks take, you can amend your planner. If you remain short of time, learn some of the tactics used by successful mature students: rise early to fit in study when interruptions are few; have planned, dedicated 'study weekends'; and always be prepared for short study opportunities (see Box 2.2).

See Planning your study sessions in this chapter; see Exams: Time planning and preparation in Chapter 5

Box 2.2 Mind the (time) gaps and make use of them

Think of the occasions when you have unexpected time to spare, such as when you complete a task sooner than you think or when waiting for someone. Some people simply 'kill time' with unplanned activity. Others plan for it. Have several tasks you can work on and select on the basis of where you are, how long you have and whether there's a computer you can use or space for your laptop.

Planning your study sessions

Planning study sessions is an important task, one that will eventually be quick and easy to accomplish for familiar tasks. If you have not completed Activities 2.6, 2.7 and 2.8 in this chapter, do so now: it will avoid the need for 'crisis management' later. Once you have organised your study planner and have an idea of how you will divide up your time, you can begin to plan individual study sessions.

A study session is a small block of time ranging from an hour to one day. A series of them takes you towards a study goal, such as an assignment. You don't need a highly detailed plan for each; rather, you need a realistic objective. Your main goal, of course, is the successful completion of a course. But look for sub-goals. These are often assignments, group work or other activities. Identify the first sub-goal in a course and work backwards from it. Your aim is to break up larger tasks into more manageable ones. Usually there is an order in which these more manageable tasks must be done. For example, while you can begin to outline an assignment before you complete your reading, you cannot submit an assignment before writing it. It's obvious when you think about it.

Size of study sessions

The size of individual study sessions will depend on other activities in your planner and the blocks of time you can devote to study. You may be able to dedicate a day to reading and note-making or you may have to slot study sessions between other commitments.

See Planning your time in this chapter

Reading, note-making and assignments of one kind or another are likely to take up a substantial amount of your study time, so many of your study sessions will be devoted to these activities. Set a realistic objective for each session. Your objective for a session lasting one day might be 'read six journal articles' or 'a quarter of the texts on the essential reading list' if the reading list has not yet been supplied. Ideally, a session should be no more than half a day so that it matches an uninterrupted period of study. The average time people are able to concentrate fully is 90 minutes, resuming after a short refreshment break.

ACTIVITY 2.9 Study the planner you developed in Activity 2.8. Identify:

- your first study sub-goal
- where your blocks of study time appear on the planner prior to the sub-goal
- the total time you can devote to studying towards it.

On a separate sheet, list the tasks you need to do achieve the sub-goal. Beside each item, estimate how long each is likely to take (or how long you have). Don't forget to list tasks such as finding resources in the library. List these tasks as study sessions, using the blocks of time indicated on the planner. If, for example, reading and note-making take two days but your planner shows that you must spread this over four days, then you need several 'reading and note-making' study sessions, each no more than a morning or afternoon. Some of them may be only one hour long, slotted between other scheduled activities. Before you diarise these sessions, carry out the next activity.

Many people like to have a study activity plan for the week and for each day, too. What is not planned probably won't get done – and having a study plan helps you to monitor your progress.

Setting SMART objectives

You need one more planning technique to ensure you achieve what you intend: SMART objectives. You'll be expected to use these at work where you need to achieve tasks 'on time and on budget'. SMART is an acronym, so each letter refers to a word that is a criterion to be met.

Specific. Objectives for a task or study session should be specific, such as 'Map out project and produce draft plan for discussion' or 'Plan essay – write headings and what content to put under each'.

Measurable. You need to know whether you have achieved your objective. In the examples above, achievement of the objectives will be a) a draft project plan and b) a document with headings and notes on content.

Acceptable (to you and to stakeholders – these are people who have an interest or 'stake' in what you are doing). It's no use setting an objective which you have no intention of meeting. The agreement of others is necessary when you work in a team or group, for example. A second interpretation of **A** is Achievable. Others include Assignable (who will do it), Agreed and Attainable, depending on the context.

Realistic. Objectives should be achievable within the resources available. Planning to do one day's worth of reading in an hour is not realistic.

Timed. Objectives should have a time frame. You might judge that producing the document with headings and notes will take 90 minutes.

An example of a SMART objective is: write essay outline with headings and brief outline of content as a first step in preparing an assignment in 90 minutes. The objective is specific; it's measurable (you should have an outline for the assignment at the end), it's acceptable to you; it's realistic (you can achieve it with the resources you have) and 90 minutes is sufficient time – and, importantly, there *is* a time frame.

> **ACTIVITY 2.10** Return to the study sessions you developed in Activity 2.9. Write SMART objectives for each session. As you approach the planning of study sessions for the subsequent sub-goals, check them for SMART-ness.

This activity was probably more difficult than listing the tasks and working out study sessions in Activity 2.9. SMART helps you to monitor your progress. If you don't meet a goal, you'll have a good idea why and be able to rectify problems. If you invariably achieve your goals try extending them so they are a little more challenging. Try fitting more into study sessions or increase the intellectual demand by producing a proper summary of your notes after each item of reading, for example. You may be tempted to reward yourself for additional efforts but this could be a mistake, as Box 2.3 suggests.

Box 2.3 Should you reward yourself for achieving goals?

Is rewarding yourself for achieving a goal a good thing? Not always. Some activities are rewarding in themselves. They are *intrinsically* rewarding. Like art and sport, learning is considered to be one of these activities. When such activities receive an external or *extrinsic* reward the effect can be negative. The activity becomes less intrinsically rewarding and may cease altogether. (This is why sometimes, in workplaces, rewards can have a negative effect on performance.) Good outcomes reinforce good work: the effort of producing high-quality assignments will produce good grades, and ultimately, degree success. These are rewards worth having and waiting for. Small, occasional rewards can help you to begin or finish tasks that you find difficult initially, however. Don't confuse rewards with support and encouragement – these always help!

Prioritising

Often, there are too many items on weekly and daily *To Do* lists when tasks other than study are added. If so, prioritise some tasks and activities and reschedule others. To do this you may find a priority matrix useful: the principles are so commonly used in workplaces that most people don't use a matrix – they just think that way about tasks. The essential elements of the matrix are set out in Figure 2.5. The priority matrix is the basis of the popular 'In Tray' task often used in selecting people for jobs; the ability to prioritise is an essential skill.

Tasks in Cell 1 of the priority matrix should be done first because they are both urgent and important; tasks in Cell 2 should follow; tasks in Cell 3 should be fitted in around those in Cells 1 and 2; tasks in Cell 4 should be crossed off your list. If there are tasks that will become urgent or important or both, then note them for action later. The hardest part of using a priority matrix is deciding what is *most* important.

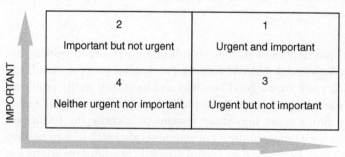

Figure 2.5 Priority matrix

This section of the book and the activities helped you to work backwards from goals and sub-goals, organise and manage your work to achieve your academic goal more easily and prepare you for professional life.

How long does it take to prepare an assignment?

Assignments need preparation. In your professional life, you'll be expected to break down tasks, work out the sequence of activities and have a realistic estimate of how long they will take, so why not use these techniques now? While complex forms of bar charts such as Gantt charts are popular in organisations for planning large projects, a network diagram is useful for smaller ones. It is used to break down a project into smaller components, show the relationship between them, the time needed for each and how long the project will take overall. Preparing an assignment can be regarded as a small project. A completed network diagram for this is shown in Figure 2.6. It is self-explanatory. The numbered tasks and arrows indicate the order in which the preparatory tasks need to be done and the time needed. To calculate the overall time you need, you add the times for individual tasks together.

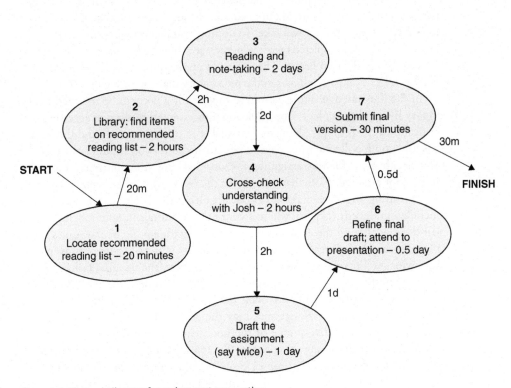

Figure 2.6 Network diagram for assignment preparation

ACTIVITY 2.11 Consider the preparation for your next assignment. Your aim is to produce a diagram like the one shown in Figure 2.6. First consider all the tasks you need to accomplish. Then start your diagram by drawing circles (called 'nodes') for individual activities, as in Figure 2.6. Label the nodes and number them in the order in which they need to be done. Now connect the activities with lines in the same sequential order. Estimate how long each activity will take (you will become more accurate with experience) and label each connecting line with the time estimate. Properly speaking, the connecting lines should be proportionate to the time taken, but this is not necessary unless your diagram is to be used in a more formal context.

Now add up the times along each line: the total is how long it will take you to produce your assignment, from start to finish. Bear in mind that you are likely to have to continue attending lectures and seminars, and carry out pre- and post-lecture reading while writing your assignment, so the sum of days on the network diagram – the total time estimated – needs to be planned as a series of study sessions.

If you need to save time, review the individual components. In the example, is Task 4, the meeting with Josh, essential? Could the time spent drafting the assignment be reduced by careful planning of the structure first?

For many tasks and projects, particularly those that involve more than one person, activities can be carried out in parallel. In such cases it's possible to calculate the shortest time a project will take. To do this, you identify not only the essential tasks that must be completed before another starts, but the *longest tasks* that must be finished before the next begins. Then you add up the durations of those tasks. This will be the 'critical path', shown in the preparatory diagram in Figure 2.7.

In the illustrated example, you have to wait for a book to be returned to the library by another student. The book contains essential reading so accessing it is critical but, frustratingly, the book is available in print form only and the library has told you it will take three days to be returned once you submit your request. You decide that, for this assignment, cross-checking your understanding with Josh is not essential. Note that waiting for the book (4) occurs in parallel to your other reading and note-making (5) but acquiring the book takes longer so it is included in the critical path, whereas your other reading and note-making is not. (In the diagram, all the activities on the *critical* path are in circular nodes while the one that isn't – reading and note-making – is not. Diagram conventions vary widely.) The total time on the critical path lines (the essential tasks with the longest lines) is the shortest time it will take you to produce the assignment.

Notice how the wait for the book holds you up, providing 'slack time' you could use productively. Notice too, how the critical path time would change if you found an alternative source of the book chapters during your reading and note-taking task. These are the concepts that inform Gantt charts and the software that uses Gantt charts for complex projects. You will encounter these in your studies: in professional life, effective management of complex tasks and projects is essential in delivering outputs and is likely to feature in performance appraisals.

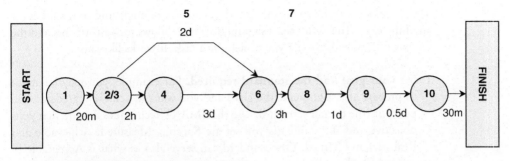

1 Locate recommended reading list – 20 minutes
2 Library: find recommended reading – 2 hours
3 Request book – (zero time)
4 Wait for book – 3 days
5 Read and make notes – 2 days
6 Collect book and read essential chapters – 3 hours
7 Cross-check understanding with Josh – *identified as not essential*
8 Draft the assignment, say twice – 1 day
9 Refine final draft; attend to presentation – 0.5 day
10 Submit final version – 30 minutes (online submission)

Figure 2.7 Preparatory diagram for a critical path analysis

Monitoring your progress

How do you rectify problems if your progress towards a goal is not going to plan? Professionals use a common but powerful management control tool: the control loop shown in Figure 2.8.

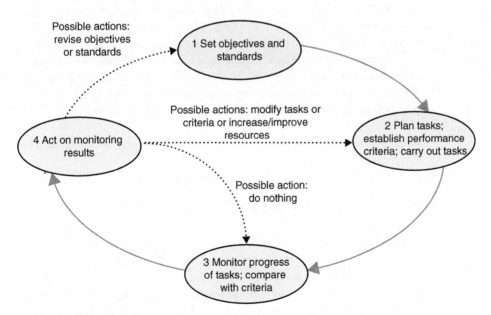

Figure 2.8 The control loop

The name of the technique may suggest a rigid way of managing your studies (or anything else). This is not so. It's useful because it allows for adjustments and the remedy of problems so that you *do* achieve a task. It works like this:

1. **Set your goal and the standard required.** For example, you may be about to prepare an assignment (the goal) and you want to achieve a grade of 100 per cent (the overall standard). Use the SMART technique. Be sure that your objective and the standards you set are **S**pecific, **M**easured, **A**chievable and **R**ealistic, and **T**imed. (The standard can serve also as what is **A**cceptable in your SM**A**RT goal).

2. **Identify and plan each of the tasks necessary to achieve the goal.** When planning each main task establish performance criteria. Use SMART objectives again, paying attention to how you will 'measure' whether a task has been done to the required standard. Your objectives for a reading task might be: *Read the six 'essential' items on the list and ensure understanding of the concepts by 26 November.* But how will you measure 'understanding'? You might decide to write a short summary of each text in your own words. (You can make use of these when writing your assignment). Note that when you state the number of texts, the deadline and a measure for 'understanding', you have three performance criteria for the task.

3. **Monitor your progress.** As you progress through the tasks in the appropriate order, you check on how long you are taking and whether you are meeting the performance criteria. In the example of reading, there are three key criteria to meet and you check your performance against these.

4. **Act on the results of your monitoring.** Few tasks proceed exactly to plan. For example, in your reading task, you discover that one text requires more time and effort to read than you anticipated but it is a key text. It means you might not be able to read all six texts. Worse, a long-standing commitment at the weekend means you can't 'gain time' by sacrificing some social time. Doing nothing about the situation is not an option: you won't be allowed to submit your assignment late. Alternatively, you could revise your overall standard (getting 100 per cent for your assignment may be too optimistic). However, your best initial course of action is to consider the tasks you set yourself.

- Might you improve your understanding of the difficult text by talking to other students who have read it?
- Is there another text that explains the difficult one more simply?
- Can you read on the train?
- Can you save time on another task?

Note that some of these remedies involve trying to save time (that is, increasing one of your resources or spreading it more thinly). You might want to improve other resources such as a better understanding of what you read – a cognitive resource. Invariably, the way to increase resources is planning because it releases time otherwise wasted or spent inefficiently. Fortunately, many improvements come naturally with practice. Next time you plan an assignment, you'll do it better. But you also need to monitor your progress, not only to quickly rectify

See *Using SMART objectives* in this chapter; see *Reading techniques and strategies* and *How to make reading notes* in Chapter 4 problems but, importantly, to learn and inform what you do and also identify any learning or support needs you have. Whatever field of work you enter after university you will need to plan, self-monitor, learn and develop your practice, so it's wise to acquire these skills now.

ACTIVITY 2.12 Using the network diagram you created in Activity 2.11, construct a control loop for a learning task. Set objectives and standards and establish performance criteria, ensuring that all are SMART. Then use it to monitor your progress as you move towards your goal. See how you can *systematically* keep track and make adjustments in a number of ways: you can modify the tasks you planned, adjust the performance criteria for each or increase your resources, such as by finding more time. You can also revise your objectives or standards. When you have used the control loop reflect on how it informed what you did and what you learned about yourself and your work. The control loop is a powerful tool and it's small wonder that it's ever-present in workplaces. Its origins and variations are set out in Box 2.4.

Box 2.4 About the control loop

The control loop originated in the field of mathematics and engineering in the nineteenth century. Business and management practitioners and academics have many ways of drawing it and there is more than one name for it – some call it the Plan-Do-Check-Act model. But all of the forms have four main stages and incorporate the all-important feedback loops that allow remedies to be put in place to stay on track.

Monitoring progress using a learning diary

Some students monitor their learning progression by keeping a learning diary. A learning diary is a record you keep of your study activities and their impact on your thinking, knowledge and skills. In a sense, it's a conversation with yourself. Some courses or learning activities formally require students to keep a learning diary. Learning diaries are usually expected to be *reflective* – you look back on and review what you have done, how you did it, how you felt about it and the effect it had on you. Record in your diary:

- what you did and when
- how long it took
- how you did it (the methods or techniques you used)
- why you chose these methods or techniques
- what you found particularly challenging and why this was so
- what problems you found and how you resolved them

- whether and how your thinking, knowledge or skills changed as a result of carrying out the task
- your views on your performance or output
- how you felt about any of the above
- your conclusions
- actions (what you would do if you had to repeat the task and improve on your effectiveness and/or performance)
- how you will act on your conclusions.

Not only do you learn from analysing and critically reflecting on study tasks, you can monitor your performance and plan improvements. Extracts from a learning diary are set out in Table 2.2. At regular intervals, look back at what you wrote to make sure you acted on your conclusions. Always do this before you begin an assignment and check it again before you submit the assignment. Did you act on your own advice?

To gain value from a learning diary it's vital to avoid being descriptive, that is, just stating what you did. Effective monitoring and improvement comes about through analysing how you went about a task and critically reflecting on your performance of it. Through this process you gain insight into how you learn and how to improve your learning skills. You learn *how* to learn.

See Critical reflection in Chapter 6

Some professionals keep learning diaries. They find them useful for their own development and as a record they can draw on for annual appraisals.

The writer of the diary extract in Table 2.2, a female student, has made some practical and personal discoveries, or is in the process of making them:

- planning is difficult without a full understanding of what's required
- understanding and learning are satisfying
- this satisfaction might be lost if she focuses *only* on what is needed for an assignment
- organised summaries of her reading are helpful and allow her to be selective later
- linking academic topics with the 'real' world has value (not yet fully explored by the diary writer)
- distractions and misjudgements about time can disrupt plans but there are ways of putting them back on course
- getting behind with study can lead to demotivation (again, not yet fully explored by the diary writer)
- short study sessions can be made use of if planned well
- scan reading is a useful way of deciding where time and effort is well spent
- critiquing reading material happens when you engage with it fully
- it takes practice to use formal structures for writing
- assignment guidance needs to be kept in mind: trying to fit elements in later often doesn't work without rewriting.

These discoveries may seem commonplace when written as a list. However, discovering them for oneself makes them personal, valuable and more memorable. They constitute self-knowledge which will help the learner to understand how he or she learns.

Table 2.2 **Extracts from a learning diary**

Diary entry checklist

What, when, how long; how and why. Challenges/problems, why, solutions adopted. Performance. Knowledge/skills gains. Feelings. Conclusions. Actions.

14 October

Spent the morning study session organising tasks for the rest of the week. It took a lot longer than I thought. First, I couldn't find the assessment criteria. Then I realised I needed all the reading to hand to see how long it would take me. I ended up guessing. I felt less organised at the end of the session than I did at the start! Felt a bit downhearted till I realised I'd learned that you can't organise anything without knowing WHAT you're trying to organise, so – a gap in my planning skills, but one I've overcome just by going through the process. Overall conclusion: a learning experience. I've written myself a checklist for next time I have a written assignment.

[...]

16 October

Spent two hours reading two journal articles. Enjoyed them, then realised that I'd made lots of unstructured notes without referring to the assessment guidance. I don't think it mattered because it meant I wasn't being selective, just trying to understand. I made a quick summary of the main points of each paper. I think I'll carry on reading and making notes this way – I think I'm happier getting the whole picture than just extracting what I need. However, if I'm going to do this I'll have to scan read papers first to make sure they're worth the time ... I like the fact that I've started to question what I'm reading and today I think I found a flaw in an argument. I don't know if I'm brave enough to put that in the assignment! Afterthought: I think making notes is helping my understanding. Not sure why yet.

[...]

18 October

Bad day! Nothing but interruptions and not much time between lectures. I thought I could fit in a couple of hours of study but managed only one. Felt demotivated when I realised. I'll get up an hour earlier tomorrow to catch up. Must switch off phone when reading. Perhaps I wanted to be distracted. Perhaps on busy days I'll do shorter tasks. Need to think about this when planning study.

[...]

20 October

Wow, my summaries of the papers I read really helped in drafting and writing the assignment! It was easy to select the points I needed.

[...]

21 October

Submitted the assignment with an hour to spare having decided there was no time to make any more changes. I spent my morning and afternoon study sessions refining it, only to realise to my horror that I hadn't looked at the guidance and checklist again after I started writing yesterday. When I checked I could see that I hadn't included some things, or they were in the wrong place. Structuring and writing has definitely been the most difficult part. I have the 'narrative' in my head but when I write it, it's stilted because of the formal structure needed. I don't think I'll have done as well as I hoped.

Table 2.2 (cont.)

I did enjoy the reading I did though; I'll look at advertising in a different light ... trying to guess the different marketing strategies for products when I go shopping will be fun and it'll help me remember what I read. So, not ecstatic about my writing performance but I'm happy to find that my concentration is better than I thought it was ... maybe I work better under pressure. I can do better next time if I keep the checklist to hand from when I begin to outline an assignment and then keep checking before I start the refinement. The problem was that when I'd finished the report I could see what I'd left out but I couldn't see how to fit it in. Think I'll ask Debbie if we can have a look at each other's work, now that we've submitted.

Working with study buddies and critical friends

Tom always liked to study alone; it was quicker. Working with anyone else was frustrating because of differences in perspective. His first 'proper' job after university has been a shock. To demonstrate team skills on his CV and at his interview, he relied heavily on a few mandatory peer-work activities. It hasn't taken long for him to realise that his professional interpersonal skills are poor. He's struggled to work with colleagues and to participate in meetings; often he sits in silence as others present, share and critique ideas without causing offence.

He finds it impressive when discussions produce problem solutions that he didn't anticipate. Tom notices that colleagues who work together successfully are more willing to help and support one another, making work life more enjoyable and productive. Sometimes there are disagreements but people don't take them personally. Tom begins to model some of the behaviours he knows he lacks.

Modern organisations expect graduates to be capable of working with other people, including in groups and teams. The UK's Management and Leadership National Occupational Standards (2012) lists more than 20 attributes and skills that people working in business and management should have in order to be able to work with others effectively. You are likely to gain some experience at university because there will be times when you are required to participate in various forms of peer-work. But there are many more opportunities – if you create them yourself.

Many universities recommend that students form small, informal study groups because they recognise the benefits. Provided the group is well organised, you develop professional skills, achieve more than you would alone and gain much-needed social support.

If you want to set up an informal group then use the comprehensive guidance in Chapter 8, *Working with others*. Covered in the following pages are various forms of one-to-one work with peers. You won't want or need to use them all. Select whichever suit you best – but be prepared to step outside your 'comfort zone' when you work with others. While you provide support for one another, the aim is not to confirm your own perspectives but to gain new ones.

Study buddies

A study buddy is a fellow student, studying the same course or courses as you, with whom you study to make learning more enjoyable and productive. You share your newly acquired knowledge and understanding on a regular basis. Choose a person who:

- you get along with
- wants to use sessions to work not socialise
- works at roughly the same pace as you do
- is reliable and trustworthy
- understands the idea of mutual study support.

As informal as the relationship sounds, there are rules of engagement that require discipline. Both of you need to:

- be committed
- be willing to provide encouragement and support
- feel able to challenge each other's understanding respectfully
- have a shared goal for each meeting
- agree on where and when you meet
- start and end meetings on time
- prepare for each meeting
- not allow discussion to drift off course.

Study buddies keep in regular touch, discussing their understanding of lectures, reading material and concepts and what they find difficult, testing out ideas for assignments, presentations and other learning activities. You might also find it useful to go through lecture and reading notes together. If there's a difficult study task coming up, simply doing some preparation together can overcome procrastination and increase your motivation. Always work on assignments individually after the discussion phase, however.

When revising for exams it's useful to practise answering exam questions with brief outlines of content. Making up exam questions and testing each other's knowledge is a good revision technique: you'll identify gaps in your own – and your study buddy's – knowledge.

A degree of friendly competition is healthy to avoid a situation in which you and your buddy always agree. If there is serious disagreement over interpretation of study material, look at the study material together, consider possible meanings and narrow them down to the most likely one. Alternatively, be tolerant of differences of opinion.

Agree with your study buddy that you will tell each other if the relationship isn't working. If your meetings have become social events you may have found a good friend but have 'lost' your study buddy. Some universities run buddy mentoring systems. Established students help new students settle in over the first semester. If this is what you need, ask if your university provides this service.

Critical friends

Everything from projects to governments can have critical friends. Critical friendship is a relatively modern idea, emanating from the field of education where it is much used. The aims are two-fold: to provide support as a friend would and to challenge by asking provocative questions or by providing critiques of a person's (or team's) work. The critical friend does not offer advice, but facilitates reflection and learning.

Critical friends are harder to find than study buddies because a critical friend needs to be 'outside' your situation and have a depth and breadth of knowledge. This rules out many of the students studying the same courses as you and many of your peers. However, you may find a critical friend among final-year students or postgraduates studying for higher degrees. Those who plan to have a career in teaching might be interested, along with those who have worked in business and management. Having experience of being a critical friend is a useful addition to a CV (curriculum vitae). You are looking for a person who:

- you trust and respect
- has a strong motivation to help develop others
- has the knowledge and experience to ask questions that cause you to think and reflect
- understands the role (the person may need to seek detailed information)
- understands the balance between support and challenge
- is willing to understand what you are studying or trying to do
- has good critical-thinking skills
- has good communication and interpersonal skills
- expects you to make up your own mind
- has sufficient time for regular contact
- is supportive and reliable.

In work settings, confidentiality is a vital attribute. In both study and work settings, for each session you set out what issue, problem or work you want to discuss and your critical friend agrees to engage with it. During the session you expect to be questioned and challenged so that you explore your thinking and assumptions, make sense of what you have learned, are aware of your knowledge needs and know how to meet them. A critical friend can help by providing alternative perspectives on an issue. At the end of the session, your critical friend helps you to review what you have learned. A risk with critical friends is that they err on the side of friendship and resist critique in order to protect your feelings. For your part, you must be willing for your thinking to be critiqued. An effective critical friend is able to judge how far to stretch your thinking without arousing your resistance.

The overall aim of critical friendship is to help you to improve your understanding by a process of constructive provocation. This can be uncomfortable but friendship prevents the process from being threatening or personal. Thus, the relationship needs to be based firmly on trust, mutual liking and respect.

See Critical thinking in Chapter 6 and Giving and receiving feedback in Chapter 8

Mentoring and peer relationships at work

Mentoring involves a more-experienced person assisting the development of a less experienced one. Peer relationships are more equal and mutual: you and a colleague help one another. Both are common in workplaces and they are useful to students who work while studying. This is because most business and management courses are designed to cover not only theory but how theory 'works' in practice. Mentoring – and peer relationships at work – can help you to apply your learning although you may need to create opportunities (see Box 2.5 on how to create them). This focus is slightly different from classic mentoring, which centres on personal and/or career development.

Box 2.5 Creating opportunities at work

Employed students sometimes find that they lack opportunities to apply their learning in the workplace. For example, you are likely to study staff recruitment and selection, finance, marketing and other functions which, in large organisations, may be the reserve of specialist departments. To ensure you have at least some opportunities to apply your learning, let your line manager and others in a position of influence know what topics you are studying and when. There may be a variety of ways in which you are able to make a contribution.

Developmental networks

An alternative to classical mentoring is a *developmental network* of mentors. In such a network, each mentor meets a slightly different need, according to his or her experience and expertise. The mentors in the network don't have to work in

See *Networking* in this chapter; see *Networking to create opportunities* in Chapter 9

the same organisation as you. If you choose the developmental network approach, you need to spend time cultivating a network. You must find and get to know people who can provide resources and information, support and feedback and who, at times, will challenge you. Whether you choose a traditional mentor or several people from a network, the way to make the most of such relationships is much the same.

Finding the right mentor

A mentor should be more knowledgeable than you are and be strongly motivated to help you to develop your knowledge. In a developmental network, a mentor may have more knowledge than you in just one area and his or her motivation may be some form of exchange with you. You need to identify your needs clearly to benefit from being mentored and be open to change and development. You are not seeking confirmation of what you already think or know; rather, you are looking for a different perspective from your own.

Key functions that mentors can perform include:

- arranging opportunities for you to apply your learning
- acting as a guide or role model
- providing additional information, knowledge and experience
- offering practical and/or emotional support and encouragement
- providing honest feedback and constructive advice
- challenging you to think more deeply, as a critical friend would.

Some organisations encourage or have mentoring systems. If you need to identify an informal mentor or developmental network mentors, then look for the same kinds of qualities and attributes that you would choose in a critical friend. Personal friendship is not vital but you must trust, like and respect one another.

The person must:

- be committed
- have an interest in you and your development
- be empathetic and able to listen
- be trustworthy
- help you to arrive at your own decisions (not theirs)
- understand the difference between critique (specific, helpful and forward-looking) and criticism (fault-finding).

A mentor will normally gain a sense of satisfaction from helping you to develop. In a developmental network, relationships may also be more informal and may involve some form of exchange.

The rules of engagement with mentors, informal mentors and developmental network mentors are the same as for critical friends. End relationships diplomatically if they are not working.

How peer relationships help

A peer relationship can be a viable alternative to mentoring. Although what can be provided is often more limited, relationships are less formal and easier to manage. A work colleague in the same, or a similar, role to yours and who is familiar with your work can:

- share information and technical expertise
- provide support and encouragement
- give feedback on work tasks
- be a sounding board.

A peer will expect you to provide the same for him or her (as may some developmental network mentors). Friendship isn't essential but mutual liking and respect are vital, along with a desire to help one another. This requires mutual trust. Giving and receiving feedback needs to be done sensitively. Ensure that the relationship is not a competitive one and agree that anything discussed will remain private.

See *Giving and receiving feedback* in Chapter 8

Other types of peer relationship exist including those those that are based on friendship. How you organise a peer relationship depends on its level of formality.

Networking

A network of people who provide mutual support and help is useful when you are studying and is essential in your professional life. Social networks often first consist of friends but an effective network is intentional and planned, with goals in mind. These goals may focus on study help and support right now but they soon include finding job opportunities. Networks can be informal or formal, such as those that professional associations provide.

Consider people you know or meet who you would like in your network (and why) and then make contact or quickly follow up on a first meeting while the person still remembers it. Be sure to maintain contact and build a relationship: try to be in touch with at least two different contacts each week. Social media and other networking resources are useful for finding potential contacts but make sure your network is a 'real' one based on good relationships. Reciprocity is important: help those who help you.

See *Networking to create opportunities* in Chapter 9

Developing and managing your network

Your network requires active management. Ask people in your network to suggest other people you might like to be in touch with. If you belong to university clubs or societies or do voluntary or paid work, you have further opportunities to extend your network.

Networking skills are now considered vital in the workplace: according to networking experts, connectedness between employees and between organisations can speed up information-sharing, foster collaboration, improve products and services and provide opportunities for professional development. Who knows what becomes as important as what you know. Your network will be especially valuable when you seek work or change jobs. In the meantime, it's useful when you are studying: it's a source of help when you need it.

Managing stress

At some point in your university studies you are likely to experience stress: most students do and some need professional help. Table 2.3 lists common causes of stress found by education researchers among traditional students moving directly from school to college, mature students, students with childcare responsibilities, international students who have moved to another country to study, part-time students who work and distance-learning students. Some students fit several categories, for example, distance learners who work and have childcare responsibilities.

Table 2.3 Common stressors

Common stressors
New demands that require intellectual, social or domestic adjustment
Challenges of a 'new life'
Challenges to your identity as a learner (your beliefs that shape your approach to, and experience of, learning)
Time and workload management
Finance
Homesickness
Having to meet new friends (social skills)
Having to work with others online
Lack of IT skills
Lack of social or academic confidence
Lack of study skills
Balancing study and other responsibilities (time pressure)
Reduced social and leisure time
Isolation
Difficulty in organising flexible childcare
Commitment clashes
Mismatch between school and university holidays
New demands because of cultural differences
Loss of, or reduction in, social support network
Concerns about returning home
Discrimination (including cultural and religious)
Difficulties complying with religious doctrine or rules

ACTIVITY 2.13 Identify your current and anticipated stressors. Identify one key stressor. Make notes on the specific circumstances to use in the next activity. If you are not currently experiencing any stress, work with a friend who is and who is willing to share details with you.

Some stressors, such as time and workload management, finance, lack of confidence and challenges to learning identity are common among students. Isolation tends to feature more among international students studying away from home and students who are too 'time poor' to spend time with other students. Disabled students and those from minority ethnic groups may be exposed to other stressors.

Coping and individual differences

Not all students succumb to symptoms of stress such as changes in sleeping or eating patterns, feelings of anxiety, irritability, headaches or depression. So why can one student cope well with a difficult situation while another copes less well?

One difference between students lies in beliefs, perceptions, values and attitudes – everyone's are different. They are subject to strong cultural differences, too: people assess and interpret the meaning of situations differently. So the same situation may be more stressful to one student and less stressful to another. The other difference lies in 'coping strategies': poor strategies are associated with downward spirals. For example, students who are stressed by lack of time may forgo sleep to catch up and become sleep-deprived. They are then less able to cope, which leads to more stress. This has a negative impact on academic performance and health. (Stress suppresses the immune system, increasing the risk of illness.)

The good thing about effective (or 'adaptive') coping strategies is that you can learn them. A well-respected theory of stress and coping has been developed, tested and refined by Richard Lazarus and colleagues over several decades. Figure 2.9 shows the basic mechanisms in this coping process.

The coping process

Consider Marc's case

My academic grades have been average so far, though I always set out to do better than this. My tutors believe in my ability to do better but, if I'm honest, I've never bothered to follow the advice on planning the structure of my written work: there's always something more pressing to do. To help my finances I work 20 hours a week part-time; I know it's too much and I need to find another job but it's hard to find work that fits around study. Now, a really important assignment is due. It carries 50 per cent of the total marks for continuous assessment on the course. The remainder of the course grade rests on an exam and I'm already feeling anxious about that. I should have started preparing for the assignment a week ago because I've other commitments coming up: it's my sister's wedding next weekend and I've also got to prepare a presentation for an assignment on the other course I'm studying. I've written the notes for it but I have to use PowerPoint and it takes me ages because it's only the second time I've used it. Today, on top of all that, my employer asked me to work more hours this week and he made it clear that it would be easy to replace me if I declined.

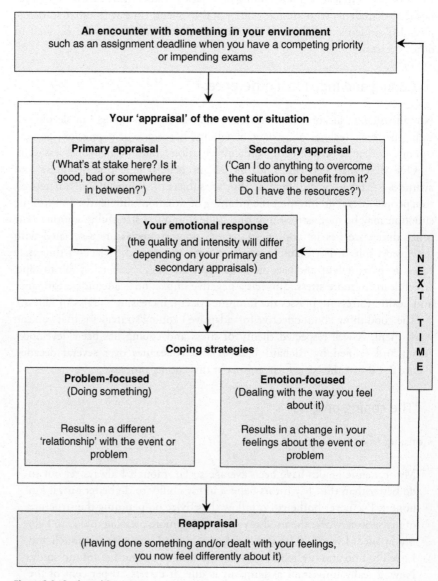

Figure 2.9 Coping with events

Adapted from Folkman and Lazarus, 1988

Marc's first reaction is that the situation is potentially harmful to his grades (his primary appraisal). His second is the thought that he doesn't have time to do any additional work for the assignment (his secondary appraisal). He feels out of control of the situation (his emotional reaction).

A poor, or maladaptive, coping strategy at this stage would be to muddle through with the prospect of a poor grade, increasing anxiety about the end-of-course exam and concerns about his overall degree success. That would be typical of Marc's previous behaviour. Marc, however, has decided to make a change (positive changes are often made during crises).

Adaptive strategies

An adaptive strategy is one that is usually both emotion- and problem-focused. First Marc 'manages' his emotional reaction (an emotion-focused strategy). He goes for a run to calm himself; then he talks to close friends to help him put things in perspective. They offer support and help which he builds into his problem-based strategy. The key issues, he decides, are a) time and timing of the assignment and b) lack of expertise with essay structures.

There is nothing he can do about the time out for his sister's wedding: that's something he has to accept. Work is a different matter, though. Marc decides to talk to his employer. He needs to decline the overtime and he also prepares himself to be given notice to quit. He's decided that a short-term finance problem is preferable to putting his goal of a university degree at risk.

Marc's employer is sympathetic to his dilemma but tells Marc firmly he should have said earlier that 20 hours a week was proving too much and that he could not work overtime. He allows Marc to work his normal hours but tells him to look for another job at the end of the semester. Marc accepts this with some relief. He decides he can use his time on his assignment more effectively if he finds out more about it and gets some formal help with structure.

Marc talks to his tutor who arranges support. His tutor also tells him about the university's financial help for students, which he decides to follow up after the assignment deadline. Marc's friends offer him their summaries of key reading to help him catch up and they agree to share and discuss essay structures next week – they're interested in the advice Marc receives. One friend, Amal, offers to help Marc use PowerPoint for his presentation. Marc realises that his lack of skill in using PowerPoint is the reason he's been putting off this assignment. They have fun doing it.

Dealing with emotions

As Marc works stepwise through his solutions, he finds his emotions aren't constant – sometimes he feels out of control, anxious and frustrated that he can't work faster – but he deals with them by reminding himself that he has a plan and he'll manage as long as he doesn't allow himself to be distracted. His Plan B is to ask his tutor if he can submit his assignment late, but he knows that's likely to increase time-pressure later on. He realises he'll need to take the same positive approach to revising for the exam.

By taking control of the situation, Marc coped well with it. Getting help took time – and he had to 'manage' his anxieties about this – with the result that he spent fewer hours on each task, but he used this time more effectively. He reflected that previously he had avoided seeking help because it would create more time pressure.

When Marc received his grade and feedback on his assignment

- his improved writing skills were reflected in his marks although his lack of reading let him down a little
- his tutor adopted a different view of him ('I'm pleased to see you're taking responsibility for your learning')
- he gave his presentation (it wasn't great but he'd learned a lot about using PowerPoint)
- he was honest with his employer
- he didn't lose his job immediately
- his financial difficulties remained but he'd see what could be done.

The outcomes were mixed and imperfect, of course, but they were *good enough* in the circumstances and he'd taken a first step along a new path. Next time his emotional response will be more positive.

Developing insight

In using adaptive coping strategies, you will need to be honest, insightful and creative. You'll need to be aware of your appraisals of situations and identify any assumptions, for example, about your resources. A student who is juggling studying with childcare may realise that friends who used to help with childminding have been lost through lack of time. It would be worth spending time rekindling these friendships, making new ones or organising a mutual-help group.

Look again at the case and identify where you think Marc displayed honesty, insightfulness and creative problem-solving. Creative solutions don't have to be new to the world, just new to you.

ACTIVITY 2.14 Using your notes from Activity 2.13, use the model to work through the current situation you (or a friend) are finding stressful. If it helps, work in a trusted group, share individual problems and have the group work on each. Try to arrive at constructive solutions that are acceptable to the problem-holder.

Working systematically to cope with a stressor normally helps, especially when you have the support of others. Sometimes professional help is needed, however. Seek it if you need to.

Culture and coping

The two coping strategies outlined, problem-focused and emotion-focused, are commonly found among Western populations with a culture of individualism and independence. Westerners are more likely to try to change the environment in order to deal with the stressor. People from 'collectivist' cultures, where there is more focus on social cohesion, may adopt other strategies. They may focus on changing themselves to deal with the stressor so that they can 'fit in' better or avoid 'rocking the boat'. They may seek social support while saying nothing about the stressful event or situation or their feelings.

The effectiveness of a coping strategy is likely to depend on the cultural context in which it is used but this research field is too new to be informative. If you are studying in a culturally diverse group of students, discussions about coping strategies will be productive and interesting.

Developing resilience

Some stressful events are short-lived; others are longer term. Whichever they are, they need to be dealt with constructively to prevent chronic stress. It's not possible to avoid adverse events and situations. Dealing with them will help you adapt and cope better – you will develop resilience.

There is no single 'recipe' for building resilience but these actions and habits are considered to be important.

- Developing and maintaining strong and positive relationships with family, friends and others. (Join groups to extend the circle of people who have an interest in your well-being.)
- Having plans or goals that are realistic and can be achieved in manageable steps (otherwise they are just wishful thinking).
- Accepting that life events and change happen and may be outside your control or influence.
- Building a positive attitude towards yourself and your abilities. (You don't have to be brilliant to succeed: make the most of what you have.)
- Finding helpful 'stress busters' such as taking exercise and avoiding unhelpful ones such as alcohol or drugs.
- Being mindful and decisive. Some problems may disappear by themselves; others don't unless you take action. Few problems are truly insurmountable, so develop a sense of proportion.
- Being resourceful: know where to get help.
- Developing good communication and problem-solving skills.

Managing others' stress

In your professional life you'll be exposed to a number of sources of stress such as workload, where and how you are expected work, insufficient control over what you do, work relationships and conflict, lack of support, unclear roles and organisational change. According to the UK's Health and Safety Executive (2007) work-related stress is a major cause of occupational ill health, poor productivity and human error. If you become a manager you may be expected to conduct stress risk assessments and minimise the impact of stress on employees you are responsible for by exploring problems and resolving them. You'll cope with workplace stress and be able to better support others if you have developed adaptive coping strategies and resilience.

Chapter summary

❖ Acquiring effective planning and management skills begins when you embark on study; they form the basis for professional skills.

❖ Students often have concerns about studying at university. Some may be unfounded; others may need remedies so that your academic performance is not negatively affected.

❖ Assessment happens in the workplace too! Constructive feedback helps you to recognise where improvements can be made. Assessment can be formative (low stakes) or summative (high stakes).

❖ Having a place to study helps you to be organised. But you need discipline to avoid interruptions and distractions.

❖ Developing a study strategy – a high-level plan for your studies – helps you to use your resources effectively. Workplace techniques can help you to assess what may hinder your efforts to achieve your goal and to analyse the causes so that you can remove or reduce them. Then you devise an implementation plan to do this. It's a process that you find in all workplaces.

❖ Planning your time well begins by understanding how you currently spend it. Drawing up an overall plan for the semester involves seeking information. Block out uninterrupted periods of study that you can protect.

❖ Plan study sessions by setting objectives that are SMART (Specific, Measurable, Acceptable, Realistic and Timed).

❖ Use scheduling tools and techniques to work out how long it will take to write an assignment. Even if you do this only once, you can use the concepts for planning study activities.

❖ The control loop is a powerful management tool that you can use to monitor your progress towards any goal and make timely adjustments, just as you would at work. Using it will become second nature.

❖ Keeping a learning diary can help you to critically reflect on your learning progress.

❖ Studying with others brings learning benefits. Organise your own peer support by finding a study buddy or critical friend. If you are studying while working, mentors or creating a developmental network or workplace peer support can help you to apply your new knowledge in the workplace.

❖ Stress is common among students. A formal model of coping helps you to identify adaptive strategies and develop resilience. In professional life you may have to manage the stress of other staff, too.

References

BBC (2016) *Skillswise* [Online]. Available at www.bbc.co.uk/skillswise/maths (Accessed 15 April 2016).

Folkman, S. and Lazarus, R.S. (1988) 'Coping as a mediator of emotion', *Journal of Personality and Social Psychology*, vol. 53, no. 3, pp. 466–475.

Health and Safety Executive (2007) *Managing the causes of work-related stress: a step-by-step approach using the management standards*, 2nd edn, The Health and Safety Executive [Online]. Available at www.hse.gov.uk/pubns/books/hsg218.htm (Accessed 5 February 2016).

Lewin, K. (1947) 'Frontiers in group dynamics: concept, method and reality in social science; social equilibrium and social change', *Human Relations*, vol. 1, no. 5, pp. 5–41.

Management and Leadership National Occupational Standards (2012) Skills CFA [Online]. Available at www.skillscfa.org/images/pdfs/National%20Occupational%20Standards/Management%20and%20Leadership/2012/Management%20and%20Leadership.pdf (Accessed 23 February 2016).

McKenzie, K. and Schweitzer, R.D. (2001) 'Who succeeds at university? Factors predicting academic performance in first year Australian university students', *Higher Education Research and Development*, vol. 20, no. 1, pp. 21–33.

National Careers Service (2016) [Online]. Available at https://nationalcareers-service.direct.gov.uk/Pages/Home.aspx (Accessed 15 April 2016).

OpenLearn (2016) The Open University [Online]. Available at www.open.edu/openlearn/(Accessed 15 April 2016).

The Open University (2011) *B/BZX628 Managing 1: managing and managing people*, Milton Keynes, The Open University.

Tyler, S. (2001). Management development at IBM: report to IBM and The Open University Business School, *The Open University Business School*.

CHAPTER THREE

How you learn

You *know* you can learn, otherwise you would not be studying at university. So why would you want to know *how* you learn? The reason is that you can improve how you learn. You can become an efficient and effective learner: an expert one. This expertise lasts a lifetime and is sought by organisations who want employees to have *lifelong learning skills* to meet ever-changing organisational needs.

Becoming more expert at learning is about using your existing learning resources fully and, in doing so, increasing them. But first, you need to recognise that you may have fixed learning patterns or ideas that hinder the way you use your personal resources and limit improvements. Discovering them may be uncomfortable but the rewards will be great.

ACTIVITY 3.1 Your conception of learning – your informal, personal theory of learning – can be a barrier to effective learning. Which one of the following statements most closely matches the one you hold?

1. When I'm learning something I aim to abstract the meaning.
2. I think learning is largely about increasing the amount of knowledge I have.

3. Learning means memorising information so that I can recall it when I need to.
4. I interpret information so that I can understand the world around me.
5. For me, learning is about acquiring facts and procedures that I can apply.
6. I believe that learning is the process by which I change as a person.

Adapted from original research by Säljö, 1979 and Marton et al., 1993

If you chose Statement 2, 3 or 5 then you hold an unhelpful view of learning. You see it as an accumulation of information to be memorised and reproduced. This is necessary for learning but there is more to learning than that.

Statements 1, 4 and 6 represent more helpful views. In the order they appear in the list, they set out a progression beyond memorising and reproducing: first there is abstraction of meaning from information, then using meaning to understand the world and finally, seeing learning as a process that changes you by developing your thinking and your views about the world. A first step to unlocking your abilities is to recognise unhelpful personal conceptions and to ask yourself *why* you adopted them.

Josie believes she is thorough, systematic and good at her job. She has a well-rehearsed routine for compiling weekly sales reports, which she produces swiftly and sends to her line manager. But her new line manager has asked her to present an overview to the team. She assumes a summary of the reports will suffice but at the presentation she is embarrassed when she's unable to answer questions about trends and forecasts. Reflecting on her 'weekly-reports routine' with her line manager afterwards, she admits: *No, there's not much point in having an efficient routine if I don't stop to make sense of the figures.* Over the following week, she realises that she has many such routines that are quick and efficient but need only the bare minimum of thought. Working out what she needs to change is disconcerting. Josie realises that her belief in her competence is based on her efficiency and her routines, not on understanding issues and having fingertip knowledge of sales.

The example underlines the importance of the *how and why* of learning and not just the *what* – what must be learned; what must be done. *How and why* form the foundations of good learning which remain with you long after factual knowledge is forgotten or superseded. This chapter takes you on a journey through different types of knowledge, how you acquire them and how you can transfer your knowledge to the workplace. Being aware helps you to become a truly effective learner.

What happens when you learn?

Understanding different types of knowledge and learning processes is important to becoming a better learner: you can become conscious of what you are learning and how you are learning it.

Learning is a universal process that begins in the simplest way: something we do produces a consequence. We clumsily hit a dangling toy; the toy swings to and fro. We learn about cause and effect. Gradually, through our actions and experiences, we begin to make sense of the world of objects, actions and people. Our sense-making is a kind of jigsaw. The pieces fit together to form a concept or idea. Our first concept of 'bear' may be that of a small soft toy that moves when we make it move. But when we discover that there are real, live bears our concept of bears has to assimilate some extra pieces of the jigsaw. Sometimes, however, the jigsaw requires a radical change.

This happens when new information conflicts with our current conception. The new pieces of jigsaw just won't fit. For example, we learn that some mammals give birth to live young; then we discover that some reptiles give birth to live young and some mammals lay eggs. Our 'animal concept' jigsaw needs to be reconfigured to accommodate the information, probably in this case by changing the defining characteristics of our animal categories. And so the conceptual jigsaws keep being added to and/or reformed throughout life. Consider how digital technology has changed conceptions of communication and how these have changed twenty-first-century models of how to do business.

When we construct our jigsaws we don't simply memorise information, storing it for later recall. We abstract, or draw out, key elements of information. Consider a table. What does an object need for us to call it a table? We'd probably say: *Four legs supporting a flat surface*. We generalise this to all objects with four legs and a flat surface, incorporating along the way, three-legged tables and flat objects that can serve as tables. We construct knowledge in this personal, individual way, but many of our constructions are similar to those of other people of the same culture because our constructs are influenced by culture. The following activity illustrates the notion of a concept and of abstraction.

ACTIVITY 3.2: Draw a chair from memory, without looking at one. Now draw the chair you are sitting on, without looking at it. Lastly, compare your drawing of the chair you are sitting on with the actual chair.

Your drawing of a chair from memory is, more or less, your concept of a chair. It probably doesn't match any particular chair: it's an abstraction. It is not an accumulation of all the chairs you have ever seen and used but captures their quintessential features. Your drawing of the chair you are sitting on probably doesn't look much like the actual chair. You probably hadn't noticed details such as the shape of the back and the seat, the type or angle of the legs. When you compare both drawings you may find that, in fact, they are quite similar. Your 'chair concept' influenced your drawing of a particular chair whose detail is relatively unimportant. Do you now have a better idea of a concept and abstraction?

The capacity to abstract has the advantage of removing us from the present – the *concrete* experience we are having right now. We can *think* about tables, chairs and many more complex things in the abstract. We can treat a concept almost as a physical object. We can examine its parts; we can deconstruct it; we can critically analyse it: *Why is this part here? Is it consistent with this other part?* We can 'play' with the parts and try to reconstruct them differently; we can combine elements of different concepts. We can also ask hypothetical questions, such as *What if our organisation used the blockchain system used by Bitcoin for transactions?* Hypothetical – *What if?* – thinking is a useful way to explore what doesn't yet exist, except in our minds. Innovators, entrepreneurs, senior managers and risk assessors all think in this way, as do keen employees wanting to help an organisation improve what it does and how it does it.

Much of your knowledge will be in the form of concepts or theories (a number of integrated concepts). Many will be acquired indirectly by reading because culture allows us to bypass direct experience: other people can tell us what they know from their experience or thinking. Knowledge can take different forms: think of riding a bike. You might be able to draw a bicycle, but can you draw how to balance yourself on two wheels? So, before moving on to how to learn more effectively, you need to know about different types of knowledge and how they are acquired.

Types of knowledge

Consider the following case.

Ewan has fulfilled his ambition to open a small fine-dining restaurant. He spent time developing his ideas for the restaurant, finding a location and creating a business plan. He now has a chain of three restaurants with an average of ten employees in each. His restaurants have a reputation for creative menus that change regularly.

Curious by nature and a keen experimenter, Ewan reads recipe books only for inspiration. Some of his experiments fail and fewer still become menu items: dishes must appeal to more than one or two customers. When an experiment passes all his criteria for success (including cost and preparation time) he demonstrates the making of the dish to his chefs. He takes particular care over the order of preparation and the timing. For some dishes it's important to prepare ingredients in particular ways. As an experienced chef himself he is impressively fast at wielding sharp knives – and still retains all his fingers!

Ewan must coach and manage all his staff so they develop their skills and perform at their best. In the restaurant business, wages are low and staff turnover is often high, so he tries to make his staff feel appreciated: he encourages them to make decisions for themselves to increase their commitment and job satisfaction. His staff teams are culturally mixed and he strives to understand these cultural differences to help staff work together harmoniously. He's found it helpful to identify his own cultural values, beliefs and behaviours as a starting point to understanding those of other people. When people ask him what the most difficult part of his job is he says it's dealing with staff.

One aspect of his job is to ensure that food storage, handling and hygiene meet health and safety regulations. Here, staff training is well worth the time. When he can, he likes to deal directly with customers. It's an ideal way to gain feedback on dishes and to ensure quality of service by his staff. For example, waiters need to have good knowledge of the dishes, the wine list and where ingredients are sourced. Ewan's role allows him to do what he enjoys: experimenting, improving his knowledge and creating new menus. He is very creative but he takes a systematic approach – not only to the tasks he sets himself but to the way he learns.

Your first thoughts on reading the case are likely to be that running a small chain of fine-dining restaurants is hard work. You are probably right!

ACTIVITY 3.3 *Part 1* – Read the case again and count the number of different types of knowledge that Ewan uses. You might also consider an area of your own life and identify the different sorts of knowledge you use.

It should be clear that Ewan possesses different kinds of knowledge. Chopping vegetables fast is not the same kind of knowledge as knowing about food-safety requirements. Understanding customers and staff requires a different sort of knowledge, too, as does the knowledge that Ewan uses when he experiments with dishes. You probably counted at least four types. Distinguishing between the types of knowledge is usually more difficult, however.

There are many ways of doing this but each presents some difficulties. Knowledge has a habit of changing from one type to another. For example, say you learn a numerical code to open a safe. This is explicit knowledge that you can state verbally: *The code is 205672*. After opening the safe many times, you forget the numbers but you know the spatial pattern of key presses on the keypad. Your knowledge has been transformed from explicit to implicit (often called 'tacit') knowledge. What was once knowledge that could be stated verbally is now encoded differently in the brain and expressed through a different output channel. Your brain has made a short-cut.

Different types of knowledge are used in combination when people carry out highly practised tasks. Virtuoso job performance is like this: some aspects can be carried out automatically, leaving you free to focus on what needs your conscious attention.

Here is one way of categorising different types of knowledge, based on the work of the late Benjamin Bloom and developed by David R. Krathwohl (2002) and others:

- knowing what
- knowing why
- knowing how
- knowing how you know.

Bloom's work remains very popular and you may encounter it during your studies.

Knowing what

This knowledge can be stated (it is *propositional*). It includes **factual knowledge** (for example, egg white is a protein, ovalbumin) and **conceptual knowledge** (for example, ovalbumin belongs to a category of raising agents, along with sodium bicarbonate and yeast). The difference between factual knowledge and conceptual knowledge is that a 'fact' is a single knowledge element ('egg white is protein') while conceptual knowledge combines and relates a number of knowledge elements into an organised, integrated set of elements (such as raising agents and their function when combined with other ingredients with which they interact). Conceptual knowledge includes knowing about principles, norms and rules that form the basis of a chain of reasoning.

Formal knowledge

Conceptual knowledge can be **formal**. Much formal conceptual knowledge is gained empirically from systematic and controlled observation of some kind. In the field of business and management, research often focuses on the practices of organisations and employees. Then, conceptual knowledge is *abstracted* from practices observed. From many observations of group dynamics, for example, a pattern is found and expressed as stages of group formation. The research results are refined into a concept or theory (a number of integrated concepts) and then *generalised*: the concept or theory will state something about group dynamics in general rather than the dynamics of a particular group in a specific context.

These formal theories or concepts are what you are likely to encounter in your studies. They are often codified or structured (their elements are systematically arranged and set out) like the theories of microbiology that underpin the food-hygiene regulations Ewan uses. These regulations form part of Ewan's conceptual knowledge. Formal theories – and conceptual knowledge – are modified, or even abandoned, on the basis of contrary or new evidence. This is the way formal conceptual knowledge is developed.

Informal theories

Theories can be **informal**, too. These are important in professional life even though they may not have the structure of formal theories. They can range from *expert* to *naive* depending on how much knowledge and experience a person has.

An example of a naive theory is attributing an inedible cake to using the 'wrong' flour because of not knowing the function of raising agents or gluten in flour. An expert informal theory is based on extensive formal knowledge, personal experience and learning.

Expert informal theories may lack the systematic development and structure of formal theory but they combine different sorts of factual and conceptual knowledge, including specific knowledge of an organisation, job role or task. Ewan's informal theory of food is an expert one gained through years of experimentation and practice, combined with formal knowledge. He's also willing to challenge his knowledge and question it on the basis of his experiments, which produce new evidence that may not fit his current conceptions. *Knowing what* can include **personal knowledge**, ranging from the foods we like to how our behaviour is shaped by our culture. Our informal theories and personal knowledge influence our behaviour.

Ill-informed personal theories or concepts based on *unfounded* beliefs can have a negative impact on others. If you believe that people from culture X are quarrelsome, your belief will influence your behaviour towards them. If you later discover that people in culture X are highly vocal and are expected to express their views freely, your personal theory or concept will change. You then regard culture X as expressive rather than quarrelsome and you are likely to be more tolerant. Similarly, if you have unfounded negative beliefs about your abilities (*I can't*) you restrict your learning until you revise your beliefs. Your unfounded negative belief prevents you from trying or experimenting: it's a self-limiting belief.

Knowing why

Ewan would not create a dish of pasta, bread, rice and potato. He *knows why*. It's not only because such a dish would be unappealing. It is not nutritionally balanced: it contains an excess of carbohydrates and lacks a balance of ingredients, textures and flavours. Knowing *why* when we acquire knowledge is particularly important. Equally, questioning our factual or conceptual information or our personal beliefs can lead to further knowledge. Knowing *that* (or *what*) without knowing *why* is often not really knowledge at all. Imagine that Ewan didn't know why he should follow food-hygiene regulations. He wouldn't be able to use them with understanding. A robot could be programmed to check levels of pathogens on work surfaces but it would have no understanding of why it did so.

Knowing why also extends to Ewan's behaviour towards his staff. It's not just that he wants to keep them engaged and committed. His attempts to understand his own culture and beliefs are attempts to understand why he thinks and behaves as he does so that he can better understand and work with people from other cultures. His self-knowledge and self-awareness help him to understand interpersonal differences. Understanding the *why* of our own emotional, social and cultural knowledge is important in professional life.

Knowing how

Knowing *how* can be *procedural* knowledge such as chopping vegetables or riding a bike, usually learned by practice, but it includes any knowledge that is so well-practised that it has taken on the quality of being second nature. Experienced managers can set agendas and run meetings because they are accomplished practitioners and know how meetings 'go'. They have a routine or process or procedure that they follow.

Ways or methods of doing things, along with skills and techniques, come under the heading of 'knowing how'. Knowing how also includes knowing *when* to use a process, skill or technique. *Know-how* is valued in organisations. If the know-how needed in a particular task is difficult to learn, an employee may work with a person *with* the know-how who guides, shows, advises and so on. This is particularly the case where know-how is implicit, such as how to knead bread dough to the right texture. When bread-making machines were first developed, bakers were studied to find out how they did it – and their implicit (tacit) knowledge was turned into explicit knowledge that could be programmed into the machines.

Much of the informal knowledge in an organisation is possessed by individuals and this knowledge can be lost to the organisation when a person leaves or retires. Some organisations implement knowledge management strategies to ensure such knowledge is not lost.

Successful strategies tend to use a mix of codifying and storing information for reuse later, and person-to-person contact and communication. In the case study of Ewan, consider how much of his work is based on knowing how. What strategy does he use for passing on his creative know-how to his chefs? Consider too, your own know-how and the strategies you use to pass it on.

Knowing how you know

Knowing *how you know* is what's known as metacognitive knowledge. It covers *knowing about* knowing and the **self-regulation** of learning. In previous sections of this book you have thought strategically about studying, how to plan study tasks, to monitor your progress and to reflect on the outcome. If you do this mindfully, paying attention to and being aware of your thinking, then you know *how you know*. You are able to regulate your learning and improve it.

Ewan exercises control over his learning by being systematic. You'll look in more detail at self-regulation of learning later.

ACTIVITY 3.3 *Part 2* – Now return to the scenario and try to *identify* the types of knowledge and skills that Ewan uses. Notice that it can be difficult to isolate different types of knowledge and skills because they are often used in combination.

Cultural, social and emotional knowledge

It is easy to think of learning and gaining knowledge as something we do in formal settings. However, to function successfully in the world we need to acquire and use cultural, social and emotional knowledge.

Cultural knowledge

Consider Ewan, again, running his restaurants. He reveals his cultural knowledge in the dishes he creates. He doesn't have to consciously consider whether to put cat or dog meat on a menu in the UK. While it's legal to do so, he 'just knows' that it would be unacceptable to the majority of his customers. Cultural knowledge is often like this. We may not know we possess cultural knowledge until we encounter the practices or beliefs of a different culture. Researchers who study internationalisation, where other-culture knowledge is vital, find that it helps if we first understand our own cultural beliefs and practices.

ACTIVITY 3.4 Consider to what extent your beliefs about food are influenced by culture rather than what is edible in your environment. Identify items that *might* be edible, such as non-poisonous weeds, insects, amphibians, reptiles, mammals and so on, but that you would not eat, and say why you wouldn't. If you can, pose the same questions to a person from a very different culture from your own and compare responses.

You probably uncovered some cultural knowledge about what doesn't count as food in your own culture and why not. An example is: *Cats are not food in my culture. We regard cats as pets and we don't eat pets.* You may have had more difficulty with fish and rabbits! You may have needed to define a 'pet' if you also decided that eating non-pets such as squirrels and hedgehogs is not acceptable either. You will have gained cultural insight and probably some knowledge of your prejudices (we all have them).

Social knowledge

Our social knowledge is culturally influenced, too. We know what behaviour is socially acceptable when we meet people we don't know, adapting according to the formality of the context. We know 'how it goes' when we visit a restaurant. Something stops us from entering the restaurant and sitting on another diner's lap or pouring our soup into a glass and drinking it.

If you think about the way your world is organised, you may realise that these are *social activity systems*. A social activity system is made up of objects (for example, in a restaurant these include tables, chairs), rules (pay before you leave), norms (if tables and chairs are provided, don't sit on the floor), conventions (in some restaurants, wait to be seated; in a café, find a table yourself), divisions of labour (the tasks of waiting at table and cooking the food) and formal relationships between people (the manager is in charge of the restaurant staff, for example). Note that conventions are more dependent on the context than norms and so vary more. Social norms are often a reference point – a social compass – for people and they feel uneasy transgressing them. In some situations, however, people feel that they are 'released' from some social norms. Students have a reputation for this at times!

Note that the physical aspects of particular environments, such as the restaurant, are culturally prescribed and aid you in terms of knowing and remembering what to do or *how things go*. Your knowledge of social activity systems, such as visiting a restaurant, may feel as if it's your own but it's likely to be similar to that of other people in the same culture or social group.

Organisations are full of activity systems: they are designed or have evolved to meet multiple goals. In the case of restaurants, the commercial goal is to turn hungry people into satisfied, well-fed ones by transforming ingredients into appetising dishes while making a profit. However, they draw heavily on established activity systems in the process.

ACTIVITY 3.5 Recall something you have done recently such as visiting the hairdresser or the library. Now think of it as an activity system. Note down the objects, rules, norms, conventions, divisions of labour and formal relationships you encountered or were aware of. There will be some interaction between, for example, objects and norms or conventions. You may find it easier to draw a diagram of the various elements of the activity system with arrows showing the relationship between them.

When you completed the activity you were probably surprised at the complexity of your notes or diagram. Consider how complex a system would be if it involved many activity systems, each one interacting in some way. This is how an organisation would look if you documented all its activity systems.

Emotional knowledge

Emotional knowledge is what we use to recognise, understand and manage emotions – our own and those of others. Organisational leaders and managers, if they want to win over the hearts and minds of employees and influence them, must recognise and understand the feelings of staff and manage those feelings, for example, by acknowledging concerns.

In the scenario, Ewan uses his emotional knowledge in managing his staff. Paying his employees more would make his restaurant meals more expensive than those of his competitors. Instead, he tries to help his staff achieve job satisfaction by encouraging them to take decisions appropriate to their role. It might be easier to give them orders but Ewan would not like to be managed in that way himself.

He uses his emotional knowledge and makes the assumption that others feel the same way as he does.

He listens to his staff and customers and tries to see things from their perspective. Using *empathy*, he gains understanding of different perspectives. Empathy is predominantly a cognitive skill (it is different from sympathy) requiring reasoning to try to understand others. Empathy allows us to make sense of the behaviour of others and how they feel, make 'connections' with them and predict what they might do next so that we can respond accordingly (Allison et al., 2011; Wheelwright and Baron-Cohen, 2011).

See *Six steps to empathy* in Chapter 8

Empathy and sympathy

Most people are capable of empathy. We empathise with a friend who has missed an assignment deadline and we may also feel sympathy, that is, feel a degree of distress. We can do this because we know or can imagine how it *feels* (sympathy) or can *understand* how the friend feels (empathy). In order to empathise, we must believe that people think and feel even though we can't experience their thoughts or feelings. A practical consequence is that we constantly assess what others might be thinking or feeling and what they know. Our assessments and interpretations shape our responses.

We normally also know when not to make assumptions. When beginning a conversation with a person we don't know well we often start by asking if he or she knows about the matter we want to discuss. When we talk to a fellow student studying the same course, however, we might just say: *I found that article on X a bit lacking in detail.* When we assess the level of knowledge people might have we adjust our own behaviour and what we say accordingly. In short, we are doing no less than attempting to mind-read.

In some situations, there is more room for error than others. A common mistake made by students when writing assignments is to (rightly) assume that a tutor knows about topic X. However, what the tutor wants is an assignment that sets out a student's understanding of topic X, making no assumptions about the tutor's knowledge!

Learning by doing

The focus of learning when we are students is often on learning from books or instruction. We don't have to experience something first-hand to learn about it. But this is not the only way we learn. We also *learn by doing* – a feature of learning in the workplace. Learning by doing is often referred to as experiential learning – the learning you do through direct experience. David Kolb, the renowned North American educational theorist, together with Ron Fry developed a formal model of such learning that sets out a *cycle* of experiential learning, shown in Figure 3.1. This is the kind of learning you do when you perform your professional work role and is simulated during your studies when

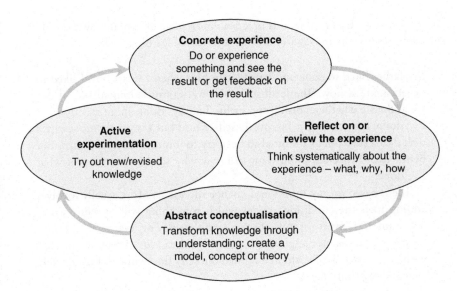

Figure 3.1 The experiential learning cycle

Based on original work by Fry and Kolb, 1979

you carry out learning activities such as role play. (You also learn by doing whenever you *act*, of course: when you structure an assignment, seek sources of information, work with others and so on.)

The model describes a cyclical process and what you need to do to learn from experience.

1. You do or experience something that you consciously attend to.
2. You reflect on the experience. You try to make sense of what you did, why and how. Reflection involves thinking systematically, analytically and critically about your action or experience. You need to be prepared to question what you did or how you responded to the situation and explore more desirable actions or responses. You may need to consider the personal beliefs and values that influenced your action or behaviour. Effective reflection takes courage!
3. You conceptualise. As a result of your reflection, you *abstract* from the concrete experience the most important ideas and create a model or concept. In doing this, many details of your actions may be lost. Abstract conceptualisation removes you from the 'here and now' of an experience.
4. You engage in active experimentation. In this step you test your conceptual understanding when you next carry out the same action or experience a similar situation. By reflecting on *that* experience, you refine your conceptual knowledge, which then informs future actions. Experimenting involves making or using opportunities to experiment and taking calculated risks. Your insights and experiments change your practices and responses to situations. The cycle never stops.

In the scenario, Ewan gained his practical knowledge of cooking by *doing*. Here he describes how he moves around the experiential learning cycle.

My father liked to cook and let me help him when I was a boy. I liked to experiment, as now. The feedback from my actions is immediate – I can see and taste whether a dish is successful. I always think about exactly what I've done, how and why. I'm overly self-critical but I want to know why a dish didn't turn out as I wanted so I can try to improve on it. If it turns out better than expected, I still want to know why so that I can repeat what I've done.

Then, based on my thinking, I change my theory. This usually involves adding to it the conditions under which something will or won't work. Sometimes, I overturn my theory completely. For example, a friend developed intolerance to gluten in wheat. It led to a lot of experimentation with gluten-free flours. After I'd figured out why they worked, I completely changed my thinking.

Yes, you can learn about cooking from a book but there's no substitute for actually doing it.

A criticism of Kolb and Fry's model is that there is little evidence that people invariably use every step. Often they use *trial and error*, moving between concrete experience and testing. That is, they do something and if it doesn't work to their satisfaction, they simply try something different next time. They omit the reflection and conceptualisation stages. It takes conscious effort and motivation to move around the cycle systematically. Moving around it is essential both in formal education and in the workplace.

The problem of learning styles

What kind of learner are you? Do you have a preferred style of learning? These questions are common ones and you might encounter them in your studies. But it can be counter-productive to categorise yourself in this way.

Attempts have been made to identify 'learning styles' or 'learning preferences' based on whether learners prefer to experience, feel, think, watch or do, or to learn visually, verbally, alone or in a social setting. There is little empirical evidence to support these ideas, however. Learners who use them can limit their opportunities for learning. At university, much knowledge results from reading and producing assignments. In the workplace, what you need to learn will be presented in a variety of ways. For example, information may be given verbally in meetings and briefings; verbally and visually during presentations and practical demonstrations; and in written form in reports and memos. If you define yourself as having a preference, say, for 'visual learning' you may pay less attention to information presented in another form. You need to develop all your information input channels. The advantage of using many input channels is that you establish more neural connections and are more able to readily retrieve information.

It is useful to remember this 'many channels' idea when making presentations to others. Your presentations will be more memorable if you use a variety of ways of presenting information: in addition to conceptual interpretations of the information, use pictures, diagrams, descriptions and demonstrations.

How do you go about your learning?

Is there a general approach to learning that you can adopt to help you become an expert learner? First, consider your approach to your learning now.

ACTIVITY 3.6 In Appendix 1 of this book you will find the *Approaches to learning and studying inventory: self-score version*. Complete the inventory and then use the scoring system provided. At the end of the activity you should have identified your current approach to learning.

Approaches to learning

Research by Noel Entwistle and his colleagues (for example, Entwistle, 2013, 2000; Entwistle and McCune, 2004) has shown that learners take one of several approaches to learning, based on particular characteristics. These are described below (Tyler and Entwistle, 2007) with permission from The Open University.

1. Deep approaches

Active deep approach. Learners currently using this approach are characterised by their intention to understand what they study, although they may decide to memorise some things when they decide that memorising is best. They are interested in ideas and in relating them to one another. They question and use evidence critically; they seek out the main points and aim to gain an overview; they draw conclusions. They see the purpose of a task or its use in a wider context than the study situation.

Another strong characteristic of this approach is *monitoring*. Learners ensure that their work meets their own requirements as well as assessment demands. They monitor their understanding of what they are studying, check their own reasoning and pay attention to feedback. They also monitor their general skills such as communication and locating learning resources.

One or more secondary characteristics complete the active deep approach: *organised studying* and *effort management*. Learners are systematic, prepare for study sessions, organise their time, prioritise, and work steadily through a course. They also channel their efforts and push themselves. They focus on their studies and keep going even when things aren't going too well. They don't seem to find concentration a problem and can force themselves to stay focused even when they are bored by what they are studying.

Deep approach without much effort. Learners currently adopting this approach are similar to those with an active deep approach, except that *organised studying* and *effort management* are not much in evidence.

2. Surface approaches

Active surface approach. Learners who describe themselves in this way often study without much sense of purpose. They are primarily concerned with memorising information with a view to reproducing it when required, for example, in assignments and tests. Material may be memorised without understanding. Learning is unreflective; information is accepted unthinkingly and knowledge may be fragmented. Rarely do learners with this characteristic stray beyond the syllabus of a course.

Like those who adopt an active deep approach to learning, however, they also possess the characteristics of *organised studying* and *effort management* but usually in more moderate levels. Learners with an active surface approach often study quite hard but may wonder why they don't do well.

Surface approach without much effort. In learners currently adopting this approach, the *organised studying* and *effort management* characteristics are absent or present only at low levels. The approach is characterised by unreflective learning and routine memorisation or following procedures without thinking about them just to complete the required work.

3. Organised and managed approach

In learners with this approach the *organised studying* and *effort management* characteristics are dominant. Other characteristics may be present but at more moderate levels. These learners take neither a deep nor surface approach but organise their studies and manage their efforts to achieve good outcomes. The learner may be someone who is very keen to succeed in terms of course grades, but who is less concerned with understanding than someone using a deep approach. Previously, this approach was termed 'strategic' but it is not as clearly identifiable as the deep and surface approaches.

4. Mixed approach

A few patterns may show fairly high levels of both deep and surface approaches, with moderate levels of monitoring, organised study and effort management. The presence of both deep and surface approaches is contradictory and seemingly implausible, but research indicates that learners describing themselves in this way may have a misunderstanding of what is involved in learning and a lack of awareness of how to use learning support.

Profile of a learner

Looking back to a previous learning situation, you can probably recognise some of these approaches: the person who was disorganised and concerned only with scraping over the hurdles of assessment; the student who was motivated by academic success; the person who constantly interrupted with questions starting with 'if' and 'why'.

What is important to understand, however, is that the learner characteristics which make up each of the recognisable approaches to learning are not mutually exclusive. Learners can have elements of a number of them. This is why your completed questionnaire provides a *profile* of your approach. An *ideal* profile would show a combination of strengths in four characteristics: the deep approach; monitoring; organised studying; and effort management. Few learners have this profile, but it is one you should aspire to.

Approaches are not fixed

Our approach to learning is not fixed. Consider situations in which you are pressed for time or anxious, or you need to learn something uninteresting or irrelevant to you. Consider the difference between studying for a university degree that will be career enhancing, and learning about your new mobile phone. Your approach to learning is influenced by your time, your interest and the value you place on particular knowledge. But your approach to learning does matter if you intend to succeed in your studies – and in the workplace. A deep approach will produce a deeper understanding of what you are learning. Moreover, a deep approach among managers is associated with applying learning in the workplace *and* the important 'diffusion' of knowledge that happens when new knowledge is used with others at work (Murphy and Tyler, 2005). Interestingly, perhaps, approaches to learning are not often or consistently associated with academic learning outcomes in terms of course grades, although surface learners often perform less well. The organised and managed approach is usually successful but the deep approaches are associated with success when understanding is required.

Developing an effective approach

When you carried out Activity 3.6, you discovered your current approach to learning. This is the first step in developing a more effective approach. If you identified a profile that was not predominantly deep and monitoring, or with too little organisation and effort management, you need to identify your beliefs and attitudes to learning and modify unhelpful ones. You may need to think again about what learning is.

You also need to adopt learning methods that develop your understanding and the quality and depth of your thinking. You'll find a number of ways of doing this in this book. You may find you need to organise your time better, to make way for experimenting with and developing better ways of learning. Disorganised study wastes time, and deep learning takes longer, at least in the short term. If you currently take an organised and managed approach it may involve taking shortcuts that limit your learning. If you already possess a deep approach you may need to adopt techniques to produce efficiencies to avoid overload, without damaging your understanding.

The key to changing your approach depends on both *attitude* and *intention*. If you think differently about learning, you behave differently. Moreover, you have to *want* to behave differently. Learning how to learn, including the accompanying change in attitude, is not comfortable but you will come to readily accept a degree of discomfort when you associate this with effective learning.

In your professional work you need a desire to understand, together with commitment and the skills required to learn. Organisations will expect you to identify your learning needs, plan how to meet them and acquire the necessary knowledge effectively and efficiently. 'Good' learning may be a little more demanding but there are few, if any, shortcuts. Fortunately, 'good' learning endures for a lifetime.

Becoming an expert learner

It has been said that we know how to be taught, but not necessarily how to learn. We can be novices at learning – and novices share some of the same characteristics as surface learners. University learning *seems* like a simple process of acquiring knowledge but in reality it develops thinking. The pattern of this development has been studied among university students. Figure 3.2 shows the progression in thinking that occurs as concepts of learning change from 'reproduction' when a learner simply memorises information to 'transforming' when knowledge changes the learner as a person.

On the first step of the ladder, students see 'facts' as separate entities, accepting them even if they contradict one another. Each 'fact' is equal, hence the term *dualism* for this kind of thinking – opposing facts can exist side by side. On the final step of the ladder when students leave university, however, they realise that knowledge is not absolute but 'relative', that is, it is not independent of the way in which it was derived. It can be challenged. Students can see that knowledge is provisional, ready to be revised in light of new evidence. Thus, they are able to examine different perspectives and assess how well each is supported by evidence. Students therefore become more expert learners as a result of the development of their thinking. No longer are 'facts' accepted as 'true'. You can help this development along by consciously attending to *how* you learn.

Learning how to learn

When you set about a learning task, if you go about it mindfully, paying attention to your thoughts and actions, you can learn *how to learn* and improve

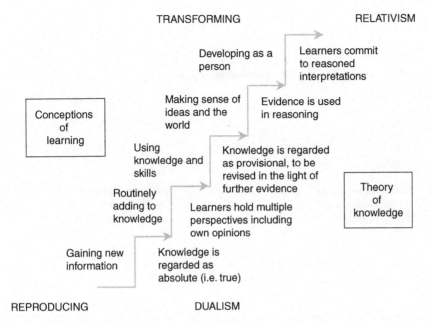

TRANSFORMING   RELATIVISM

Developing as a person

Learners commit to reasoned interpretations

Conceptions of learning

Making sense of ideas and the world

Evidence is used in reasoning

Using knowledge and skills

Knowledge is regarded as provisional, to be revised in the light of further evidence

Routinely adding to knowledge

Theory of knowledge

Learners hold multiple perspectives including own opinions

Gaining new information

Knowledge is regarded as absolute (i.e. true)

REPRODUCING   DUALISM

Figure 3.2 Concepts of learning and their development

Adapted from Entwistle, 2000 based on original research by Perry, 1970

your learning. Repeating the same pattern of learning, one that is not modified by previous learning tasks, won't help you. Yet many students approach every formal learning task in the same way. They miss opportunities to learn how they might have done better. Knowing how to learn is a special kind of knowledge. It is effortful initially but practice makes it a habit that you take into the workplace.

Good learners manage their learning by a process known as *self-regulation of learning*. There are many models of self-regulation but most converge on the same or similar factors. A model developed over several decades is that by Barry J. Zimmerman, a pioneer of self-regulated learning (for example, Zimmerman, 2008). Figure 3.3 sets out Zimmerman's basic model. Like all models of self-regulation it is both cyclical and iterative, that is, you can move backward and forward around the circle. The model focuses on internal, metacognitive conditions:

- your self-beliefs
- your motivation
- your analysis of a task and what's required
- your assessment of your current knowledge of a topic
- your knowledge of the skills, strategies, methods and tactics you can bring to the task
- your use of these skills, strategies and methods *mindfully* so that you can monitor whether they are working
- how you maintain your attention, concentration and effort
- how you reflect on the outcome.

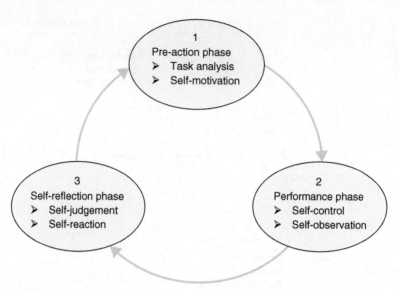

Figure 3.3 Self-regulation of learning: the cycle

Adapted from Zimmerman, 2002

The pre-action phase

Two clusters of factors are important in the pre-action phase – **task analysis** and **self-motivation**. **Task analysis** involves working out what the task is, what's required and what strategies, methods and skills you need to do it. It involves setting a goal for the task. This might be to understand a particular theory using a set of journal articles. In this case you bring your 'reading and understanding strategy' to the task. This strategy may involve methods and skills such as scan reading the material first, arranging it in some kind of reading order, then reading it fully, making notes and summarising to check your understanding.

Self-motivation refers to a cluster of factors, the most important of which is *self-efficacy*. This is your belief in your capability to carry out the task. Self-efficacy is quite task-specific and will depend on whether the last, similar task you carried out turned out well or not. If it didn't then your self-efficacy for the current task will be lower.

How self-efficacy works

Self-efficacy is what makes you summon up your resolve and get on with something. It influences your motivation and persistence in carrying out the task and influences effort management: the time you devote to the task and the maintenance of your focus, attention and concentration. Learners with high self-efficacy increase their efforts to overcome difficulties, while learners with low self-efficacy may procrastinate – put off a task or allow themselves to be distracted – or they may reduce their efforts and skim over 'difficult' sub-tasks.

You have some control over your level of self-efficacy. If it is low because the previous outcome was not successful, then you can increase it by working out what went wrong, attribute the causes accurately and aim to put things right *this time*. Remind yourself that you *do* have belief in your general ability to learn, otherwise you would not be studying at university. Also remind yourself of your ability to get things done.

Motivation and expectation

In addition to self-efficacy, self-motivation refers to your expectations about the outcome. You are more motivated if you expect success, but it is important to be realistic. If you are overconfident you will be disappointed when the result doesn't meet your expectations. Alternatively, you might have low expectations of success because you believe you lack sufficient ability. This can be a self-fulfilling prophecy: your attention, motivation, persistence and effort management suffer as a result and the outcome will be the disappointment you anticipated.

Goal orientation

A third component of self-motivation is goal orientation – whether your goal is a *good performance* (a good outcome) or whether it is *appropriation* (where you generate your own knowledge by a process of understanding and interpretation). Appropriation involves a deep approach to learning and is the appropriate goal for learners. You are likely to have an appropriation goal if you have an intrinsic interest in the material to be studied and aim to become knowledgeable. The problem with performance goals is that they focus on the external value of the goal rather than the satisfaction of learning. This means learners' interest may be extrinsic: they are more interested in the result than the knowledge gained.

See *How do you go about your learning?* in this chapter

The value you place on your learning goal is vital in shaping your thinking in the pre-action phase. If you consider a goal to be fairly unimportant, you may plan to make little effort. It's a common response to 'unimportant' goals.

Other pre-action factors

Researchers believe that other factors at play in the pre-action stage include planning activities, time-management skills and control of the study environment – for example, avoiding noise and distractions. Many learners may go through the pre-action phase without being aware of it. Self-regulated learning is about being mindful of your thoughts and considering the range of actions and decisions you are going to take because they influence how you carry out the task.

ACTIVITY 3.7 Recall a recent learning task. What thoughts did you have before you began work on it? Did you consciously think about the task, what was required and how you would approach it? Were you aware of your feelings about it: your level of motivation, your confidence in achieving the task and your expectations of success? What can you learn from the thoughts you had? Check your answer using the information on the pre-action phase.

Performance phase

The performance phase requires **self-control** and **self-observation**. You need **self-control** in using the strategies, methods and tactics you have chosen in the pre-action phase and in maintaining their use. Control also needs to be exerted over paying attention: you need to keep yourself focused and maintain your effort and motivation.

To be aware of all of this, you need to be **self-observant.** Then you can make adjustments. For example, should the task be easier than anticipated you might feel more motivated and decide to increase the standard you set in the pre-action phase. Or you might decide to experiment with your learning strategies, methods or tactics, or work on improving a study skill such as note-making. If the task is less interesting than anticipated, you might find ways of maintaining your motivation and effort, perhaps by assessing your progress through the task and re-focusing (*The less time I waste, the sooner I'll finish*). Should the task be more difficult than expected, you might decide to spend more time monitoring your understanding of the material (*I don't understand that; I must be reading too quickly* or *I don't understand my notes – I've been writing down what I read, not my interpretation*). You might also decide you need help.

These are the behaviours of self-regulated learners who maintain a metacognitive awareness of what they are doing during a task. Some researchers believe that emotion control is important, too, in reducing or dealing with intrusive, negative thoughts or anxieties that can distract you. These might arise, for example, as a result of low self-efficacy (*I can't do this*) or a focus on performance (*What if I get a low mark?*).

The influence of pre-action factors on performance

During the performance phase learners draw on their prior knowledge and study skills. Problems can arise if, in the pre-action phase, you are overconfident and have decided a task will be easy, or if you have set an unrealistically high standard for the outcome (goal). Then the task may turn out to be more complex and difficult than you anticipated and you find that your prior knowledge, learning strategies, methods and skills are insufficient. Your performance suffers if you aren't exerting sufficient self-control to identify the problems and see how you can rectify them. You may become confused and 'lost'. Rather than muddle on, you need to stop and return to the pre-action phase.

ACTIVITY 3.8 In the learning task you considered in Activity 3.7, think about how you performed the task. Was it easier or more difficult than expected? Were you aware of your level of motivation and effort and the ways in which you controlled and maintained them? Did you change the strategies or methods you used to achieve the task and why was this? Did you note any gaps in the knowledge and skills you believed you had before the task – and what did you do about them? Check your answer using the information on the performance phase.

Self-reflection phase

The self-reflection phase involves various types of **self-judgement** and **self-reaction**.

Self-judgement

Self-judgement refers to self-evaluation when you compare the actual learning outcome with the outcome and standard you set. If there are discrepancies, learners try to attribute causes. These attributions of causes can be categorised as:

- internal – causes over which the learner has control
- external – causes outside the learner's control.

Learners whose assessments of their ability are positive and accurate normally attribute causes to internal factors within their control. (*Everything took longer because my note-making wasn't good … I was just copying the text at times.*) Learners who are overconfident before performing the task often attribute causes to external factors outside their control. (*The tutor set a task that was too hard.*) It's important to note that the terms *internal* and *external* refer to the degree of control a person *believes* he or she has, not whether the cause exists *within or outside* the learner. Thus, learners with low self-efficacy often attribute the cause to a lack of ability which *looks* like an internal cause but is an external one if the learner believes that ability is fixed and nothing can be done about it.

Self-reaction

Self-reaction refers to the feelings that result from self-judgement. Satisfaction with the task outcome, or the learner's approach to it, is reinforcing. It increases self-efficacy, including the motivation to learn next time. Lack of satisfaction is also positive and adaptive if the learner has accurately identified *internal* reasons for discrepancies and makes plans to rectify them next time. Making mistakes is a vital part of learning – *the* most valuable trigger for learning, many researchers believe. When discrepancies are wrongly attributed to *external* causes, however, the opposite can occur. External attributions allow overconfident learners to defensively preserve unrealistic views of themselves and so fail to carry over 'lessons' to subsequent study tasks. Learners with low self-efficacy who attribute discrepancies to their own lack of ability will carry over the same low, or lower, self-efficacy to subsequent tasks.

Overconfidence and low self-efficacy can be associated, of course: overconfidence is often a way of covering up negative feelings about one's own ability, although very high self-efficacy can also lead to overconfidence, too. The trick is to make an accurate assessment of your current ability, plus a little optimism! (You can always improve your ability over time.)

ACTIVITY 3.9 Using the same learning task as you did for the two previous activities, consider the self-judgements you made about your performance of the learning task and the feelings you had.

- To what did you attribute any discrepancies between your expectations and what actually happened?
- Did you make a mental note of anything you might change next time you carry out a similar task?
- Did you feel better or worse about yourself and your abilities?
- If you felt worse, what might you do about this next time?

Check your answer using the text on the self-reflection phase.

An advantage to becoming a self-regulated learner by working on your metacognitive awareness is that you develop the knowledge you need for lifelong learning. Your know-how paves the way to increasingly independent and autonomous learning. It is a vital attribute to offer employers and, if you are already working, you will be able to enhance your professional learning and performance. The following case is set in a workplace but the behaviour of Charlie, the central character, is typical of many students.

Charlie is new to the organisation and to the innovative Project Z, which requires team members to develop and master new processes quickly. Charlie's manager asks him to develop a 10-minute presentation on Project Z and has provided a short, written brief that Charlie can find on the project's SharePoint. Charlie readily agrees. It should be easy, he thinks, because he's prepared lots of presentations before despite some unfortunate mishaps beyond his control. He checks to see that the presentation brief is on SharePoint before he takes a long weekend's leave.

On his return, he has an hour to spare at the end of the day and he sets to work, telling himself: *I know the project's aims and objectives off by heart. I'll just organise a few slides that set them out.* He quickly identifies 'the headlines' from the original project proposal and asks a secretary to insert his text into PowerPoint slides. He knows he should really master PowerPoint but there are two systems diagrams that need to be resized to fit the slide format. 'Right, that'll do,' Charlie says when he takes a look at the slides the next day. Charlie's manager calls by to see Charlie later in the week. 'Is everything going all right with the presentation, Charlie? Any questions or anything I can help with?' Charlie tells him the presentation is already done. 'I'll look through the slides, then,' Charlie's manager replies.

Later Charlie's manager calls by again. 'Charlie, the audience is the project team's support staff. They're all conversant with the project's objectives. What they really need is a summary of the implementation plan that the core project team discussed at the last meeting. Didn't you read the brief?' Charlie makes an excuse about his holiday disrupting work. Afterwards he thinks to himself: *That was dreadful. But I'm not going to feel bad about it. My manager should have simply told me what he wanted when he first asked me to do the presentation.*

ACTIVITY 3.10 Identify how Charlie set himself up for failure and learned little or nothing from carrying out the task. Check your answer using all three phases of self-regulated learning.

Using self-regulated learning in the workplace

In the world of formal education, learning is the primary purpose of all you do. In the world of work, organisations exist for other purposes. Learning for its own sake – out of curiosity – is a luxury few organisations can afford. Learning is valued and expected, nonetheless. The increasing complexity of work and ever-changing demands are not the only reasons that employees need to learn, nor the need for innovation. Often, the reasons are more mundane: many work practices, activities and tasks rely on employee learning for their continuity.

Organisations differ in how they promote and support employee learning. Each organisation has its own learning culture ('the way learning is done round here') and these cultures can be very different. In some organisations, learning is structured, actively promoted and supported in a variety of ways from teamwork to job rotation. In many others, there appears to be no obvious provision for employee learning at all. This is because it is unstructured, on-the-job learning which is often taken for granted and unremarked upon.

In fact, an impressive amount of this type of learning takes place in every organisation, every day, whatever the learning culture of the organisation and regardless of sector and type. Learning needs arise and are met as employees carry out their work. Work and learning are often interdependent. The learning goal *is* the work goal because employees know that organisations value output and productivity – and that may be what promotion and career prospects depend on.

Making time to reflect

This emphasis on productivity – on outcomes rather than process – means that, in particular, there may be little time for the reflection needed for effective, self-regulated learning. What does all this mean for employees? It means that you need to be attentive to your learning in the following ways.

- Identify your own learning needs.
- Set your own learning goals.
- Identify resources and make effective use of colleagues.
- Make efforts to attend to and make space for the process of learning, including the important reflection phase. You may need to negotiate with line managers for 'learning time'. Using the phrase 'skill development' will often produce a positive response.
- Find sources of feedback on process as well as outcomes at work; here, peers or colleagues you work with can help.
- Accept that you may not gain all the necessary learning in one attempt because of time and resource demands. This means prioritising your learning needs and achieving them in small bites each time you carry out the same or similar tasks. It can be frustrating to have to spread mastery over several similar tasks, but a benefit is that you will be able to practise and consolidate what you learned last time.

Note the high degree of responsibility you need to take for your workplace learning – and, if you are or become a manager, your role in the learning of other employees. In the workplace, employees who are self-regulated learners are likely to experience richer learning and achieve their career aspirations. The study of self-regulation of learning at work is a relatively new field of research and one with which organisations themselves have yet to fully engage. Graduates who know how to exercise self-regulation and can demonstrate the benefits will be the pioneers in the organisations they work for.

Transferring your knowledge and skills

You are probably studying, or intending to study, courses on organisational strategy, marketing, finance, leadership, operations and human resources to name but a few key topics. You expect to use this knowledge in your work as a business and management professional. To do this you need to *transfer* it.

Transfer of knowledge from one context to another can be relatively simple, such as when you transfer your car-driving knowledge and skills to driving a small truck, but this is not always the case. You may understand something of group problem-solving from your university studies but be unable to recognise and solve a problem involving a workplace team. Things often look and seem different in a workplace context and you may struggle to 'map' what you know to the new situation.

Transfer does not happen automatically. Indeed, current knowledge and skills can hinder transfer such as when, for example, knowledge of pronunciation in one's native language hinders the pronunciation of words in a different language. This so-called *negative transfer* can sometimes be a problem. Transfer is easier when the new context in which the knowledge and skills are to be used is very similar to the one in which learning took place: the context is *near*. It is harder when the contexts are very different or *far*. Moreover, far contexts can look near when they are not and vice versa. Consider the following examples.

Jane and Akira are business and management graduates in their first jobs in different non-for-profit health organisations. Jane attends a meeting at which the discussion centres on the possibility of changing public behaviour to reduce the number of cases of Vitamin D deficiency without increasing skin cancer risk by over-exposure to sunshine or other sources of ultraviolet light. The science is complicated. The variety of factors involved, in addition to skin type and diet, mean it is impossible to provide guidance on 'ideal' exposure time. There is little evidence that Vitamin D supplements are effective and the active ingredient in tanning creams and sprays is under scrutiny for links to cancer. Jane is sure that the result of the meeting will be about 'selling the benefits' of limited sun exposure but she sits in silence as she tries to see exactly how her marketing knowledge can be used in this complex and confusing context.

Akira is attending a meeting, too, but on the introduction of a new system for allocating work in a part of the organisation in which pay is relatively low. The system should increase workflow. Akira quickly outlines to the meeting a marketing plan to 'sell the benefits'. He is dismayed when a manager tells him that 'selling the benefits' is just one part of a wider change management plan that's needed. *The full engagement of staff is needed and they'll resent a marketing approach*, the manager says.

In Jane's case her marketing knowledge – and her assumptions – are hindering her ability to capture the important features of the situation. She'd be wise to use her problem-solving skills first. In Akira's case, he's too ready to map his marketing knowledge to the communications feature of the situation, which requires a broader approach using his knowledge of human resource management and change management. Both have failed to transfer their knowledge.

At the heart of effective transfer are the 'deep' approach to learning and 'learning how to learn'. These help you to acquire the other skills you need for rapid transfer and extending your knowledge.

See *How do you go about your learning?* in this chapter

Fortunately, the skills and behaviours that are important in knowledge transfer are ones you can begin to practise now. Transfer of learning involves more than a simple pattern of 'learn-it-here, apply-it-there' use of previously acquired knowledge (Perkins and Salomon, 2012). They use the example of a person noting the high price of oranges and relating it to prior information on poor weather conditions in key growing areas and theoretical knowledge of supply and demand. The concept of transfer is a difficult one and transfer is hard to achieve in practice because it requires effort and skills. Your first task is to search for connections between the context in which your learning took place and the different one in which your knowledge may be relevant. Perkins and Salomon (1992) succinctly set out the six key elements of learning transfer.

1. **Thorough and diverse practice.** Practise your skills and knowledge in as many different contexts as possible. At university you will follow a number of courses, each providing a different context. You can apply knowledge from one (or more) to another, for example, applying financial knowledge to marketing. Courses that take a problem-based approach to learning will be especially useful. If you are working while studying, your place of work provides more contexts in which to practise. If you are not, you can apply your knowledge and skills in other areas of your life. When you shop for a product you can switch roles from customer to management professional to consider what the organisation's marketing strategy is and whether and why it is effective. You can apply your knowledge and skills more easily if you belong to a voluntary organisation or club and are involved in aspects of organisation.

2. **Explicit abstraction.** Transfer of knowledge and skills depends on whether you have 'abstracted' the critical attributes of a concept, situation or problem. Understanding the underlying principles or features aids transfer. Asking why and 'self testing' what you know ensure that you deepen your understanding and knowledge – and fill gaps. As you study, focus purposefully on understanding underlying concepts and principles. Then apply these to everyday life. For example, if you are studying marketing and business ethics, consider how an ethical marketer would sell the can of beans you are buying.

3. **Active self-monitoring.** Monitoring your learning is a component of learning how to learn or self-regulation of learning, covered in this chapter. Practise this whenever you study. It can be interesting to be aware of, and monitor, the different strategies you use for different learning tasks, ranging from formal study to looking up a bus timetable. What are the differences between the strategies and what are the similarities? Why might this be? Differences can often be traced to approaches to learning, with 'surface' approaches being applied to low-priority learning (such as bus times).

4. **Mindfulness.** Mindfulness has no standard definition. Rather, it refers to a general state of awareness of what one is thinking, feeling and doing and attending to one's surroundings, which are likely to include other people. It also means temporarily reserving judgement: being judgemental has the effect of redirecting attention elsewhere. Being mindful allows you to 'step back' mentally and be more aware. By noticing and attending to what you might otherwise ignore or take for granted, you gain new knowledge about yourself, how you are doing something and the situation around you. Mindfulness is often used in organisations in the context of safety or 'safety cultures' and risk awareness. Individuals are encouraged to be alert to the complex nature

of work and its demands rather than rely on authority and rules. It has also become a popular topic among writers on business and management and has been taken up by a wide range of organisations to help reduce stress and improve empathy and communication. The advantage of mindfulness is that it can be practised anywhere and is equally valuable in study as it is in the workplace.

See *Six steps to empathy* in Chapter 8

5. **Frequent practice.** Frequent repetitions of knowledge transfer help you to remember the knowledge you have and extend it as you apply it to different situations in different contexts. Organisations often waste spending on staff training and development by failing to follow up short programmes with opportunities – and time – for people to quickly and repeatedly apply the knowledge they have gained. As a student, you create your opportunities; as an employee, you can request them, too, as well as creating them.

6. **Structure learning for transfer.** It's possible to structure learning with transfer in mind. Good educators do this. They set learning objectives and design programmes of learning with transfer in mind; they provide practice opportunities during the programme and give feedback. In workplaces they provide support for transfer when the programme has ended. Support includes opportunities, time, the involvement of other key staff such as line managers and sometimes refresher programmes. Consider these factors as you learn; use them when you are working and when you support other people's learning.

ACTIVITY 3.11 Consider your current way of studying. Do you think about how your knowledge might be used in specific situations in an organisation – or in your daily life? Take something you learned recently and work out where and how you can apply it. Mindfulness should prevent you from making hasty judgements.

Practise the skills of transfer as you study different topics and in other areas of your life. The habit will help you to learn in and from different contexts throughout your life. When you transfer your learning you consolidate and extend your knowledge. At the same time your knowledge contributes to your intuition – a feeling of 'knowing'. The better one's knowledge, the better one's intuition or instincts. In turn, you make better decisions.

Learning and changing

The content of this chapter may have surprised you. You may have asked *What does a business and management student need to know about the psychology of learning?* Learning is not just about memorising but also about thoroughgoing revisions to your knowledge, self-beliefs and ways of thinking – revisions that you encourage and manage as you study. Changes are sometimes incremental and sometimes radical: students can sometimes feel that, suddenly, all they understood about something lies in fragments. Provided they continue to study and to think, however, a new way of understanding emerges.

Never be afraid to challenge or abandon old, unhelpful ways of thinking: this is the nature of learning. You are learning about learning to succeed at university, to become a lifelong learner, to support the learning of others in the workplace and to help the organisation you work for – or will do – to develop a positive learning culture.

Chapter summary

- ❖ Your concept of learning may hinder your progress. Recognise unhelpful concepts and make efforts to change them.
- ❖ Knowledge is *constructed*. Learn how to deconstruct it by critical examination. Organisations want 'good thinkers' who can help them improve what they do and how they do it.
- ❖ Knowledge has various forms: knowing what; knowing why; knowing how; and knowing how you know.
- ❖ Learning can be uncomfortable when you encounter information that doesn't fit your current conceptions. When you study your understanding is in a constant state of change.
- ❖ Cultural, social and emotional knowledge are as vital as formal knowledge in order to function in the world. Insights help you to understand yourself, others and how our social world is organised.
- ❖ Learning by doing and reflection are important in the learning process. They are the primary ways in which you learn in the workplace.
- ❖ How do you go about your learning? The ASSIST inventory can help you to identify your own approach and to improve it. In this way you can help yourself to become the kind of expert learner that employers want.
- ❖ Learning how to learn involves metacognitive processes that you can practise as you study. You self-regulate your learning by understanding and exercising control over it. You need to do this in the workplace.
- ❖ Organisations expect you to take responsibility for your learning. You may also be required to manage the learning of others. Be a workplace learning pioneer.
- ❖ The transfer of knowledge to contexts other than the one in which you acquired it is a vital skill. You can practise as you study.

References

Allison, C., Baron-Cohen, S., Wheelwright, S.J., Stone, M.H. and Muncer, S.J. (2011) 'Psychometric analysis of the Empathy Quotient (EQ)', *Personality and Individual Differences*, vol. 51, no. 7, pp. 829–835.

Entwistle, N.J. (2000) 'Promoting deep learning through teaching and assessment: conceptual frameworks and educational contexts', *TLRP Conference, Leicester*, November [Online]. Available at www.tlrp.org/pub/acadpub/Entwistle2000.pdf (Accessed 16 April 2016).

Entwistle, N.J. (2013) *Styles of learning and teaching: an integrated outline of educational psychology for students, teachers and lecturers*, London, Routledge.

Entwistle, N.J. and McCune, V. (2004) 'The conceptual bases of study strategy inventories', *Educational Psychology Review*, vol. 16, no. 4, pp. 325–345.

Fry, R. and Kolb, D. (1979) 'Experiential learning theory and learning experiences in liberal arts education', *New Directions for Experiential Learning*, vol. 6, no. 1, pp. 79–92.

Krathwohl, D.R. (2002) 'A revision of Bloom's Taxonomy: an overview', *Theory Into Practice*, vol. 41, no. 4, pp. 212–218.

Marton, F., Dall'Alba, G. and Beaty, E. (1993) 'Conceptions of learning', *International Journal of Educational Research*, vol. 19, no. 3, pp. 277–300.

Murphy, S.M. and Tyler, S. (2005) 'The relationship between learning approaches to part-time study of management courses and transfer of learning to the workplace', *Educational Psychology*, vol. 25, no. 5, pp. 455–469.

Perkins, D.N. and Salomon, G. (1992) *Transfer of learning. Contribution to the International Encyclopedia of Education*, 2nd edn, Oxford, Pergamon Press.

Perkins, D.N. and Salomon, G. (2012) 'Knowledge to go: a motivational and dispositional view of transfer', *Educational Psychologist*, vol. 47, no. 3, pp. 248–258 [Online]. DOI: 10.1080/00461520.2012.693354 (Accessed 1 August 2016).

Perry, W.G. (1970) *Forms of ethical and intellectual development in the college years: a scheme*, New York, Holt, Rinehart and Winston.

Säljö, R. (1979) 'Learning about learning', *Higher Education*, vol. 8, no. 4, pp. 443–451 [Online]. Available at http://link.springer.com/10.1007/BF01680533 (Accessed March 6, 2016).

Tyler, S. and Entwistle, N.J. (2007) 'Approaches to learning and studying inventory: self-score version', in Tyler, S. (ed), *The manager's good study guide*, 3rd edn, Milton Keynes, The Open University.

Wheelwright, S. and Baron-Cohen, S. (2011) 'Systemising and empathising', in Fein, D.A. (ed), *The neuropsychology of autism*, Oxford, Oxford University Press.

Zimmerman, B. (2002) 'Becoming a self-regulated learner: an overview', *Theory into Practice*, vol. 41, no. 2, pp. 64–70.

Zimmerman, B.J. (2008) 'Investigating self-regulation and motivation: historical background, methodological developments, and future prospects', *American Educational Research Journal*, vol. 45, no. 1, pp. 166–183.

CHAPTER FOUR

Reading, making notes and finding information

Oliver has read the report on likely causes of a failure of scaffolding during building repairs. He re-reads it for the key points and then makes a list of implications for the company. He also lists a series of questions for the reports' authors: he needs clarification on some points and more information on others. He calls them. Later he meets the Health and Safety Manager, Nancy. At the end of the meeting Nancy says: 'I can see you're on top of this, Oliver. Get back to me with some suggestions to deal with safety issues. I realise that the contractors were largely responsible but the accident doesn't sit well with company values. We need to look more closely at our systems and processes.'

As the scenario shows, in professional work you need to be confident that you've understood accurately and engaged critically with what you have read or heard. If you haven't, then your interpretation of information will lack authority when you have to comment or report back. Not only that, unsound interpretations can have negative consequences for organisations. Many people are mistakenly overconfident. Study at university is an ideal opportunity to hone the skills you need later: you probably do more reading and note-making at university than at any other time in your life. Indeed, the amount of reading is often challenging.

More often than not, too, you have to seek out your own sources of information and ensure that they are reliable. Sourcing high-quality information and accurate, critical interpretation of material are needed before actions are taken that can have significant effects on an organisation and its employees. For this reason, it's best to master these skills now. In this chapter you learn the fundamental skills of reading critically, note-making and seeking and evaluating information, all of which you need for study and for your professional work.

Reading strategies and techniques

When you sit down to read are you aware of *why* you are reading – and does the purpose affect *how* you read? You can probably answer these questions intuitively but it is easier to identify purposes with examples.

ACTIVITY 4.1 Consider the scenarios below and then respond to the questions that follow.

1. Gary has arrived at the dental surgery a little early for his appointment. He picks up a magazine in the reception area and casually turns the pages, looking for something interesting to read while he waits.
2. Kaara has already read a number of academic articles for her assignment. She wants to use a diagram she saw and now she's trying to find it.
3. Laurence is searching for a book on human resource management that covers managing volunteers in the not-for-profit sector. He finds two books with a chapter that appears to cover this and is about to make his selection.
4. Suyin has just finished reading a financial report at work and is now monitoring her understanding of it by revisiting the key points.
5. Aaron is reading a text in order to critically review it for an assignment.
6. Meredith has just bought a flat-packed shelving unit which requires construction. She is studying the diagrams she found in the box.
7. Otho must read a case study about an operations management problem in a large company. He's in a hurry and wants to extract just the main points of the case as quickly as possible but he's finding the language used is complex and the terms are technical. He can't seem to identify the main points by glancing through the text.
8. Maria has logged into the library to find items on a reading list. Her first search term produces a number of choices. She browses the journal titles and looks at the latest contents list of one of them. One article looks intriguing. She looks through it quickly and, then, without much more thought, settles down to read it. It covers an area of knowledge she

didn't know existed but which helps her to understand a topic she has just studied – and it changes her perspective.

In each case, identify the purpose each person has in mind as he or she reads. Then try to describe the different ways in which the characters are approaching their reading. Otho's purpose is set out but can you identify his problem? Maria's purpose and behaviour may be quite difficult to understand but consider how purpose and reading behaviour might change. Read on to check your responses.

The differences in the way the readers approach their reading reflect the *purpose*. In Scenario 1, Gary simply wants to pass time. This means his reading is casual, without focus, and takes little effort. It is easy for him to see from the title of the magazine and the headlines what kind of article to expect. The 'point' of each one will probably be quite simple, such as a celebrity making a new film. The language used will be very accessible. The shorter the words and sentences, the easier a text is to read. Gary can assess all this without reading every word.

When we study, we generally do not have Gary's purpose in mind, but we might sometimes use a similar, if more systematic, reading technique. Note that Gary might change his reading behaviour if he finds an article that he finds engaging. This is what happened in the case of Maria. Her purpose wasn't to pass time; she browsed – 'just looking' out of interest – and changed both her purpose and approach to her reading when she found something relevant to her studies.

Compare Gary's behaviour with that of Aaron in Scenario 5. Aaron's purpose is to fully understand the text before him. He needs to read it 'cover to cover', probably re-reading parts to check his understanding. Like Aaron, Meredith in Scenario 6 has set out to read for understanding because she needs to apply – accurately – what she reads. In the remaining scenarios, the characters are reading with the purpose of assessing whether the content is appropriate: they are selectively reading by *scanning* or *skimming* – or both in turn. Scanning, skimming, and *reading for understanding* are all reading techniques and strategies that are influenced by a reader's purpose. Scanning is looking at selected elements and omitting large parts of text, while skimming is glancing quickly through a text. Like Maria, you might do both before reading for understanding. Otho's problem is that he has chosen the wrong technique for the reading material. Read on to see why.

Reading selectively

Scanning

Scanning is ideal for getting an overview of a text or to extract specific items of information. You might read the first and last sections of a text (they may be labelled *Introduction* and *Conclusion*) and then the first and last parts of any subsections, paying particular attention to any key points, summaries and diagrams. You don't read a text from cover to cover; when you scan it, you omit large parts of it. Scanning is also useful when you are searching for key points of information to decide whether to spend more time on the text, when you revisit a text to check your understanding or want to find something you read in the text earlier.

Gary in Scenario 1 first scans the magazine to see if there is anything worth reading. Kaara in Scenario 2 and Suyin in Scenario 4 are doing this, too. Scanning is a useful technique if you want to relocate a specific piece of information that will be easy to identify, such as a diagram, after you have read a text. All you need do is glance through each text until you locate it. If, like Laurence in Scenario 3, you are searching for a textbook that covers a particular topic, you first scan the contents page and the index and then turn to the relevant part of the book to scan the headings and subheadings. Maria in Scenario 8 *starts* by scanning: she looks at contents pages and titles of articles and the abstracts to see if they contain anything of interest. She immediately changes her reading strategy (and purpose), however, when she finds something intriguing.

Skimming

Skimming is used to decide if a text covers the material a reader wants. You quickly glance through the whole text to identify key terms or see if they are present. From this, you can quickly assess whether a book is accessible and covers what you need in sufficient detail and at an appropriate level of complexity. Skimming is normally sufficient to make a comparison between one textbook and another. Lawrence in Scenario 3 must skim the book chapters after scanning them. However, the ease and speed with which you can do this depends on the difficulty of the text and your familiarity with the subject matter and terms used. Otho in Scenario 7 encounters problems because the text is too complex and technical for skimming. Skimming becomes easier as you acquire knowledge of a topic and become familiar with the language and terminology.

While skimming is useful, it's not a substitute for reading a text 'cover to cover' for understanding.

Reading for understanding

When you read for understanding you read an entire text carefully. You need to do this when you are critically analysing the content, as Aaron is attempting in Scenario 5: An important part of this strategy is how you deal with difficult parts of the text or unfamiliar words. Effective readers re-read difficult passages or read on to see if the meaning becomes clear, returning to the difficult passage if it doesn't. For unfamiliar terms a specialist dictionary or glossary is a vital tool. In Scenario 6, Meredith is not dealing with complex information but she needs to read for understanding and take care not to omit steps in the process. In her case she is immediately applying the information she reads. In this scenario, understanding means being able to apply information. Practical knowledge is gained from seeing the results of applying the information. Diagrams need to be read with as much care and attention as other kinds of information.

Browsing and serendipity

Ask any professional how he or she 'discovered' something that changed his or her thinking or course of action – and those who use libraries, whether online or physical ones – and they will often mention 'serendipity', meaning a happy accident. It can occur when you simply look at the title of the book or journal next to the one you want. Serendipity is what happened to Maria in Scenario 8. You can help to create opportunities for it to occur. Serendipity happens when you browse journals and contents lists or simply walk into a library and look at the 'newly arrived' or latest editions of academic journals. If you see an interesting title you might quickly skim the contents list or text. If it looks interesting, your reading behaviour changes to reading for understanding. Sometimes a text turns out to be perspective-changing – you find something significant to knowledge needs that you didn't know you had, purely by accident. If you are short of time, however, limit your browsing and don't use it to justify (to yourself) not having read essential material. Regularly browsing for several minutes is usually the best tactic.

Using the structure of texts to aid your reading

Authors normally structure their writing to help readers. Textbooks written for students are likely to be written accessibly and have contents lists and indices. There are also chapters with headings and subheadings. Chapters often begin with an introduction which provides an overview and, in some cases, end with key points. Any textbook that seems inaccessible is one you may want to discard. Academic articles are often less accessible to read because they are written by researchers for other researchers. However, writers of academic articles use structural conventions.

As a minimum there is a title, an abstract that briefly sets out what the article covers and a conclusion at the end. Empirical research articles based on systematic observation are normally divided into headed sections:

- the abstract
- a short literature review
- hypotheses (the questions to be answered by the research)
- the method used

- how the data were analysed
- a discussion
- conclusions.

Understanding and using structures, headings and conventions can help you to hone your reading techniques and strategy for your purpose.

Reading on-screen: what you need to know

When we look at a printed page we see more than the text. A printed page is a kind of map of the terrain – we see the corners of the page, the layout of the text, the visual contrast between the text and the white space, where headings occur and where diagrams are inserted. When a text has a number of pages we can flick through them, establishing the terrain of the entire work. We can easily determine the length of a text, how many diagrams there are, and how accessible it might be.

It is much harder to navigate digital text on-screen. We see only one 'page' at a time, the whole text can only be scrolled or clicked through and it's more difficult to 'look back' to re-read earlier content. It's easy to lose track of 'where we are' in a text. Research into on-screen reading among students reveals a fairly negative picture: they read in a more cursory way – scanning or skimming – and comprehend less. They also seem to fail to use the same process of self-regulation they employ when reading printed material. Why? It appears that reading on-screen text requires more cognitive resources, such as attention and what's known as working memory. This is the memory you use to calculate, say, whether you have enough cash to cover the items you're taking to the supermarket till. You keep several things in mind at once.

See Learning how to learn in Chapter 3

On-screen reading is also tiring, reducing the cognitive resources available. Students who want to read for understanding are more likely to print off digital text. Sustained attention without distraction is needed to read for understanding and printed text offers benefits over on-screen text. However, if on-screen reading is your only option, two tactics seem to be effective in extracting the same information from digital and printed texts: tests on the content and re-reading.

Tactics for on-screen reading

If you decide to read digital text on-screen, then do the following to create a 'map' of the text and to incorporate re-reading and testing your understanding.

- Approach the on-screen text as if you were reading it in print form – identify explicitly the purpose of your reading.
- Scan the text to create a basic 'map' of it (if the text is in .pdf format look at the page 'thumbnails') or skim read the content to build a richer 'map'.

See *How to make reading notes* in this chapter

- Then, assuming you are reading for understanding, read the text carefully while managing your concentration and effort.
- Make jottings and notes.
- Re-read the text or specific parts to verify your understanding.
- Test your understanding in some way, perhaps by producing a short summary *without* referring to your notes.

Course materials written for study online normally have helpful features such as short sentences and paragraphs and 'next' buttons to eliminate scrolling. Texts often include prompts to re-read, questions about the content and activities to ensure that you have understood. There may be a contents list, an indication of how long a text is and even the time you should set aside to read it. A high proportion of your on-screen reading, however, is likely to be textbooks, which may be digital facsimiles of print versions and academic articles in a .pdf format. These will not share the same design features of high-quality, online teaching material. So, whenever you read on-screen, use good practices that won't compromise your learning.

Reading strategies and techniques in action

See *Reading strategies and techniques* in this chapter

What to read is a decision you do not often have to make as an undergraduate unless you want to 'read around' or read further. Educators normally produce lists of essential reading for you; these are often called indicative reading lists. You may have to make choices if optional readings are also listed and, here, you can be guided by your interest. Usually, however, you have to decide on the order in which you read the essential items. How do you do this? Read *Reading strategies and techniques* at the beginning of this chapter if you have not already done so before attempting Activity 4.2.

ACTIVITY 4.2

Simon has seven academic articles to read on a particular topic. His tutor has listed the articles by the authors' names in alphabetical order. Simon wants to understand the content as fully as possible but he doesn't have much time. He accesses the articles in the order they appear on the list and starts reading. Soon he finds he's in a muddle. Two articles set out the topic very clearly but rather differently; another one seems to challenge all previous research findings. Finally, the last paper reveals that there are different 'schools of thought' on the topic which inform the different approaches to research. *I wish I'd read that first,* Simon thinks. *I'm confused now about where each article 'fits' into the research narrative. But I haven't got time to read all the articles again.*

What should Simon have done? Can he rectify his problem even at this late stage?

Simon would have avoided problems by doing the following.

1. Scan each article to get an overview OR skim each for a better idea of the content and scope. The appropriateness of each tactic depends on the accessibility of the texts and the reader's familiarity with the subject matter. If one article or textbook section provides an overview of the topic or a review of the research literature, this text should be the first one to read. (If there is a choice, select the most accessible one to read first.) Such works normally provide a context for other research articles which may be more-narrowly focused. Then consider the dates of the remaining articles. It's usual to read in date order because newer research tends to question, overturn or elaborate on earlier work or refer back to it. Indeed, a set of academic articles may be chosen by educators to represent the historical development of a research field. Then organise the articles in the order they will be read.
2. Read the articles cover to cover only when they are placed in a logical reading order.

It's not too late for Simon to rectify his problem. He can scan the texts and place them in an appropriate order. He can then skim read them, amending the notes he made while he was reading for understanding. It will take a little time but it is better than remaining muddled.

Monitoring your understanding and reading critically

Reading a text to fully understand the content demands more than focused and careful reading. When you study you are doing more than trying to memorise information in order to reproduce it later. You need to understand the information and to turn it into your own knowledge. You need to do two things to achieve this:

- monitor your understanding
- read critically.

Monitoring your understanding

To monitor your understanding as you read, stop at the end of each section of the text or paragraph or page, whichever is most appropriate, to summarise your understanding. Ask yourself the questions in Table 4.1 at relevant points as you move through the text.

You may need to re-read parts of a text, especially if you encounter information that seems to contradict what you read earlier in the article. Sometimes you *will* find contradictory information or arguments that are

Table 4.1 Reading questions

Questions	Where to look for answers
What questions or phenomena is this article supposed to answer or address?	Introduction
Why are these questions or phenomena – and proposed answers – important?	The questions posed by the author or from the literature reviewed and any suggested answers
What are the main points of the article (so far)?	Middle sections of the text (method, data collection and analysis or the theoretical arguments of the author or from the research literature)
What is the author's argument (so far)?	Discussion/conclusion
How do the author's points and arguments answer the questions?	Discussion/conclusion
Do I understand why the article was written and all the main points?	At the end, when you review your understanding

flawed or lack coherence. When you monitor your understanding in this way you can be more confident that you understand the text well enough to read it critically at the same time.

Some educators suggest reading difficult parts of texts aloud or sub-vocally – that is, under your breath. This is not advisable, however. We often use an 'inner voice' for thinking and it has been found that sub-vocal reading or reading aloud suppresses this verbal thinking.

see *Note-making* in this chapter

Knowledge transformation

Your aim when you read is to *transform* what you read into your *own* knowledge. To do this you need to read critically. This process is vital to the transformation because your critique becomes part of your new knowledge. Your transformed knowledge is more extensive. The transformation process is set out in Table 4.2.

The transformation model is often used in business processes, particularly operations management. The process is shown in Figure 4.1.

In the transformation process, you take inputs and transform them in some way to produce different outputs or those with higher value than the input. Think of a bakery buying in raw ingredients and producing freshly baked bread. The transformation process is vital to the finished product. Within the overall transformation process many small transformation processes take place: a micro output is the input for another micro operation.

Inputs comprise resources including raw materials, people, their knowledge and skills, time, rules, working practices and criteria for success; transformation involves the use of these to produce outputs that meet the criteria for success. The outputs reflect the adequacy of inputs and the transformation.

Table 4.2 Knowledge transformation

Your untransformed knowledge	'The authors of this study claim that *Behaviour A* is a common phenomenon because they have found it occurs in *Situations X, Y and Z*.'
The transformation process	In transforming this knowledge you look closely at the descriptions of *Situations X, Y and Z* and question whether they are very different. You find that all three situations are similar in important respects. This means the authors have overstated their claim that *Behaviour A* is common. The authors have over-generalised their findings. They would have to do more research to support their claim.
Your own transformed knowledge	'The authors of the study claim that *Behaviour A* is a common phenomenon because they have found it occurs in *Situations X, Y and Z*. However, the authors have overstated their claim because all three situations are very similar, i.e. they all involve project teams which need to adhere to deadlines. Thus, *Behaviour A* may not be as common as the authors state and may not be found among other types of team involved in non-project work. The authors have over-generalised their findings. They would have to do more research to support their claim that *Behaviour A* is common. Therefore, I will accept the authors' argument only in a limited or qualified way.'

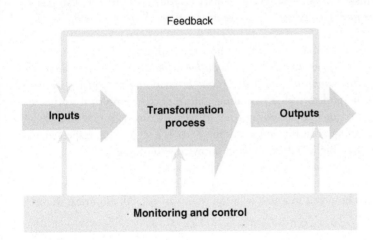

Figure 4.1 The transformation process

Feedback from outputs is needed to adjust inputs and transformation processes so the output can be maintained or improved or changed. For example, customer complaints may lead to staff training or buying better-quality flour (a change in inputs) or modifications in the way the dough is kneaded (a change in the transformation process). Inputs, transformation processes and outputs need to be monitored to check on quality and progress and for divergence.

ACTIVITY 4.3 How might you monitor your reading and use your own feedback on the outputs? Identify the inputs and the processes you use. How might you adjust or improve the inputs and/or the transformation process?

You would monitor your output by first reviewing your transformed knowledge. If this revealed that the transformation was not wholly effective, for example, and you found you had not understood (your objective) you would modify what you do. You might decide to change the way you make notes to improve your focus (a transformation process) or you might select fewer or less-demanding texts (an input). If monitoring revealed good understanding and you read faster than anticipated, you might adjust by reading more texts or more demanding ones. When you work on your personal inputs and processes, the outputs improve: you become better at achieving your purpose!

How to read critically

When you read critically you are not being negative; rather you are taking control of a text. You go beyond simply being able to restate what the text covered. You question all the important aspects of the content and look for answers in the text: you check to see if the authors address your questions satisfactorily. If they don't, the unanswered question becomes part of your critique, for example: *In discussing their findings, the authors make an assertion, X, that is unsupported by evidence.*

Better still, if you can, try to work out how the authors might have supported their assertion: *To support the assertion the authors would have had to conduct the study under further conditions, such as D and E.* In doing so you justify your criticisms. It is helpful to realise that almost all important empirical studies are challenged, refined or overturned by later studies. This is how new knowledge is created. In reading critically you are doing what is a legitimate, respected and essential practice in higher education and knowledge-building.

Critical reading is easier if you know the protocols (rules) and conventions for empirical research in business and management. These methodological protocols and conventions help you to know what questions to ask. All empirical research work should:

- set out the purpose of the study
- justify the purpose, normally by referring to previous research literature
- state the questions addressed and why these are important ones
- be explicit about how the research was conducted
- state what data were collected
- set out how the data were analysed
- state clearly the conclusions reached.

Quantitative and qualitative data

Research methods fall into one of two broad categories: those designed to gather quantitative data and those designed to gather qualitative data.

The quantitative approach

The quantitative approach aims to seek 'objective' facts that identify causal relationships between factors, for example, between motivation and productivity. Hypotheses – research questions – are posed and then tested by collecting evidence to support or refute them. The approach gets its name from the numeric quantification of what is being measured, such as amounts and frequencies. It's possible to quantify more or less anything, however – for example, eye movements can be tracked to discover how frequently and how long people respond to advertisements. In this example, the numbers tell you about attention and novelty rather than the subjective states of individuals. Some quantitative studies assess context or beliefs or feelings about something, but they are designed to isolate what is being measured from its usual context. Numerical data are easy to analyse statistically, given a sufficient sample size.

Quantitative research methods belong to a long tradition of experimental science, which aims to provide theoretical knowledge. They are useful for the study of well-defined behaviours or attitudes, for comparisons and for large, representative samples. Findings can often be generalised.

The qualitative approach

The qualitative approach to research is concerned with context and the subjective realm. It is based on the idea that the social world is made up of personal interpretations that are not necessarily generalisable to other contexts. Data are collected from multiple sources such as observation and interviews in natural settings such as workplaces, often together with 'secondary' data collected for other purposes. The aim of the approach is to capture meaning – the *how* and *why* – within a deep, rich picture. The approach, which embraces a variety of types of case study, generally precludes the use of very large samples and findings are often not generalisable without further research. Qualitative methods are commonly used in research into organisations and behaviour.

The strengths and weaknesses of both approaches are often overstated. Depending on design, both approaches can be used to:

- explore new or un-researched phenomena
- build or extend theory
- test hypotheses
- try to replicate findings to confirm or refute an explanation or theory
- challenge or refute the findings of previous research.

Both approaches can result in purely descriptive findings and, in some instances, case studies may be designed to create a particularly rich and insightful picture. Regardless of approach, not all findings are generalisable to contexts other than the one studied.

The distinction between quantitative and qualitative data is somewhat artificial because, in many research studies, both types of data are collected, for example, via questionnaires and interviews. A more fundamental distinction is that the traditional, scientific approach and the case-based approach follow different conventions. These are discussed in *Deductive and inductive reasoning in research* in Chapter 6.

Case studies aim to capture context, while traditional research methods often aim to remove it. No inquiry is ever 'context-free' however: the interests and moral, social and political values of researchers inform their decisions about what is important to study.

> **ACTIVITY 4.4** You have decided on a research question: To what extent does 'healthy eating' advertising influence people's purchasing decisions? What do you *believe* the answer will be? *Why* do you believe this?

When you reflect on why you believe what you do about such advertising, consider whether your belief is based on how it influences your own purchasing decisions. Might the advertising equally influence people of different ages and backgrounds? It is likely that your answers are biased by your beliefs. This is clearly illustrated in Box 4.1. Researchers try to systematically identify and remove biases that might affect the design and interpretation of the data. However, research is invariably influenced by the social and cultural contexts that shape people's views of the social world and their subjective beliefs.

Box 4.1 The Pygmalion effect

Robert Rosenthal, a well-known North American psychologist, active in the twentieth century, studied both types of bias – beliefs (internal) and context (external) – over a number of years. He found that researchers who expected particular findings were likely to find them, even when the subjects of the research were animals. His work on external bias in research in the 1950s and 1960s was rejected by academic journals. But it could be ignored no longer after the famous 'Pygmalion in the classroom' study was carried out. The Pygmalion study (Rosenthal and Jacobson, 1968) showed how culture and then-current theories of education and human development shaped teachers' expectations of young students. The 'Pygmalion effect' remains controversial (for example, Jussim and Harber, 2005): the idea of external bias is still rejected by some while the notion of classroom injustice has entered popular imagination uncritically.

What to question, when and where

In general, research studies can contain one or more of the following problems, which then cast doubt on an author's argument and conclusions. Table 4.3 is a checklist to use when reading research studies. It sets out the possible flaws you may find.

Table 4.3 Checklist for research studies

Potential problem	Description
Poor connection with previous research	Previous research work may be overlooked, ignored, misinterpreted or used too selectively.
Uncritical assessment of prior research	Faults and flaws in previous work may have been replicated. Refuted or unconfirmed theory may have been used.
'Confirmation bias'	The attempt to disconfirm a proposition or hypothesis can be inadequate or there is only an attempt to confirm it.
Inappropriate design or method	The design of a study may not address the research question well or the method or design is not wholly appropriate to the situation being studied.
Flawed design or method	Insufficient account may be taken of the many factors that can influence the behaviour or practices studied.
Design of questionnaires, inventories etc.	Questionnaires, inventories and scales may be poorly developed and then used uncritically by other researchers.
Insufficient information	Researchers may give insufficient information about the sample, data collection and how the data were analysed.
Inadequate data	The data gathered may not be sufficient or adequate to address the research question or phenomenon.
Faulty data analysis	The data can be analysed in a way that doesn't fully answer the research question – and may address a subtly different one.
Flawed interpretation of results	The results may be open to more than one interpretation. Evidence to support alternative explanations (or disconfirmation) may have been ignored. Conflicting findings from the literature may be ignored.
Unstated or unsupported assumptions	Assumptions – the acceptance of something as true – are unstated or unsupported by evidence.
Unstated limitations	Authors may fail to draw attention to the limitations of a study, such as narrowness of context, unrepresentative sample, low response rate to a survey, missing data.
Logical flaws	Contradictions in arguments, other logical flaws and gaps can occur anywhere.
Over-generalisation of findings	Conclusions can be too widely drawn and make unsupported assumptions about their relevance to other contexts.

The list of potential gaps and flaws is far from exhaustive but is sufficient to indicate what you might find and where. Problems differ according to the nature of the research and the approach taken. Nevertheless, you should not accept uncritically the research studies you read. Researchers may base their work on theoretical models refuted by previous research, use concepts uncritically or use previous literature selectively. The use of commercially developed questionnaires, inventories and scales is problematic because details of their development are rarely available. There is no way of knowing whether they measure what they purport to. Studies by practitioners need careful reading, too, because there is often a gap between new knowledge and its integration into practice. Why is all this such a problem? It is because flawed studies cannot provide useful new knowledge.

Test your understanding

Now test your understanding of how critical reading applies to research studies. You do not need to read the academic works referred to.

ACTIVITY 4.5

Geert Hofstede studied dimensions of national culture among mostly professional men in a single multinational organisation, IBM. In almost equal measure the questionnaire-based study (Hofstede, 1980) has been criticised and used uncritically in subsequent studies. Criticisms range from the methodological, such as sampling bias (professional males), to the theoretical, such as the confounding factor of organisational culture, which is not the same as national culture.

Now answer the following questions without referring to any literature:

1. Do you think the cultural dimensions Hofstede identified among male professionals at IBM *necessarily* apply to women, to all IBM employees, to employees in different organisations, or to employees in, say, a Chinese organisation?
2. How could researchers find out whether Hofstede's dimensions are *generalisable* to people in other contexts and cultures?
3. What if national cultures have changed since Hofstede carried out his work? How could a researcher find out?

Logic alone suggests that the answer to all the 'sampling' questions is *No*; that the answer to the second question is *Test the dimensions rigorously in other settings*; and that the answer to the third is *Test the dimensions using a sample population as similar to the original one as possible*. Logic is a good starting point for reading critically. But what if Hofstede did not fully distinguish between national culture and values? It is vital for researchers to define precisely the phenomenon they are studying and for you to question their definitions. For example, a critique of

Hofstede's work by Galit Ailon (2008) argues that Hofstede's notion of *culture* was reduced to *values*, which were then reduced to a set of questions in an IBM questionnaire. The notion of *national society* was reduced to middle-class males in IBM's marketing and service division personnel. Often, when you read, your questions lead you to more reading!

Using critical questions

When you read critically you ask questions of definitions, arguments, theoretical perspectives, research designs, the development or choice of instruments of measurement, data gathering, analyses, interpretations and conclusions. Critical questions usually begin with *What? Why? Who? Where? How? When?*

Where? and *When?* may not be obvious questions. However, *where* the research was carried out is important in terms of the context of study and the extent to which findings might be generalised. For example, communication behaviour is highly influenced by culture. *When* the research was carried out is also important because the wider context may have changed.

Start your critical reading by scanning the article to extract the stated purpose of the study and the key assertions made. Then read the paper to understand and assess the author's arguments and the evidence provided to support them. Ask questions of the author as you read, as if in conversation with him or her. Be the sceptic who is saying to the author: *Convince me that I should accept what you are saying.*

See *Reading strategies and techniques* in this chapter

You may find it helpful to postpone making proper notes initially. Instead you can make margin notes to record your questions and queries while underlining key phrases and sentences (provided you have your own copy of the text). This speeds up your reading and helps you to focus the content and your critical stance to it. Then skim read the article for the purpose of 'proper' note-making. Note each criticism you have made and, where possible, how each could be addressed. Support your own assertions either with logical argument or evidence from other research articles.

See *Note-making* in this chapter

The more you practise reading critically, the more knowledge you gain. The more knowledge you gain, the easier critical reading becomes: it's a virtuous circle. As a bonus, critical reading will help you to become a more accomplished writer because you have greater awareness of the need for logical arguments that are supported by evidence and of the care needed to draw legitimate conclusions.

The purposes of note-making

We make notes for many different purposes. Consider the situations below and then carry out Activity 4.6.

It's been a long day at work. Treasa, a product manager, arrives home to a dark hallway. No spare light bulbs! She adds *buy light bulb* to her personal 'to do' list for tomorrow, which reminds her that she hasn't made a proper shopping list. The phone rings. It's a friend who wants to pass on the phone number of a plumber.

Treasa's job involves providing the sales team with relevant product and marketing information, including reviews of the product data of competitors. She also needs to critically assess the appropriateness of advertising material, to design market research initiatives and to prepare product forecasts. She needs to liaise with outside agencies and she frequently compiles reports, attends meetings and gives presentations. Making notes has become second-nature in her job: she makes critical reading notes on promotion material and competitor product data, notes for meetings and notes for the preparation of reports, forecasts and presentations.

Today, Treasa attended a sales team meeting. A secretary took notes, recording key points of discussions, the decisions taken, who is responsible for various actions and by when they need to be completed. The secretary works to a set formula for each meeting.

ACTIVITY 4.6 What is the difference between the notes Treasa makes when she's at home and those she makes at work? What is the secretary doing? Which types of notes are most like those you need when you are studying?

In personal life, people make notes as *aids to memory*: phone numbers, shopping lists and 'to do' lists. This is what Treasa is doing at home. At work, the notes she makes are only partly aids to memory and not all are of the same type: it depends on her purpose – what she will use her notes *for*. The secretary is not *making* notes but simply *taking* notes because all she needs to do is make an accurate record of the meeting. The notes don't represent her own interpretation of the discussions. The notes will be subject to scrutiny later to ensure that they accurately reflect the business of the meeting: the notes are a précis or synopsis for the purpose of record-keeping.

When you are a student your note-making will be most like that of Treasa at work. You need to make notes on your reading, lectures and other teaching sessions, for and during team work, for presentations and other purposes such as preparing for assignments. The problem is that many students find that their notes are not useful. This is because they have been made with no clear, specific purpose. Coupled with the absence of proper methods and formats, the notes can be meaningless later. This is a problem because there is rarely time to re-read the original material or to watch or listen again to lectures and other types of teaching sessions that are digitally recorded.

A vital part of making any notes is *using your own words* to aid understanding, concentration, focus and thinking. It helps you to follow the logic and narrative or arguments, too. You *know* if you have not understood; you *know* if you have simply been note-*taking* without the full engagement you need for note-*making*. Making notes helps you to make connections between concepts and ideas, providing you with 'the bigger picture' for which successful students strive. The satisfaction that this deeper understanding brings helps you to enjoy note-making rather than seeing it as a necessary chore.

'In your own words'

What does *in your own words* mean when concepts, models and processes have names and when definitions are precise? It does not mean finding your own terms or definitions. Imagine you have just read an interesting text on whether poor economic situations or environmental degradation should be addressed first by policymakers. Various economists and business leaders have given informed opinions. To your surprise, all agree that environmental degradation should be addressed first on the grounds that environment degradation, if left unchecked, will be more costly to rectify later, if at all, leading to further economic deterioration. The implications for organisations' corporate responsibilities appear to be significant. You have copious notes copied verbatim from the text. Excited by what you have read, you phone a student friend to tell her about it. Do you read her your notes or do you tell her the key points of the arguments, adding your questions and critique? You do the latter, of course. The words you use will be your own, while retaining all the formal terms used (although you should be able explain what they mean).

ACTIVITY 4.7 Enlist the help of a student friend. Select two equally short academic texts to read critically – one for you and one for your friend. Meet again when you have each completed the reading and made notes. Then, *without referring to your notes*, tell each other in turn what the key points and arguments are, together with your critical comments. When you have carried out the activity you will know what 'using your own words' means. If you found it difficult to use your own words, you will know where you faltered and why.

Succinct delivery 'in your own words' of the results of your critical reading is a skill required in the workplace, where time and attention spans can be short. If you are reporting to senior managers at work they may require you to present a carefully considered but concise one-page summary of a document or report that is 30 pages long.

How to make reading notes

You are likely to make different type of notes when you study. Making succinct, clear and critical notes on your reading material is probably the

See *Using critical questions* in this chapter

most important of these types. Your main purpose will be one of the four set out below.

1. To identify all the key points and arguments AND the results of your critique, insights and thoughts.
2. To do the above but selectively if, for example, you want to consider only ethical issues or to address a specific question. Note that this means selective extraction of points, not selective reading of a text.
3. To make connections and synthesise concepts, arguments and evidence from a number of sources that you have critically read.
4. To distil a topic or set of readings into notes for an assignment or to revise for an exam, including key critical comments.

See *Preparing for and sitting exams* in Chapter 5

When you read a text it is better to make very brief notes first to allow you to focus on reading the text critically and then to make fuller notes at the end, as set out in the following guidance.

Make 'jottings'. As you critically read the text use a pen and highlighter (or digital equivalents if you are reading on-screen) to make margin notes and underline or highlight main points, key terms and phrases and your critical comments, provided you own the copy. Take care not to highlight too much – it will be hard to read later. If you don't own the text and there is no digital copy, have a note book to hand and very briefly record the main points and your critical comments or queries, also noting the page and paragraph number. Something as simple as 'p37 para 2 Sample size?' is sufficient. Alternatively, note in one or two words the main points and your critical comments in a spray diagram. To create one, place the key concept in the centre then branch outwards to linked ones. You can add sub-branches to include more sub-concepts and ideas. Your aim is to *briefly* record important ideas and your critical comments: your focus is on reading, understanding and critiquing at this stage. A spray diagram allows you do this because it is quick to draw: you don't have to consider the connections between concepts although this often happens as you draw.

Figures 4.2 and 4.3 show, respectively, a spray design for a theoretical article and a completed spray diagram for a 20-page textbook chapter on operations planning and control.

Select an appropriate format for your fuller notes. When you have completed your in-depth reading, write proper notes. Formats range from a simple series of headings to multiple-column tables. The more columns you have, however, the more difficult it is to insert notes. A two-column tabular form distinguishes between the content of the text in one column and your own critical comments in the other. An outline is shown in Table 4.4.

If you omit a second column, you'll need to find a way of identifying your critical comments. If you don't, you may later inadvertently attribute your own comments to the author of the text. Try using different coloured pens or font colour, or noting all your critical comments separately and adding them to the end of your notes under a separate heading.

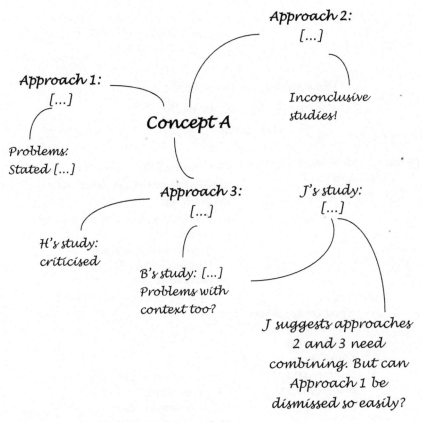

Figure 4.2 Simple spray diagram for a theoretical article

Create and use headings. Adjust and elaborate the sets of headings that follow to create a simple set that meets your needs. Then use the headings to structure your notes as you write them. Headings help you to organise and structure your thoughts and make your notes easier to use later, too.

Headings for notes on research articles and case studies

1. **The full reference for the text.** Use the referencing style required by your university, normally Harvard.
2. **The purpose(s) of your reading.** If you are reading in order to write an assignment, state the assignment question. However, take care that the question is not so narrow that you could not answer another, related one that might appear in an exam. Your reading may have more than one purpose, for example, peer-work and a later written assignment. Listing the purposes of your reading helps you to focus on your needs and keep them in mind even if they are simply to *understand* topic X.
3. **A brief description of what the author is trying to achieve and why.** Note whether the authors are putting forward a theory or model, testing

See *How to cite and reference* in Chapter 5

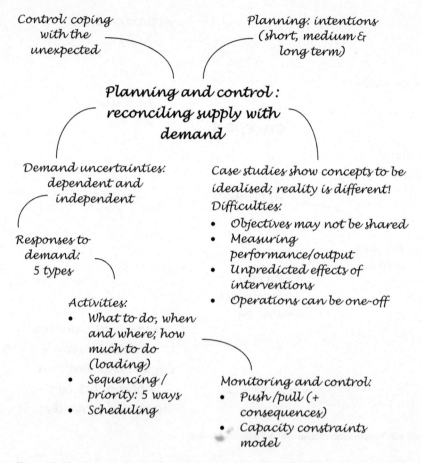

Figure 4.3 Simple spray diagram for a textbook chapter on operations planning and control

one, or testing the practical application of one. Note, too, why the authors are doing this.

4. **The authors' findings in brief.**

5. **The theoretical framework or perspective adopted by the authors and brief details of key items of supporting literature (or background).** *From this point include your critical reading comments.* Set out the theoretical position, what informs it and if there is any prior evidence to support it.

6. **Details of the study.** For *research articles* you may want to sub-divide this section to cover the research design or method, data gathering and analysis, the interpretation and the findings. For *case studies* you may want to sub-divide this section to cover the context, data types and analysis, the interpretation and the findings. For both types of article, be sure to include your critical evaluation of each aspect. It's useful to think in terms of strengths and weaknesses – and how weaknesses could have been avoided.

7. **The authors' conclusions.** The authors need to support their arguments and to refute alternative ones. Note the authors' arguments together with the strengths and weaknesses. Note any assumptions made. Indicate the breadth of the authors' claims and how generalisable these are to other contexts. Note

Table 4.4 Outline of two-column format for notes on a research article

Full details of source material	My comments
My reading purpose	
The research question and its importance (what the author is trying to achieve and why)	
Findings in brief	
Background (theoretical framework; previous research literature)	

Approach 1
  Study 1
  [...]	

Approach 2
  Study 1
  [...]	

Approach 3
  Study 1
  [...]	

Method	
Data and analysis	
Discussion	
Conclusion	
Use to me	

any implications of the findings for theory or for practical application or the contribution the work makes to theory or practice. Include your own comments on what further work is needed to confirm/refute/generalise the findings or to test the theory/model. Note the research question or questions you believe emerge from the work.

8. **What use you can make of the material.** This relates to the purpose of your reading. If you are reading in order to address a specific assignment question, note the relevant issues and identify diagrams that might be useful, with page numbers.

An outline of a two-column notes format for empirical work is shown in Table 4.4.

Headings for notes on articles and book chapters that consist of argument and evidence only

1. **The full reference for the text**
2. **The purpose(s) of your reading**
3. **A brief description of what the author is trying to achieve and why**
4. **The theoretical framework or perspective adopted by the authors and brief details of other background**

5. **The main arguments**
6. **Supporting evidence** – normally, this is based on the research of others, which is cited and referenced. Note briefly any details of the evidence (and any problems you detect): you may need them later.
7. **Strengths and weaknesses of the arguments**
8. **What use you can make of the material.**

Synthesising notes from a variety of sources for assignments and distilling notes for exam preparation are covered in Chapter 5. A question that students commonly ask is *How long should notes be?* Box 4.2 sets out what you need to consider.

Box 4.2 How long should notes be?

Ideally, notes are short and well organised, cover the main points and are easy to read. However, the length doesn't matter as much as the other features: it's a matter of purpose, circumstance and preference. If you don't own a copy of an article or book, you might make more notes because the text will not be to hand if you need to refer to it again. If you enjoy making detailed critiques and connections to other research work, your notes will also be relatively long, extending to, say, three or four handwritten pages for a 10–15 page academic article.

Notes that are too long often fail the test of being well organised, covering the main points and being easy to read. This is because students copy long passages of a text verbatim or they use note-making as a cognitive tool. That is, they use 'writing while reading' to focus their concentration, understanding and thinking. Long notes are often of limited use later and it takes time to make a fresh set of shorter, structured notes from the long ones. Practise making margin and other brief notes while you read and then compose well-organised and well-structured ones.

Notes that are too short can present similar problems of usability. When you need the notes, you find they aren't sufficiently comprehensive and contain little more than several descriptive sentences. Your notes are too short if they don't cover your interpretation and critical comments.

Checking your notes

When you have made your notes, read them to make sure they make sense. Mistakes such as writing *now* instead of *not* can cause problems later. If you have quoted verbatim anything the authors have said, place it in quotation marks to distinguish it from your own words and check that you have quoted correctly. Confine quotations to short statements that illustrate a point or state something more succinctly than you can in your own words. Also check the original text if you are unsure what your notes mean. Adjust headings as necessary and use subheadings where these will make your notes easier to read later.

Making notes on lectures and other sessions

Note-making during lectures, other teaching and learning sessions and peer-work can be difficult and result in notes that are unreadable later. Your note-making purpose for lectures is to identify all the key points and arguments together with your own thoughts, comments and criticisms. However, making notes during lectures is not easy. This is because you are doing five things simultaneously:

1. listening
2. working out the meaning of what's said
3. making connections with what was said earlier or in a previous lecture or what you have read
4. formulating questions to resolve queries
5. writing.

You may also be trying to participate if the teaching or learning session is interactive or involves peer-work. There is a lot to accomplish quickly (though considerably less if you have prepared) and it can result in a high cognitive 'load' – in other words, too much for your brain to deal with properly. For these reasons, note-making is ideally a three-step process.

1. Prepare
2. Record
3. Review/refine.

The time is well spent because the three steps help you to consolidate and remember the material. The process is the same for interactive or peer-work sessions but the recording stage may consist of making fewer notes that you refine and elaborate later. Making audio recordings of sessions or lectures is normally unhelpful because they save no time: you need to listen again in order to make notes.

Step 1: Preparation

Preparation is vital if the session involves group work such as seminars: you won't be able to make informed contributions otherwise. If the preparatory work involves critical reading then one purpose of your reading notes and how you use them will relate to the nature of the task with other students.

See *How to read critically* in this chapter

Preparation helps you to engage better with lectures and other types of teaching session, too: you reduce the cognitive load and understand the content better. If you can, work through the reading list before the session. This is essential for seminars and tutorials. Preparation also allows you to formulate questions that might be answered in the session or that you can ask. If you are very short of time, read an overview of the topic: textbooks are generally useful for this. If you are a student who often struggles to understand teaching sessions, make a habit of at least some preparation. Your tutor should be able to recommend a suitable overview to read beforehand if there is no set textbook for the course.

Step 2: Recording

Record all the key points and arguments. As you listen to and note the main points, consider their logical flow. Be alert to words such as:

- *but* and *however*, which signify that what has been said is about to be qualified (perhaps a theory or a research study is about to be critiqued or contested by subsequent work)
- *because*, which signifies reasons for something
- *therefore*, which signifies consequences.

Listen for gaps. If the lecturer states that there are five important issues to consider in marketing communications and then mentions only four, ask what the fifth one is. (Lecturers are human: they sometimes forget!)

Listen critically. When you note the main points of what is said, add your own thoughts and questions. Distinguish between the points that the lecturer or session tutor is making and your own thoughts and questions, or comments by other students. A tabular format for notes allows you to make such distinctions: you use one column for what the lecturer said and another for your thoughts and questions. Alternatively, draw a wide margin to the right of your notes pages and use that for thoughts, comments and questions.

Note any examples of concepts or practices. Examples aid understanding and recall.

Note any sources of information that are given. These usually consist of names of authors and the date of the work. If a source of important information is not given, ask for it at the end of the session.

Ask in advance if there any any handouts. Lectures and other teaching sessions may contain PowerPoint slides, video clips or web pages.

> *Slides*: If a handout of the slides is available in advance, annotate this as each slide is discussed. If there is no handout, you won't have time to copy out what is on a slide. Listen and make notes on what the items mean then get a copy of the slides at the end.
>
> *Webpages*: Make a note of the webpage URL and take notes on what the lecturer says *about* the content, not on the content itself other than a few words of description. You can look at the website again later if you need to.
>
> *Video clips*: The notes you make depend on the nature of the video clip. Clips are often used for illustration so make notes as you would for an example of practice.

Lecture notes written by the lecturer, if available, are not normally released until a lecture is over. Make your own notes during a session and check them against the handout. If lecture notes are supplied in advance, it is unwise to try to read and annotate them during the lecture. It is not possible to listen and read simultaneously – or to read and speak, or to write and speak – try it! Further, lecturers may not follow what is in the handout, they may deliver the information in a different order, or the handout may be confined to a list including references. In all cases, there is unlikely to be space for annotation.

At this stage your notes will probably not be tidy ones. There may be omissions and you may not have answers to your questions. In the third stage of the process you refine your notes and fill in gaps so that they are structured and usable later.

If you are making notes during a seminar, tutorial or any other session that involves interaction with educators and peers, listen and contribute. Record quickly only key points (including your own). Your notes will be untidy but can be refined immediately after sessions while your recall is still good. Your notes will be shaped by your purpose: many interactive sessions involve problem-solving or application so you may need very selective notes. One question that often arises is whether you should make notes by hand or use a computer. Box 4.3 provides an answer.

Box 4.3 Are handwritten notes best?

Handwriting your notes is better than using a laptop computer. Pam Mueller and Daniel Oppenheimer (2014) found that students who used laptops for note-making in lectures tended to take verbatim notes and were less likely to recall conceptual information a week later. Students who made handwritten notes took fewer, less verbatim notes and were better at later recall. The recall difference remained even when students were allowed to study their notes before the recall test. It's likely that the students who made handwritten notes processed, synthesised and summarised in their own words what they heard: they seemed to have processed the information more deeply.

Step 3: Review and refine

In the third phase of note-making, after the session, you review and refine your notes. This means reading and rewriting them in an organised way. Fill in any gaps and insert answers to questions. If new questions are raised as you do this, you seek answers to these too. There are many formats you can use. Multiple-column formats are popular but they require notes to be very brief: fuller notes are difficult to insert and may be difficult to read later. A single- or double-column format is probably best.

Structuring your lecture notes: headings

The headings you use depend on the nature of the lecture or session. Look at the notes you made during the session and decide what headings will be suitable. The example that follows is appropriate for a traditional lecture in which one or more concepts or theories are being discussed together with the research evidence. Experiment with formats and headings. What's important is that headings should allow you to capture all the key points as a logical *narrative* that is easy to follow. To distinguish your own thoughts and comments from other content, use a different coloured pen or font, add a *My thoughts and comments* heading at the end, or use a two-column format.

Notes for interactive sessions may be briefer – and different – depending on the nature of the session. There is a huge variety of types, from traditional seminars in which each student prepares and presents a perspective on one or more journal articles to those involving role play. In these cases, decide what kind of notes best meets your purpose(s).

Lecture notes

1. **Title of the lecture.**
2. **Concept(s) under discussion.** Include a definition. Definitions are often contested, so note any challenges to the definition.
3. **Main theories/perspectives or schools of thought.** Include the authors' names and dates when the theories were published, in date order.
4. **Differences between the theories.**
5. **Research evidence for each theory.** Include researchers' names and dates; the strength of the evidence; problems with the evidence (the critique, if any, provided in the session).
6. **Important points raised.** This is the place to include anything said in the session, including answers to questions, that don't seem to fit anywhere else in the notes.
7. **Conclusions.**
8. **Brief summary of the above.** Some students prefer to place summaries under the title of the lecture, but summaries are often written last. If you are writing your notes by hand, the summary will be difficult to insert unless you have left space for it.
9. **Questions to follow up.** These will be your own questions to remind you to ask your tutor or to seek answers to in your reading.
10. **Full references to the work referred to.** You may not need this heading if your tutor has provided a list that you can append to your notes. If not, you may need to consult academic articles mentioned in the session. If you have the full references, you can access them easily in the library.

There are many lecturing styles and some lecture content lends itself to a historical narrative in which concepts, theories and research evidence are set out chronologically. However, the headings shown can still be used. Concepts, theories and research evidence can be put in date order under Headings 2, 3 and 5. If a lecturer makes his or her notes available after a lecture, assess them in terms of how useful they will be. The point about your own notes is that they are your *own*. Making your own notes consolidates your knowledge and aids recall.

Consolidating and making connections: re-reading your notes

Good note-making results in notes that make sense when you read them and that you can rely on later. Their value goes beyond this, however, if you re-read them regularly. Re-reading helps you in two ways:

1. **It helps you to make connections.** Making connections between ideas, between topics and even between different areas of business and management increases your knowledge at very little 'cost'. You gradually build a bigger picture of your discipline. This helps while you are studying and when you become a practitioner. If you can see the financial implications of a marketing plan, for example, or the human resource implications of operations management, your knowledge has broader value. The sum is greater than the individual parts.
2. **It helps recall.** If you sit an exam at a later date, think of re-reading your notes as part of the revision process. Frequency of re-reading aids recall far better than one long revision session. Preparation for assignments will be easier, too: you will find it easier to plan your work.

When to re-read your notes

Appropriate times to re-read your notes are:

- when you have completed all your reading on a sub-topic: you may find you can add to your notes based on the connections you make
- when you prepare an assignment on the sub-topic
- when (or before) you move on to a new topic
- at the end of a semester
- before or when a new semester begins
- when you revise for an exam
- at any time you realise you can't recall what you studied.

Successful students re-read their notes regularly. A useful practice is to mentally review the topics you have studied: if you can't recall them in any detail, then re-read your notes. Ideally, re-read your notes as soon as you *begin* to forget. You should find your recall improves each time and the periods between re-reading grow longer. Eventually, just a short phrase or key word and the authors and date of relevant research triggers the recall of all the salient points of a whole sub-topic or topic. You then have 'fingertip' knowledge – the kind you need in order to apply it easily.

Finding and evaluating sources of information

When you study, your educators often decide what you should read. You accept that the material they have chosen is fit for purpose. But what happens when you must find information for yourself? Will you go to Wikipedia or a commercial business and management website for information? Will you believe everything you read? How do you know if the information is current and accurate?

See
Plagiarism: Recognising plagiarism and
Avoiding plagiarism in
Chapter 5

It's surprising how many students use questionable internet resources and even copy and paste, or paraphrase, large amounts of text into their written assignments. But would these students use unreliable sources when they are business and management practitioners and high-quality information is needed to make a decision? Consider the following scenarios:

1. Your organisation wants to extend its operations across Europe to take early advantage of new market growth. It is seeking to acquire at least one strategically located smaller company. A shortlist of potential candidates has been drawn up and you've been asked to develop profiles on each. The investigation you've been tasked with must remain confidential so you cannot approach the companies directly. Some of the information you need is commercially sensitive so it won't be freely or easily available. Much rests on the quality and reliability of your sources.
2. A for-profit health care company has resisted using workers from employment agencies – a key marketing message – but is now re-considering its policy. You have been asked to investigate whether the use of agency workers has a negative impact on the well-being of patients.
3. Stock control problems are believed to be the cause of a company's falling sales because of delays in fulfilling orders. Should the company adopt a new inventory management system – and if so, which one will work best? You have been asked to supply the answers.
4. A university wants to increase its market by attracting non-traditional students. It has many alumni, a subset of whom is retired. There is an active alumni community in which the time- and cash-rich retirees are active, but unlike the working-age alumni they are not attracted to the university's 'keeping up with your field' courses. The university wants to predict how many retired alumni might be attracted to short, general-interest courses before deciding to trial a scheme. You have been asked to make this prediction.

Workplace decision-making is important and it can be complex. In Scenarios 1 and 2 what is needed is accurate descriptive information (*What do we know about X*). In Scenario 1, information is needed to value the target companies. In Scenario 2 the descriptive information will also require 'weighing up'. Information is often needed to explain the reasons for something (*Why did X happen?*) as in Scenario 3, or to make predictions (*How likely is it that X will happen?*) as in Scenario 4. Problem-solving and decision-making can have significant implications for organisations, so high-quality information is important.

With so much readily available information – good and bad – finding information and assessing its quality requires particular skills. These are known collectively as information literacy. Organisations require these skills and you can acquire them as you study. Information literacy embraces a certain amount of digital literacy, too, because much information is readily available online in one form or another.

When seeking and evaluating sources of information, you need to be disciplined and systematic. These are the steps you need to take.

Step 1: Clarify your purpose and carry out preliminary work
Step 2: Extract your search terms and know where to search
Step 3: Carry out the search
Step 4: Evaluate the results
Step 5: Organise your sources
Step 6: Organise the material
Step 7: (optional) Keep up to date

There are covered in detail below; Scenario 2 is used as an example in some steps.

Step 1: Clarify your purpose and carry out preliminary work

Consider why you need the information. Do you want to:

- find data
- support an argument
- illustrate a point
- get an overview of a topic or issue
- find a critical review
- find a different perspective
- solve a problem?

When you have defined your purpose, identify what you *already* know. This helps you to identify key gaps in your knowledge – what you need to know. Then you can formulate the question you want to answer. You may need to do this more than once because the information you find is likely to raise further questions that you were not aware of initially. If you have a series of questions, decide which one you should ask first. Some secondary ones may be answered as you find answers to the primary one.

In Scenario 2, for example, you assess the information you have and realise you have only your company's marketing material that sets out the (unspecified) benefits of patients being able to build relationships with their carers. Thus, you begin by setting out a general question: *Does the use of agency carers have any impact on patient well-being?* You realise that you have made an assumption: that the use of *agency* carers means lack of continuity. You should probably look at your company's records to look at *staff* turnover and sector benchmarks for turnover, if there are any. You also realise that agency care in other countries might operate differently: up-to-date information on practices elsewhere would be useful. You decide not to revise your question at this stage, but you note these issues for later.

When you have formulated your question, decide whether you want research findings, the opinions of pressure groups, company data, state or government department policy, ethical or legal perspectives or public opinion. Decide, too, whether you need current or historical work. When researching organisations, both may be appropriate. If you already have *some* information, make use of any key sources cited. Note the authors' names or full references if given so that you can find more up-to-date work by them.

In Scenario 2, you decide that up-to-date, country-specific research information is needed initially, ideally focusing on the health outcomes of patients cared for by agency nurses compared with patients who are cared for by directly employed staff.

Step 2: Extract your search terms and know where to search

When you have formulated your question and assessed your information needs, extract key words, phrases and possible sources. Choose words and phrases appropriate to the type of literature you need: specialist terms will be needed for formal literature. These terms, in different combinations, are those you use in your information search.

In Scenario 2, you choose: agency carers, patient well-being, psychological impact and health outcomes. Then you look for alternatives to these; agency nurses, health impact, medical outcomes and psychological outcomes. Then you decide on appropriate sources of the information you need. Common sources of information in the UK include:

- newspapers and magazines; such as, respectively: *The Financial Times* and *Business and Strategy*
- scholarly media such as academic journals that contain descriptions and reports of research and academic discussion such as the *Journal of Business Economics and Management*
- professional bodies whose target audience is often practitioners who want practical information, such as the *Chartered Institute of Management Accountants* (CIMA), the *British Standards Institute* (BSI), and the *Chartered Institute of Personnel and Development*, CIPD (many have websites)
- trade media such as *The Caterer, Retail Week, The Entrepreneur* and *Materials Recycling World*
- books, including eBooks
- the government and its agencies (which include regulatory bodies) such as the *Financial Conduct Authority* (FCA) which regulates financial services and *Companies House*, which offers both free and paid-for information about organisations
- organisations that provide reports and data including the *Office for National Statistics*, which offers official data, *YouGov* and the *Centre for Retail Research*
- blogs such as *The Small Business Blog* and discussion forums such as *UKbusinessFORUMS*.

The list of sources, many of which are online, is far from exhaustive. The formal way of categorising information is one that identifies 'distance' from the original source.

Primary **sources** refer to 'first-hand' information, such as an academic research article by the person who carried out the research. A company's financial statements, eyewitness accounts, government statistics and a novel perspective by a newspaper columnist are also primary sources.

Secondary **sources** refer to information 'once removed'. These include reviews of research literature by people not involved in the research, articles, trade magazines or practitioner websites that interpret primary sources. Books, other than autobiographies, are usually secondary sources.

Tertiary **sources** refer to information 'twice removed', for example, a practitioner website article based on secondary sources or a newspaper review of a book.

As information becomes more distant from the primary source, it can become oversimplified and distorted. However, primary sources are not a guarantee of high-quality, accurate information. Research articles published in academic journals are generally peer-reviewed for quality before publication. This peer-review process is considered to be the gold standard in publishing but studies may still be flawed or lacking in some way. Similarly, a person's first-hand testimony and witness reports may be biased. Depending on your purpose, sometimes biases don't matter: an advertisement can provide insights into how an organisation likes to portray itself to the public.

More 'distant' secondary information is not necessarily lacking in quality or accuracy. Secondary sources such as quality trade publications and newspapers can provide information on the reasons why an organisation has been in the public eye, for example. Others such as textbooks and academic reviews can provide overviews, useful critiques and interpretations of a topic.

Necessarily, primary sources are where you will find the most up-to-date information but peer-reviewed material can take time to be published. Secondary sources, such as books, will not contain the latest research findings even if they are newly published. However, they may contain primary material such as new perspectives and insights. In general, tertiary sources (and even more distant ones) should be avoided but they can still have their uses: marketing and public relations professionals may use Twitter, for example, to assess the effectiveness or reach of their campaigns.

Step 3: Carry out the search

Your main access points to information are:

- library databases (a database is a searchable, organised collection)
- the databases of government and statutory bodies
- the internet (a disorganised database)
- book sellers
- the media (newspapers, magazines and periodicals).

A database lists publications in one or more fields or disciplines. Expect to find a mix of books, journals and articles in a single database; some also list audio and audiovisual material. First, identify the databases that cover your discipline or research area. Look for descriptions of coverage. For example the academic database *Business Source Complete* covers scholarly articles in the fields of business and economics. But if you were looking for market survey information you might try *Mintel*, or for newspaper and trade press material, *Nexis*.

In many cases, the full digital content of an item can be downloaded. Not all material is free of charge, although items are often free to students. The internet can be a good source of information if you use scholarly search engines such as Google Scholar, although items are not necessarily available for free download. A non-scholarly search, however, will identify a huge number of sources whose quality will be harder to evaluate. Internet searches require particular care and are covered in the next section of this chapter.

To search a database, insert keywords into the 'search fields' in the database to look for relevant material. Library databases allow you to narrow your search in ways that internet search engines do not. If your database search returns too few or too many items, then adjust your search terms. For example, you might want to set date or geographical limitations or use fewer terms. As you search, you may find other key words or phrases that are more selective than those you have chosen. If so, amend yours.

When the database returns a list of items, scan the titles and ignore those that don't meet your needs. Read the summaries or abstracts of items that seem to be relevant and select potentially useful ones. If you are able to, view the whole text. If it seems to cover what you need, download the item. If you can't view the whole item note the full reference (the authors, date, title of the article, journal name, volume and part number). Then find the print version in the library to make your assessment. Also note the full reference of any other work that *might* be useful (and where you found it), should you want to return to it. This is your initial choice of material, which you now need to evaluate more fully. Be selective: a single overview or review article can be an excellent place to start.

Step 4: Evaluate the results

How do you know whether to believe all that you read? First assess the quality of information. Two questions are important.

1. Is the source – the publication – credible?
2. What makes the writer likely to be a reliable source?

Peer-reviewed articles in an academic journal are likely to be credible. However, research invariably requires funding – by governments, companies, pressure groups, political parties and trusts (non-profit organisations that hold and distribute assets to fund specific causes). The work may reflect the funder's interests. Assumed credibility is often judged by the number of others who have used the work and have cited it in their own articles. In general, work with many citations has been found to be interesting or useful, although discredited work is often highly cited too. You can check how often a work has been cited by looking it up on the internet, using the Google search engine. The listing shows the number of citations. (You can also search for critiques of an author's work if he or she is sufficiently well known.)

When assessing empirical work (that is, work based on observation or experiment), you have to judge whether it is sound, that is, it has no obvious flaws. Scan read it first. If you have concerns, don't use the material: there may be better choices. If not, you may want to use the study anyway but you will need to set out its shortcomings. Most empirical work has imperfections of one kind or another. A common method of checking claims is triangulation, set out in Box 4.4.

Box 4.4 Triangulation

Triangulation, originally a method used by navigators to check physical location by using at least three reference points, is often used in research, particularly in case studies. Triangulation can involve using different theories, methods and types of information to study a phenomenon. It can overcome flaws in a single research method and is useful in the study of complex, hard-to-study phenomena. It is useful for assessing the accuracy of information, too. For example, if a company makes claims about its rapid growth, these claims can be checked against formal financial data elsewhere and against sector performance ('benchmarking') data. Triangulation does not mean looking for the *same* information from three or more sources: inaccurate data may have simply been reused by other sources.

Step 5: Organise your sources

List and organise your sources of information. For an article, record the author, date of publication, title of the work, who published the work and where, page numbers (if given), and when and where you found it. If you accessed the work online, copy and record the URL (the web address) or DOI (a permanent URL that doesn't change) and the date you accessed it. Free or paid-for reference management software can capture the full references of particular sources (and store digital material). A free one, *Mendeley*, is easy to use for journal articles, books and reports. *Endnote* is popular among academics but the full version is not free.

When you use sources of information in your written work or presentations you need to attribute them. Cite authors when you mention their work *and* provide a full reference at the end of your text. These are the established ways of crediting authors for their work. They allow your readers to consult the sources themselves if they want to. The conventions ensure that you avoid

See *How to cite and reference* and *Recognising plagiarism* and *Avoiding plagiarism* in Chapter 5

what is known as plagiarism – using the work of others as if it were your own. Organising sources is a necessary chore but it you don't do it you'll waste time by trying to find missing sources again or by altering your text to work around them.

Step 6: Organise the material

The usual method of organising academic articles is to download digital copies and 'file' them in folders. Often .pdf files are labelled with long numbers so when you save them replace the number with the first author's name and date or the title of the article to make it easy to find them in your filing system. Reference management software normally stores downloads for you by author name.

Step 7: (optional) Keep up to date

If you want or need to keep up to date with a topic or field, subscribe to mailing lists and news groups to receive alerts on new articles. The search engine Google maintains a list that you can find by using the search term *Google groups*.

Internet searches

The internet is the modern-day equivalent of the Wild West: it's lawless. This means internet searches for non-academic information are problematic. There are huge amounts of poor-quality information – incomplete, inaccurate and misleading – to trip up the unwary. The traditional method of publishing, whereby professional gatekeepers filter information to try to ensure credibility, is largely absent. It costs nothing to publish material and there is no quality control: everyone can be an author. When you visit a webpage, quickly assess

- the author's qualifications
- the reputation of the host organisation or sponsor
- the quality of the content.

If in doubt, don't use the material. Authors may not provide any details of what qualifies them to be a reliable source; websites that host the material may blur the line between advertising and content and some are funded by organisations seeking to subvert public opinion. Content may be detailed, well-presented and well-structured but heavily biased and even prejudicial. Other websites may exist only to attract advertising revenue. These often host very short articles with appealing titles and text that makes bold and unsupported claims.

   When assessing websites, look for the first-level domain name in the URL – the address. This tells you something about the sponsor organisation. Some common domain names are **.edu** or **.ac** for educational institutions. The 'second-level' domain name is usually an abbreviation of the organisation's name, followed by the initials of a country. So, for example, the website of The Open University in the UK is www.open.ac.uk. Other common first-level domain names are set out below.

- Companies including newspapers and professional bodies such as the *Chartered Institute of Marketing* in the UK use **.com** or **.co** as domain names. An alternative to these is **.biz**.
- Government websites use **.gov** including municipal government sites such as the *City of London Corporation*, UK.
- Non-profit organisations such as the *Small Business Advisory Service* in the UK use **.org**.

There are exceptions, however. Some UK organisations use an abbreviation of their second-level domain followed by the initials of the country. An example is *The British Library* (www.bl.uk). This is the case, too, in parts of Europe and beyond where universities do the same, such as the *University of Turin* in Italy (www.unito.it).

When you locate a potentially useful website as part of a search, assess it on the basis of:

- its 'credentials'; websites likely to provide authoritative information include those of professional bodies such as the *Association of Chartered Certified Accountants*, universities, many governments, learned societies such as the *British Academy of Management*, and independent bodies such as the *Institute for Employment Studies*
- why the site was created; purposes range from informing to promoting particular beliefs or attracting advertising
- the date the website was created or updated, if available.

The British Academy for the Humanities and Social Sciences provides an online directory of UK-based associations and learned societies in its field. High-quality websites provide details of the authors of texts or articles, their status, sponsors (who funds them) and sometimes the authors' other publications. Information that *must* conform to certain standards or country laws is normally sound. Examples are published financial statements of organisations and the specifications and descriptions of products made or distributed by a company in a country where UK trade descriptions and consumer rights laws apply.

Potentially useful websites can be bookmarked (saved to 'favourites' on your web browser) and fully evaluated later. If you decided to use the material you find, record the name of the webpage, the owner, the URL (web address) or DOI (the permanent link) and the date you accessed it. If a website contains vital information you want to read offline, you can download the material if the website permits this or copy and paste it into a Word document to file on your computer, adding at the top the information you need to cite the author and provide a full reference. If you do this, don't share the document with others: you may infringe copyright laws. You can share only the URL. Internet-based social bookmarking services allow you to store and organise online resource lists (and sometimes content) and to access your list from any computer. The services are not designed to be private, however, and it is easy to be overwhelmed and distracted by other people's submissions, thinly veiled commercial material and advertising.

A final point about internet searches is that it is important to use more than one search engine. This is because search engines such as Google personalise their lists of results on the basis of your prior searches. In effect, they are pre-selecting what you see. Make sure your internet searches are skilled and informed.

Assessing sources: test your understanding

Activity 4.8 is designed for you to assess how well you have understood the issues of sourcing information. First read the sections of this chapter on *Finding and evaluation sources of information* and *Internet searches* if you have not already done so.

ACTIVITY 4.8

You are a UK student preparing a marketing assignment that focuses on e-commerce and customer communication. You want to illustrate the rise of internet-based marketing in general but you can find very little information on small and medium-size enterprises (SMEs). Looking for material online, you come across a website (.com) offering free results from previously commissioned surveys. One survey asked respondents if their business had a website. Over 90 per cent of 1,872 small- and medium-sized businesses in the USA said they did. The metrics are hard to understand and there is little more useful information provided, apart from the date of the survey which is two years old. The website looks like a good quality one run by a for-profit company that conducts surveys.

Then you find an e-commerce monitoring report on a UK government department website (.gov). The report, focused on the UK, is detailed and comprehensive but a summary of key data shows the proportion of e-commerce turnover by size of company. It's not quite what you were looking for but, interestingly, it shows that e-commerce among small companies increased as a proportion of turnover during the four-year monitoring period more than it did for larger companies, apart from very large enterprises. The most recent data were collected two years ago and the report shows this year's date.

You find a third source, the website of an independent UK-based non-profit organisation (.org) devoted to retail research. An article, funded by a shopping voucher organisation, compares online sales across EU countries and the USA. It is short and accessible. However, it provides no breakdown of the companies by size. Data were collected from shoppers and online traders although the figures seem to have been combined with statistics from government departments: there is a caveat about these. Exact sources and the method used are not given. The data appear to be gathered last year but could be older because secondary data have been used, too. You notice that this website carries several advertisements at the end of the article. All three organisations give full information about themselves including contact details, but omit the date on the creation and frequency of update of their websites.

1. Should you use the USA survey results?
2. Should you spend more time 'sampling' the government report or will the summary of information be sufficient if you rethink the illustration you want?
3. Is the information on the third website reliable and relevant?
4. How relevant is the lack of information on creation dates and frequency of updates in the case of these three websites?
5. Which data best address your purpose?

Hide the following guidance until you have arrived at your answers!

1. You should not use the data. Insufficient information is provided. Who are the respondents and what kinds of businesses do they run? Who funded the study – a website design company with a vested interest? Are the definitions of small, medium and large businesses the same in the USA as elsewhere?
2. The summary of information on the second website would be sufficient for illustration purposes, provided you check to see how the data were collected and from whom. If you included data from this website it would add authority to your illustration but you might need to rethink it to cover the UK only.
3. The advertisements on an independent non-profit organisation suggest that this is the way it funds itself, along with commissioned work. Specific caveats about the data inspire confidence. The study is probably reliable but the lack of data sources and method should make you wary. The data could be used – with your own caveats – to suggest trends and country comparisons for brief illustrative, indicative purposes only, if nothing else were available.
4. As the dates of the reports and, in two cases, of the data collection, are provided, the creation dates and update frequency of the websites are less important in your evaluation of quality (provided you have confidence in the websites).
5. The first website doesn't address e-commerce and the third website doesn't address size of organisations, so neither fits your purpose. The government website doesn't *exactly* match your purpose. Thus, you might come to one of two conclusions. The first is that you have not yet located the information you need (but for illustrations don't spend too long looking). The second is that you could use the data on the government website if you changed your illustration slightly and narrowed it to cover the UK only. You could show

Table 4.5 Information quality checklist

Criterion	What to check
Relevant	Relevance of the information to your purpose
Trustworthy	Reliability and trustworthiness of the source
Clear	Comprehensible. Avoid sources that are too detailed or complex for your purposes (or simply indecipherable)
Sufficient	Sufficient for your purpose. A one-sentence description of a concept won't provide enough detail for you to apply it; a whole book can provide too much. An overview may be enough to guide further reading, even if it contains contested interpretations. At other times you may need very accurate and detailed information, for example, statistics and financial data
Necessary	Vital to your purpose ('need to know'). Relevant information may be interesting and 'nice to know' but beware information overload. Background information can be essential, however

that, in the UK, the relative gap between smaller and larger enterprises is closing in terms of proportion of turnover from internet-based commerce. In fact, it's a more 'business-like' illustration than one that simply states, in general, the number of SMEs which have websites. 'In general' doesn't specify location and a proportion of websites could be static pages providing opening hours and contact details only, with no online facility for e-commerce. By considering the data, you can identify assumptions you have made. Learning leads to more learning!

Information quality: a checklist

Quality of information easily outweighs quantity. Criteria are often used formally or informally to assess information against fitness for purpose in organisations. The criteria normally include a cost–benefit analysis: the cost of gathering and processing information must not outweigh its value. When you are a student this means you should not spend too long chasing an elusive item of information. When you find it, it may not be as valuable as you hoped. Moreover, there may be high-quality secondary sources that refer to it. Use the criteria in Table 4.5 as a checklist for the information you gather.

Chapter summary

❖ At university and in the workplace you need to be confident that you read accurately and critically, that is, questioning what you read. The quality of your own work – including decision-making – depends on your interpretation of what you read and your skill in finding and assessing information.

❖ Reading strategies reflect your purpose for reading a text. Selective reading techniques – scanning and skimming – are useful for choosing material and gaining an overview. Full understanding involves cover-to-cover reading.

❖ On-screen reading is cognitively demanding but there are techniques to help you focus on digital material.

❖ Reading critically and monitoring your understanding of a text is vital. Ask questions as you read and write a summary.

❖ Your aim when you read for understanding is to transform the information – combined with your critique – into your own knowledge. In this transformation process – a concept from operations management – inputs are changed into outputs with more value. The inputs, transformation and outputs require monitoring.

❖ Methodological conventions for empirical work help you to read critically, looking for omissions, flawed logic, biases and alternative explanations. Using critical questions aids the process.

❖ Make notes with an objective in mind. It's important to use your own words because this improves your understanding.

❖ Making notes is normally a two-step process when reading. In Step 1 you use jottings or spray diagrams; in Step 2 you write up your notes using a structure that's easy to follow later when you next read them.

❖ Making notes during lectures and interactive learning sessions is demanding. Ideally, three steps are involved: preparation; recording (by hand); reviewing and refining. Full preparation is essential for peer-work sessions. Reviewing and refining your notes means rewriting them using an appropriate structure.

❖ Re-read your notes regularly. Frequent revisiting means you remember what you learned and your knowledge is at your finger tips.

❖ Sometimes you need to find your own sources of information when studying. In the workplace you invariably need to do this. Information literacy is an important skill that requires a systematic approach, knowledge, techniques and organisation.

❖ When seeking sources of information, first clarify your purpose and consider what you *already* know. Then formulate the questions for which you want answers and devise search terms.

❖ Sources of information can be primary (first-hand), secondary (once removed) or tertiary (twice removed) depending on your questions. Familiarise yourself with access points for information.

❖ When you carry out your search you make an initial choice based on relevance. Then you evaluate the results based on the credibility of the source and soundness of the information. A technique known as triangulation can help.

❖ You need to record details of your sources or information and organise the material. Using reference management software makes these tasks easy. There are simple ways of keeping up to date with a topic or sector if you want to.

❖ The internet is a disorganised information database with no rules or regulations. Much information is incomplete, inaccurate and misleading. High-quality sources exist but you need to know how to make assessments.

References

Ailon, G. (2008) 'Mirror, mirror on the wall: culture's consequences in a value test of its own design', *Academy of Management Review*, vol. 33, no. 4, pp. 885–904.

Association of Chartered Certified Accountants (n.d.) [Online]. Available at www.accaglobal.com/uk/en.html (Accessed 18 April 2016).

British Academy of Management (2016) [Online]. Available at www.bam.ac.uk/ (Accessed 18 April 2016).

British Standards Institute (BSI) (2016) [Online]. Available at www.bsigroup.com/ (Accessed 18 April 2016).

Business and Strategy (2016) [Online]. Available at www.strategy-business.com/ (Accessed 18 April 2016).

Business Source Complete (2016) [Online]. Available at www.ebscohost.com/academic/business-source-complete (Accessed 18 April 2016).

Centre for Retail Research (2014) *Online Retailing: Britain, Europe, US and Canada 2014* [Online]. Available at www.retailresearch.org/onlineretailing.php (Accessed 13 October 2014).

Centre for Retail Research (2016) [Online]. Available at www.retailresearch.org/ (Accessed 18 April 2016).

Chartered Institute of Management Accountants (CIMA) (n.d.) [Online]. Available at www.cimaglobal.com/ (Accessed 18 April 2016).

Chartered Institute of Marketing (n.d.) [Online]. Available at www.cim.co.uk/ (Accessed 18 April 2016).

Chartered Institute of Personnel and Development, CIPD (2016) [Online]. Available at www.cipd.co.uk/ (Accessed 18 April 2016).

City of London Corporation (n.d.) [Online]. Available at www.cityoflondon.gov.uk/Pages/default.aspx (Accessed 18 April 2016).

Financial Conduct Authority (FCA) (2016) [Online]. Available at www.fca.org.uk/ (Accessed 18 April 2016).

Google Consumer Surveys (2012) *Why doesn't your company have a website?* [Online]. Available at www.google.com/insights/consumersurveys/view?survey=ri4o3b47ht6na (Accessed 13 October 2014).

Google Groups (n.d.) [Online]. Available at https://groups.google.com/forum/#!overview (Accessed 18 April 2016).

Hofstede, G. (1980) *Culture's consequences: international differences in work-related values*, Berkeley Hills, California, Sage Publishing Inc.

Institute for Employment Studies (2016) [Online]. Available at www.employment-studies.co.uk/ (Accessed 18 April 2016).

Journal of Business Economics and Management (2016) [Online]. Available at www.tandfonline.com/toc/tbem20/current (Accessed 18 April 2016).

Jussim, L. and Harber, K.D. (2005) 'Teacher expectations and self-fulfilling prophecies: knowns and unknowns, resolved and unresolved controversies', *Personality and Social Psychology Review*, vol. 9, no. 2, pp. 131–155.

Materials Recycling World (n.d.) [Online]. Available at www.mrw.co.uk/ (Accessed 18 April 2016).

Mintel (n.d.) [Online]. Available at www.mintel.com/ (Accessed 18 April 2016).

Mueller, P. and Oppenheimer, D.M. (2014) 'The pen is mightier than the keyboard: advantages of longhand over laptop note taking', *Psychological Science*, vol. 25, no. 6, pp. 1159–1168 [Online]. DOI: 10.1177/0956797614524581 (Accessed 5 May 2016).

Nexis (2016) [Online]. Available at www.nexis.com/ (Accessed 18 April 2016).

Office for National Statistics (2014) *Monitoring ecommerce: 2014* [Online]. Available at www.ons.gov.uk/ons/rel/rdit2/measuring-e-commerce/2014/art-indicators.html (Accessed 13 October 2014).

Office for National Statistics (n.d.) [Online]. Available at www.ons.gov.uk/ (Accessed 18 April 2016).

Retail Week (n.d.) [Online]. Available at www.retail-week.com/ (Accessed 18 April 2016).

Rosenthal, R. and Jacobson, L. (1968) 'Pygmalion in the classroom, newly expanded edition', *The Urban Review*', vol. 3, no. 1, pp. 16–20.

Small Business Advisory Service (2016) [Online]. Available at www.smallbusiness.co.uk/ (Accessed 18 April 2016).

The British Academy for the Humanities and Social Sciences (2016) [Online]. Available at www.britac.ac.uk/ (Accessed 18 April 2016).

The Caterer (2016) [Online]. Available at www.thecaterer-magazine.co.uk/ (Accessed 18 April 2016).

The Entrepreneur (2016) [Online]. Available at www.entrepreneur.com/magazine (Accessed 18 April 2016).

The Financial Times (2016) [Online]. Available at www.ft.com/home/uk (Accessed 18 April 2016).

The Small Business Blog (2016) [Online]. Available at http://sme-blog.com/ (Accessed 18 April 2016).

UKbusinessFORUMS (n.d.) [Online]. Available at www.ukbusinessforums.co.uk/ (Accessed 18 April 2016).

YouGov (n.d.) [Online]. Available at https://yougov.co.uk/ (Accessed 18 April 2016).

Writing assignments and preparing for exams

Writing as communication

Writing is about *communicating*. To dispel any doubts, carry out the activity below.

ACTIVITY 5.1 Read the following two email messages to staff in an organisation and then answer the questions.

Message 1

The Q3 budget forecast has been completed and indicates that [the organisation] is forecast to achieve a net outturn position of £46.4m for 20XX/XX, an adverse variance of £3.2m to the revised budget. New customer acquisition in October was impacted adversely by a number of factors including (a) closure of the London office due to fire while rebuilding and refurbishing took place, during which time there was major disruption to business; (b) security changes to the website resulting in a period where new customers could not register for new accounts; and (c) the temporary loss of the facility. This lower-than-budgeted new customer acquisition has impacted on both the forecast income and costs and the forecast net impact is the £3.2m shortfall. In an endeavour to ameliorate this shortfall, all staff are encouraged to exercise tighter cost control particularly with respect to discretionary expenditure during the final quarter of 20XX/XX.

Message 2

All staff are requested to reduce spending and expenses. The organisation's third quarter profit is likely to be £3.2m less than the £46.4m forecast because of three main factors:

1. Temporary closure of the London office due to fire.
2. Security changes to the website which led to delays in new customers being able to open accounts.
3. Technical problems with the website.

These factors reduced new customer numbers and, therefore, income. We would be grateful for your co-operation in minimising spending and expense claims.

Which email message would you prefer to receive? Which is easier to understand and why? Consider:
- how the recipients of each message are treated
- whether the reason for the message is immediately clear
- whether each message was designed to be an email rather than, say, a memo or a formal letter
- how each message is set out
- the jargon used in each.

Most people would be likely to prefer Message 2 because the writer has considered *who* the message is for, *why* it is being sent, the *medium* (email) and, therefore, how it will be read (on-screen). Such considerations influence wording and style. Thus, the writer has *focused* on the audience and the content. Jargon and unnecessary words have been removed, leaving only the relevant content set out in a *well-organised* way so that the *progression* through the narrative or 'story' is clear. The writer has considered *presentation* and set out the text in a visually accessible way. The result is a shorter message that is both easier to read and more likely to be well received. Both messages use writing conventions (sentences and paragraphs) and correct grammar, spelling and punctuation. These, however, while essential to good writing, do not alone 'do the job'.

This chapter guides you through the principles of good writing for any purpose. Common assessment criteria, formats for essays and reports, and preparation for exams are covered too. How to polish your writing is set out in Appendix 2 of this book.

Principles of good writing

Seven principles of good writing apply whenever you are composing text. These are set out below.

Seven principles of good writing

Principle 1
The audience and method: to whom and how

An informational item in a newsletter, a formal memo and an informal email, for example, will differ as a result of:
- your audience
- the medium you use.

Principle 2
Purpose and content: why and what

The *purpose* of your communication – *why* – will differ each time you write. You might be:
- writing an advisory note on different marketing methods for the university drama society
- preparing a report comparing and contrasting different marketing methods for an organisation's managers
- critiquing different methods of marketing from an ethical perspective for a study assignment
- presenting a well-argued case for adopting a particular method of marketing.

Your purpose determines the *content*. Your work won't be a simple demonstration of all you know about marketing methods.

Principle 3
Refinement of purpose: understanding what's required

In the workplace and at university the purpose of your writing is often defined for you: you receive a brief. So:
- read the brief (assignment question) in detail.

Each word or phrase tells you what's required. A brief requiring you to *analyse and evaluate* fundraising methods and make a recommendation or to *critique* different methods from the perspectives of environmental sustainability and ethics means examining in detail, identifying weaknesses and strengths, weighing up and so on. Overlooking significant terms in a brief can mean missing the point and, in a student assignment, low marks.

See Table 5.1 *Common terms in assignment questions* in this chapter

Principle 4
Structure and organisation

The intended content needs to be organised into a logical *chain* of linked ideas. Often, there are several threads that need to be woven together. You need to do the following.
Identify appropriate content:
- what to include to meet your purposes
- how you will support your assertions and argument (evidence illustrations and examples).

Plan a logical structure:
- work out the sequence of the main ideas
- know what links one idea with another
- decide where and how each thread will be woven in
- write headings and side headings.

A common problem is not being able to identify links or where threads fit. Standing back from your plan helps. Often, it's a matter of identifying *gaps* in content, *making new connections* or understanding that you've made unwarranted assumptions about connections. Don't start writing until you have a clear narrative or route map for the work. Know where you will start and end, what comes in the middle and how it all fits together.

Principle 5
Clarity

Express yourself clearly. Complex language and sentences reduce accessibility and frustrate readers. Use plain language. Aim to:

* say it simply: regularly ask yourself *What am I trying to say?*

The better informed that people are about a subject the more simply they can write about it. Also reduce 'clutter'. Imagine someone has told you to cut 100 words from your finished text. Delete superfluous words and repetitions and rewrite sentences more simply. Editing your own work is an important skill in professional life.

Principle 6
Appropriate style

If you want your work to conform to your intended purpose, attend to your choice of words and the construction of sentences and paragraphs. Consider the terms you might use to link ideas or to indicate consequences, conditionality, contrast, emphasis, disjunctions or lack of continuity and difference. Useful words include:

therefore	if	however	in addition
as a result	in contrast	but	similarly
in consequence	that is	conversely	alternatively
because	in comparison	despite	arguably

These words tell the reader what to expect next without telling them directly. You need to:
* choose words that convey what you want to say
* help the reader by linking ideas and sentences meaningfully.

Principle 7
Conventions

Spelling errors, poor grammar, inadequate use of paragraphs and other conventions such as punctuation don't command authority. Check your spelling and grammar. Set your computer spell-checker to English (the choice between UK and USA depends on your location and context) and use it. When in doubt, use a conventional dictionary. Read your penultimate draft carefully: many simple typing errors slip past spelling checkers. Grammar checkers are not helpful. They often present incorrect alternatives, even if your original choice was correct. Look up correct use. Always:
* check your spelling and grammar
* use writing conventions.

Grammar

Many people struggle to write grammatically. Use Appendix 2 now to test yourself on using apostrophes. The appendix also provides guidance on other aspects of grammar and word use.

Why am I assessed?

Assessment is a fact of life. In professional life, your performance is 'measured' in a variety of ways – by your managers, peers and sometimes by customers and by employees who report to you. Their feedback helps you to improve your performance so that it meets prescribed and/or agreed standards. When you are a student, assignments test whether and how well you have learned what your educators intended.

Assessment is not always formal. In the workplace *self-assessment* is important. You know, for example, if a presentation went well and you work out for yourself how to do better next time. At university, self-assessment is used for the same reason. For example, you may be asked to carry out an activity and then to reflect on what you did. *Peer assessment* may also be used by educators. Its primary purpose is normally to encourage you to learn from seeing the work of fellow students, much as you learn at work. These forms of assessment are called *formative*. They may not be awarded marks but they may be compulsory: you have to do them.

See *Critical reflection* in Chapter 6

Mark or grade-earning assignments, known as summative assessment, cause most apprehension among students. This chapter covers written, summative assignments.

Understanding assignment requirements

The requirements for study assignments can seem very stringent. Where do these requirements come from? First, there are overarching objectives or learning outcomes for your overall degree course and for each year or level of study. These often incorporate higher education goals and often professional ones too. They state what you will be able to do after successful completion. Ideally, courses are developed in ways that help students to achieve these outcomes so that, for example, practical outcomes will involve designing courses with practical work. In developing courses, educators tease apart the overarching learning outcomes into more specific, detailed ones that they embed into the content and the assessment regime. These specific outcomes align with the overarching ones. Your educators then assess your performance against a set of criteria designed to deliver each specific outcome. Ideally, these outcomes and criteria are made explicit to students. You can visualise this as a *pyramid of purpose*, which organisations use to ensure high-level goals are strategically aligned with day-to-day activities. Figure 5.1 shows the general idea.

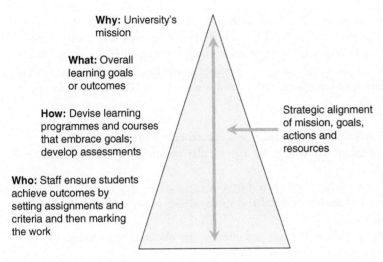

Figure 5.1 Degree programme pyramid of purpose

The learning outcomes of a course are likely to be stated using practical 'action' verbs. This makes the outcomes easier to measure. Here is an example of the expected outcomes of a marketing course.

By the end of the course students will be able to:

- describe and explain common marketing practices, tools and techniques
- demonstrate understanding of the role of marketing strategies and their 'fit' within organisations
- demonstrate understanding of ethical, environmental sustainability and legal issues in marketing
- critically evaluate marketing practices in the context of particular organisations
- apply knowledge to cases and scenarios
- plan a simple marketing campaign
- plan the implementation of a campaign
- understand and apply evaluation techniques
- plan an evaluation.

The list is also likely to include some learning objectives that are not directly related to the course content but more generally to your degree programme such as:

- participate effectively in a small group
- apply information literacy skills to relevant internet content
- take personal responsibility for learning
- communicate effectively.

To achieve all these outcomes you are expected to carry out relevant activities ranging from reading and information-seeking to (perhaps) problem-solving and group work. Assessed work tests whether or not you are doing so. Each item of assessed work targets a particular subset of objectives – no single assignment is likely to cover them all. The objectives in this subset are then broken down into elements that can be used as criteria for the assessed work. These criteria tell you – and the marker – what is required. For example, the criteria for an assessment that covers planning a case-based marketing campaign may focus on the application of knowledge, ethics and sustainability. The criteria may specify that a student:

- understands relevant knowledge, with reference to course material
- applies relevant knowledge to a particular organisation, taking account of context
- demonstrates logical and critical thinking
- identifies and analyses ethical and sustainability issues and how these will be remedied
- demonstrates understanding and effective use of planning techniques
- supports ideas with evidence/reasons
- structures and organises material logically
- presents campaign plan clearly
- uses management/marketing terminology.

Your assignment is marked on how well your work meets each criterion. Guidance and checklists provided by tutors may be even more detailed. In particular, distance-learning students may receive precise guidance on structure and appropriate content. Checklists of criteria are useful to 'test' your work against. A checklist for presentation is set out below. It is adapted from an assessment booklet for a problem-based assignment requiring a report structure (The Open University, 2012).

In the presentation of your report, markers are looking for:

- clarity of writing
- use of report structure
- consistent use of headings and subheadings
- inclusion of relevant diagrams
- clear titles for diagrams and tables
- full referencing, with citations in the report itself and, where necessary, use of quotation marks
- use of management vocabulary and language.

Other checklists cover different elements of the assignment. They set out in detail what readers want, the purpose of writing and how the text should be structured and organised. Together they match the principles of good writing set out earlier in this chapter.

The key difference between student assignments and writing in other contexts is that, as a student, you often have fewer choices. You often need to work within the confines of course content, to demonstrate your knowledge in particular ways and to meet other specific requirements related to the objectives of courses. For assignments that cover tasks such as group work, expect criteria that go beyond any written component. The criteria often include participation and the nature and quality of your inputs. Students who aim for high grades read assignment questions, guidance and criteria very closely indeed.

How to interpret assignment questions

Accurate reading and interpretation of assignment questions is essential. Individual words and phrases tell you what is required. They tell you the focus or perspective you should adopt, your choice of content and your treatment of it. You are never asked to *Write about Topic X*, which might result in a text that contains all you know about Topic X. This would be literally pointless with no focus or central case or argument. Sadly, some student assignments are like this because words and phrases in the assignment question have been overlooked or become obscured in the writing process. Inexperienced students often think that if they write everything they know about a topic they are bound to cover the assignment question somehow. Offering an assignment that fits the criteria is the key to good results.

Common terms

Some common terms used in assignment questions and instructions are set out in Table 5.1. The terms are rarely used alone. Common combinations include *describe and explain* and *compare and contrast*. Analytical thinking and a critical stance are invariably needed whatever the assignment question. For example, being asked to *define* a concept can look deceptively simple. Definitions can be highly contested with competing ones based on evidence gathered from different perspectives. That evidence may be incomplete or flawed in various ways. You discover these shortcomings through analysis and critique of the evidence.

Evaluate means to analytically weigh up the *pro et contra* – the pros and cons – of something. *Critique* includes analysis and evaluation. *Summarise* is often necessary in all your assignments when you draw conclusions from your analysis or draw together various strands of an argument. One term *entails* others. The terms, then, are normally shorthand for more complex thinking than the assignment title suggests. They indicate the *dominant* approach needed.

Work assignments often contain few words to guide you; the requirements are indicated by the context. You may be asked to *Prepare a report on the X marketing campaign*. Then, you must identify for yourself the terms, or combinations, that are appropriate to the context and readers' needs. A report on a completed marketing campaign would normally be a critical evaluation ending in 'lessons learned', for example, while a report on a proposed campaign might be an analysis of the plan and its implementation together with suggestions for improvement.

Table 5.1 Common terms in assignment questions

Term	Meaning
Define	Give a precise meaning of something, often a concept
Describe	Provide a detailed account
Explain	Give reasons for something, usually involving *how* and *why*. There may be more than one explanation
Discuss	Investigate, examine or analyse, usually with the use of argument. It can involve comparison and evaluation
Interpret	Make the meaning of something clear and present your own informed judgement. It usually involves explaining a concept, theory or practice in detail and how it works
Compare	Identify similarities. This often involves identifying differences, too. You need detailed understanding of what you are comparing (usually concepts, theories, practices or solutions)
Contrast	Identify differences. This usually involves identifying similarities, too. You set theories, practices, events, solutions and so on against one another and draw out differences
Analyse	Separate out the component parts of a concept, theory, event or problem and systematically examine each in detail. The instructions should tell you why you are doing this: to identify the underlying principles, identify causes or to critically examine
Evaluate	Appraise something. You weigh up the worth of a concept, theory, solution, practice or course of action – its strengths, weaknesses and limitations. It almost always involves analysis
Critique	Question closely and systematically. You analyse and evaluate a concept, theory, practice, situation or course of action, and provide support, qualified support or rejection of it. You set out your reasoning and support any assertions you make
Justify	Set out the grounds for something, usually your criticisms, decision or conclusion
Review	Critically examine something such as a course of action or literature on a topic
Summarise	Gather the key points or issues raised

In the following activity, an assignment title includes a statement and the term *discuss*. Titles like these are common in traditional assignments. While you may not encounter assignments with such titles, the activity is useful for *deconstructing* assignment questions.

> **ACTIVITY 5.2** You are given an assignment with the title: *Leaders are born, not made. Discuss.* What do you think you are required to do? You don't need any knowledge of the topic to carry out the activity. Make brief notes on:
>
> 1. How you might explore the assignment title.
> 2. What the instruction *discuss* means.

1. You will have noted that the assignment title is not set out as question but as a statement. So, when exploring the assignment title, you may have considered alternative ones such as:
   Leaders are made, not born

Leaders are neither born nor made
Leaders are made by circumstances.

Devising alternative statements helps you to research different definitions and perspectives.

2. Table 5.1 indicated that the instruction, *Discuss*, doesn't mean *write about the statement in general.* You are likely to have identified that it means *Consider evidence that supports or challenges the statement.* If you devised several alternative statements then look for evidence for each one. You may have noted that you should look not only for evidence that supports a statement but also for counter-evidence, too, that is, evidence that refutes it and may support a different one.

   Finally, although the title says *Discuss* you may have noted that you need to critically examine the evidence and evaluate it – weigh up the evidence for and against the statement (and alternative statements). You might also have realised that a conclusion is needed that summarises your considered view.

Such explorations of assignment questions are useful to carry out with fellow students: *debate* the question. Sharing perspectives helps you to understand what's needed.

Content and structure

Activity 5.2 explored *content* requirements for one type of assignment question. There are many forms but all written work has some common *structural* features no matter what the question is. For example, you introduce a topic and set out your approach, move on to detailed analysis and draw a conclusion that briefly summarises the evidence you have considered, the decision or judgement you have reached and your justification for it. Reports may go further to include options for action, recommendations or an implementation or action plan. There are standard frameworks for organising your content to set it out in an orderly way. These are covered later in this chapter.

Writing student assignments: the process

When preparing an assignment many students focus heavily on demands that relate to content – knowledge and understanding, interpretation, selection of relevant material and so on, that is, the *cognitive* demands. But *task* demands are equally important. Planning, systematic preparation and a logical production process help to ensure you demonstrate your ability. Work that is produced in haste and poorly presented does you no justice. A good assignment writing process is set out in Table 5.2.

   The sections that follow cover in more detail the tasks of outlining and structuring, which students find difficult. Recognising knowledge gaps is dealt

Table 5.2 Producing a written assignment

Tasks	What to do
Understand the requirements	1. Study the assignment question, assessment criteria, any guidance and checklists. Be clear about what you are being asked to do, how, and the standards expected. 2. Check the deadline for submitting the work, how and where you must submit it, the format and length. If you anticipate difficulties, check the rules and procedures for time extensions if these are allowed: early requests are more likely to be granted than last-minute ones except in exceptional circumstances. 3. Read the feedback on your previous assignment: it helps you to improve your work.
Plan your time	1. Devise a schedule that includes all the remaining tasks in this table. 2. Take account of reading you have done that is relevant to the assignment and whether you need to do more. 3. Leave some contingency time. Scheduling becomes easier with experience.
Assess your resources and develop an outline	1. Identify what you already know that addresses the question. To do this, organise your reading notes together with any notes from lectures, tutorials and/or seminars. Create an initial outline for the assignment using the required structure, making brief notes under appropriate sections. Indicate the maximum word count for each section. Use headings and subheadings and don't lose sight of the assignment question! 2. Identify what you don't know, that is, gaps in your knowledge. Record these gaps in your outline. 3. Identify potentially useful diagrams and ways of presenting information if appropriate.
Carry out library work	1. Carry out any further essential reading; make reading notes. 2. Find the information you need to fill your knowledge gaps; make reading notes.
Refine your outline	1. Incorporate elements of your new reading notes into your outline. Indicate how you intend to draw in and link different threads of content or strands of argument. Weaving content and making connections is often the hardest part of outlining. 2. It's useful to mentally rehearse what you want to say: it may reveal new gaps in knowledge or understanding. The assignment narrative should now be clear in the outline; if not, work on it.
Produce a draft	1. Create a first draft. This 'tests' your outline. Do more research if you find further knowledge gaps. 2. Use the checklists (and previous feedback) to critique your work: it's easier to make additions and changes early in the writing process. Some students use a highlighter pen to indicate description, discussion, analysis and so on. Then they delete text that is contributing little. 3. Refine your first draft; the result will be your second draft. Rewrite your first draft if necessary: it's quicker than major restructuring. Use the checklists again.
Polish your work	1. Polish your work to produce a third draft. Edit the draft; check the spelling and grammar; improve the presentation; make a final check on the word count. 2. Award a tentative mark to compare with your actual mark later. This helps you to assess your own standards.

See *How long does it take to prepare an assignment?* in Chapter 2 and Appendix 2 *Effective writing*

with first, however, because gaps can occur any time in the writing process. 'Time-poor' students often ignore or fail to notice such gaps and so limit the understanding and knowledge to be gained through remedying them.

Recognising and filling knowledge gaps

How do you recognise a knowledge gap? If you find it hard to answer *what*, *why* and *how* at any point when planning or preparing an assignment, then you have identified one. Knowledge gaps can prevent you from understanding and making connections between different content elements and weaving them together. Confusion can result. Stop and step back. Try to identify the knowledge gap. Common causes are:

- having insufficient information for or against an argument or theory
- not knowing how empirical findings relate to a particular theory
- missing the significance or meaning of empirical findings
- confusion over how different research findings support or challenge each other
- failing to see how research findings can be applied to work situations.

Once you identify your knowledge gap, it's usually easy to fill it. Scan or skim academic articles you read earlier to see if you missed conceptual connections that didn't seem significant then. Alternatively, find an article that reviews the topic, a textbook chapter that provides a synopsis or a descriptive case study in which a concept was applied. Discussing problems and queries with other students is useful, too.

Also review your current conceptual understanding. Sometimes students put together a conceptual jigsaw puzzle only to find new pieces don't fit. You may have to reconfigure your existing knowledge. Accepting reinterpretation and modification as a necessary part of learning (and that it's normal to have moments of confusion) help you to feel in control. Learning is an iterative process in which you move back and forth between existing knowledge and new information. With each iteration you increase your knowledge.

Organising your ideas: the initial outline

You may have all the ingredients for an excellent assignment but you need to organise them. Start by reviewing what you already know that addresses the assignment question. This allows you to tackle any obvious knowledge gaps immediately, although gaps can become apparent at any stage. Use your reading notes and any relevant lecture, tutorial or seminar material and reading notes to do this. You may need to do more reading later. If your assignment involves an investigation into a workplace situation some knowledge needs won't be evident until you explore it.

See *Recognising and filling knowledge gaps* in this chapter

When you have completed your review and met immediate knowledge needs, create an outline that structures the assignment. Refine the outline as you identify unforeseen knowledge gaps. Your final outline serves as a brief, structured, note-form version of your assignment that you refer to when writing. It disciplines your

See *Recognising and filling knowledge gaps* in this chapter

writing. An example of an initial outline for an essay is shown below. Structures for essays and reports are covered later in the chapter. The example is not a model; rather, it shows the process of outlining.

Kai's essay outline

Kai is planning an essay that requires him to *Discuss the empirical evidence on performance-related pay to promote productivity.* He has already analysed the words and phrases in the title: *discuss the empirical evidence* (what he needs to do); *performance-related pay* (the topic area); *productivity* (the sub-topic). These tell him what to include and, importantly, what to exclude.

He has also noted the guidance provided on the basic structure – an introduction, a main section with subsections and a conclusion. Generic checklists cover what each part should contain. The checklist for the introduction instructs him to include *in brief:*

Why this topic is important and topical
The background to the topic
Your case, argument, position or main areas of discussion
Your justification

This checklist also reminds him to use words and phrases from the essay title. The checklist for the conclusion includes items such as:

A summary of the main points/findings
Your overall view

It reminds students not to introduce any new information in the conclusion but says they can include implications or suggestions for future research or for practice.

Kai begins by assessing what he knows and organising his reading notes. He makes these headings and subheadings:

Introduction
Main section
   1. Evidence to support the use of performance-related pay (PRP)
   2. Evidence against the use of PRP
Conclusion

He decides that three articles will be useful for the introduction. Seven fit well under the two *Evidence* headings. The three remaining ones aren't *for* or *against*. He decides that these contain material that explains the mixed findings, so he inserts another subheading in the main section:

   3. Why the findings might be mixed

Kai works iteratively, moving back and forth, and becomes engaged with identifying links between ideas. While making notes under *Conclusion* he finds he's now unsure what his main argument will be, so he indicates this. He thinks he will mention implications for practice in his conclusion. Then, satisfied he has organised what he knows, he now has time to address what he doesn't yet know – his knowledge gaps. To fill them he will first scan or skim the articles again for links or information that didn't seem relevant when he first read them. Then he will look for further material to answer his remaining questions. As he does this, he will refine his outline until it's possible to use it as the basis for the first draft of his assignment. Kai's initial outline is set out in Table 5.3.

Table 5.3 Kai's initial outline

Introduction

The use of performance-related pay to promote productivity in the workplace is a relevant and important topic because of the needs of organisations to increase output in the face of competition, according to X (date). X says the reason for this competition is globalisation. X is cryptic ... would globalisation affect, say, the public sector which is also experiencing rises in the use of PRP? Look up something on contract culture?

Use Y (date) for background: the resurgence of interest in PRP is a result of the move towards low-trust relationships within organisations. Do Y's reasons conflict with X's or is it that competition results in organisations with low-trust employee relationships? Read articles again or look up more research. Still doesn't make sense in terms of the public sector.

H (date): Empirical work in the late twentieth century emanated from work on the motivational theories F (authors, date) and G (authors, date). Mixed findings, depending on key variables studied. Is anything different now?

My case: write later. Mostly, 'it depends' – and what this means for practice.

My justification: write later.

Evidence for PRP

Set out F and G theories in brief and how PRP is 'supposed' to work. Diagram?

J (date): if goals are clear and compensation is adequate with management support for merit pay, then PRP works. Study in brief: [...] Include my comments on type of organisation/employees studied.

K and L (date): PRP works for structured jobs that aren't very complex and when performance goals are clear and easily measured. Study in brief: [...] Include my comments on trust/security.

[...Kai adds two more studies]

Evidence against the use of PRP

M (date): a substantial part of the incentive effect turns out to be the result of higher-productivity workers replacing lower-productivity workers. Study in brief: [...] How much increased productivity is due to each factor isn't clear; a different type of study would be needed to differentiate. This and other studies mentioned don't say how long the PRP effects last so there's a time factor to add to the mix of PRP effects along with inflow of higher-productivity workers.

N (date): PRP doesn't work if employees don't see the relationship between performance and rewards. Study in brief: [...] Basic and fundamental point; the relationship may not be easy to see in many jobs.

P (date): negative outcome when PRP is used with employees in occupations which are intrinsically motivating, i.e. bring job satisfaction just by doing them. Study in brief: [...] N mentions some other studies where outcomes were negative: look them up; they make a strong case against ill-considered introduction of PRP by managers.

(continued)

Table 5.3 (cont.)

Why findings might be mixed

Q (date): it depends on the following contextual variables […]. Types of studies reviewed: […] The table in the paper is the best summary.

R (date): it depends on the employee's level in the organisation and role and on the quality of the appraisal of performance responsibilities. Study in brief: […] Q cites other studies – is it the same in all organisations?

S (date): theories F and G may be flawed. Suggests the theories aren't universally applicable and puts forward alternatives. The alternatives are quite complex so best to just mention how they differ from theories F and G and the perspective they take. I think the alternatives are just untested ideas but see if there are findings to support or refute any of them.

Conclusion

Does PRP work? It depends, and theories F and G may be flawed.

Implications for practice: overall – context-dependent but don't introduce PRP just because everyone is doing it. Illustrate with one of O's examples.

Revisit and draw in introductory material – globalisation, competition and changed relationships with employees. Does this really explain why everyone seems to be doing it when it's so hard to make it work and the underlying theories may not work? Has the history been forgotten or has something changed? Do some research – it's a bit of a puzzle!

The example doesn't show the iterative process Kai used. Understanding that organising ideas is iterative is important because many students feel that they *should* be able to work through ideas on paper in a serial way. However, this is rare even among professional writers.

Note that the outline is tentative, unfinished and is likely to contain misconceptions requiring correction later. It illustrates how to organise what you know and identify what you need to find out as you try to fit together your current knowledge and ideas into a logical and critical narrative. This is the value of outlining and why it's important to adopt a critical stance from the start.

> **ACTIVITY 5.3** Use the outlining technique next time you prepare an assignment. Save all the paperwork you produce including a copy of the assignment you submit and review it to fully understand knowledge gain through iteration. It will be reassuring and confidence-building. It will also provide useful insights if you are required to reflect on your learning in a log, blog or diary.

Assignment structures: essays and reports

There are two common forms of assignments: *essays* and *reports*. Report structures differ slightly according to whether or not they are reports on empirical research you have carried out.

Essay structure

Essay structures have three main parts: the introduction, the main body and the conclusion.

The introduction. Here you introduce the topic and say how you will address the assignment question. Try to reflect the question in the first sentence or two. Define concepts or technical terms used in the question and, if necessary, say how you have interpreted the question. You can also justify omissions.

An assignment question that asks *Discuss the empirical research on PRP to promote productivity* contains no clues as to why PRP might be an important issue, if and why taking a historical perspective might be useful and the implications of research findings for practice. Neither does it specifically direct you to take a critical stance. These are all issues you might address in the introduction. Guidance or checklists may indicate that your introduction should state why the topic is important and relevant, the background and so on. Thus, you might begin your introduction with the following statements:

> The use of PRP to promote productivity in the workplace is a relevant and important topic because of a recent resurgence in its use in all sectors, although different reasons for this resurgence are put forward (X, date, Y, date, Z, date).
>
> PRP was first introduced in the twentieth century, based on two motivational theories, F and G, that related effort to reward. However, research at that time revealed very mixed findings: PRP did not invariably increase productivity and sometimes reduced it.
>
> This essay critically discusses historical and more recent research findings, analyses the possible reasons for the resurgence of PRP and considers the implications of past failures of PRP for today's practitioners.
>
> Given the size of the literature on PRP, only those studies that focus on productivity are considered together with causal factors of increased or decreased productivity.
>
> The conclusions drawn are [...]

Note how the introduction restates the question and gives the reader a clear picture of the perspective the writer has adopted and what to expect.

The main body. This is where you set out and consider the balance of evidence to develop your case or argument. You can visualise an essay's shape. The top (the introduction) and the bottom (the conclusion) are narrow, while the middle (the main body) is the widest part. Within this overall shape there is a chain of smaller, similar shapes as shown in Figure 5.2. These represent new material or sub-topics. As they are drawn in, they need to be introduced, developed with the use of evidence and then briefly concluded. They need to be linked to your overall argument and/or the content immediately before or after. You make these links in the mini-introduction or the mini-conclusion, or both. There are no hard and fast rules but linking is vital to achieve a flow of logical argument and narrative. Know *why* you are including something.

See Table 6.3 in Chapter 6

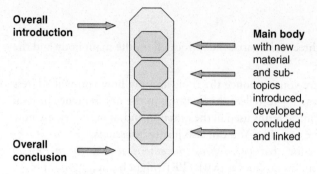

Figure 5.2 The shape and structure of an essay

In the assignment question, *Discuss the empirical research on performance-related pay to promote productivity*, each smaller shape can be given headings that match your intended content:

Background and reasons for resurgence of PRP
Evidence for PRP
Evidence against PRP
Explanations for mixed findings.

It's possible to nest a series of even smaller shapes within these as you draw in different pieces of evidence. In practice, the smallest shapes-within-shapes are individual paragraphs. This is how the main body of an essay takes shape.

The conclusion. A conclusion reminds readers of what the essay has considered by summarising, that is, by drawing together *in brief* all the main findings, points of argument and justifications. Then a concluding statement is made. It should follow logically from the summary and be justified by it, so that no further justification is needed.

A conclusion contains no new or additional material although it is acceptable to include the implications for future research or for practice. If you wanted to draw in new research articles to explore implications for practitioners, however, you would include these in the main body of the essay. There are always choices but the essay title and word count influence how much space to devote to sub-topics. Don't allow a sub-topic, however engaging, to draw you away from the main topic. The last sentences of a conclusion generally make links to the title of the essay by using words and phrases from it to 'close the loop'.

Table 5.4 sets out the basic essay structure with generic content guidance.

ACTIVITY 5.4 Select an essay you have written and see how the content compares with the structure and content guidance in Table 5.4. It may be more or less detailed than the guidance you were given. It's unwise to disregard guidance that tutors give you but you may see additional ways of enhancing your work. If you have not yet written any essays, use Table 5.4 as additional guidance for your first essay.

Indicate where you could improve the structure and content. Set aside a little time to do this; it is not an activity you can carry out in a few minutes if you want to improve your marks next time.

You may find it helpful to use highlighter pens to identify the various parts of your essay. If you can't identify some parts this is likely to mean one of two things: the content is in the wrong place and would be much more powerful somewhere else or it should not be in the essay at all. Table 5.4 should help you with this identification task. Finally, add headings and subheadings. Use the terms *Introduction* and *Conclusion* for these parts of your work; for the main body use terms and phrases appropriate to the content.

see *How to cite and reference* in this chapter

Table 5.4 Essay structure with generic content guidance

Essay section	Content guidance
Introduction	1. State what the topic is and why it is important and relevant, reflecting the essay question in the first sentences 2. If necessary, explain any concepts or terms used in the question or if definitions are highly contested, say so and discuss in the main body of the essay 3. Briefly set out the background 4. If necessary, state how you have interpreted the question 5. State how you are addressing the question 6. Justify omissions or additions

Main body	1. Introduce evidence
	2. Develop your discussion of it
	3. Summarise and link to previous content and/or to what follows
	4. Repeat 1, 2 and 3 as necessary
	Reminders:
	  • Ensure that you build your case as you move through the main body
	  • Construct your content in accordance with the essay question, for example, *discuss, evaluate, compare and contrast*
	  • Take a critical stance whether or not the question explicitly requires it

Conclusion	1. State what the essay covered 2. Summarise the key findings 3. State your conclusion (supported by the evidence) 4. Set out implications for future research and/or for practice 5. Include a final sentence that reflects the title of the essay Reminder: • Don't include any new material in the conclusion
Reference section	1. Provide in list form the full references to sources of information you cited in your essay; adopt whatever style is specified by your university (usually Harvard style)

Report structures

Report structures are often used for problem-based assignments and for the analysis of descriptive case studies and scenarios. They are commonly used in workplaces, too. Reports have many parts, identified by headings, which make them easier for others to read – and to read selectively.

A report has much the same basic structure as an essay: there is an introduction, a middle part (usually made up of several parts) and a conclusion. The logical progression of content elements is the same, as is the need to adopt a critical stance, be analytical and explore and evaluate ideas. Educators who claim that reports are 'descriptive' have not read a good report! The obvious differences between reports and essays are that reports have:

- additional presentational elements such as a cover page, an executive summary, a contents page
- content divided up under sections/headings, often numbered
- diagrams, tables, charts and bullet points as appropriate
- business-like or matter-of-fact language (sentences may be short)
- appendices if necessary.

The key difference is *the type of content*. Report formats are used when the author evaluates a past action, tries to resolve a problem or plans to do something such as make improvements. Reports are likely to:

- critically analyse and evaluate a problem or situation
- present data/information
- critically apply concepts, models and theories rather than critique them (although shortcomings should be identified)
- put forward realistic and practical recommendations or plans of action
- provide an implementation plan to deliver the recommendations or to carry out any proposed action.

Report writers can be creative as well as critical: problem-solving requires both. Solving problems also demands identifying assumptions – your own as well as those of other people. This can mean questioning received wisdom or usual practice. Sometimes you need to make sensible or reasonable assumptions because information is lacking. This is often the situation when you are reading cases studies. Reasonable assumptions have to be made about staff behaviour, for example, and whether novel solutions are likely to be welcome.

See *Recognising assumptions*; *Critical thinking*; *Using critical thinking for investigations* in Chapter 6

Whereas when you write an essay you can critique an argument without necessarily putting forward an alternative one, in a report you are almost duty-bound to be both critical and constructive. Reports *can* be descriptive if they deal with events that have already happened. But, even so, it is invariably better to critically evaluate what happened in order to identify more advantageous courses of action so that lessons can be learned. Report-writing is equally demanding as essay-writing. Despite all the headings that seemingly break up the content, the report elements must be linked logically. It is a report on your detailed, critical analysis of a situation and your – justified – choice of solution, one that is appropriate to the context. The concise and factual language may disguise your efforts but your excellent thinking will be evident in the incisive and insightful way you treat the issue.

Table 5.5 provides guidance on structure and content; Activity 5.5 helps you to improve your report-writing. When writing reports for study assignments, also attend to specific guidance or checklists you have been given. If you are required to apply theory to resolve a problem or 'solve' a case, then you should also read *Applying theory* in Chapter 6. This sets out how to do it, given that theory can be flawed or not quite 'fit' the context you are dealing with.

See *Setting SMART objectives* in Chapter 2; see *How to cite and reference* in this chapter; see *Using critical thinking for investigations* in Chapter 6

ACTIVITY 5.5 Select a report you have written and see how the content compares with the structure and content guidance in Table 5.5. Don't disregard any guidance you have been given by tutors but use the table to see if there are additional ways of enhancing the structure and content.

As in Activity 5.4, use highlighter pens to identify the various parts of your report. For example, highlight in yellow all the sentences relating to analysis to see if they are in the first main analysis section. Highlight in green all the recommendations you make to see if they are all under the heading *Recommendations*. See what is in the wrong place or should not be in the report at all. Adjust or add headings and subheadings.

Set aside some time to do this and then review what you have done before attempting your next report. If you have not yet written any reports, use Table 5.5 as additional guidance for your first one.

Table 5.5 Problem-based report structure with generic contents guidance

Report component	Content guidance
Title page	Set out • an informative title, conveying what the report is about • the author • the date
Executive summary	Set out a very brief guide to what's in the report including: • the issue the report considers • the purpose of the report • main evidence/analysis • conclusions • recommendations for action
Contents page	Set out • a list of headings with page numbers, including the reference section and appendices if any • titles of tables and diagrams with page numbers if the report is a long one

(continued)

Table 5.5 (cont.)

Report component	Content guidance
Introduction	Identify and describe • the problem and its impact (why it is an issue and to whom) • the background to the problem • the purpose of the report and its scope (the limits or boundary you have set and why) For student assignments involving workplace issues it is helpful to include • your role and information about the organisation that is relevant to the issue or problem (this provides context for the marker)
Main sections	
1. Analysis	Set out • your choice of factors to analyse and why • assumptions (your information is likely to be incomplete) • your analysis of causes and contributory factors using relevant theories and concepts • diagrams, where these add value to the analysis
2. Conclusions to the analysis	These are your conclusions *to the analysis.* Set out • the overview you have gained • the main causes and contributory factors that your analysis revealed • any limitations of your analysis (such as lack of information about some aspect of the problem)
3. Recommendations	Set out • criteria for a solution (for example, limits of cost, time, resources; minimum disruption); options for possible solutions; your choice and justification • specific recommendations for action based on theory where relevant. Make sure your recommendations are SMART • any assumptions you have had to make in your recommendations • negative implications arising from your recommendations and how to minimise their impact • advantages and disadvantages of your recommendations to save your reader having to work this out for him or herself
4. Implementation plan (optional depending on assignment brief)	Set out, if required • how your recommendations will be implemented – a schedule may be useful
References	List the full references to sources of information you cited in your report; adopt the style specified by your university (usually Harvard)
Appendices	Appendices should include only supplementary material that supports statements in the report, not essential material

Tips to help readers

- Use standard headings for components of the report but adapt them to customise your report. For example, change *Analysis* to *Analysis of X*. Create subheadings such as *The communication climate* and *Communication channels* as you analyse different elements of the problem or situation.

- Keep the presentation simple. Use diagrams that make information instantly understandable. Avoid unnecessary graphics, for example, pictures on the title page. These can be unwelcome when sent by email. Some universities have a size limit on assignments submitted electronically.
- If you use colour for diagrams and charts, make sure they convert well to greyscale if the report needs to be printed.

Case-based report

Case studies or scenarios are frequently used by educators. You may be asked to 'explain' a descriptive case or scenario using models, theories and concepts but to do this you need to analyse it. For assignments involving descriptive cases and scenarios, a report structure is usual. The structure is the same as for a problem-based report, as set out in Table 5.5. The difference in content is that the problem (or workplace situation) is contained in the case study or scenario.

Note that descriptive cases and scenarios are different from *theoretical* case studies, which you may be asked to analyse, although this is not a common feature of undergraduate study. The method for analysing theoretical cases is set out briefly in Chapter 6. For the analysis of theoretical cases you may be asked to set out your work in a report structure *or* essay format. If you use a report structure, you omit the sections for Recommendations and Implementation.

See Applying theory to problems and scenarios in Chapter 6

Research report

Research reports, that is, reports on your own research, are structured like the research articles you read in academic journals. They follow the same conventions. The structure is set out in Table 5.6.

Use the research report format even if you are conducting a simple survey. Readers want to know why and how you conducted the survey, if one had been carried out before and so on. The format is designed so that reports contain sufficient information for a reader to replicate the survey or research.

> **ACTIVITY 5.6** See how well a research report you have written – or one you are planning – compares with the structure and content guidance in Table 5.6 in addition to any guidance you have been given. Use the instructions in Activity 5.5 to do this. Alternatively, select an academic research article and assess how well it conforms to Table 5.6. Identify any differences and possible reasons for them.

Word counts

In professional life a report can be as short as a page or as long as a book: it depends on the subject matter. When you are a student, educators adopt

Table 5.6 Research report structure and generic content description

Report component	Content guidance
Title page	Set out • an informative title, conveying what the report is about • the author • date
Abstract	The abstract summarises the report. Set out • its purpose • methods used • main findings • main conclusions and significance
Table of contents if required	Set out • a list of headings with page numbers, including the reference section and appendices if any • tables and diagrams with page numbers under relevant section headings
Introduction	Set out • the purpose of the study and why it is important or relevant • relevant background information
Review of literature	Set out • your review of the literature • how it establishes the reason for your empirical work • your research question(s) and its relevance (which should emerge easily from the review)
Method	Set out • any theory on which you based the study • justification of its use (and its limitations) • who the participants were and how they were selected • the instructions you used • how you carried out the study • any survey or interview questions you used (if there were many, put the full set in an appendix) • any limitations of the method • how you dealt with ethical issues, such as withholding information from participants to avoid biasing their responses Give enough detail for the study to be repeated by another person
Results	Set out • the results • details of any statistical analysis used
Discussion	Set out • the findings • whether your research question (hypothesis) was supported and how well • other possible explanations for the results and/or results that could not be explained • any limitations of the study and/or assumptions • implications of the results for theory or practice

Table 5.6 (cont.)

Report component	Content guidance
Conclusion	Set out • a summary of the discussion • a conclusion about the most likely explanation for the results
References	List the full references to sources of information you cited in your report; adopt the style specified by your university (usually Harvard)
Appendices	Appendices should not include essential information, only supplementary material that supports statements in the report (you may want to include data or a questionnaire you referred to in the report)

standard lengths for written assignments: long enough for you to demonstrate your knowledge and reasoning and short enough for ease of marking. Word limits are also essential to ensure fairness and to allow time for variety in assignments and learning activities. Many benefits of brevity are directly relevant in the workplace; you learn to prioritise and select content and to write concisely.

Common lengths for student essays and reports range from 1,000 words to about 2,500. Check the assignment guidance carefully. Some guidance suggests the proportion of the overall word count you should use for each part of your assignment. However, if you are told only the *maximum marks* for each part or section, it can be a mistake to divide up the word count in proportion to the marks. This is because the marks may not be based on length but on the quality of what you write or the difficulties students have with that part of the assignment. Use marks only as a rough guide.

Consequences of too many or too few words

If you exceed the overall word count you may be penalised. Markers may allow a 5 per cent or 10 per cent overrun but deduct marks after that. Check your university's rules. While keeping within the word count is the usual concern of students, writing too little can be a problem. Even if the quality of what you write is good, you cannot achieve maximum marks if there is insufficient content. Try to write *to* the word length. Make sure you have sufficient material, that you provide enough detail and that you discuss the meaning or significance of it. Seek help if you find it hard to reach the required length. Suggested percentages of the overall word count are set out below for essays in Table 5.7 and for problem- and case-based reports in Table 5.8.

The reference list is normally included in the word count. It may earn marks for presentation; marks may be deducted if it is not present.

Table 5.7 Suggested word-count percentages for essay sections

Introduction	5% – 10%
	Several paragraphs are sufficient; more than 15% of the total word length is too long
Main body	75% – 85%
Conclusion	10% – 15%

Table 5.8 Suggested word-count percentages for report sections

Introduction	15–20%
Main sections	80–85% of the overall word count but individual sections will vary according to content
	• In general, the conclusion to the analysis should be the shortest main section
	• The analysis and recommendations should be of about equal length
	• Expect to receive guidance if an implementation plan is required, although the use of time charts can dramatically reduce word count

The following are not normally included in the word count:

- cover page
- executive summary
- contents page
- appendices.

The content of these is not usually mark-earning but the presence of the items may earn marks for presentation; marks may be deducted if they are not (excluding appendices). Never use appendices for essential information: markers may not read them. The length of an executive summary varies according to the overall length of the report. For a report of 2,500 words, half a page of text is generally sufficient.

Research reports

Use the problem-based and case-based report guidance above but adjust the percentages you use for the main sections according to the nature of the work carried out. In general, the discussion section contains the most words and the conclusion the fewest. Exclusions from the word count are normally the same as for problem-based and case-based reports. In effect, the abstract replaces the executive summary and a contents page is not always necessary.

Building and supporting an argument

When you write or make a presentation your aim is usually to put forward a point of view, case or argument – preferably an informed, balanced and considered one if you want it to be credible and respected. There are conventions for building a case or argument when the aim is justification. A well-known one that is widely used to help students is that of the British philosopher Stephen E. Toulmin (1922–2009).

Argumentation

Toulmin's structure has a number of specific elements.

1. **The claim** – this is the statement or claim being made (for example, *We need to move to larger offices*).
2. **The data or grounds** – these are the facts, figures or other evidence on which the claim is based (*Three of our 15 staff have insufficient space*).
3. **The warrant** – this a statement that shows that the claim follows logically from the data or grounds (*Employees are supposed to have at least 11 cubic metres of space*).
4. **The backing** – this is information that validates, justifies or supports the warrant; it answers any questions about the warrant and provides additional support (*The UK Workplace Health, Safety and Welfare Regulations states this – it's the law*).
5. **The rebuttal** – this recognises exceptions or restrictions to the claim or anything that might undermine the grounds, warrant or backing; it can be a counter argument to a real or potential challenge (*I don't think the unused storeroom will solve our problems because it's very small … but it's worth considering*).
6. **The qualifier** – the degree of certainty attached to the claim (*We'll need to move offices* if *the storeroom is not sufficiently large*).

All arguments need a claim, ground and warrant (which may be self-evident or assumed – a potential problem) but not all require backing, rebuttal and a qualifier. Toulmin's structure works well for short arguments, particularly in conversations between people when critical dialogue is needed: the strength of one person's argument is discovered through questions from one or more others and the first person's responses. These can uncover unjustified claims. The structure may be harder to follow in complex ones, however. Table 5.9 sets out how to use it in an essay and Table 5.10 in problem-based assignments.

Argument structure for essays

For essays, you don't *have* to set out the warrant (or backing) if a claim is supported by the grounds on which it is considered to be warranted. In practice, however, you'll want to 'interrogate' the grounds and see or show how they support the

Table 5.9 Argument structure for an essay

Toulmin element	How to cover the element	Notes
CLAIM	State the claim: *This essay argues that…*	The claim can be the position you take; it can *already* be a qualified claim or position.
DATA/GROUNDS	Set out the evidence	This is evidence on which the claim is based.
WARRANT	State: • why this evidence is relevant to the claim • how this evidence supports (justifies) the claim • whether it is sufficient to support the claim • whether it is effective in supporting the claim	Justify that the claim follows from the grounds. You question and decide whether the grounds support the claim. In doing so you also reveal any assumptions made.
BACKING	• Show the validity (and credibility) of the warrant • Provide further information if the warrant needs more support	Assess the credibility of source/accuracy of the warrant – perhaps other sources can verify?
	Repeat the process for each ground you use. Each will normally come from an individual research study.	
REBUTTAL(S)	Provide rebuttal(s). State: • evidence rebuts that the claim • why this evidence rebuts the claim • whether this evidence is sufficient to rebut the claim	Some rebuttals will be from academic articles that set out alternative positions, or from critiques.
	Repeat the process for each rebuttal you include. **Some rebuttals will be your own**, arising from your critical analysis of the evidence; you might want to comment on the rebuttals, too. A rebuttal is an argument in itself and may need to be set out with a claim, grounds, warrant and backing.	
Qualifier	Indicate the degree of certainty attached to your claim or the position taken (*if, but, some, depending*).	You may already have included the qualifier in your introduction but discuss it.
Qualified claim	Qualify your original claim here if you have not already done so.	A claim can be *refuted* or qualified.

See *Logical reasoning* and *Using critical thinking for investigations* in Chapter 6

claim. You can set out rebuttals after each item of evidence or gather them together. It depends on whether exceptions to the claim arise from each piece of evidence presented or whether they arise from elsewhere.

Argument structure for reports

In problem-solving, when you are diagnosing a problem you invariably need a warrant. For example, you claim that a project has failed because it has been poorly managed. You analyse the failure and identify a number of relevant factors (your data – the symptoms of the problem). These lead you to believe

Table 5.10 Argument structure for a report

Toulmin element	How to cover the element	Notes
Claim (qualified)	State the claim: *The X project failed primarily because of failure to set realistic objectives.*	The claim has already been qualified (*primarily*).
Data/grounds (reasons for the claim)	Give evidence: • Set out the evidence: the 'symptoms' of the problem.	Evidence on which the claim is based.
Warrant	Show that the grounds support the claim: *These symptoms are consistent with problems arising from failure to set realistic objectives* (invoking the management control loop). State: • why this is relevant to the claim • how this supports the claim (how it justifies it) • whether it is sufficient to support the claim • whether it is effective in supporting the claim.	When you show how the grounds support the claim do so *critically*. Reveal any assumptions made.
Backing	Assess the validity (and credibility) of the warrant and provide further information if the warrant needs more support.	Consider the credibility of the source/accuracy of the warrant – perhaps other sources can verify? Invoke management control loop's history of successful use in the workplace.
Rebuttal(s)	Set out rebuttal(s). State: • evidence that rebuts the claim • why this evidence rebuts the claim • whether this evidence is sufficient to rebut the claim.	A rebuttal is an argument in itself and may need to be set out with a claim, grounds, warrant and backing. There may be data that didn't quite fit the claim.
Qualifier	State the degree of certainty you can attach to the claim.	In a report you are likely to have included the qualifier in your claim but discuss it.
Qualified claim	State your qualified claim here if you have not already done so.	Reports are generally retrospective, so it's usual to provide the qualified claim in the introduction.

the problem is a failure in setting realistic objectives. This is your warrant (since these 'symptoms' typically suggest a failure to set realistic objectives). Then you must back your warrant (you support your 'diagnosis' by evidencing the formal work done on management control which involves setting realistic objectives or its common use in practice). In most cases, the warrant will involve use of theory. Detailed guidance on this is provided in the subsection on *Applying theory* in Chapter 6.

Table 5.10 sets out *the structure of the argument* rather than the report itself. Each time that you make a claim, use data and then apply theory you go through

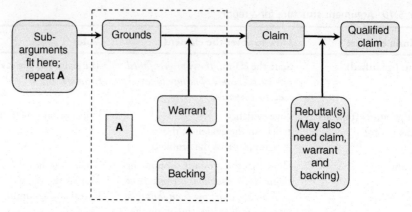

Figure 5.3 Schema for Toulmin's structure

Adapted from Toulmin, 1958

the claim-grounds-warrant-backing sequence. You need to do this, for example, when you set out a claim in a solution to a problem, use 'case' data and apply a theory to inform a proposal or action.

Toulmin's structure is useful in checking that you or others are putting forward justifiable, robust arguments. You can use it when reading and in *critical dialogues* in which others question the speaker and the speaker responds. A schema of Toulmin's basic structure is easy to draw but when sub-arguments and rebuttals requiring claims, warrants and backing are included, the schema becomes very complex indeed. A schema is set out in Figure 5.3 showing where sub-arguments generally fit. For each ground and for each sub-argument, **A** must be repeated as shown.

Practise using the argumentation structure

Carry out Activity 5.7 to see how Toulmin's structure works.

ACTIVITY 5.7 Read the case study below, then answer the questions that follow.

Jane puts forward a case to save costs on IT support. This is a requirement since costs are rising on account of increased user demand. Currently, staff phone or email the IT help desk, which then allocates the work to in-house IT engineers. 'Outside' specialists are contracted in when necessary. Jane makes a case for outsourcing the IT support service which she argues will save money. Engineers would be located on-site and staff would email requests for assistance on a first-come, first served basis. Jane supports her case by presenting the annual cost of providing in-house IT support and the estimated cost of outsourcing, which is less.

Committee members put forward the following comments and questions:

- Has Jane factored in the savings of having a help desk? Not all IT problems need an engineer: sometimes staff want quick verbal help, for example, on how to renew a password.
- Some IT problems are more urgent than others. It makes sense to prioritise IT support if problems affect staff taking customer orders, for example.
- Many IT problems result from the organisation being multi-platform and allowing staff to use many different types for software for which engineers sometimes have insufficient knowledge. In other organisations, computers use the same operating system and repertoire of software so that updating and fixes can be done centrally. Costs could be reduced by reducing demand on IT support services.

Now:

1. Identify Jane's claim, grounds, warrant and backing.
2. Identify rebuttals.
3. Can Jane qualify her claim?
4. What assumptions did she make that weakened her argument?

You probably identified Jane's *claim* as the statement that outsourcing would save money. Her *grounds* are the figures that show that outsourcing would be cheaper than the current in-house system. Her *warrant* is rising costs, which she *backs* with a statement about increasing demands on IT support. The *rebuttals* come from other committee members: that her case seems not to have taken account of any potential savings of having a help desk, her failure to consider the need to prioritise requests for IT support and the strong possibility of reducing demand on the service. From these rebuttals, it's easy to see Jane's *assumptions*: that all calls for support are equally urgent and important; that engineers are invariably required; and that requests for support cannot be reduced. Jane could *qualify* her argument only by stating that outsourcing *might* be an option for *some* parts of IT support *but* that further investigation is needed.

Problems of scope

The key weakness of Jane's argument is its *scope*. It is limited to the cost of running IT support in-house rather than consideration of how demand might be reduced or the function of the help desk. Scope is an important but little-mentioned aspect of building strong arguments and it's difficult to assess: too wide and an argument can become too vague or lengthy; too narrow and an argument can easily fail to anticipate counter-arguments. Problems with scope are a feature of solving problems in scenarios, descriptive cases and, in particular, workplace situations.

Toulmin's structure is an *ideal* and it is not universally applicable to all types of argument. The principles work well, however, for conventional argument when you need to make a case either in writing or verbally. You use it in critical dialogue to discover the strength of an argument – your own and those of others. Questions and responses establish logical links between statements and the justification for them. Be open to questions when presenting an argument and make a habit of engaging critically with willing peers.

See *Study buddies* and *Critical friends* in Chapter 2

Recognising plagiarism

A word you hear frequently as a student is *plagiarism*. What is plagiarism and is it something only students do? Read the scenario in Activity 5.8 and then answer the question.

ACTIVITY 5.8

There is a temporary warehousing problem at work. Elsa has an idea for a solution and discusses it with a colleague, Klaes. At a meeting, Klaes puts forward Elsa's idea as his own and says nothing when he's complemented by the operations manager – after all, Elsa is not present. Later that week, Elsa writes a short report on addressing volatility in consumer demand. Searching for figures, she finds a draft report that contains useful material, elegantly and concisely written by someone who has left the organisation. She copies and pastes large parts of it into her report, wondering whether to cite the author. She makes a calculated decision not to. Elsa's report is well received by senior managers, one of whom asks to use extracts in a presentation, crediting her as the author. She readily agrees.

What's wrong with what Klaes and Elsa have done?

One's own work is one's own, whether ideas in a conversation or material in a text, an illustration, photograph or video. Using other people's work and taking credit for it, as Klaes and Elsa did, is plagiarism – a form of fraud. You must credit your sources of information. If not, you will be found out. At work, sooner or later you will gain a reputation for taking credit for other people's ideas. When studying, failures to cite original sources in your assignments will be identified and you may be penalised.

See *Moral and ethical reasoning* in Chapter 6

The internet has made plagiarism easy for students. It's not unusual to find assignments constructed from text copied from Wikipedia. Universities commonly use text-matching and text-similarity detection systems that compare thousands of student assignments – past and current – with one another and with internet sources in many languages. Turnitin, a well-known company that provides detection services, carried out a survey among educators and identified ten common types of plagiarism (Turnitin, 2012). They are set out below in order of 'plagiarism intent' with discussion added.

Ten types of plagiarism

1. **CLONE**
   Using another person's work word-for-word. Here, students use another student's assignment or text from the internet. They are easily identified by markers because invariably they don't address exactly the same question and they cite sources not mentioned in lectures, course materials or on reading lists.

2. **CTRL-C**
   Copying large amounts of text from a single source. Students use chunks of text and insert a few linking words or phrases.

3. **FIND–REPLACE**
   Copying from a single source but changing words and phrases. The changes may be an attempt to disguise the plagiarism, to personalise the text or to try to address the assignment question.

4. **REMIX**
   Copying sentences and paragraphs from multiple sources and making the copied material fit together by paraphrasing and changing and/or inserting words and phrases.

5. **RECYCLE**
   Using your own previous work without citing it. This is self-plagiarism. Marks from your assignments normally count towards your degree and it is wrong to be credited twice for the same work. Tutors *may* mark a reused assignment but give marks only for content that applies to the current assignment question. Thus, the reused work earns few marks: previous assignments rarely address a new assignment question. In professional life there is normally no problem with reusing extracts from previous work or presenting an updated version of it, provided you cite the source.

6. **HYBRID**
   Copying from various sources including in-text citations but failing to cite the origins of the copied material. In this type of plagiarism, an assignment credits primary sources of information but not the secondary sources whose authors have done the hard work of reading and reviewing the primary sources.

7. **MASHUP**
   Copying material from several different sources. Provided the use of such material is not excessive, the practice is not wrong *per se*. What's wrong is the failure to cite the sources and to place the copied text in quotation marks.

8. **404 ERROR**
   Copying from one or more sources and providing non-existent or inaccurate citations. The rule is to give enough information about a source so that

readers can find it for themselves. Cited sources that don't match real sources raise suspicion.

9. **AGGREGATOR**

    Citing sources fully and accurately but copying from them to such an extent that very few words are the student's own, however much thought went into the selection of copied material. *In your own words* is the key to assignment writing: it demonstrates *your* thinking and reasoning.

10. **RE-TWEET**

    Using proper citation but following a source's wording and/or structure. This method is often used by students who find it hard to think through and transform what they read into their own knowledge. It is true that experienced writers often express ideas elegantly, but higher education is about making efforts to extract meaning and learning to think effectively.

Plagiarism isn't confined to these ten types. Another form of plagiarism arises from sharing too closely when you work with other students. The rule here is: collaborate, then write your assignment individually, citing and referencing ideas that are not your own (there is a method of crediting other students' ideas and group discussions). Where very close collaboration is required, educators may award a mark to the group rather than to individuals.

It's unlikely that students set out to be blatant plagiarists. In this author's experience, small, unnoticed, acts of plagiarism grow into larger ones. It's not unusual for such students, when finally caught out, to protest: *No one has ever said anything before*. This is no defence. Find out what penalties your university imposes on offenders.

> **ACTIVITY 5.9** Read through the list of plagiarism types again and reflect on your own writing habits. If you tend to adopt one or more of the approaches on the list, consider why you do it. While a few students want a university degree without making the necessary effort, others have problems with understanding what they read and putting it into their own words. Some are afraid of misinterpreting or oversimplifying. Yet others leave insufficient time to prepare an assignment. Plagiarism may be accidental when you are new to study, too, but you can become sensitive to it and develop an approach that avoids it. Learning to write without plagiarising is an important skill.

Avoiding plagiarism

It would be odd if we didn't repeat something that has been said or written before. Some match between words and phrases you use in assignments and your sources of information is inevitable because there are standard ways of referring to concepts and theoretical positions, describing organisations and so on. When you use material from lectures, tutorials, academic papers and so on, however, you need to express the meaning in your own words and cite the source.

Sometimes you want to repeat something that has been expressed in a particularly apt or concise way. Provided the copied material does not amount to more than a sentence or two, it is acceptable to *place it in quotation marks and cite the source.*

> 'Use quotation marks and cite the source along with the page number from which the quotation was taken, especially if the source is a book. It's also a good idea to set the quoted text apart from your own works like this.'
>
> Bloggs, 2016, p. 16

Always cite the source of definitions and use quotation marks if you repeat the definition word-for-word.

Do the above, and only the above, and you will avoid plagiarism. Don't copy and paste material. Consider what the material means. There is always a risk of getting the meaning or significance wrong but learning often proceeds by making mistakes. If using your own words is difficult then try explaining it, or imagine explaining it, to someone else. It's easier to identify misunderstandings and then refer back to the source. You must still cite the source, of course, giving a full reference at the end of your assignment. By practising the skill of interpretation, you gain knowledge that makes it easier to find flaws in your source's ideas or argument. This is more rewarding than copying.

How to cite and reference

Identifying your sources of information by citing and referencing demonstrates professionalism. You show you are selecting and making informed use of accepted or authoritative sources of new ideas and, by expressing these ideas in your own words, you show you understand them.

When you *cite* a source, you mention briefly in the text the author and date of the work. When you provide a *reference* for the work you set out full details of the source at the end of the document. There is a variety of citation and referencing styles depending on the subject matter, the style of writing and the audience. The preferred style of universities is Harvard. It sets out what information to give and the order in which to give it; this style requires a reference list (see Box 5.1 for the formal difference between a reference list and a bibliography). A problem arises, however, in that there is no definitive guide to Harvard style and so many variations are used. These differ in minor ways, such as punctuation. Your university library will almost certainly provide its own guide, which you should follow.

Box 5.1 Reference lists and bibliographies

A *reference list* provides full details of the sources you cited in your work whereas a bibliography gives full details of all the sources that informed your work – including those you did not cite because you did not quote or paraphrase from them. The terms are sometimes used interchangeably, however: some citing and referencing styles use the term 'bibliography' to mean a list of cited sources only. Other informal and formal terms you may encounter include:

- *Selected bibliography* – a list that covers a selection of uncited sources
- *Annotated bibliography* – a list that also contains notes on the usefulness and quality of the sources
- *Further reading* – a list of recommended additional sources of information for readers.

You are not normally asked to use these forms of referencing but your reading material will sometimes use them.

Harvard style covers all types of sources and media including blogs, wikis, Twitter, podcasts, newspapers online, images, audiovisual material, conference papers, patents as well as specialised business material ranging from bond prospectuses to commercial databases.

In-text citations, Harvard style

The general rules for in-text citations are set out below. Follow your university guidelines on the use of punctuation.

1. **Name + date for most sources.** Place the author's surname and the year of publication in your text as near to the cited material as possible: (Smith, 2012). Alternatively, make it part of the sentence: 'Smith (2012) has stated …' Do the same when citing the author of a chapter in a multi-authored book. In the case of websites provide the name of the author or the website owner and the date the website was created or last revised. Use the same name + date method for citing informal sources, for example, a forum message.
2. **Name + date + page number for books.** The preferred style for books is the inclusion of page numbers when citing and/or quoting from them:

   Not all problems are resolved this way, according to Smith (2014, p. 205).
   or
   As Smith (2014, p. 7) points out: 'The model itself may be flawed …'

3. **Use et al. when there are more than three authors.** If there are three authors give all three names: (Smith, Brown and Jones, 2009). If there are more than three give the first author's surname followed by et al. (meaning *and others*): (Brown et al., 2016).

4. **Secondary sources: cite both sources.** When referring to original work mentioned in another, secondary, source, cite both sources in the text: (Williams, 2009, cited in Taylor, 2015). In your reference list at the end of your work, list only the work that you have read – Taylor.
5. **Distinguish one article from another.** When several sources have the same date and author, distinguish each by adding a, b, c… after the year, for example (Smith, 2015a) and (Smith, 2015b) or (Smith 2015a, 2015b).
6. **When citing more than one source, order them by date.** When you cite two or more sources together, list them in date order with the most recent date first and separate them with a semicolon: (Jones, 2016; Smith, 2015a, 2015b, 2008; Brown, 1976)
7. **Cite the source of diagrams.** Give the author's or originator's surname and the date of publication, for example (Jones, 2015, p. 7). If you change the diagram indicate this: (Based on Jones, 2015, p. 7); or (Adapted from Jones, 2015, p. 7). You use 'based on' if you customise a diagram, for example, using the same labels or elements but different text. You use 'adapted' if you change the labels, too. You might do this if for example the original diagram includes *Shareholders* and the organisation you refer to has none.

Reference lists, Harvard style

Include a full reference list at the end of your assignment. List the references in alphabetical order of authors' surnames. If there are several items by one author, place them in chronological order starting with the earliest. If two or more have the same authors and date, order them by the letter (a, b, c) that you used in the in-text citation.

The information you provide varies slightly according to whether you are listing a book, a multi-authored book which may have a volume editor, a journal article, a webpage or another source. Examples are given in Table 5.11.

Ebooks, ejournal articles, websites and other online sources

The referencing system for digital material is identical to that for printed material except that it is necessary to:

- provide the **URL** (web address) of the source or the **permalink** (a permanent link that doesn't change) provided by the publisher or the **Digital Object Identifier (DOI);** the permalink or DOI is preferable to the URL which can change
- insert **[Online]** after the title of the material or, in the case of ejournals, before the URL
- include **the date** you accessed the material (if a URL changes, the accessed date shows when the material was available)
- use the abbreviation **n.d. (no date)** where no date is given (n.d. can be used in citations, too).

Table 5.11 Referencing printed sources

Source	Full reference
Books Author's surname, initials, year of publication, title, edition (if not the first), place of publication, publisher.	Gardener, M.R. and Green, V. (2016) *Marketing and Ecological Sustainability*, 2nd edn, London, Mill.
Edited books Editor(s) surnames and initials, ed. or eds, year of publication, title, edition (if not the first), place of publication, publisher.	Good, V. and Noble, S.O. (eds) (2014) *Socially Responsible Businesses: A Manual of Good Practice*, New York, Perfection Press.
Contribution in a book Contributing author's surname, initials, year of publication, title of contribution, in, surname of editor(s) of publication, initials, followed by the name/s of the editor/s (ed. or eds), title of book, place of publication, publisher, page numbers.	Risk, A. (2015) 'Gambling with investments,' in Cautious, I. (ed), *Financial Growth*, Oxford, Bigger Books, pp. 21–31.
Article in a journal Author's surname, initials, year of publication, title of article, title of journal, volume number, part number, page numbers.	Smart, I.B. (2016) 'Learning organisations: do they exist?', *Practical Management*, vol. 9, no. 3, pp. 17–23.
Newspaper article (1) Author's surname, initials (or newspaper title), year of publication, article title, newspaper title, day, month and page number(s).	Fast, B. (2014) 'Green light for high speed trains', *The Daily Bulletin*, 14 February, p. 22.
Newspaper article (2) If the author's name is not given, use the newspaper title as the 'author'.	The Daily Bulletin (2013) 'Green light for high speed trains', 19 May, p. 22.
Publication/report from an organisation Name of author (or issuing body), year of publication, title of publication, place of publication, issuing body, report number (if there is one).	Summing, U.P. (2013) *Counting the cost of counting*, Brussels, The Central Statistics Centre, Report 104.

An example is:

Carter, S., Mwaura, S., Ram, M., Trehan, K. and Jones, T. (2015) 'Barriers to ethnic minority and women's enterprise: existing evidence, policy tensions and unsettled questions', *International Small Business Journal*, vol. 33, no. 1, pp. 49–69 [Online]. DOI: 10.1177/0266242614556823 (Accessed 21 March 2016).

Journal articles accessed online may not give page numbers. Table 5.12 gives examples of online-only sources. It may be difficult to use all the conventions because providers have not yet adopted universal standards. Provide whatever information you can.

Check that authors of emails and forum messages are happy for you to use material that was not intended to be in the public domain.

Harvard style made easy

There are many online guides to Harvard style and there are online reference style 'generators' that format references for you. The easiest way to cite and reference in

Table 5.12 Referencing online-only sources

Source	Full reference
Website	The Open University (2015) *Business and management* [Online]. Available at www. open.ac.uk/courses/find/business-and-management (Accessed 21 March 2016).
Online article	The Carbon Trust (2015) Ice pigging technology offers dairy industry significant savings, *The Carbon Trust* [Online]. Available at www.carbontrust.com/about-us/ press/2015/04/ice-pigging-technology-offers-dairy-industry-significant-savings (Accessed 21 March 2016).
Blog	Fletcher, N. and Wearden, G. (2016) Recession jitters knock global stock markets to fresh lows, *The Guardian Market Forces*, 11 February [Blog]. Available at www. theguardian.com/business/marketforceslive/2016/feb/11/recession-global-stock-markets-lows-federal-reserve-economy (Accessed 21 March 2016).
Wiki	Wikipedia (2016) *Strategic Thinking* [Online]. 30 January 2016 [Online]. Available at https://en.wikipedia.org/wiki/Strategic_thinking (Accessed 21 March 2016).
YouTube	*Unconscious Bias@Work* (2014) YouTube video, added by Google Ventures [Online]. Available at www.youtube.com/watch?v=nLjFTHTgEVU (Accessed 30 July 2016).
Email	Evans, K. (2016) Email to Evan Hughes, 3 January.
Forum message	Williams, G. (2016) 'Profitable campaigning', forum message to *UK Business Lab The Foyer*, 20 February.

Harvard style, however, is to use free or paid-for reference management software such as *Mendeley* or *Endnote* for capturing, organising and storing references. These software management systems format citations and references, insert citations into your work and then automatically create a formatted reference list. Guides, online generators and reference management software may use slightly different versions of Harvard style. Ask your university which software it provides or recommends.

> **ACTIVITY 5.10** When you next prepare an assignment, highlight all the in-text citations you have made, then highlight the text where in-text citations are missing. In each case, insert the correct in-text citation. Then compare your reference list with the forms of reference shown above; add missing ones (look up styles for sources such as patents or standards that are not listed). What kinds of errors did you make? You can do this activity using a recent assignment. If you can't recall the details of a source, insert the correct *form* of in-text citation and reference.

You may have identified three main types of error: forgetting to insert citations; overlooking citations when you created your reference list and having incomplete information to reference a source fully. Errors of omission often occur as you write because inserting citations can interrupt your flow. You can do as Wikipedia editors do and insert *Citation needed* or, best of all, train yourself to stop and insert names and dates. Citations can become lost as you redraft your assignment, so take care to retain them. Reference lists can be incomplete because in-text citations have been overlooked or because full information has not been retained. One way to avoid overlooking citations is to highlight them as you write. Using reference management software can solve many such problems including incomplete information.

Is your work ready to submit?

When do you consider your assignment is ready to submit? Many students carry out a spelling check and consider the job done. To be sure of the best marks possible, check that your work meets the objectives set out below.

You have answered the assignment question. If your outline addressed it but your finished text does not, use the outline to change or remove material.

You wrote what you planned to. If your assignment does not match your outline try to identify why. A common cause is including too much detail on one aspect of the question. Put this right by removing detail.

You have consistently used the required structure (for example, essay, report, research report). Check your assignment against the required structure. Make adjustments if necessary. Adding headings and side headings helps, provided your content is in the 'right' places. If not, move some of the content. It's very easy when writing reports, for example, to place conclusions and recommendations in your analysis.

Your arguments are logical and supported by evidence. Your statements and arguments should flow logically, supported by research evidence *used critically*. Add evidence or justification where necessary.

Your work demonstrates critical thinking. Avoid common-sense arguments and descriptive use of evidence. Gain marks for including alternative interpretations of research findings, for example, or for pointing out possible reasons for conflicting findings.

See Appendix 2
Effective writing

Your text is clear, grammatical and spelt correctly. Check clarity and sentence construction. Ask a trusted friend or colleague to read your assignment or, at least, read it *aloud* to yourself (errors will become evident).

Your diagrams, charts and graphs are labelled. Labels instantly tell the reader what they are looking at.

You have cited sources and given full references. Carry out Activity 5.10 in this chapter.

You have kept to the word count. If you checked your word count as you wrote, you won't be far off the required length. To shorten a text, find more concise ways of expressing what you have written. If your text is far too long, create a shorter version that covers the *essential* content. Editing may unbalance it.

Please your marker

Your work is uniquely yours and you will be familiar with every page. However, consider the marker who may have many similar assignments to read on-screen or in print form. Make the marker's life easier and learn professional habits as you study. Do the following:

1. Put your name on the cover page together with the name(s) of the recipient(s).
2. Under the title of your assignment or the assignment question add the date and course title.
3. Use page numbers. This is helpful even if your assignment is read on-screen. Page numbers help readers to navigate through your assignment.
4. Include a file reference – normally the document name and pathway to it – so that the assignment can be easily retrieved from an archive. In this case it will probably be your own archive but in the workplace it is likely to be an organisational one containing many documents. Put the file reference in a header or footer. Acquire good habits now.
5. Include any reference numbers, for example, your student number, on the first or cover page and as a header or footer. Your work will be easier to identify. In professional life, using several subtle forms of identification is better than writing your name in 36-point type on the cover page.

It is customary to sign reports at the end of the text (but before the appendices and references), digitally or by hand. This is not normally required for assignments but it may be required by some universities and in workplaces.

> **ACTIVITY 5.11** Audit a piece of work you are about to submit or have already submitted using the checklist and guidance above. Consider what would help the marker or reader. In professional life you need to audit and edit any work that is circulated to others, so become accustomed to doing this every time you write.

Preparing for and sitting exams

Examinations are less common than they once were. Continuous assessment is often preferred by educators because it allows a wider range of student knowledge and skills to be tested. Examinations can still be an important part of assessment, however, and there are benefits. Revising a whole course can consolidate and increase your knowledge by helping you make links you didn't see before. Exams can be an opportunity to demonstrate your understanding and higher-order thinking skills if you plan, revise and practise.

Exams range from those involving multiple-choice questions where you select an answer from a range of options, to those where you are given material, such as a case study, to study beforehand and the questions are provided in the exam room. The traditional and perhaps most common paper is one that comprises a number of essay-type questions from which you can choose a fixed number to answer. Sometimes question papers are divided into sections to ensure that you cover a range of topics. Some may contain a mix of question types, for example, multiple-choice and an essay, or multiple-choice and 'short-answer' questions. Case-based and problem-based examinations, which require you to apply your knowledge, are often regarded as more appropriate for business and management students, however.

Student marks for exams are commonly lower than for coursework. Understanding this helps to put your performance into perspective. It is usually possible to get full marks *only* in exams that consist wholly of multiple-choice questions although, in other types of exam, markers are sometimes encouraged to use the full range of marks (0–100%).

Instructions and rules

Many students lose marks unnecessarily by not familiarising themselves with the type of exam to be taken, by taking insufficient care with reading the instructions on the exam paper and by failing to follow exam rules. Find out what the rules are in your university. On any examined course, ask about the type of exam and look at past papers. If you are an international student, your knowledge is likely to be based on exams in your home country; these may make different demands on students.

> **ACTIVITY 5.12** *Part 1* – Read the statements in Table 5.13 and indicate whether each is *Right*, *Wrong*, or *It depends* (meaning you would have to find out as it depends on the type of exam or your university's rules).
>
> Tick Column A for *Right*; Column B for *Wrong*; and Column C for *It depends*. You can carry out the activity in a group, discuss the statements and arrive at a consensus view.

Answers are as follows. Statements 2, 14 and 18 – *Right*. Individual feedback may not be provided but it's usual to receive feedback on how *in general* students could have improved their performance. Exam preparation needs to be built into your coursework plan.

Statements 4, 5, 8, 10, 11, 12, 13, 15, 16, 17, 19 and 20 – *Wrong*. Statement 12 is wrong because a re-sit paper will contain different questions from the original paper. Statement 16 is wrong because you *do* have to think about the question to give a concise, focused answer. Statement 17 is wrong because revision is not solely about memorising but using your knowledge. Statement 19 is wrong because revision can improve your knowledge. Statement 20 is wrong because this is not the reason for using past papers in revision.

Statements 1, 3, 6, 7 and 9 – *It depends*. It depends on the type of exam (Statements 1, 2 and 6), on your university's rules (Statement 7) and on whether you arrive on time for the exam (or leave early) or have any condition that might adversely affect your performance (Statement 9).

Table 5.13 Exam quiz

Statement	A	B	C
1. I can take textbooks into the exam room	☐	☐	☐
2. Exams are strictly timed	☐	☐	☐
3. I will see the exam paper in advance	☐	☐	☐
4. I should revise by rote learning my essays	☐	☐	☐
5. Exam questions don't require a critical stance	☐	☐	☐
6. It's possible to get full marks in an exam	☐	☐	☐
7. I can use a dictionary in the exam room	☐	☐	☐
8. Notes are never allowed in the exam room	☐	☐	☐
9. Everyone gets the same amount of time to sit an exam	☐	☐	☐
10. I need to memorise detailed references to any sources of information I use	☐	☐	☐
11. I can choose when I take the exam	☐	☐	☐
12. It's best to wait for the re-sit exam so I know what the questions are	☐	☐	☐
13. In any exam I have to answer all the questions on an exam paper	☐	☐	☐
14. I will get feedback on my exam performance	☐	☐	☐
15. The exam paper instructions state: Answer one question from each of three sections. I will get marks for all my answers if I choose two questions from one section.	☐	☐	☐
16. You don't really have to think during an exam	☐	☐	☐
17. I have a great memory; I don't need to prepare for exams	☐	☐	☐
18. Exam preparation begins at the start of a course	☐	☐	☐
19. There's nothing to be gained from revising	☐	☐	☐
20. There's no point in looking at past exam papers: the same questions won't come up again	☐	☐	☐

ACTIVITY 5.12 *Part 2* – Now categorise your incorrect answers using Table 5.14. Some statements appear in more than one category. Identify your weak points (these will be collective ones if you carried out Part 1 of the activity in a group). Use the following sections of this chapter to remedy weaknesses in understanding the demands of exams and your approach to revision.

When you read the remaining sections of this chapter pay particular attention to remedies for these weaknesses.

Time planning exam revision

Plan revision time as part of your overall schedule for coursework. Then *protect* the time you have set aside for revision: start by avoiding overruns on other activities. Aim to work slightly faster than you're comfortable with – just as you are expected to in professional life. What happens is that you gradually improve

Table 5.14 Identify weaknesses

Statement numbers	Category
1, 2, 3, 6, 7, 8, 9, 11, 13, 14, 15	Rules, information about type of exam and attention to instructions on the exam paper
4, 5, 10, 16, 17, 19	Demands of exams
4, 5, 12, 17, 18, 19, 20	Approach to revision

your workspeed. It's acceptable to slow down for particularly difficult or complex tasks, however, or while you are familiarising yourself with something new. Pace yourself according to what you are doing.

ACTIVITY 5.13 Read the statements in Table 5.15 and indicate whether you have carried out or plan to carry out the activity described. Tick Column A for *Yes*, Column B for *No* and Column C for *I intend to*.

Table 5.15 Planning and preparation quiz

ACTIVITY/KNOWLEDGE	A	B	C
I have been conscientious about note-making during courses	□	□	□
I have regularly reviewed my notes to consolidate my learning and make links between topics	□	□	□
I have copies of past exam papers to hand	□	□	□
I understand the format of the exam(s) I will sit	□	□	□
I know how long it will take me to read the exam paper(s)	□	□	□
I know how long I have to answer the required number of questions on the exam paper(s)	□	□	□
I understand the marking system on each type of exam paper so I can prioritise my revision	□	□	□
I know the day, time and venue of the exam(s)	□	□	□
I know my travel arrangements to the venue(s)	□	□	□
I know if I am entitled to additional exam time	□	□	□

Your responses will tell you how prepared you are or intend to be (but remember to carry out your good intentions).

The time you allow for revision will be shorter if you have been conscientious about note-making and have regularly reviewed your notes; consolidating your learning in this way shortens revision time. In this case, allow at least several hours' revision per topic and then several hours more per topic for practice. In total, allow about one week of revision per course.

This normally means starting your revision several weeks before an exam is due because of continuing coursework. If you have not been organised and disciplined or have not understood the course well, allow more time. If the exam includes material that you see before the exam, allow additional preparation time of at least a day. For problem-based exam papers allow at least half your revision time for practice.

Past exam papers familiarise you with the format of the exam, how long you need to read a paper and how much time you have to answer each of a required number of questions. The marking system is usually set out on the paper and helps you to prioritise what you revise. In some exams, more marks are awarded for some sections or questions than others.

Make sure you know the day, time and venue of the exam and how you will get there if travel is involved. Find out about extra time to sit an exam if you have any condition that might adversely affect your performance such as dyslexia. Make the necessary arrangements with your university in advance.

See Planning your studies in Chapter 2

Revising

Revising for exams begins with organising and consolidating your notes. For many types of exam, you first produce a short version of your notes that covers a topic. Then you turn it into a list or spray diagram of words and short phrases as a reminder of concepts, research evidence, critique, examples and applications. Aim for a single list or diagram for each topic. Make your lists or diagrams memorable: number key items, use illustrations or colour. Make sure you know what each word or phrase refers to in full. Refer to the 'short version' of your notes if you don't. Quickly rehearse daily, as you move through your revision.

See Spray diagrams in Figures 4.2 and 4.3 in Chapter 4

Allow the type of exam to influence the content of your notes and revision. The focus of multiple-choice question exams is usually definitions or examples. 'Short-answer' questions (sometimes combined with multiple-choice questions) often require explanations but you won't need as much detail as for an essay-type question. 'Open book' questions, case studies and problem-based questions test your understanding and sometimes your ability to apply your knowledge. Working with other students can help.

Practising past exam papers

Use past exam papers to practise answering questions in note form. The point of practice is to:

- identify your knowledge gaps
- ensure you can use your knowledge flexibly, that is, address different questions on a topic or apply it to a case.

See Recognising and filling knowledge gaps in this chapter

For some exams, particularly those that require application of knowledge, effective revision consists mainly of practising answers using past exam papers. Whatever the type of exam, however, write some answers out in full to build up your writing speed. When you feel sufficiently confident, try answering at least one answer from a past paper under exam conditions: time yourself and do not refer to your notes. Practising under the same conditions in which you will take the exam – and experiencing important psychological states, such as apprehension – helps you to recall what you have learned. While practising in this way can be uncomfortable, studies of recall over many years show that it is effective. Moreover, you see how much you are able to write in a defined period. It helps you to avoid a common problem that students experience under exam conditions: to start answering a question in too much detail initially and then run out of time. The opposite – answers that provide too little detail – can occur, too.

Revision tips

1. Revise during the part of the day when you learn best.
2. Test your knowledge; fill gaps.
3. Revise with fellow students but do some individual revision first: it's easy to become anxious if other students seem more prepared and knowledgeable.
4. Take breaks. The number of times you revise is more important than the overall time. Reviewing your knowledge and notes during a course reduces revision time.
5. Be disciplined. Know if you are a perpetual procrastinator and don't accept your own excuses. If an unanticipated event interrupts your revision, however, stay positive: an exam tests a *selection* of your knowledge, not all of it.
6. Get enough sleep. Last-minute cramming and being tired on the day affects performance.
7. Organise what you need for the exam including identification (and know what you are *not* allowed to take into the room). Make sure you know about any other rules: if you leave the room without permission you may not be allowed back, for example.

Sitting the exam

1. Arrive at the venue in good time. Use relaxation techniques to calm nerves. Avoid anxious students: anxiety is contagious!
2. In the exam room listen to any instructions about leaving the room, asking for more paper and so on. Note how and where you identify yourself on the answer sheets or booklet.
3. Read the exam paper carefully. A misread question won't be answered well.
4. If the exam requires you to select questions, first choose which ones to answer. Base your choice on the knowledge you can bring to bear on the specific questions, not everything you know about the topics.
5. Make brief notes on how you will answer each question *before* you write any answers in full. While answering one question it's easy to forget how you were going to address others.
6. Structure your answers: write an introduction; in the main body of your answer use evidence to support statements, give examples and so on as appropriate, and then write a conclusion. If the exam is case-based or problem-based, use the conventional techniques for these.

7. Cite your sources, but don't worry if you forget a name or date: include the evidence anyway. You don't have to provide full references unless instructed.
8. After the exam, avoid students who want to discuss in detail how they answered the questions. Such students can cause anxiety among others. Relax and move on to your next study task.

What if I can't sit the exam on the day?

You won't be allowed to sit *the same* exam on a different day from other students. If you miss the exam for any reason, there may be an opportunity to take the exam later but the exam paper will be a different one. A 're-sit' exam will be on a particular day: you can't choose when it is. In some cases, often exceptional ones, universities allow an oral exam as a re-sit. In these cases, the date may be one that is convenient to the examiner and the student. Find out your university's rules for missed exams and re-sits.

Stress-busting

Simply thinking about exams can cause anxiety even among conscientious students. There are times when laughter helps.

ACTIVITY 5.14 With a group of friends devise a list of comical ways to fail an exam. Then check the list to make sure that it contains, at least, the opposites of all the guidance given in the sections on exams in this chapter.

Humour is a great stress-buster. When revising it can help to draw cartoons, make jokes about the material or, at least, take a break to watch a film or do something that makes you laugh. Imagining how good life will be after exams helps, too. And remember, failing an exam *isn't* the end of the world. You may be able to re-sit the exam and, if not, depending on your university's rules you may still be able to gain a degree. If failure is a real prospect, seek help early and know that while a university degree is highly desirable, many interesting and satisfying occupations don't require one.

Chapter summary

❖ Writing is communicating. The seven principles of good writing ensure that you know what you are communicating to whom and why, and that you do so clearly using appropriate styles and conventions.
❖ Assessment is a fact of life whether you are studying or working. There is normally strategic alignment between overarching higher education goals and the criteria educators use to assess your performance and progress through assignments. This is similar to what you find in the workplace.

❖ Guidance and checklists set out what markers are looking for in your work.

❖ Key terms in assignment questions identify the approach to take but invariably critical thinking and evaluation are required.

❖ Assignment preparation starts with a consideration of what you already know and then filling your knowledge gaps. Recognising gaps is important: know the symptoms.

❖ Outlines help you to organise your initial ideas before you produce a first draft of a text.

❖ Essays and reports have different structures. There are conventions for each type to help you place content appropriately. Use checklists for potential content and word-count guides for different sections.

❖ Knowing how to build sound arguments is an important skill you always need and helps you to achieve good marks in assignments. Toulmin's method of argumentation is commonly used with students.

❖ Citing and referencing your sources of information is required by universities and is ethical practice in workplaces. Learn how to do it easily and to recognise your weaknesses.

❖ When is your assignment ready to submit? Not before you have carried out a series of final checks!

❖ Preparing for exams requires an understanding of the demands and rules as well as planning and practising. Allow sufficient time for revision and use past papers to identify knowledge gaps. Different types of exam require different approaches to preparation but consolidation of reading notes is normally essential.

❖ Humour is a great stress-buster!

References

Endnote (2016) [Online]. Available at http://endnote.com/product-details/basic (Accessed 19 April 2016).

Mendeley (n.d.) [Online]. Available at www.mendeley.com/ (Accessed 19 April 2016).

The Open University (2012) *B628/BZX628 Managing 1: organisations and people assessment booklet*, Milton Keynes, The Open University.

Toulmin, S.E. (1958) *The uses of argument*, Cambridge, Cambridge University Press.

Turnitin (2012) *The plagiarism spectrum. Instructor insights into the 10 types of plagiarism. White paper*. Turnitin [Online]. Available at http://turnitin.com/en_us/resources/white-papers (Accessed 9 February 2016).

CHAPTER SIX

Thinking skills

Bill Gates, the founder of Microsoft, is said to write in pencil to make it easy to change his mind in light of new knowledge, thinking and ideas. It's probably not true but the point of the anecdote is to show that effective thinkers and innovators are willing to be challenged by other people and themselves. Developing skill in thinking is about being open to these challenges. You are receptive to information that can overturn your thinking, reveal flaws, improvements and present new approaches. The uncertainty that results can be disconcerting but this is a small price to pay to promote your learning. You quickly learn to focus on the pleasure of your gains rather than on the discomfort of finding your thinking wanting in some way.

This chapter covers key thinking skills you require for study and the workplace. It contains procedures and checklists for different types of thinking: logical reasoning, argumentation, critical thinking, investigative thinking, rational decision-making, applying theory and critical reflection. (Moral and ethical reasoning, systems thinking and creative thinking are covered in Chapter 7.) When you are a student the focus of these different types of thinking and the use of protocols and checklists is normally your learning activities and assignments. To make them relevant to professional (and personal, daily) life, you can shift the focus to these realms. So, familiarise yourself with the protocols and rehearse them whenever an opportunity arises. Application is important.

If you are working while studying, opportunities may include work projects or ethical dilemmas. If you are a full-time student, apply the various types of thinking to experiences and situations you encounter in your learning environment – and in your personal, domestic and social life. The protocols are often detailed and contain checklists of questions and issues. Read these carefully and then apply them to your work or chosen circumstance. Not every question or issue may seem relevant. But if you revisit them several times with different learning activities or circumstances to consider, you should find you apply more of the questions in the checklists. When you have mastered all the types of thinking and can switch from one to another seamlessly, now thinking critically, now creatively, for example, you have gained expertise that can lead you to the top of a career ladder. Organisations and society *need* effective thinkers.

Read the section *Knowledge and belief* that follows. Other sections can be read in isolation but you may need to refer specifically to the section on logical reasoning because it is fundamental to thinking skills.

Knowledge and belief

Good thinking skills are vital for effective learning and professional work. You first learn them when you study but you improve and hone them at work *as* you work. All organisations want 'good' thinkers – those who can identify and rectify a flaw in a case for change; who can 'teach themselves' through the self-correcting process of critical reflection; who can identify ethically unsound practices; work out how to improve a system and think creatively to meet the challenges of the twenty-first century. But thinking is not easy.

Knowledge was once thought to be the *result* of rational thinking: first we understood something and then we applied rational thought to decide whether or not to believe it. Now scientists advocate that the reverse is true. We appear to accept and believe without rational thought. Try answering the questions in this activity to test this.

ACTIVITY 6.1

1. Look at a familiar object. Is it the same object you saw last time you looked? How do you know?
2. Think of a moral belief you hold, such as *It's wrong to hurt others*. Where, when and how did you acquire this belief?
3. When you last met a friend you hadn't seen for several days, how did you greet each other? Why did you greet each other this way?
4. Is a shy person likely to be a gregarious leader of a social club? What makes you think not?
5. Do you believe gravity exists? Why do – or why don't – you believe so?

Your answers to the first four questions are likely to be: *I just know* or *Because it's normal.* Your answer to the last question is probably based on what you have been told, but you might not object to your view being called a belief.

As social, emotional and moral animals, we adopt the beliefs of others; we accept and believe, often without question, what we are told about the way the world is, how it works and how we should behave towards others. Many beliefs are formed as a result of unconscious processing of sensory input. For example, babies quickly acquire a factual belief in the temporal continuity of objects (*This object is the same one I saw yesterday*). It's a *belief*, however, because we have no way of knowing for certain. Over time, beliefs are elaborated, becoming more abstract. At least some beliefs can be stated (*It's right to share*). Others are revealed in behaviour such as using a knife and fork to eat a meal. Yet others unconsciously inform our conscious decisions: for example, we don't nominate shy Georgio as president of the music club.

Belief, whether in something factual, social, emotional or moral, concrete or abstract, has an interesting quality: we feel sure of something; we *know*. Our reasons for a belief may not be obvious to us, however. If asked why we believe something, we *justify* our belief by mustering evidence to support it: we don't change it. When we encounter new information, we try to make the new information fit the current belief. To 'un-believe' – to question and reject a belief – takes effortful, conscious thought. Knowing and believing, then, have an interesting relationship. It's one that makes everyday life less effortful but, without the use of conscious thought when required, it can be a barrier to learning, problem-solving and making decisions and constructive contributions in all aspects of life. Some beliefs, particularly 'deep' cultural and moral ones, are often resistant to change but there are times when it's useful to articulate and question them. It helps people to see different perspectives that also promote understanding and tolerance.

ACTIVITY 6.2 Consider whether you believe inequality among people is right or wrong. Why do you believe what you do? If you can, carry out the activity with two or three other people. First, without discussion, write down the grounds for your belief, then share and explore them in the group. Finally, reconsider your initial reasons.

The chances are that, at first, you found reasons to support your belief rather than to challenge it. Sharing reasons or evidence may then have led you to question the grounds for your belief. Finally, you might have changed your belief if you were presented with evidence that undermined or challenged it, leading you to 'un-believe' it or to believe it in a more qualified way. This might be the case if the group attempted to define inequality or specify a particular type of inequality, such as work and pay. Alternatively, you may have felt a sense of 'rightness' that put your belief beyond question, rejecting any reasons that threatened it. This is not uncommon if beliefs are moral ones. Try repeating the activity using a non-moral belief.

Being receptive and open to challenge is central to good thinking skills. You question the beliefs of others and, moreover, you challenge *your own* beliefs. You also question information you are presented with, so your belief in it is less automatic. Fundamental to thinking skills is logical reasoning, an essential everyday thinking skill necessary for other types of thinking.

Logical reasoning

Logic consists of rules that apply when we relate one statement to another. There are two kinds of formal logical reasoning, deductive and inductive.

Deductive reasoning

In deductive reasoning the conclusion of an argument *must* be valid provided the preceding statements from which it's drawn are true. An example of deductive reasoning is:

> Major proposition or premise (*p1*): All company directors are human. (All Xs are Ys.)
> Minor proposition or premise (*p2*): John is a company director. (Z is an X.)
> Conclusion (*q*): Therefore John is human. (Therefore, Z is Y.)

The first two statements are the propositions or premises of the argument on which a final, conclusive statement rests. Few would disagree with the conclusion. Now consider this argument:

> *p1*: All assembly-line operatives are human. (All Xs are Ys.)
> *p2*: This robot is an assembly-line operative. (Z is an X.)
> *q*:   Therefore this robot is human. (Therefore, Z is Y.)

The rules of logic have been correctly applied so the argument is valid, but it is unsound. So what has gone wrong? It is not true that all assembly-line operatives are exclusively robots. Thus, a deductive argument can be logically sound – the conclusion is correctly drawn – but untrue because one or more premises are untrue or faulty. In such arguments, therefore, it's important to identify the premises and access their accuracy. This isn't easy if a main premise is hidden. Consider the following argument:

> I don't know what the people on the selection panel were thinking about. They chose a biochemist as our new project manager! He'll understand the laboratory work but he doesn't have a management degree so he won't be able to deal with the researchers and technicians. I'm sure that's going to lead to all sorts of problems. Those researchers are hard to manage.

We can deconstruct this argument by identifying the hidden main premise.

   p1: Only people with management degrees understand how to manage people.
   p2: Our new project manager does not have a management degree.
   q: Therefore, our new project manager won't know how to manage people.

The flaw in the argument lies in the hidden premise *p1*. It may be true that people with management degrees understand how to manage people. But it's also true that people without management degrees can do so because they can be taught. Thus, the main premise on which the conclusion relies is untrue. Whether or not the new project manager understands how to manage people needs to be ascertained.

See *Recognising assumptions* in this chapter

Inductive reasoning

Unlike deductive reasoning, in which a conclusion *must* be true if the premises are true, inductive reasoning provides no such guarantee of truth. An inductive argument begins with specific premises but the conclusion is probabilistic: it doesn't necessarily follow from the premises. The conclusion can be unsound even if the premises are sound. An example is:

   p1: Our market research showed that 40 per cent of people asked preferred our brand.
   p2: Our sample population was representative of the UK population.
   q: Therefore, 40 per cent of the UK's adult population will prefer our brand.

The argument is valid but this conclusion doesn't *necessarily* follow from the premises: it may not be the case that 40 per cent of the UK's adult population *will or do* prefer that brand, it is simply a probability. The potential for making unsound inferences is therefore great: a conclusion will be wrong if the inference is incorrectly made or, as is often the case, a conclusion makes a generalisation that goes beyond the evidence. Consider the example again with one small change:

   p1: Our market research showed that 40 per cent of people asked preferred our brand.
   p2: Our sample population was representative of the UK population.
   q: Therefore, 40 per cent of the UK's adult population will *buy* our brand.

The premises may be faultless: perhaps the population sampling was excellent, covering all demographic groups and areas of the UK, and the sample was large. But the conclusion has now been wrongly inferred: that 40 per cent of the adult population will *buy* the brand. (People may prefer something but have insufficient funds or opportunities to buy it.) This is an example of a wrong inference that could bankrupt an organisation if acted upon.

Now consider the premises. As in deductive reasoning, they must be correct. Imagine that in the above example, 100 people were asked. The sample size is too small to be representative of the UK population. Any conclusion based on the premises would be flawed. The premises of inductive arguments must be scrutinised for accuracy and sufficiency, as well as the soundness of inferences, before they are accepted.

ACTIVITY 6.3 Here are three examples of inductive reasoning. Identify the strongest argument and explain your choice.

Argument 1

  p1:   I surveyed 100 staff members to test reactions to removing car parking facilities at our offices.

  p2:   The 100 staff were selected on the basis that they were representative of our workforce of 500.

  p3:   Their reactions were negative.

  q: We should not remove car parking facilities at our HQ.

Argument 2

  p1:   I use the car park at our offices only three times a week.

  p2:   I'm a typical employee.

  q: Staff won't mind if we reduce the car parking facilities.

Argument 3

  p1:   A study of staff use of the car park found that over a typical week 20 per cent of employees used the car park daily, 20 per cent not at all and the remaining 60 per cent three to four days a week.

  p2:   The car park has spaces for 80 per cent of the workforce.

  q: There is limited scope for reducing car parking space.

The first argument is based on staff reaction to the removal of car parking space rather than actual use. The second is based on a formal measurement (frequency) but on only one observation – and an assumption is made about the representativeness of the observer. The third argument is based on frequency of use, too, but on a survey that appeared to cover all staff and included information about the size of the car park. The least sound argument is No. 2, and the soundest is No. 3. The reasons lie in two important features of inductive arguments.

1. The relevance and sufficiency of the premises or evidence including quantity and quality.
2. The better the evidence, the more robust the conclusion.

The premises of Argument 3 best met the criteria of relevance and sufficiency so its conclusion is more robust, if rather incomplete – more detailed evidence could have helped to identify the precise limitations of space reduction. A better and more conclusive argument than No. 3 could be found: inductive arguments are not judged on whether or not they are sound, but *how* sound they are. This should invite you to question their premises and conclusions.

Deductive and inductive reasoning in research

Both deductive and inductive reasoning are used in research. Case studies, common in research into the workings of organisations, use inductive reasoning. Case studies can be:

descriptive – to show the relevance of a phenomenon
exploratory – to gain understanding of it
explanatory – to attempt to show why it occurs.

To do this systematically, researchers develop constructs about the phenomenon and ways of 'measuring' them through various types of qualitative data, and may produce testable propositions. The inductive method used is normally as follows:

- **observe** through collection of qualitative data
- **analyse** the data, often via sense-making and use of logic to look for patterns and their meaning
- **make inferences** from the analysis that are plausible or reasonable.

Traditional research methods – derived from the scientific disciplines – can then use deductive reasoning to test propositions, which can be developed from inductive inferences such as those made by Alfredo De Massis and colleagues (2015) from a study of ten small firms in Italy. Their case study findings can be restated as: *Innovation in family firms differs from that in non-family firms as a result of preservation of resources, functional authority structures, lack of incentive to experiment with risk and behavioural conservatism.* This is a proposition, or set of propositions, that can be tested experimentally with a large sample of small family-run and non-family-run businesses in several countries, perhaps using questionnaires. The method would be:

- **state proposition(s) as hypotheses – the premises**
- **gather relevant data** that can potentially confirm or disconfirm the hypotheses
- **analyse the data** and interpret results
- **draw (deduce) a conclusion** (confirmation, disconfirmation or qualified confirmation of the soundness of the premises).

In practice, case studies may take the place of traditional research methods because they can be used for comparison, to replicate findings, to build and extend theory and to narrow down or eliminate alternative explanations. They can cover single or multiple cases. They can adopt a deductive approach.

The choice of method – case study or the experimental method – depends on the nature of the phenomenon to be studied, the types of question to be asked and the degree of control researchers would like over variables, such as organisational climate or leadership style, for example, when studying strategic decision-making or employee absenteeism and turnover. Case studies control such variables with careful selection of the sample, while the experimental method can use very large randomised samples and control for such variables statistically. The fields of organisational behaviour (human behaviour in work environments) and occupational psychology (psychological theory applied to the workplace) commonly use the experimental method, adopting ways of controlling for variables statistically. Causal relationships can be established statistically.

See Applying theory to problems and scenarios in this chapter

Abductive reasoning

In daily life people often use abductive reasoning, which is not classed as formal logic and is sometimes called 'best-guess' reasoning. You start with an incomplete set of observations or statements and then 'weigh' them up to arrive at the most plausible conclusion.

When you visit a doctor, he or she is likely to use abductive reasoning. For example, you explain your symptoms (a painful toe) and say when you first noticed them. The doctor's reasoning will probably proceed like this:

Observation 1:   The toe is swollen, painful, bruised and stiff.
Observation 2:   The symptoms began when the patient tripped on a step.
Conclusion: The patient's toe is broken.

This is the doctor's 'best guess' – a medically informed one. The doctor could confirm the diagnosis with an X-ray. However, she knows that the usual treatment for a broken toe is to bind it to a neighbouring one, which she plans to do. When she tells you to return after one week, or sooner if the symptoms worsen, she is testing her conclusion. If you return a week later and the toe is less painful, her diagnosis was most likely correct. If you return earlier with worsening symptoms, the doctor knows that the first diagnosis was not quite right (or that complications have occurred) and that further observations are needed.

ACTIVITY 6.4 *Part 1* – Given the premises (observations) below, what would your 'best-guess' conclusion be? How would you test your conclusion and what measure of success might you use (that is, the evidence that would confirm your conclusion)? What evidence might refute your conclusion?

Observation 1:
'Pester power' (the persuasive power children have over adults) increases the sale of particular products such as sweets.

Observation 2:
Parents are complaining that our store stocks too many sweets.

Observation 3:
We display sweets at our supermarket checkouts.

Conclusion:

How I would test my conclusion:

Evidence that would confirm my conclusion:

Evidence that would refute my conclusion:

Your conclusion is likely to be that children are pestering their parents for sweets at the checkouts and that the number of complaints will fall if the sweets are removed from these areas. You can test this by removing sweets from the checkout displays. Your measure of success would probably be fewer complaints. No reduction would refute your conclusion: you might then try to find out if parents' complaints were related to the number of sweets on display in general.

> **ACTIVITY 6.4** *Part 2* – Now think of an example in your own life when you have made a 'best guess'. On what observations was it based and what further evidence would you need to modify or confirm your conclusion? The example can be the best guess you made about how long it would take to prepare your last assignment or a workplace decision you made on the basis of observations.

Abductive reasoning is only as sound as the premises and the plausibility of the best-guess conclusion inferred from them. The better informed you are, the better your 'best guesses' will be – and it's possible to test those guesses.

Abductive reasoning is used in research when something in the data gathered is unexpected or seems unintelligible and requires intellectual effort to arrive at a plausible explanation. It is also used with inductive reasoning in grounded theory research in which there is an attempt to discover theory from data.

Reasoning in action: an example

When we are aware of our reasoning we can form better hypotheses, test them more effectively, develop sound arguments and make better decisions. Read the sections in this chapter on deductive, inductive and abductive reasoning if you have not already done so, then consider the following example of reasoning.

See *Logical reasoning* in this chapter

The care home

A not-for-profit care home in the Alps for people with dementia has a funding problem. Government grants have been cut back and the home, which provides both residential and day care, must now rely more heavily on donations, fundraising and bequests. A board of trustees acts as a management committee. The trustees have appointed you as general manager. They are convinced that more effective fundraising efforts – and more events – are needed, based on the advice of the previous general manager. The deductive reasoning of the trustees is:

> *p1*: Financial sustainability is achieved by income exceeding costs.
> *p2*: This home is not financially sustainable.
> *q*: Therefore, this home must increase its income to exceed costs.

You want to investigate the financial situation carefully before you respond, however. You identify costs that indicate the problem is not, or not only, lack of income. Compared with sector averages, the home's staff retention is poor and absenteeism, particularly though stress-related illness, is high. In the current financial year the cost of this was €50,000, due mainly to the use of agency staff from the nearest regional city. You know that poor working conditions have a negative impact on retention and attendance. Your inductive reasoning is:

> *P1*: Low staff retention and high absenteeism cost €50,000 – more than expected judging from sector averages.
> *P2*: Poor retention and high absenteeism are symptoms of poor working conditions.
> *q*: Therefore, dealing with poor working conditions will reduce costs.

In testing your conclusion, you know you need to look for evidence to try both to confirm it and to refute it. The trustees are happy for you to investigate further when you explain that some of the home's costs seem high. You arrange meetings with staff, volunteers, residents and day visitors and their families, and with key stakeholders in the wider community such as providers of social and health services, leaders of religion and representatives of local government. You hope to get a range of views about working conditions and fundraising as well as general information.

This is what you learn and use to inform your abductive reasoning (*o* refers to 'observation').

> *o1*: Staff are often over-qualified for their jobs but initially are happy to obtain work in an area of higher-than-average unemployment.
> *o2*: They have almost no control over their work and no flexibility in work arrangements, which makes childcare and non-work life difficult.

o3: Staff are stressed and frustrated: they know how to improve work practices but there are no formal channels; suggestions are ignored or forgotten.

o4: They have no time to train volunteers although this would reduce their workloads.

o5: Volunteers say their potential is under-exploited; they are mostly left to 'mind' residents and day visitors because they are not trained to do the activities that residents and day visitors say they would enjoy. They also feel that the home would benefit from more volunteers but dementia is not well understood in the community.

o6: Families of residents and day visitors are supportive of the home but are concerned that many different staff care for their relatives.

o7: People with dementia would like to feel part of the wider community and to continue many of the activities they enjoyed before the onset of symptoms.

o8: Key stakeholders say the home is isolated from the community and doesn't communicate its mission. They would welcome opportunities for exchange.

o9: A representative of a health care group mentions a Europe-wide initiative to create 'dementia-friendly communities' to promote understanding of dementia and social inclusion. She talks about what it means to be a dementia-friendly community and how participating businesses can benefit from the custom of people with dementia, their families and carers.

q: Your best guess is that the problems are three-fold:

1. Job design and working conditions. These affect costs and quality of care and have an impact on the training of volunteers, too.
2. Lack of communication with the wider community. This affects fundraising and, therefore, income, and the number of volunteers the home is able to attract, which has an impact on quality of care.
3. Absence of a strategic network of relationships in the community and in particular with key stakeholders. This has multiple impacts not only on income generation but on the understanding of dementia in the wider community and, therefore, opportunities for participation by residents, day visitors and their families, affecting quality of care.

During follow-up discussions you test the reaction to your best guesses – you try both to confirm and refute them. Then you prepare a proposal to trustees. It is a participative change programme involving:

- the formation of semi-autonomous teams caring for the same groups of residents and day visitors
- more-flexible working
- opportunities to identify, communicate and implement improvements to systems, procedures and practice
- training for volunteers
- the formation of an advisory group of key community stakeholders.

You emphasise diplomatically to the trustees that the lack of connection between the community and the home results in poor communication about the work of the home and less-than-optimal fundraising. (This reminds you, too, that your initial reasoning on working conditions alone was rather limited.) You distribute leaflets on the creation of dementia-friendly communities to hint at the work in which the home might be involved in future.

These are the four key points to remember when thinking through an issue and arriving at conclusions.

1. Check the premises. What evidence is there to support them? Are assumptions being made?
2. Know when you are making inferences. Are the inferences sound? Are you inferring too much?
3. Are you making appropriate observations?
4. Are your 'best guesses' informed ones?

These considerations are more important when constructing sound arguments than identifying the type of reasoning you are using (though this can sometimes help). You can also assess other people's arguments, and, most importantly, your own.

Recognising assumptions

Whenever you take something for granted you are making an assumption. Assumptions are useful. When I say *We are all older than our children* I am making a *warranted* assumption because it is incontrovertible. When I say *It's a national holiday, so I'll postpone my shopping trip* I am making a *sensible* assumption (one that is not incontrovertible) that the shops will be crowded (or closed), based on my prior knowledge. If the shops are not crowded (or closed) then my assumption will be wrong: I recognise my assumption and remember its inaccuracy.

Difficulties arise when assumptions are hidden, wrong and remain unrecognised. As a result, important arguments and decisions will be flawed. If I complain *I've done everything that's expected of me, and more, but I still haven't been promoted or had a pay rise* I have made an assumption that is career-limiting (one that female employees typically make). I have assumed that doing what's expected of me (and more) will be rewarded automatically. My employers have probably made the different assumption that I'm happy with my current rewards. My assumption means that I expect my employers to notice my contributions and to reward me in the way I think I deserve. If I identify and explore my assumption it might lead me to be explicit about my contribution and ask for promotion or a pay rise.

ACTIVITY 6.5 In this two-part scenario, identify the assumptions the managers make. Some Part 1 assumptions are easier to identify than those in Part 2.

Part 1 – A construction company uses large nail guns for constructing timber framework. The nail guns cut costs by making construction much faster than using traditional hammers. The company recruited a number of apprentice carpenters last year when it won a contract for a housing development of award-winning designs that maximise the use of solar energy. Nail gun-related injuries have doubled since work started. Senior managers have ordered an investigation but it will take several weeks. Keen to avoid accidents in the meantime, they suggested the following immediate measures:

1. Ensure that all apprentices are properly trained.
2. Ensure there is adequate personal safety equipment, such as hard hats and high-impact eye protection.
3. Ensure that all teams have one person available who can administer First Aid.

Identify the assumptions that the managers have made here. You may need to read Part 2 to identify them all.

Part 2 – Three weeks later, the investigation is complete. It is reported that:

1. The largest nail guns are responsible for most accidents.
2. Apprentices are not allowed to use the largest guns in their first year of employment.
3. Most accidents occur when the nail guns are being used in awkward angles when ladders are used instead of scaffolding (as required by the company's nail gun working practices) because of space restrictions.
4. There are more injuries than officially reported.
5. First aid is invariably administered but professional medical advice is often not sought until later when even relatively minor wounds can become infected, usually because of embedded clothing and debris.

Senior managers decide that all accidents should be reported, however minor, and that anyone who is injured should be taken to hospital or the nearest 'walk-in' clinic for assessment. They can't think of an immediate solution to the sharp angles in the framework and there are a lot more houses to be built over the next four years.

What assumptions have the managers made here?

In Part 1, it's quite easy to identify the first assumption: that *apprentices* are being injured and thus require better training. The second assumption is a little harder: that the provision of personal safety equipment is sufficient to prevent injury. Such equipment may be provided but not used or not used properly. The third assumption is the most difficult: you probably needed to know from Part 2 that even minor injuries are often complicated by later infection, so First Aid alone may not be sufficient.

In Part 2, the assumptions made are that a) awkward angles can't be avoided b) the use of nail guns is essential and c) that there is only one type of heavy nail gun. The managers quickly recognised their assumptions in discussions with nail gun suppliers and the architects. First, they discovered that there are nail guns with safer trigger mechanisms. Then they discovered that the architects could modify the design of houses to reduce the number and sharpness of the angles, at least to the extent that scaffolding can be used. The architects also agreed to investigate factory prefabrication or construction at ground level and the possibility of using alternative materials to avoid the use of nail guns.

The fictional scenario illustrates typical assumptions made when quick decisions must be taken. The point is that the senior managers' initial assumptions meant that accidents were not reduced and, had an investigation not followed, they would have prevented the problem from being solved. The scenario shows how hidden assumptions can be a powerful hindrance to clear thinking.

Assumptions can be hard to identify because they can arise both *from* our experience or knowledge and *lack* of it. They can also arise from flaws in interpreting data. A famous example happened during World War II when USA fighter bombers returned with bullet holes primarily in their fuselages rather than their engines. It was decided that the fuselages need reinforcement. It took a mathematician, Abraham Wald (1902–1950), to spot the erroneous assumption: he realised that the statistics covered only *returning* aircraft. Aircraft whose engines had been hit didn't return; it was the engines that needed armouring.

Factual assumptions were used in Activity 6.5 but many assumptions are 'deeper', shaped by culture and personal circumstances. For example, when people say that child labour should be outlawed globally, they may have assumed there are free or affordable schools for children to attend and that family economies can support non-working children. Where child labour is common, there will be different assumptions.

Workplaces are a rich source of assumptions. They have their own *organisational cultures* with shared assumptions about the way things are or should be done, how to behave, communicate and carry out work roles. The reasons may have long been forgotten, but the structures, systems and behaviours can remain, maintaining the culture. You've probably encountered – or will do – the response *This is the way we do things here* when you question a work practice. Quality assurance processes, for example, often reveal long-standing assumptions. When we *recognise* our assumptions we can assess whether they are well founded. Our reasoning will improve as a result.

Biases and flaws in reasoning

You can improve your reasoning if you know where to look for errors, flaws and bias – or fallacies as they are known. Common ones are set out below.

Something out of nothing. We are predisposed to find patterns even where none exist. We 'see' relationships between unconnected events. We believe one event caused another because they happened together when, in fact, both were caused by another event not taken into account. For example, sales of paddling pools and skin protection cream, displayed alongside, increase together. The store believes that sales of the paddling pools 'cause' the additional sun cream sales. However, the nearby pharmacy also experiences more sun cream sales. The causal factor is that, with summer holidays about to start, local schools are alerting parents to the dangers of over-exposure to UV light. Always consider *how* events are linked.

Too much from too little. It's easy to misinterpret data that are incomplete and unrepresentative. We're also prone to trying to confirm hypotheses, rather than trying to refute them. This is known as confirmation bias. A classic test was developed by Peter Wason in 1968 and remains in popular use. An adapted version is used in Activity 6.6.

ACTIVITY 6.6 Ask a willing friend to carry out this test of confirmation bias with you. You are testing your friend's confirmation bias because, in order to set it up, you have to know how it works. The rule you're testing is: *If a person is drinking alcohol then that person must be over 18 years old* – or if *P* (drinking alcohol) *then Q* (over 18 years old).

First make four cards. On two of the cards write JUICE and on the other two, BEER. Then, on the reverse side of the two BEER cards write, respectively, 24 and 32, representing the ages of the beer drinkers. On the reverse side of the two JUICE cards write, respectively, 15 and 17 representing the ages of the juice drinkers. Then set out the cards as shown in Table 6.1.

Table 6.1 How to create and set out the cards

What to do	Card 1	Card 2	Card 3	Card 4
Write on the front	JUICE	BEER	15	24
Write on the reverse	17	24	JUICE	BEER
Display as	JUICE	BEER	15	24
Card as displayed represents	*not-P*	*P*	*not-Q*	*Q*

Your friend is allowed to turn over only two cards to discover the truth of the rule. One card must be a 'drink' card and one an 'age' card. Which cards does your friend turn over? Ask your friend to explain his or her choice. Is he or she 'guilty' of confirmation bias? How can you explain this bias?

If your friend turned over only the cards showing BEER and 24, he or she is demonstrating confirmation bias (unless the choice of the second card was random). The cards that could have refuted the rule – the JUICE or 15 cards in the display – have been ignored. To both confirm *and* refute the rule, your friend should turn over one card to try to confirm the rule – BEER (*if P*) or 24 (*then Q*) – and one card to try to refute it – JUICE (*if not-P*) or 15 (*then not-Q*).

If you want to demonstrate how confirmation bias can lead to inappropriate confirmation of the rule, change the age on Card 1 to 19 and the drink on Card 3 to BEER. Turn over the same cards as your friend did to 'confirm' the rule and then turn over one of the other cards to show that it refutes it. Imagine making a workplace decision with implications for staff based on this bias.

Seeing what we want to see. Our beliefs, hopes and prejudices can make us selective about the information we attend to. This is often unintentional but we should be alert to our selectivity. When people deliberately ignore information that would weaken or overturn an argument they are guilty of *cherry picking* the evidence. Examples include arguments against climate change and evolution and, more mundanely and inevitably, CVs or personal résumés.

Believing what we are told. Much of what we know comes from other people, often those in authority. If we appeal to authority *as a reason to believe something*, however, then our argument is fallacious. Similarly, appeals to peers, to past practice and to common belief or practice are invalid. They don't count as evidence or justification, even though in some parts of the world they are common cultural practice.

Ad hoc rescue. People can be unwilling to question a belief they have even where there is contradictory evidence. Instead they try to 'rescue' it. For example:

> PERSON 1: The instructions I gave were very clear.
> PERSON 2: I followed the instructions but I found that several steps were missing.
> PERSON 1: You couldn't have followed the instructions properly, then.

Appeal to the emotions. Here, the fallacy is committed not by the person making the argument but by the person it is put to. You accept an argument because it triggers emotions that override your reason. In marketing, such appeals are common. They can arouse feelings of self-worth or fear of doing the wrong thing, for example. They can also appeal to values such as caring for the environment and buying ethically produced goods.

False dilemma. False dilemmas present too few choices. They are often used by marketers. For example, you are given a choice between deluxe Brand X and basic Brand Y. The sales person intentionally withholds information about other brands that offer the same advantages as Brand X. Always consider whether there are choices you have *not* been offered (or arguments you are not aware of).

Slippery slope. In this fallacy, a chain of cause-and effect-links is made but exaggeration occurs in one or more links. For example:

> A. If we can't recruit a good HR director, staff performance won't improve.
> B. If staff performance doesn't improve, sales will be very poor.
> C. If sales are very poor, the company will fold.

A is said to lead to B, and B to C (and so on). As C is not a desired consequence, then A is avoided at all costs. In the example, unnecessary cost may be incurred to recruit a 'good' HR director. Avoid the fallacy by identifying exaggeration in a causal chain.

See *Building and supporting an argument* in Chapter 5

Critical thinking

Critical thinking enables you to improve your knowledge and become a lifelong, independent learner. You learn to accept that knowledge – your own and that of others – is provisional and can be bettered by careful and systematic questioning. In doing so you risk the discomfort of challenges, changes or revisions to your beliefs, knowledge, values and behaviours. The reward is that you become your own teacher. This independent learning is precisely what higher education is designed to promote and what organisations want, particularly in knowledge economies in which products and service innovation rely on knowledge gained and used in the workplace.

Because the expression *being critical* or *criticising* is often associated with being negative, critical thinking is often referred to as *critiquing* to distinguish it from these. A key part of scholarly tradition, it is an important part of knowledge construction – that is, constructing knowledge that is new to you or new to the world. Definitions of critical thinking differ but most embrace the idea of habitual use of a set of thinking skills based on formal and informal logic and reasoning. It requires application of knowledge, comprehension, analysis and synthesis and evaluation.

See *Logical reasoning* in this chapter; see *Bloom's taxonomy* in Chapter 2

Critical thinking cannot be taught directly. Rather it is learned with practice. This means that you need to apply consistently the principles of critical thinking to *acquire the habit of* asking incisive questions. These questions enable you to:

- evaluate the soundness of arguments (your own and those of others)
- evaluate the accuracy, relevance and significance of information
- recognise unstated assumptions
- seek and interpret information
- *find* problems as well as solve them
- test conclusions
- reconstruct or adjust your own beliefs, values and knowledge.

At first you may be nervous about using critical thinking in your studies and at work. It helps to recognise that 'facts' are often not what they appear to be: they are generally interpretations by people who are biased by self-interest, power, context and the assumptions they make. Some people, arguments or perspectives occupy a dominant or privileged position in society. This does not invalidate alternative perspectives, however. You need to consider what knowledge, experiences and contexts inform the dominant perspective and what informs the alternative ones.

See *Building and supporting an argument* in Chapter 5

In the academic world it is recognised that knowledge is not objective. When you are studying, you are normally directed to sources of information that try to be objective and to critiques that help you to pose appropriate questions. You are encouraged to think critically. Workplaces may not be so enlightened. There, you have to discover who and what shapes knowledge and learn the acceptable ways of posing critical questions.

Invariably, critical thinking involves posing '*wh*' questions such as *what, when, where, who, why, how, what if, so what and what next*. These are likely to reveal assumptions, poor reasoning, flawed logic or insufficient data and gaps in understanding. Then you seek further information and ask the '*wh*' questions again. As a result you deepen your knowledge and hone the effectiveness of your own thinking. When you *present* an argument you need to accept that others will apply their critical thinking to it. Thus, what applies to the arguments of others, for example in academic articles, also applies to those you construct yourself.

Looking beyond the surface with critical questions

The point of using critical questions is to dig and delve: you are behaving much as a forensic scientist or detective would. You look beyond the surface. You take nothing for granted and you reserve judgement about an argument or theory until you are convinced by sufficient and relevant evidence.

Table 6.2 sets out the key critical questions you would use for reading an empirical research article and the flaws to look for. Note that critical questions don't necessarily contain the '*wh*' terms *what, when, where, who, why, how, what if, so what and what next*. When thinking critically you modify questions to suit what you are critiquing. Use the '*wh*' terms as a final check to make sure your questions have covered them. After sufficient practice you will *know* how to interrogate what you read or write and do so naturally.

Adapt the questions in Table 6.2 when you are reading theoretical articles. These normally argue for a theory, or modification of an existing one, on the basis of evidence previously collected. Look for a clear exposition of how a theory is supposed to work, sufficient and relevant evidence and alternative explanations. Watch for assumptions and reasoning flaws. One way of improving your critical thinking is to critique an argument with a small group of fellow students.

ACTIVITY 6.7 With a group of friends, select a short text that puts forward an argument, preferably related to your studies. Alternatively, select an argument of interest to the whole group, for example, one for or against using on-shore wind power or the effectiveness of the penal system to prevent crime. Then, together, critique it using Table 6.2. What flaws and problems can you find?

Checking your own arguments

Just as you look for well-developed and sound arguments in the articles you read, people will look to see if your arguments are well-developed and sound.

Table 6.2 Critical questions to use when reading

What to ask: key critical questions	Possible flaws to be found
Who 1. Who is putting forward the argument? 2. Is the person likely to have a vested interest, e.g. commercial? 3. Has the person identified the perspective adopted and mentioned alternative ones (or simply omitted them)?	Bias, possibly leading to insufficiency of evidence and reasoning
What 1. What is the argument about: what are the main premises? 2. Are hidden/wrong assumptions made? 3. What are the hypotheses (predictions) to be tested? 4. From what prior research findings/arguments are the hypotheses drawn? 5. Do you trust the findings? 6. Are the hypotheses drawn logically? 7. What do they mean; what is their significance?	Insufficiency of premises Assumptions Predictions don't follow logically from the premises/evidence
When/where 1. When and where was the argument made and the evidence gathered? (Context might matter to the conclusion, particularly if it is intended to be or could be applied to practice.)	Evidence is insufficient and/or lacks relevance
How 1. How was the evidence gathered? 2. Is it of good quality? 3. Is it sufficient to support the hypotheses? 4. Is anything missing? 5. How were any data analysed?	Evidence is insufficient and/or lacks relevance Assumptions Data analysis does not address questions Spurious appeals to 'authority' of statistics and false precision
Why 1. What reasons, causes or explanations are given for the findings? 2. Are the findings sufficient to support the explanation? 3. What is the conclusion and can it be supported?	Logical reasoning flaws Fallacies Assumptions Arguing beyond the evidence
So what 1. What is the meaning and significance of the findings and the explanation?	Arguing beyond the evidence
What if 1. Are there alternative explanations?	Logical reasoning flaws Evidence is insufficient and/or lacks relevance
What next 1. What is needed to better address the research question?	Logical reasoning flaws

When you set out an argument use Table 6.3 as a critical-thinking checklist. Arguments that set out solutions to problems have additional components to check and questions are set out later in this chapter in *Using critical thinking for investigations*.

Table 6.3 How to use critical questions when writing

Critical questions	Possible flaws to be found
Who *I* am putting forward an argument. Have I identified the perspective I have adopted and mentioned alternative ones?	Bias, possibly leading to insufficiency of evidence and reasoning
What What are the main premises of my argument? What assumptions have I made?	Insufficiency of premises Assumptions
When/where What is the context of my argument?	Evidence is insufficient and/or lacks relevance
How Is the evidence of good quality? Is it sufficient? Is any evidence missing (and why)?	Evidence is insufficient and/or lacks relevance Logical reasoning flaws Assumptions
Why Have I offered well-argued reasons, causes or explanations for the evidence? Does the evidence support my argument? What assumptions have I made?	Logical reasoning flaws Fallacies Assumptions
So what What is the significance of my explanation/argument?	Arguing beyond the evidence
What if Are there alternative explanations/arguments that the same evidence could support?	Logical reasoning flaws Evidence is insufficient and/or lacks relevance
What next What are my criticisms of my argument and what is needed to improve it?	Logical reasoning

ACTIVITY 6.8 Critique a recent assignment you have written in which you put forward an argument. Use Table 6.3 to assess whether and how well you covered the '*wh*' questions. Try to recognise flaws in your work and identify how you might avoid them next time.

Using critical questions demands effort. You do not passively state, set out, explain, note possible contradictions and so on. You actively identify, analyse, weigh up, evaluate, prioritise, work out the significance and meaning of things, make links, assess the value of an argument, draw conclusions and justify with reasons. Imagine being handed a proposal for redesigning an organisation's customer inquiry system and being asked: *What's your view of this? Is it a sound proposal? If there's anything that's wrong with it, or not covered, we need to know.* You would study the proposal with the aim of uncovering anything that might suggest the proposal is unworkable or wanting in some way.

When you think critically, the results will be evident in your reading notes and any written report or assignment. Table 6.4 shows how critical thinking works for

Table 6.4 Basic and critical thinking

Basic thinking	Critical thinking
Note the author, context and perspective taken	Assess for possible biases, contextual limitations and unstated alternative perspectives
Describe the argument	Identify the main premises and their significance
Describe the theory	Evaluate the importance and relevance of the theory; assess its weaknesses/limitations and relative value
	If possible, weigh up whether competing theories have higher relative value
Set out how the theory is supposed to work	Evaluate how likely it is the theory will work, given any weaknesses/limitations
Describe the evidence	Evaluate the evidence for relevance and sufficiency
AND	Identify flaws and assumptions
	Justify your assessment of the evidence and how it is put forward
Set out the methods used	Assess the appropriateness of the methods used
Identify the different components of the evidence	Assess the relative importance of different elements of the evidence
Identify the links between items	Look for contradictions and whether they are or can be explained
State the conclusion drawn	Assess the validity of the conclusion on the basis of the relevance and sufficiency of the evidence and the soundness of the reasoning

notes and assignments involving theory and evidence. You keep basic descriptions and explanations brief and to the point in order to include the results of your critical thinking.

If your assignments better match the first column of Table 6.4 you are likely to earn the comment that you need to adopt a more critical stance. The marker won't be able to teach you *how* to adopt a critical stance but may offer specific suggestions such as *You might have spotted the contradiction here* or *Is this evidence sufficient to support the conclusion?*

ACTIVITY 6.9 Select a recent assignment or notes you made on empirical work involving the use of theory. Then use Table 6.4 to assess whether and how well your work demonstrates critical thinking. Consider how you might demonstrate it better next time. Together, Activities 6.8 and 6.9 provide you with a way of improving your work.

Critical thinking at work

Organisations say they want critical thinkers in order to solve problems, innovate, make better decisions, improve strategy and to plan. But graduates say that their critical thinking can be unwelcome. Critical thinking in the workplace needs to be constructive and focused on *solutions*. Here are some rules of thumb.

1. Prioritise and choose issues that are important to the organisation, or your part of it. It's wise to choose issues within your sphere of influence or control but check that you have considered wider consequences and implications. It helps to have the support of a more senior champion.
2. Set yourself a time limit and expect information to be incomplete. This is acceptable if you focus on key information and acknowledge omissions. Alternatively, make a well-argued case to spend time on the problem or issue.
3. Keep in mind the people or person who developed the proposal, system or process or made the decision you are critiquing and those who supported it. When you reveal your criticisms, these people may feel offended. Thus, the *way* in which you present your criticisms is important. Diplomacy is the key here.
4. Not all people think critically. They may be dismissive and refer to any delay in decision-making as *paralysis by analysis*. You must judge the point at which sufficient critical thinking has been done *and* how much of your critique to reveal, perhaps revealing only key points.
5. Set out clearly your solution and the anticipated benefits (but be balanced: there may be disadvantages and implications).
6. Above all, avoid deconstructing a decision, plan, argument, system or process *without* coming to a conclusion about how it can be improved or proposing an alternative.

See Beyond words: speech acts and saving face in Chapter 8

The more accomplished at critical thinking you become, the better you will be able to demonstrate its effectiveness and usefulness. Hone your skills while you are studying to make it easier to transfer, develop and use this skill at work.

Using critical thinking for investigations

When you solve problems you must think critically, logically and systematically to discover the causes and develop solutions. You do this when something has gone wrong, when an improvement is needed or when new opportunities arise. Investigative thinking is common in business and management studies because it involves *the application* of knowledge. Often you are asked to solve a workplace problem or a problem in a descriptive case or scenario.

The framework that follows uses critical questions and you should read the section *Critical thinking* in this chapter now if you have not already done so. The framework is set out as if you are acting alone, although when you investigate workplace problems the input of others is desirable and often essential. The involvement of others makes the implementation of solutions easier, too.

Activity 6.10 is designed to help you to understand the framework in the context of a real situation. In the framework, the use of theory is identified at various points but don't be too concerned about this if you have no relevant theoretical material to hand. How to apply theory is covered later in this chapter.

ACTIVITY 6.10 Think of a problem that you want to solve or an improvement that you want to make at work, at home or in your studies. You should have sufficient information about issues so that you can easily use the questions in the framework. Alternatively use a scenario.

Framework for problem-solving

1. Identify and describe the problem

This sounds deceptively easy but it requires you to have sufficient and reliable evidence of a problem. The information you gather is used in your analysis.

Questions to ask.

What is happening to suggest there is a problem?
What is the context?
Where, how and when is it happening and to whom?
What seem to be the relevant factors?
Do I have sufficient information?
What assumptions am I making?
Am I asking the right questions?
What are the consequences of the problem to others and the organisation?
Will the problem disappear with time, stay the same or worsen if nothing is done?

You may not be able to *define* the problem, that is, state its exact nature and scope, until later. However, you should be able to characterise the symptoms and consequences of the problem and how urgent, important and widespread it is. It is common for further questions to arise during problem-solving because the answer to one question leads to another. Spend time formulating appropriate questions; it will save time later.

2. Analyse the problem

No investigation can be exhaustive and normally it does not need to be, provided you can establish the main causes of a problem.

Questions to ask.

How does one factor affect another?
How do the factors fit together?
What appears to cause these factors?
What isn't known?
How complex is the problem?
How can it be simplified?
What theory is relevant and useful?
Do the factors in the theory fit the problem?
What does the theory say are the causes of the problem?
Are these the causes I've identified in the problem?
What assumptions need to be made?

See fishbone diagram and multiple cause diagrams in *Planning your studies* and the control loop in *Monitoring your progress* in Chapter 2

Use tools and techniques such as fishbone diagrams and multiple cause diagrams to help you to break down the components of a problem and establish the relationships between them and the possible causes of the problem. Process tools such as the control loop can help you to assess the realism of a project's objectives and time scales; for example, whether planning and implementation have been effective; whether monitoring of tasks is sufficient and whether the associated reporting mechanisms are working. Your choice of tools and techniques depends on the problem being investigated but none alone is likely to reveal all the aspects or complexities of a problem.

See *Recognising assumptions* and *Applying theory to problems and scenarios* in this chapter

Use relevant theory at this stage. Select the theory and apply it to the issues you have uncovered – *don't try to make the issues fit the theory*. No theory is likely to fit a set of issues perfectly; a lack of fit can indicate that there are further issues to be uncovered or that the theory itself is lacking. This is a matter of informed judgement. Setting out any shortcomings of a theory in a study assignment will earn you marks: you are demonstrating your skills of application and critical thinking.

3. Draw conclusions from your analysis

The starting point for drawing conclusions from your analysis is to make sense of your findings: you assess the whole picture in context. This helps you to distinguish between primary and secondary causes of the problem and how they fit into the wider context. At this point you will have *defined* the problem: you know what kind of problem you are dealing with and you are in a better position to remedy it.

Questions to ask.

What does all this mean?
What are the primary and secondary causes of the problem?

4. Set criteria for a solution

Criteria for a solution are the benchmarks for a solution. They set out guiding principles so that your solution remains within constraints such as limits on resources, when it needs to be in place and how much disruption would be acceptable.

Questions to ask.

What needs to be resolved?
What kind of solution is appropriate?
When does it need to be in place?
Are there resource limitations on what can be done?
What other constraints might there be (staff availability and capabilities, existing systems, procedures, structures, commitment and/or motivation of others)?
Is a lasting solution needed or would it be too disruptive?
Would a partial solution or a short-term one be effective?
What is the impact on other parts of the organisation?
What would be acceptable to the organisation itself?

5. Identify options for a solution; select one and justify it

An effective solution does two things: it resolves the problem and does so within the constraints (that is, it meets the criteria set). If there is more than one possible solution, identify the options and then select one on the basis of how well it matches the criteria. If you have a number of options it is useful to draw up a decision tree or an evaluation matrix. Score each option according to how well it meets each criterion. Then select the one that meets most criteria well. When you have made your selection, justify your choice.

See decision tree and evaluation matrix in *Decision-making* in this chapter

Questions to ask.

How might the causes of the problem be resolved?
What options are there?
How well would each option resolve the problem?
Which one best fits the criteria for a solution?
How likely is it that this option will work?
What are the advantages of this option over the others?

6. Develop recommendations or an action plan

Set out your solution as a series of recommendations or a plan of action. Use relevant theory where this helps: it is often essential if your recommendations involve, for example, a change in programme or the redesign of communication channels. Your recommendations or plan should be subject to considerations such as busy times, holidays, committee cycles and incorporate any needs such as communication and staff training. You may have to allow time to seek approval, agree resources, seek the support and commitment of staff and reduce anticipated resistance. Good recommendations or planned actions are SMART: they should be Specific, Measurable, Agreed/Accountable, Realistic and Timely.

See setting SMART objectives in *Planning your study sessions* in Chapter 2

To provide a convincing argument, set out the advantages of your solution and any new opportunities that might arise from it. Also identify disadvantages and implications, however. If these need to be remedied, say how this can be done.

An action plan sets out the process for carrying out the proposed or planned actions, how they will be co-ordinated, the costs and the commitment needed. A full plan involves identifying and scheduling tasks.

Questions to ask.

Can theory help in the formulation of recommendations?
Are the recommendations SMART?
What are the advantages and disadvantages?
Can any disadvantages and negative implications be remedied?
Are there any other implications or opportunities created?
On whom does the solution depend and who will be accountable for it?
How will I seek approval and resources?

See commitment plan in *Decision-making* in this chapter

Who will be involved in the solution (and how)?
How will the solution be communicated?
Who might not be committed it and how might resistance be reduced?

7. Monitor the implementation and evaluate the results

See control loop in *Monitoring your progress* in Chapter 2

This step is possible only if your recommendations or action plans are implemented. If they are, you need to work out how to monitor the implementation and evaluate the outcome. Monitoring allows you to make necessary adjustments if things don't go to plan while evaluation allows you to assess whether and how well your solution has worked and draw valuable lessons for the future.

Monitoring can often be achieved by using some form of the control loop. Evaluation requires additional forward thinking: you consider what success would 'look like' and what you need to measure to assess whether or not you have achieved it. Then you make your measurements using observation or by gathering evidence in other ways. Evaluation is a complex subject beyond the scope of this book but simple evaluations are often sufficient.

Questions to ask.

How will I monitor the implementation?
How will I know whether the solution has worked?
What will 'success' look like?
How much time and resources do I have?
What should I measure?

Are the measures valid and sufficient measures of the solution – do they measure what they are supposed to?

Are the data collected representative and reliable?

What can be learned from the results of the evaluation?

Problem-solving provides an effective vehicle for critical thinking and application of knowledge and theory, at university and at work. You demonstrate your thinking skills while being constructive: you aim to fix the problems that your critical analysis has revealed. You also become an effective reviewer of plans by others to solve a problem or make changes.

Decision-making

What will you eat for lunch?

Should you ask Adrian for a lift to the station or get a taxi?

What should you do in the summer vacation?

What career path is right for you?

Decisions can be trivial with few consequences or they can be life-changing. At work, decisions are just the same: sometimes they can be trivial, such as where to place the new water cooler; at other times they can be vital and risky, leading to an organisation's success or failure. Sometimes we can be misled into thinking a decision is a trivial one when it isn't: the consequences and implications of a minor decision can be great. Yet we often make them unsystematically without sufficient consideration.

A decision tree is a useful device when deciding between options. One is shown in Figure 6.1 *What to do this summer*, which shows three main options, each with two or more sub-options. Note the convention: circles represent decision points.

A decision tree won't help in the absence of a process, however. There are a number of steps to take and you normally draw up your decision tree in Step 3.

Decision-making process

Step 1 – Know why you are making a decision. You are deciding what to do this summer. You want to cover your living expenses but there seem to be many ways of doing this; working abroad would be fun. You know that any plans you make depend on the opportunities that exist but you want a good idea of where to focus your time and energy.

Step 2 – Gather information. You learn from the *Seasonworkers* website and others that short periods of work abroad are possible; harvesting jobs and working as an au pair sound attractive possibilities and there are many opportunities. The work experience you gain may not be very relevant, however. You discover opportunities near home for relevant work experience opportunities involving work placements and internships. Your local job centre is advertising various job opportunities: some are well paid but the hours are unsocial.

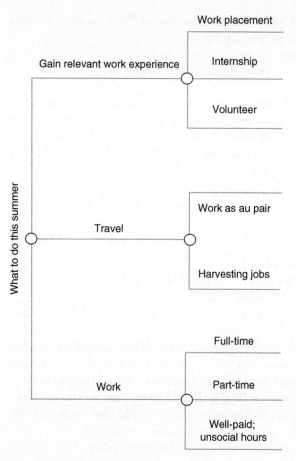

Figure 6.1 What to do this summer

Step 3 – Generate specific options. At this point you draw up your decision tree, showing your main options and sub-options, as in Figure 6.1. You carry out more detailed research into the options and sub-options but it's still hard to decide.

Step 4 – Develop criteria in order to evaluate the options. You consider your wants and needs carefully and draw up criteria to help you decide between options. They are:

- covers living expenses (£X,XXX)
- provides work experience
- must be enjoyable
- provides new non-work experiences.

Step 5 – Evaluate options against the criteria to find the best match. This is not always easy if the criteria don't carry equal weight; criteria may be faulty or contain omissions, too. Evaluating options in such situations is covered in a later subsection. You apply the criteria and make your decision.

Step 6 – Act, monitor and learn. The next step is to act on your decision and monitor the results: if your decision didn't deliver the expected results you would identify why this was so and use this knowledge next time. The decision-making process is shown in Figure 6.2.

ACTIVITY 6.11 Familiarise yourself with the process in Figure 6.2. If you have no current decision to make, then choose a simple one such as deciding how to spend your free time this weekend. In defining your purpose, consider how many hours you want to fill. An option is not an option if it occupies more time than you have available. Gathering data or information means working out realistically how long it takes to organise an event with friends, travel time if any, and so on. Your criteria should be specific. Enjoyment is too broad a term and might cover more precise items such as keeping fit, being outside or seeing non-university friends and family.

The activity involves much more than people think it will. This is because when we make simple decisions we don't think about them much: decision-making carries a high cognitive burden. It's effortful. When one option is very obviously better than another (*Replace the broken office chair or make do without one*) or when the consequences are minimal (*Shall I have the apple or the banana?*) there is no point in spending time deliberating. In the workplace, however, you not only have to make many decisions but you are often required to justify them. For that reason it's useful to have a process for making those that matter.

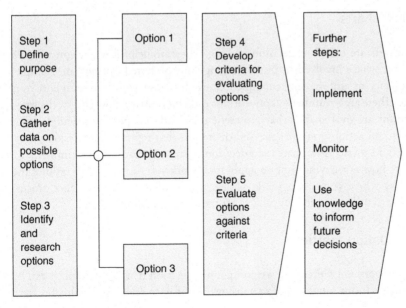

Figure 6.2 The decision-making process

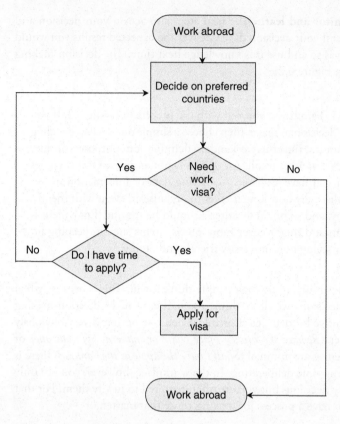

Figure 6.3 Flow chart for working abroad

Flow charts

Flow charts are useful in decision-making. They are helpful when you want to work out what's involved in implementing your preferred option, for example. Complexity or unforeseen consequences might cause you to re-evaluate your choice. There are a number of conventions used for drawing flow charts: the most important are oval shapes that represent start and end points, rectangles that represent an action you can take and diamonds that represent a decision point. Figure 6.3 shows a flow chart for a decision to work abroad for the summer.

Note how not having time to apply for a work visa causes you to rethink the countries where you might work. Unless you want to communicate a process formally to other people, flow charts are more easily drawn by hand.

Evaluation matrices

When options are difficult to weigh up, an evaluation matrix is useful. It can be used in situations ranging from choosing a holiday to selecting candidates for a

Table 6.5 An evaluation matrix

Criteria and weightings

Options	Meet client needs		Cost savings		Ease for clients		Client satisfaction		Totals	
	Weighting = 5		Weighting = 4		Weighting = 3		Weighting = 1			
	Raw score	W'ted score	Raw score	W'ted score	Raw score	W'ted score	Raw score	W'ted score	Raw score	W'ted score
Unit merger	5	25	5	20	2	6	1	4	16	55
Increase first-line services	4	20	3	12	4	12	3	3	15	47
Reduce services	2	19	5	20	1	3	1	1	9	43

job. The one shown in Table 6.5 concerns a health care service needing to cut costs. To create an evaluation matrix do the following.

1. List what your options are. In the case of a health care service needing to cut costs, the options may be to merge with other providers to enable funding to go further, to limit provision to first-line services only or to reduce services overall.
2. Consider the criteria by which the options will be judged. In the above example, meeting clients' medical *needs* might be placed above their *wants* such as retaining a local service. Meeting medical needs might be a vital criterion, more so than cost reduction, with practical ease for clients (travel and so on) being slightly less important. Patients' wants, although a consideration, might be less important still.

   Think hard about criteria. When you are problem-solving or selecting new staff, some criteria will be essential or, at least, more important than others and need to be given greater weight than those that are desirable. Some writers suggest creating two matrices, one for essential criteria to use as a filtering device first and another for desirable criteria. This avoids a situation in which one option has the highest overall score but only because it scores higher on desirable rather than essential criteria.
3. Give each criterion a weighting, depending on how important it is. In the above example, meeting clients' medical needs is weighted higher than others. Avoid giving criteria very similar weightings.
4. For each criterion, give each *option* a raw score of 1–5 (or 1–10) on how well it meets it.
5. Then multiply the weighted score of the criterion with the raw score for the option. So, if the weighting for a criterion is 5 and the option meets this criterion with a score of 2, multiply 5 x 2 to arrive at a weighted score of 10.
6. Add all the weighted scores across each row for each option. The one with the highest score is the one you would choose.

ACTIVITY 6.12 Consider your professional career. What factors might persuade you that one job or career choice is better than another? First consider several career choices that may be open to you (the options) and then how you would judge (your criteria). Your criteria might include a high salary or status, opportunities for career development, job satisfaction, work that challenges you and good working conditions. Create an evaluation matrix to help you decide.

Are the results in line with what you thought or do they surprise you? If the option that yields the highest score disappoints you, then look again at your criteria. Should high financial reward (which may come with a long commute and less free time) be weighted more heavily than job satisfaction and a good work–life balance? What sacrifices are you prepared to make in the short-term and what would make you happy over the longer term? You may want to return to this activity when you have read the final chapter of this book.

Commitment plans

Workplace decisions often need to be made quickly and sometimes with a degree of confidentiality, for example, because of potential disruption or job losses. Ensuring the agreement of all concerned may not be possible. Workplace decisions (and personal ones) can be met with resistance from some stakeholders.

A commitment plan helps you to chart where you might encounter resistance and how much effort is likely to be needed to overcome it. Consider the health care example used for the evaluation matrix. Assume the option to merge units has been chosen. The stakeholders include the managers of two health care units (A and B) and the respective staff and patients.

The senior managers of Unit A, trying to cut costs, may support the merger; those in Unit B may not welcome the disruption but are unlikely to resist the change. Some staff in both units might actively resist the change if their jobs are threatened or they face relocation. Unit A patients might resist the change initially but might welcome improved medical care. Families of Unit A patients and the local community might be resistant as a result of increased travel costs. Unit B patients and their families may have no opinion if, for them, care and ease of use are unaffected. The community local to Unit B might welcome the merger because of the potential economic benefit. Where would you put your efforts in overcoming resistance?

In Figure 6.4, O represents the current position of a stakeholder group; X indicates the commitment change needed; the length of the arrow between O and X indicates the effort required to gain the commitment. More commitment is needed from some stakeholders because they will need to lead the change and ensure its successful implementation. When you have their commitment, they can help overcome resistance among other stakeholders. The commitment plan can be used for individual role-holders where this is appropriate.

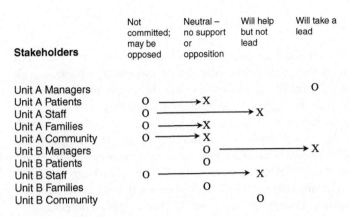

Stakeholders	Not committed; may be opposed	Neutral – no support or opposition	Will help but not lead	Will take a lead
Unit A Managers				O
Unit A Patients	O ——→X			
Unit A Staff	O ———————→ X			
Unit A Families	O ——→X			
Unit A Community	O ——→ X			
Unit B Managers		O ———————→ X		
Unit B Patients		O		
Unit B Staff	O ———————→ X			
Unit B Families		O		
Unit B Community			O	

Figure 6.4 Commitment plan

Adapted and reproduced with permission (The Open University, 2012)

The commitment plan indicates that it would be wise to focus on two stakeholder groups.

1. Unit A staff, who in turn may help to convince Unit A patients and families of the benefits of the merger. How Unit A managers implement the change is crucial in overcoming opposition or a lack of commitment.
2. Unit B managers who can help to overcome resistance and lack of commitment of Unit B staff. The Unit B community might be engaged to create a positive climate in which it's easier to change staff views, too.

Using tools and techniques for decision-making won't guarantee that you make optimal decisions but they help you to think analytically and critically.

ACTIVITY 6.13 Based on the outcome of Activity 6.12, identify all those people who have an interest in your decision – the stakeholders. These people are likely to include family members, friends and anyone affected by your decision. Develop a commitment plan to show their likely level of commitment (or lack of it) and how much 'movement' is required for them to support your decision.

Applying theory to problems and scenarios

Students – and practitioners – often have difficulty in applying theory to problem situations and scenarios. Common problems include selecting factors from a problem in order to fit a theory and taking an unsystematic approach to both the problem and theory. This section shows you how to apply theory in a way that also reveals flaws and problems with the theory itself. Some problems arise because of the way in which theory was developed; these are addressed first.

Theory and practice: a rough terrain

What use is theory to business and management practitioners? Surely they need practical information they can use immediately? The seemingly separate worlds of practice – what happens in the real world – and theory can produce a rough terrain that's difficult to navigate for practitioners and students alike.

Theoretical, case-based research can seem highly relevant to practitioners but it can be highly context-dependent. It has been conducted at a particular time and place. Findings may be of limited use in other contexts. Conversely, research based on traditional methods seeks to explain underlying principles but has less to say about context. In trying to free itself from context, it can seem irrelevant to practitioners and it can be difficult to apply. Understanding the relationship between the two kinds of research is important. It is also important throughout to note the distinction between theoretical and descriptive (or exploratory) case studies: the former purport to explain a phenomenon while the latter are often used in study situations in place of a problem to resolve. A common problem for students when reading research studies based on traditional methods is terminology. This is briefly covered in Box 6.1.

See Deductive and inductive reasoning in research and Abductive reasoning in *Logical reasoning* in this chapter

---

Box 6.1 What's in a name?

There no absolute agreement, even among scientists, on the terminology used for seemingly immutable facts, theories, hypotheses and models. The descriptions below are useful rules of thumb.

Hypothesis

A hypothesis is a testable proposition or statement such as *Money motivates employees to work harder.* The hypothesis is then tested by making observations which either support it or do not. A hypothesis supported by evidence may sometimes be called a theory but theories normally have a broader application. A hypothesis not supported by evidence is probably just a wrong one.

Theory

A theory is an attempt to explain a phenomenon. Hypotheses about the phenomenon have been supported by evidence (observations). A theory can be refined or refuted on the basis of further observations. In business and management the word theory is often used interchangeably with '*model*'. To have explanatory power, a theory must be valid – it must explain what it purports to. A theory must also be reliable – if more observations are made they should produce the same result. There are other types of validity and reliability but these are vital ones. Robust theories should be able to predict future behaviour or phenomena.

Concept/construct

These are 'bundles' of associated or related ideas. We can have personal constructs or concepts but there are also theoretical ones. Your concept of happiness may mean having a job and a satisfying social life. In social science, however, the construct or concept of happiness, or subjective well-being, includes feelings of control over good and bad experiences, a sense of mastery, and having the motivation to create positive experiences for oneself.

Fact

Only scientific laws can truly be called facts. Everything else is provisional and can be overturned or refuted. By the same measure, nothing can ever be proven (with the exception of mathematical theorems). So, in the language of the philosophy of science, there are no truths, only approximations to be improved on.

The relationship between context-dependent and traditional research is set out in Figure 6.5. Note the relevance–rigour axis.

If you take a step backwards, you can see that rigorous theory provides a tidied-up, conceptually more robust explanation of the messy, real world. So what is the problem? It is that studies that seem relevant are more attractive to practitioners but may lack sufficient theoretical rigour. At the same time, studies that seem abstract and irrelevant to the real world are less attractive but may have more rigour and so have more explanatory and predictive power. So how do you overcome these problems?

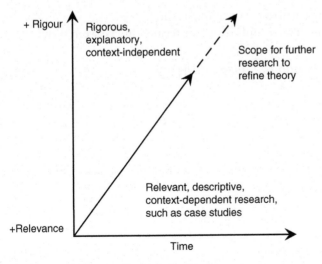

Figure 6.5 The relevance-rigour relationship
Claes and Tyler, 2013

A stepwise process for applying theory

Most courses of study expect you to understand theory, apply it to practice and, in so doing, bring practice to bear on theory and reveal theoretical flaws. The 'real world' of practice is often brought to you via *descriptive* – non-theoretical – case studies, scenarios or your own workplace situations. This helps you to critically analyse situations and apply your learning at work to improve your knowledge and professional practice.

What follows is a stepwise process to help you whenever you are asked to analyse and apply theory to a problem, scenario or descriptive case. The method also helps you to uncover problems with theory. It has been devised for use in analysing problem situations and scenarios. It is adapted from the way in which theoretical case studies are analysed, which students are not normally expected to do at undergraduate level. You can use the method with theory from theoretical case studies or traditional research methods.

Step 1 – Analyse the scenario or problem situation

See fishbone diagram and multiple cause diagram in *Planning your studies* in Chapter 2; see rich picture in *Systems thinking* in Chapter 8

Analyse the scenario or problem situation such as poor performance in branch X of supermarket chain Y. Identify and *abstract* all the factors you find and the relationships between them. The factors may exist at different levels in the organisation, from individuals to overarching management systems. Fishbone and multiple cause diagrams or rich pictures can help you to do this. By analysing the problem situation *before* applying theory you avoid the pitfall of fitting the situation to the theory rather than the theory to the situation.

Your outputs at the end of Step 1 should be:

1. What the problem situation or scenario is about.
2. The factors that you have identified and the relationship between them.

Step 2 – Understand the relevant theory

Consider the theory you are to apply and try to understand it fully. If the theory is one you have chosen yourself then, as you work through Step 2, be prepared to find that you have chosen one that is inappropriate to the situation and you need to select a different one.

The theory you choose (or are instructed to use) may be from a theoretical case study or one resulting from traditional research methods. Be sure that you understand:

- What it is a theory *of*.
- What it is supposed to explain.
- How it does this.
- What the causal relationships are said to be.
- To whom, where and when these apply, if stated.

Your output from Step 2 should be:

1. A description of the theory including factors and causes.

Step 3 – Apply the theory

From your Step 1 analysis of the problem situation, select those factors that the theory deals with. If there are too many factors, choose the most important ones at the appropriate level: if the theory deals with individuals, then choose factors at that level; if the theory deals with groups, then choose factors at that level. Then apply the theory to these factors. When you apply the theory you are also testing its *fit* with the factors you identified from the situation. Do this systematically. Ask these questions:

- Does the theory address the factors I've identified in 'my' situation?
- Does it explain how these factors are caused in 'my' situation?

At this point you should be able to make causal links between the factors in the problem situation that lead to, for example, poor performance. You may have to return to the problem situation if you have not identified a factor that the theory identifies, although you may not find it.

Your outputs at the end of Step 3 should be:

1. The factors in your situation that the theory appears to fit.
2. Their causes (and causal relationships) according to the theory.

Step 4 – Recontextualising

In this step you fully recontextualise the problem situation factors you have identified and applied the theory to at some level (individuals, teams or the organisation, for example). You need to see if the *fit* between the problem situation factors and the theory remains when you take full account of the problem context.

In what ways are working conditions affecting performance in branch X in the problem situation? Which workers are affected and when? Are they affected in the way the theory suggests? As you work through Step 4 expect some loss of fit between the problem situation *in context* and the theory. A theory developed 10 years ago in a commercial setting in the USA may have limited application to a problem in a UK not-for-profit organisation operating with volunteers. It may not fit a situation in which, for example, people work for non-standard rewards. Note any such problems.

Your outputs from Step 4 should be:

1. How the theory explains what is described in the context of the problem situation. Your notes should include specific causal factors and how these led to, for example, the poor performance in branch X of supermarket Y.

2. Any information that was missing from the problem situation that was needed to apply the theory fully.
3. Any limitations you found with the theory itself.

When resolving a real workplace problem you are likely to find missing information as you move back and forth iteratively between theory, problem factors and problem context. A theory may identify particular causal or contributory factors and if you haven't identified these in Step 1, you need to seek further information on the problem or the context to see if those factors are present. If some key factors are not present or you find different and important ones, you may need more than one theory to resolve the situation. In such cases you need to repeat Steps 2, 3 and 4 for each theory used, returning to Step 1 as necessary.

In Step 4 you are not only systematically applying theory to a practical situation but also discovering the ways in which the theory is imperfect (most are). One way of thinking about business and management theories and models is as ideas that *provoke* you to explore and critically analyse situations systematically, think for yourself and improve your professional knowledge.

Structuring your overall outputs

Your outputs from all four steps can be structured in a number of ways, depending on what you have been asked for. This may be a report or presentation. Whatever the form, you will have high-quality information to inform your argument.

If you have worked on a scenario you have been given, with the instruction to analyse it and apply theory, your outputs will be those listed at the end of each step. Further steps are needed for workplace situations or scenarios where you have been asked to resolve the problem. Often you are required to set out criteria for a solution, develop and decide between options, make recommendations and develop an implementation plan. These are covered in *Using critical thinking for investigations* in this chapter.

Activity 6.14 is designed to help you practise analysis and abstraction, two important features of the four steps described.

ACTIVITY 6.14 With two or more fellow students choose a scenario and carry out Step 1. Then select a theory you studied recently and carry out Step 2. Choose a theoretical case study if you can so you have a rich context from which to abstract the theory. Use the questions to fully analyse and understand the theory. When you next need to apply theory to a scenario or problem situation you will be familiar with two of the four steps.

Analysing theoretical case studies

If you have been asked to analyse a *theoretical* case study, the same method can be used. Instead of extracting factors from a problem scenario, however, you first isolate them *from the case* (Step 1). Then you try to understand and apply the theory to the factors (Steps 2 and 3). Finally, you recontextualise them (Step 4). In this way you analyse the theoretical case to assess it for flaws.

Critical reflection

When you critically reflect, you *think back* on your actions. In doing so you become less likely to repeat mistakes and more likely to make improvements. You acquire *self*-knowledge at the same time.

Critical reflection is an important way of improving your study and work practices. It is more than a simple examination of action: you consider how your habits, beliefs, values, attitudes, expectations, behaviours and practices helped or hindered an action. Reflecting on *how, why* and *what if* helps you to achieve deeper understanding and personal growth.

Critical reflection is a cyclical process: you reflect, then plan and implement the changes you want to make; then reflect again. It is metacognitive, disciplined, systematic and involves thinking critically. You can do it alone or with trusted others.

See Knowing how you know in *Types of Knowledge* in Chapter 3; see *Critical thinking* in this chapter

While critical reflection often focuses on the personal realm of an action – your habits, beliefs, values, attitudes, behaviours and practices – it can also focus on the interpersonal, that is, your interactions with other people. The focus can be still wider, too, on your actions and thinking in relation to the social, political and cultural world around you. In this case you relate an action to the wider context to try to understand what influenced you, what constraints might have been imposed on you and what might prevent your acting differently next time. This enables you to make decisions about your future actions and whether to try to influence or modify the wider environment in particular ways.

ACTIVITY 6.15 Consider the following scenarios and decide what 'realm' – the personal, interpersonal and wider context – is being reflected on. How comfortable do you feel about reflecting on such issues yourself?

1. Magda is organising a regular meeting. After she has circulated the revised draft agenda with a request for confirmation, her new line manager asks: 'Would it be possible to organise these meetings more quickly, Magda?' Magda decides to reflect on her work practice. If she can understand her discomfort at being asked to

work faster, she can develop her knowledge and practice and rise to the challenge of new timescales.

2. Joey is late again. Geoff, impatient and in a hurry to attend a meeting, tells him angrily to keep better time or lose his job. Later Geoff discovers that Joey's partner has serious post-natal depression. Geoff seeks out a trusted senior colleague to help him reflect on his habitual behaviour towards staff. The outcome of critical reflection for Geoff would be a more considered and empathetic approach.

3. A hospital is acting on criticisms of poor leadership at all levels. A number of managers, including Moira, have been enrolled on a leadership course that requires participants to critically reflect on their attempts to lead in ways that inspire and empower others. When Moira reflects, she might find that her own beliefs and values inhibit the kind of leadership the hospital aspires to. Or she may find that the culture and hierarchical structure of the institution obstruct staff empowerment. If so, she is not in a position to change the institution but she might try to influence it.

You are likely to have decided that Scenario 1 focuses on the person realm; Scenario 2 on the interpersonal realm and Scenario 3 on the wider context. You are also likely to have indicated that reflection might take you out of your 'comfort zone'.

Critical reflection *can* be uncomfortable. In Magda's case she may feel at ease with working in a particular way because she's over-conscientious. Perhaps she lacks confidence in her abilities and so double-checks all her work without adding to its quality. Reflection can be uncomfortable for different reasons, however. Moira might realise that the desired behaviours espoused by the hospital are not actually acceptable in the organisation. Discrepancies between what an organisation says it does or wants and what it actually does or allows are common. This is difficult to deal with; thus, not all the outcomes of reflection can be acted upon. General focal points for critical reflection are set out in Table 6.6.

Aids to critical reflection

Many professionals keep critical reflection logs or diaries to aid their professional development. When you are studying, it helps to be able to critically reflect on your learning experiences and your academic and personal development. Learning logs and diaries were covered in Chapter 2. These are sometimes required as part of assessed work. You are expected to demonstrate awareness of a learning experience or your personal development, be able to evaluate it, and say what you would change or modify to achieve a better outcome. You can improve a basic learning diary by considering which of the critical reflection focal points in Table 6.6 might be relevant and add these to the ones set out in Chapter 2. Then, when you critically reflect on your learning processes you will use higher-order thinking – metacognition – that enables you to exercise control over cognition.

Table 6.6 Focal points for critical reflection

What happened	What is the wider context and its influence
What you did	
Why you did it	What is your evaluation of this influence
The impact on you	Can you influence the wider context and why you might want to
The impact on others	
Your feelings about it	How this might be done
Why you felt that way	Who would benefit
The feelings and perceptions of others involved, likely or known	What you will do next time
	Whether your habits and beliefs will cause you to repeat the same pattern of behaviour
How you did it, including methods and strategies	
Why you chose these	Whether you can change these habits and beliefs
Their effectiveness	
Whether they were appropriate	If not, why not
If so, how they could be made more effective	How you will feel when you've fulfilled the intention
	What it will mean to you and your development
What could have helped and why	
What hindered or obstructed you	Whether you know yourself better after this reflection.
Why this was	
What you can do about the hindrances or obstructions	The assumptions you made and are making

Make a habit of critical reflection. It prepares you for it in the workplace where you must learn in the absence of formal teaching.

> **ACTIVITY 6.16** Consider a recent learning experience and systematically use items from Table 6.6 that are relevant to the experience. At the end, identify what you learned about yourself as a result of critically reflecting on the experience.

Critical reflection is a powerful skill and learning tool. While you may receive formal training and development in the workplace, critical reflection helps you to transfer your knowledge to practice. You also better understand – and can improve – your practices. You become more aware of your thinking, assumptions and behaviours. Rather than accepting the status quo, you can ask: Why do I do things this way? Why are things this way in this organisation? You discover the differences between what *is*, what is *expected* and what *might be* – and why. Enlightened organisations regard critical reflection as a vital learning tool and may also use it collectively to develop organisational learning.

Chapter summary

❖ Good thinking skills are required at university and in the workplace where you are expected to make decisions, improve practices, solve problems and to learn, using the self-correcting process of critical reflection.

❖ Your thinking improves with challenges – from other people and those you present to yourself.

❖ Logic is the foundation for thinking skills that you need for study and the workplace. It is also fundamental to the way in which empirical research is done. In everyday reasoning people often use abductive or *best-guess* reasoning. The more informed you are, the better your guesses.

❖ Important aspects of sound reasoning are being able to identify assumptions, logical flaws and biases. Hidden, wrong assumptions can result in unsound arguments and decisions. Logical fallacies are common, too, but do you know how to recognise them?

❖ Critical thinking is essential in the development of lifelong learning skills and in everyday activities such as analysing and resolving problems. Using 'wh' questions helps you to improve your critical thinking.

❖ When you are solving problems, using a framework can help you to identify what questions to ask at each stage.

❖ Decisions can be made systematically and rationally. Tools such as decision trees, flow charts and evaluation matrices are helpful but are insufficient alone: a process is needed, too.

❖ Theory can be robust but seem remote from practice. Conversely, case studies seem highly relevant to practitioners but may have limitations. Application of theory is nonetheless vital to effective business and management practice. A stepwise method helps you to apply theory and identify problems with it.

❖ Critical reflection is a powerful learning tool. It is vital when you study and crucial in the workplace, where much learning is informal and self-directed. Critical reflection can be uncomfortable but rewarding. Many professionals keep critical reflection logs or diaries.

References

Claes, B. and Tyler, S. (2013) Applying theory to case studies. Personal conversations, September 2013.

De Massis, A., Frattini, F., Pizzurno, E. and Cassica, L. (2015) 'Product innovation in family versus nonfamily firms: an exploratory analysis', *Journal of Small Business Management*, vol. 53, no. 1, pp. 1–36.

Seasonworkers (n.d.) [Online]. Available at www.seasonworkers.com/summerjobs/ (Accessed 4 April 2016).

The Open University (2012) *B628/BZX628 Managing 1: managing organisations and people*, Milton Keynes, The Open University, p. 365.

Wald, A. (1943) 'A method of estimating plane vulnerability based on damage of survivors', Statistical Research Group, Columbia University, CRC 432, Center for Naval Analyses, reprinted July 1980.

Wason, P.C. (1968) 'Reasoning about a rule', *Quarterly Journal of Experimental Psychology*, vol. 20, no. 3, pp. 273–281 [Online]. DOI: 10.1080/14640746808400161 (Accessed 20 April 2016).

CHAPTER SEVEN

Complex thinking skills

Complex thinking skills are those that interweave a number of others, including but not confined to the fundamental ones covered in Chapter 6 such as logical reasoning, critical thinking and problem-solving. Complex thinking can be messy and uncertain; many conclusions are possible and, importantly, it is much harder to be objective. It is possible to be systematic, however, although self-awareness is required.

So, which complex thinking skills serve you well both in your study of business and management and in professional practice? **Ethical thinking** is expected by employers while **creative thinking** is highly desired but rare to find. **'Soft' systems thinking** – applied to human activity systems – is vital to organisations but is even rarer, perhaps not least because few business and management degree programmes include it.

This chapter is not an easy one because it takes you through how to think ethically and creatively using frameworks and one well-known method of analysing the soft systems you find in every organisation (including your university). It assumes that, while you may be required to think ethically and creatively during your studies, you may receive little tuition. As systems thinking is rarely taught, this section of the chapter assumes no prior knowledge and no teaching of the subject even in an introductory way.

To help you, extended scenarios and cases are used together with activities to make the text accessible. The associated activities require time and a systematic approach. Attempting them is valuable, however, and you should be able to use these complex thinking skills to broaden your perspective in your studies, in the workplace and in other realms of your life.

Moral and ethical reasoning

An internet advertisement claims that for around $400 a 'quantum device' will 'soften' man-made electricity in your home so your body can 'resonate with its own frequencies', reducing stress and bringing harmony to family relationships.

A manager ends a romantic relationship with a junior staff member and then quietly bullies and harasses her, constantly fault-finding and undermining her decisions till she resigns with her self-confidence destroyed.

An organisation knows that its mining process is prone to releasing methane, a greenhouse gas, into the atmosphere but it 'buries the data' in order to gain permission to extend its operations.

All these behaviours are unethical. Would you want to work for an organisation that used or condoned them? Ethics is a large and complex discipline covering domains from moral values to theory and application. Business ethics is but one aspect, but a vitally important one: unethical organisations cause damage while more ethical ones are often the most successful.

Most people have deeply-held moral values that guide their behaviour. We acquire many of them early in life. From instructions such as *Don't hurt Freddy!* and *Help Sara pick up the toys* we abstract general principles. We learn: *It's wrong to hurt people*; *It's good to co-operate*. Compliance or non-compliance results in reward or punishment. We then internalise these principles as our own and develop *conscience*. We no longer need external reward or punishment; rather, we reward or punish ourselves by feeling good or bad about our particular actions. As adults we can *reason* about right and wrong.

Human society develops moral values and 'rules' or standards in the first place because we are social animals, predisposed to co-operate, to be just and fair. This ensures the survival and well-being of ourselves and others and avoids unnecessary suffering or harm. Thus, for the common good, we forgo some of our freedom to be wholly selfish.

Morals, etiquette and laws

What distinguishes moral principles from other kinds is that moral principles have consequences to human welfare, animals and the environment whereas amoral ones don't. Moral ones take precedence over self-interest. They should not be confused with etiquette – codes of polite behaviour – or law. It might break the rules of etiquette to wear a swimsuit to a traditional wedding but it is not immoral. Laws normally arrange society's moral values into a systematic code but this cannot embrace all human behaviour. It may be legal to refuse to help a person in distress but it might not be moral to do so if harm is caused. Laws can be unjust, too. Once, when slavery was legal, it was illegal to steal a slave but it would not be immoral to steal one in order to free the slave. Morality also differs from religion in which a supernatural authority – rather than conscience or reason – defines what is right and wrong.

Philosophers generally agree on a minimal set of moral standards or principles that correspond to valuing life, safety, health, fairness and justice, happiness, peace, respect, and freedom:

Don't kill innocent people
Cause no unnecessary pain or injury
Don't steal or cheat
Keep promises
Don't deprive a person of his or her freedom
Tell the truth
Treat others as equals
Help others
Reciprocate when others help you
Obey just laws

Questions of justification

Philosophers are not particularly interested in how we acquire our moral values or standards, but in whether they are justified. In pursuit of assessing and trying to justify right and wrong, philosophers have concerned themselves with, variously

- the act
- the consequences
- the character of the 'actor'
- the motives of the 'actor'.

To understand the significance, imagine you are intent on kidnapping your employer for ransom and by chance you do so just as he is about to set fire to his business premises in order to make a false insurance claim. The fire would threaten the lives of the night security staff. Your action prevents the fire and ensures the safety of the staff. Do we judge what you did as right on the basis of consequences? On the other hand if, as a humane individual rather than a kidnapper, you discover your employer's plan and try to stop him lighting the fire but fail, resulting in the security staff being injured, do we evaluate what you did as wrong on the basis of the consequences? Do we dismiss your act, character and motives? What about the person who has the right intentions but fails to act or the person who simply follows rules without integrity? Would we not prefer to be with others whom we can trust to invariably 'act right' *and* have the compassion and courage to speak out against injustice?

Ethics in the workplace

Now consider the world of business and management. Should you cheat, lie and bribe to win a contract that will keep your staff employed? What effect might that have on business in general? How hard might it be to carry your personal morality into the workplace if you are faced with the choice: *Cheat or lose your job*?

ACTIVITY 7.1 Consider the infamous case of Ford and its new Pinto car in the USA, based on an article in the investigative magazine *Mother Jones* (Dowie, 1977), then answer the seven questions that follow.

Faced with fierce competition from manufacturers of small cars in other countries, Ford was designing its own small car on a fast-track schedule. But there was a problem. The car failed safety tests because the design and location of the fuel tank made it likely to fracture and ignite on impact. Ford decided to go ahead with production anyway. Why? Ford took a strictly rational and economic decision, conducting a cost–benefit analysis. It weighed the cost of redesign at $11 per car against the cost of law suits as a result of a probable 180 deaths and the same number of injuries. When deaths did occur, its defence was that it was legally justified in refraining from changing the design because the cost of doing so was greater than the benefit to society of making the change. Ford had, in fact, decided that 180 deaths and 180 injuries were acceptable.

1. Would you have done the same thing, faced with a tight production schedule?
2. Could you have been persuaded to go along with the decision, perhaps knowing that you might lose your job if you didn't?
3. How much does the consequence of Ford's action – death and injury – influence your thinking?
4. Would Ford's decision have been ethically sound if, by chance, no deaths and injuries had occurred?
5. Is 'legal' the same as 'ethical'?
6. As an ordinary citizen, is your verdict different? Why?
7. Do businesses have ethical responsibilities? Can we rely on them to always be ethical?

These questions, which may be difficult to answer, take us to the complex heart of ethics in business. Adam Smith (1723–1790), considered to be the founder of modern economic theory, argued that by nature we are self-interested and the pursuit of this self-interest results in what is good for society (Smith, 1776). This societal good comes about by an 'invisible (guiding) hand'. According to this thesis, organisations are behaving in a perfectly moral way when they are motivated by profit because they engage in activities that lead to societal 'good'. What prevents unbridled self-interest is competition: a ruthless profiteer soon finds that another organisation offers a better or cheaper product.

Since Smith's time, society and business have changed. Smith's 'invisible hand' is often the highly visible hand of governments which impose regulations on businesses and provide some societal benefits that the self-interest motive was supposed to bring about: free education, health care and so on. But large businesses have considerable power to influence governments, often acting to prevent the imposition of further regulation. Tobacco and fossil fuel lobbyists, the food industry and the US firearms lobby are examples of such corporate or corporate-funded power, to which politicians and bureaucrats are not immune.

According to *Mother Jones*, Ford successfully opposed safety regulations that would have prevented the Pinto fuel tank problem. One key message it delivered was that drivers and poor road design caused accidents, not cars. How sound is that argument? Moreover, if you knew that a product wasn't safe, would you buy it? How would you know it wasn't safe?

Corporate social responsibility

In the last few decades, the concept of corporate social responsibility (CSR) has evolved. Organisations voluntarily take responsibility for their impact on society and the environment, for example, by reducing waste and pollution, ensuring that human rights are upheld and by behaving ethically towards employees, consumers and other stakeholders. Some critics of CSR claim that it is an attempt by organisations to avoid further state regulation: it is the strategy of 'enlightened' self-interest.

The adoption of CSR does not necessarily mean that organisations behave as morally as ordinary citizens would want them to. Some organisations claiming to be socially responsible may fail to change their structure and systems to embed responsible ways of behaving. Even if many have not made this fundamental mistake, we should ask two questions. Do organisations embed social responsibility into *all* their thinking, decisions and activities? What kinds of conflicts might arise between profit and 'doing the right thing'?

Individual and cultural dimensions

A pertinent issue is how ordinary people come to think and behave differently as owners or employees of organisations, making unethical decisions or condoning them or accepting them without question. Many writers on business ethics point to two main causes. First, there is naiveté: people don't question unethical behaviour or decisions because they are doing what they were asked, don't understand the consequences or don't have sufficient information to judge. These are poor defences. Second, when individuals join an organisation they become socialised or acculturated into 'the way things are done here', whether ethical or not. They willingly fit into a world in which bottom lines, margins and sales or performance targets are not subject to ethical considerations. They come to think and behave in ways that, as ordinary citizens, they would not. They would probably say their role demands it of them. For example:

- the risk of losing a contract is weighed against designing a product with lower CO_2 emissions
- meeting sales targets is deemed more important than ending manipulative selling practices
- a decision to outsource is based on the cost savings of moving production to a country where regulations on pollution and on health and safety at work are less stringent or not strictly enforced
- the 'bottom line' means that natural resources are used unsustainably (faster than they can be replaced) or that the use of finite resources continues when renewable alternatives are available.

In effect, decisions in some organisations are based primarily on profit, efficiencies and expedience. Further, in every organisation where there is moral wrongdoing, there are many people who knowingly and willingly aid and abet it. You don't have to be a decision-maker to do moral wrongs.

The three Cs of business ethics

Business ethics are commonly considered to be summarised in three Cs:

Compliance with the rules, the law, moral principles, community and societal expectations

Contribution to society though the usefulness, value and quality of what the organisation does, the jobs it provides and the prosperity they bring

Consequences – intended and unintended – of an organisation's activities. Consequences need to be carefully considered and addressed to minimise harm. They can be internal as well as external; they can be reputational; they can include consequences for other organisations and the industry or sector.

A framework for ethical decision-making

When you are making ethical decisions a framework is helpful. This one is adapted from Santa Clara University, USA (2015):

1. *Recognise an ethical issue*
   Could this decision or situation be damaging to someone or to some group?
   Does this decision involve a choice between a good and bad alternative, or between two good ones or two bad ones?
2. *Get the facts*
   What are the relevant facts of the case?
   What facts are not known? Can I know more?
   Do I know enough to make a decision?

What individuals and groups have an important stake in the outcome?

Are some concerns more important than others? Why?

What are the options for acting?

Have all the relevant people and groups been consulted?

Have I identified creative options?

3. *Evaluate alternative actions*

Which option will do *most good* and *least harm*?

Which option best respects the *rights* of all stakeholders?

Which option treats people *justly* (equally or proportionately)?

Which option best serves the common good (the whole community, not just some members)?

Which option leads me to act as the *virtuous* person I want to be?

4. *Make a decision and test it*

Which option best addresses the situation?

Can I justify my decision?

How are others likely to react to it?

5. *Act and reflect on the outcome*

How can my decision be implemented with the greatest care and attention to the concerns of all stakeholders?

How did my decision turn out and what have I learned from this specific situation?

ACTIVITY 7.2 First carry out Activity 7.1 if you have not already done so. Now address the questions again this time using the three Cs and the framework. Why do you think Ford make the wrong decision? It still may not be easy to arrive at answers but your thinking will be more informed.

You are likely to have considered:

- Your own susceptibility to acculturation of this kind; the strength of your moral character; whether it would be ethical for an organisation to dismiss a person who disagreed with a decision based on well-justified moral principles (Questions 1 and 2).
- That the risk of serious harm is sufficient to decide not to do something: Ford's decision in the knowledge of the failed safety tests would not have been ethical even if no deaths and injuries had occurred (Questions 3 and 4).
- Being ethical is not the same as being legally compliant (Question 5).
- Your own personal moral values and standards (Question 6).
- That businesses *do* have ethical responsibilities but that we shouldn't rely on organisations always to behave ethically (Question 7).

Practise thinking ethically when you study: *it will be expected of you*. Always consider what conflicts might arise between a business or management decision and 'doing the right thing'. Consider how decisions, practices and activities have an impact not only on profit and loss but also on staff and other stakeholders: in other words, consider the social and environmental costs and benefits now and in the future. These 'triple' bottom lines (and reporting) are now common; indeed a 'quadruple' bottom line involving adaptive innovation to maintain and improve sustainable profit, the impact on people and the environment, is being introduced by organisations. Familiarity with business ethics prepares you for professional life, enabling you to recognise conflicts more readily and be adept at considering how to avoid them to arrive at 'win–win' solutions.

Systems thinking

Consider these two examples of systems thinking.

Toyota and economies of flow

Ford was once master of economies of scale in car manufacturing, forecasting what customers might want, drawing up schedules and setting budgets and targets. Toyota, then a struggling car manufacturer, needed to change. But instead of copying Ford, it decided to respond directly to customer demand and make cars to order. To do this it needed to shorten 'end-to-end' time between an order and a car rolling off the production line. It did so by focusing on economies of *flow* and by involving workers themselves. Whereas Ford took 10 days to change a pressing machine to make different parts, Toyota learned to do it in 10 minutes. Under Ford's 'command and control' leadership suppliers were given the specification for each part without further information; Toyota, to avoid carrying a large inventory of parts, worked closely with its suppliers. The suppliers worked both 'hands on' with Toyota production workers and with Toyota's design teams. By working in this way, the suppliers knew what a part was supposed to do and could help to design improvements, which Toyota actively encouraged. Toyota workers themselves identified small changes that shortened a process by a few seconds. The firm's style of leadership made it easy for learning to occur. Eventually, Toyota could produce a car to order in less time and more cheaply than its competitors. Today, its systems thinking continues to evolve and develop.

Social care and misplaced targets

In the UK it is the local authorities who provide adult social care. A damning report listed failings in the level and quality of care, despite many local authorities meeting a wide range of targets. Five local authorities embarked on a learning journey. Shock followed shock as they discovered they did not know clients' real needs or how long it took to meet them. The available data focused on the authorities' own internal processes and their performance measures were detached from the purpose of the system that was supposed to deliver care. A request for help could take up to 230 days to be fulfilled and there were 81 steps in the process. There was waste in the system: duplication, rework and work that was simply unnecessary. After several months of learning and changes, one local authority cut 'end-to-end' time from several months to three days and the number of steps to 11. The better service cost less.

The Toyota and social care examples, based on Seddon and Caulkin (2007), show the power of systems thinking and learning in organisations. However, managers are often trained to manage the parts but not to see the whole. Moreover, leaders may even inadvertently block organisational learning by adopting a leadership style that makes it difficult. But what exactly is a system? Carry out Activity 7.3 to explore your own ideas about systems.

ACTIVITY 7.3 *Part 1* – Carry out this activity in a group if possible. Consider the following processes that we often refer to as systems. Answer the questions below as individuals and then compare your responses with those of others in the group.

1. *An automated system for putting bicycle parts together. Each part is added at the right time in a highly structured process to create a finished bicycle.*
2. *The human respiratory system.*
3. *An organisation's marketing system.*
4. *The public transport system in the UK or another country.*
5. *The weather system.*

    What appears to be the same about all five systems?
    What is different?
    Are they all systems?
    Is it possible to have complete knowledge of a system?
    Which system is easiest to envisage and why?
    Could you make interventions in any of the systems?
    Would or could you be aware of all the consequences of an intervention?
    Would an engineer, a respiratory consultant, a manager, a bus driver and
      a meteorologist share your perspectives on the systems?

The activity is challenging and you will return to it later when you have familiarised yourself with the defining characteristics of systems, set out below.

Characteristics of systems

A system is not reducible. A system is more than the sum of its parts. Its workings cannot be attributed to any one individual part and so a system is not reducible to its parts. Think of a sports team: it is more than a group of individuals, a set of rules and the equipment used; it cannot be reduced to any one of these components.

There are different kinds of systems. Systems can be natural, ecological ones, such as the weather system; or mechanistic, engineered ones such as automated production lines and clocks; or living systems such as the internal workings of plants and animals; or they can be social systems involving human activity. Organisations are human activity systems. Some things we refer to as systems, such as 'the transport system', may not be systems at all if they are 'fragmented and unco-ordinated' (Checkland, 2011).

Approaches to analysing what we can properly call systems differ according to whether a system is a 'hard' mechanistic, engineered one or a 'soft' human activity system. In organisations, soft systems approaches are used even if 'hard' mechanistic systems are nested within soft ones.

The components of a system are interconnected. Components are connected to one another; they interact and have interdependencies, like the components of a bicycle. Remove one part or rearrange the parts and the system works differently (or not at all). The behaviour of highly complex systems is hard or impossible to predict because a change or intervention in one part can lead to unintended and unforeseen consequences in another part. The irreducibility of a system lies in these interconnections and interdependencies. When considering systems it's not possible to use simple cause-and-effect thinking.

Some systems, such as the weather system, are so complex that they are considered to be chaotic: we do not, and probably cannot, have sufficient knowledge to foresee consequences. In less complex, non-chaotic systems, unintended consequences are usually accidental. An example is a marketing department's decision to offer regular promotions to increase revenue. Customers learn to wait for price reductions before buying. This introduces fluctuation in demand for which the existing supply system was not designed, resulting in higher costs.

Components of a system can be intangible. Components are not necessarily tangible and concrete such as objects and people. They can be intangible and abstract such as the beliefs, norms and assumptions that shape behaviour. Learning is a component of a system that has value but has no physical presence: we see only its manifestations.

Systems *do* something. Systems have a function. A system *does* something by taking inputs and transforming them into (desired) outputs. In the social care example, the inputs are people who need care; the outputs are the same people whose need has been satisfied. The transformation process involves using resources and actions to achieve the output. In the social care example, transformation processes for logging and assessing needs lost touch with the system's purpose of fulfilling needs.

Feedback mechanisms are an essential part of systems. These help a system to maintain a steady state and to adapt or learn. A feedback loop in an automated bicycle production line might pause robotic arms and delivery of parts if there were a delay up the line. In the social care example, it could be argued that the feedback mechanisms were of the wrong sort. Meeting targets can provide distorted feedback that does not properly relate to overall purpose. In the UK, targets used in the health and social care systems are believed to have become dissociated from the act of care.

Systems have boundaries and operate in a context. Because a system consists of components that connect to and interact with each other, it can be said to have a boundary around it. Everything outside is the external environment in which the system operates and which can affect it. The bicycle production line system exists with other organisational systems to manage suppliers who make the parts and reach customers who need bicycles. While it might be easy to draw a boundary around an 'engineered' system, boundaries are harder to draw around human activity systems.

Systems can have subsystems. A system can have its own subsystems. It is useful to think of systems as layered or nested: one system is a subsystem of a larger one. Figure 7.1 shows a customer service system comprising four subsystems, three of them relying on a nested 'hard' IT tracking system.

A system is what you decide it is. The issue of boundaries is complex because systems don't really exist: in most approaches to systems thinking they are regarded as *constructs* we use to make sense of activities (Reynolds and Holwell, 2010). What is included in a system depends on your perspective (including your knowledge, interests and beliefs and the social and cultural context). Each person, therefore, has a different perspective on a system and the nature of any problems within it.

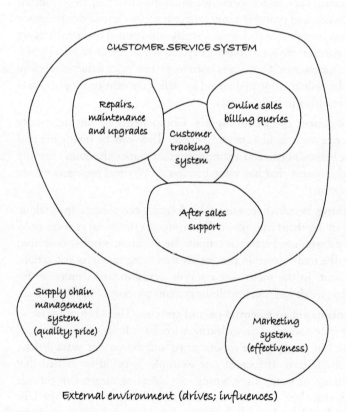

Figure 7.1 A customer service system

Table 7.1 Different perspectives of a system

Manager	Project leader	Team member	Perspectives
Why			Increase profits
What	Why		Expand customer base
How	What	Why	Create new products
	How	What	Research and development
		How	Project X

Adapted from Checkland, 2000

Perspectives on why to do something, what to do and how to do it depend on where a person is 'located' in a system. Table 7.1 shows locations and perspectives of a manager, a project leader and a project team member in a product-creation system. Checkland (2000) advises considering at least one layer above and one below the layer of interest. A layer of interest is 'what'; the layer above is 'why' and the layer below is 'how'.

ACTIVITY 7.3 *Part 2* – Return now to *Part 1* of the activity and revise your responses based on the characteristics of systems.

You are likely to have decided that one system – the public transport 'system' – is not a system at all. Not all parts are interconnected and so no boundary can be drawn, whatever perspective is taken. Only some *elements* of public transport can be considered to be systems, and each has many subsystems. The other four examples are systems but of different kinds and complexity; complete knowledge is usually not possible and the consequences of interventions are not necessarily predictable. The automated system was probably the easiest to envisage because it seems more bounded. If you drew a boundary around any one of the four systems, however, you might have to adopt a particular perspective to decide what to include and exclude. The people listed in the last question would have different perspectives.

Many universities do not teach systems thinking to business and management students. Yet it is valued by organisations. Who would not want to achieve more with less or achieve it more sustainably and ethically? In the West, achieving all three is a pressing concern given climate change, shrinking finite resources and the cost of providing essential services to a growing population. Most systems thinkers say that what is needed is a different kind of leadership and professionals who are capable of systems thinking.

Identifying a systems problem

Think of a mess, muddle or difficult-to-manage situation. Perhaps an organisation's sales are up but profits are down. Interventions increase sales but profits remain stubbornly low while costs rise more than predicted. Or the system works from an organisational perspective but fails to deliver a timely service to clients. Interventions make matters worse or produce unintended consequences elsewhere in the system. Problems can lie in the components of a system themselves or in the connections, or both. Examples of what is often identified are:

- duplication of work or 'rework', such as when client information is recorded more than once or when mistakes are made, needing correction later
- bottlenecks that hold up work 'downstream': 'local' work-arounds lead to unintended consequences or rework
- time wasted through poor location of equipment or other processes
- subsystems such as logging and fixing of IT problems that stubbornly fail to lock into place with other system components
- feedback mechanisms that don't deliver appropriate information
- ill-conceived cost savings that increase costs elsewhere
- depletion of a limited resource because increased productivity requires more of it.

All such problems create waste and inefficiency. Staff may be aware of inefficiencies but are unable to make improvements. Management systems can be part of the problem if they consider only performance and overlook what staff actually do. Not all systems are problematic in this way, of course, and the benefit of systems thinking is that it can be used to improve a system that isn't 'broken'. Thus, systems thinking can be a way of problem-finding with the aim of rethinking a system to make it do more.

One approach to 'soft' systems

Understanding and working with unstructured soft systems is different from the type of problem-solving adopted for, say, structured mechanistic systems. Even so, there are many different approaches and methods to soft systems. Arguably the best known is soft systems methodology (SSM), developed and modified by Peter Checkland and colleagues over many years at Lancaster University in the UK. By 'methodology' Checkland (2011) means a set of guiding principles: *there is no fixed, single method*. The principles involve much iteration. For introductory purposes, they are used more simply in the example of a tennis club in which you are cast in the role of the problem-solver.

Scenario: The tennis club

A tennis club run by volunteers provides free coaching for youngsters in a deprived area. The club is successful at fundraising and gaining sponsorship but there is a high turnover of members: youngsters leave as quickly as others join. A voluntary committee, chaired by Ken, runs the club; the club's coaches are also volunteers and some were once professional tennis players. Ken wants to curb the high turnover of youngsters. He knows you're studying business and management and thinks you might be able to help. Ken is the 'client' and the 'problem-holder' – the person who wants something done.

The committee includes Mark, a marketing consultant, who is highly respected because of his skill in fundraising, attracting sponsorship from local companies and producing publicity material that brings in new youngsters. Ken thinks Mark's publicity may be attracting new members who have unrealistic sporting expectations as a result of Mark's marketing messages, however. Ken takes an informal approach to chairing the committee, believing that his key task is to keep the committee members and coaches happy and committed.

You agree to help, and set to work. First you find out as much about the club as you can. You know there are likely to be a number of issues that contribute to the high turnover; indeed, turnover may be a symptom of deeper problems. You put aside what the problem *might* be while you do your fact-finding, however.

Most committee members and some coaches tell you that their goal is helping youngsters to acquire life skills such as discipline through 'playing by the rules' and practice. Some coaches disagree, believing they are helping youngsters to realise their sporting potential. The role of the coaches is important and several have an exceptional ability to engage the youngsters. Ken has no formal authority but is experienced in avoiding conflict; some committee members and coaches find this difficult because it often results in a lack of opportunity to discuss improvements in the way the club operates.

In your discussions with the youngsters you find that some aspire to applying for the free scholarships that a new tennis academy is offering in the town; others enjoy what the club currently offers. Those who intend to leave say the club doesn't offer enough coaching or that there is too much emphasis on tennis and not enough on the social activity.

Mark's view is that the club is poorly managed, has unclear objectives and doesn't take proper account of the new academy's offer to promising young players. He says he has to make many decisions independently because the committee doesn't engage much with what he does; most meetings focus on day-to-day concerns. Mark's publicity material emphasises sport because that is the distinctive function of the club, he says.

Joan, a committee member who manages the coaches, is uncomfortable in her role. She admits to focusing on the coaching rotas. She knows coaches have different views about their work but 'they all have good intentions'. Besides, coaches who can work with often difficult-to-manage youngsters are hard to find.

You consider the whole situation of the club and its components: structural elements that don't change much, such as the committee, activities and processes and how they interact. You also consider the roles people play, how performance is monitored, how 'power' works in the club and who possesses it, who the stakeholders are, the individuals and their views, and the conflicts.

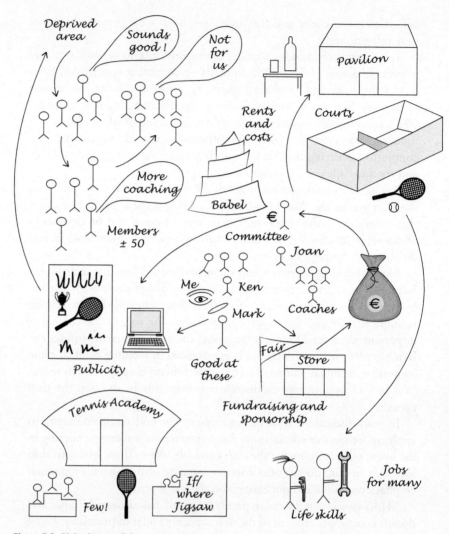

Figure 7.2 Rich picture of the tennis club

Without thinking about systems or trying to define what the problem might be, you draw a 'rich picture' of the tennis club (shown in Figure 7.2) identifying everything you think is relevant. Ideally, you would have liked to draw the picture with others in the club to capture their representations. Instead of the rich picture, you could have listed a few short statements but you find it easy to work visually.

Then you step back, away from the real world. You want to consider particular 'systems of interest'. You derive the following ones from your rich picture:

- a system to meet the needs of youngsters
- a system to ensure a shared vision and values

- a system to manage coaches
- a system to raise funds
- a system to produce and approve publicity to attract and retain members.

Each system of interest involves some kind of transformation of inputs to outputs. To make sure you can describe each system of interest comprehensively but concisely you create a 'root definition' for each one. You identify:

- the **customers**, clients or beneficiaries of the transformation
- *who* is involved in the transformation (the **'actors'**)
- the **transformation** – *what* is changed and how
- **why this is worthwhile** – the values and thinking that justify the transformation
- who could stop an activity (the **problem owner**)
- anything in the **environment** that might restrict or constrain the activities.

You know that each system of interest can be considered from various perspectives. Perspectives on what to do, how to do it and why something is done will be different for, say, the coaches and their manager. You also consider the performance of the activity by assessing efficacy – the power or capacity to do something; efficiency (how economically resources are used to meet an objective) and effectiveness (how well the objectives are met). These are known as the '3Es'. In the management of the coaches, for example, the manager needs the capacity to manage volunteers; the main resource is time, and the effectiveness of the management needs to be measured.

Then, for each system of interest you model an *ideal* system. The first one is a system for producing and approving publicity from the perspective of the person carrying out the activities. For *this* system you make the following identifications:

Customers: youngsters in the community
Actors: publicity producer; committee
Transformation: club's mission transformed into appropriate, attractive messages
Why it's worthwhile (world view): to improve the life chances of deprived youngsters
Owner: committee
Environment: reductions in funding; lack of cheap or free advertising space.

When drawn up, your ideal system looks something like Figure 7.3. It has a boundary around the ideal system; monitoring and control of the activities lie outside the boundary.

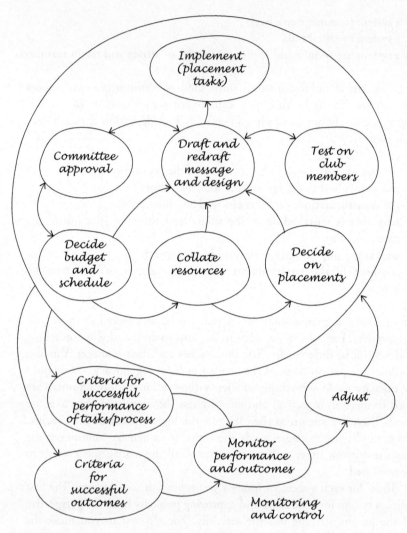

Figure 7.3 A system to produce and approve publicity

Your 'ideal systems' are drawn quite simply and quickly, as in Figure 7.3. You carry on until you have several ideal systems. One is a system for ensuring a shared vision and values. It involves establishing (and regularly refreshing) the club's mission and values. It has components for the induction of volunteers, monitoring, performance measures and regular feedback from youngsters.

Then you take your drawings to Ken. You plan to use your 'models' to discuss with him, the committee and coaches how the 'real world' of the club behaves, the ways in which it differs from the models and the improvements that can be made in the real world. Most committee members and coaches are delighted with the opportunity to discuss the models. Ken notes their insights, suggestions and enthusiasm; he supports the idea of changes that he didn't envisage at the outset, realising that they can be addressed constructively. You then adapt your 'ideal' models on the basis of the discussions, hoping the club will work out how to implement the changes for themselves.

This example has covered briefly the key steps in Checkland's SSM model (2011, 2000; Checkland and Winter, 2006). These are set out below.

Key steps

Identify the problem situation and express it. Decide what you want to explore *without* defining what you think the problem is; rather, consider your general area of interest.

Identify everything you think is relevant: the structures (things that don't change much), activities, processes and connections including performance monitoring, power hierarchies, stakeholders, people, their views and conflicts. Checkland (2000) suggests you identify key players, roles and culture, and power/politics, as set out below. If you don't then interventions to improve the system may themselves cause problems.

1. The *problem-solver* (who carries out the analysis) and the *problem owner* (who wants something done and may also be the client, although there may be a number of problem owners). Problem owners are a good source of ideas.
2. The *roles or social positions* regarded as significant by those in the problem situation, the *behaviours* expected of the role-holders and how the *performance of the role* is judged. In the example, Ken is the chairperson but he has no formal authority; he is expected to lead the club informally with the support of the committee. The performance of a role is judged informally or not at all. Organisational history informs roles, behaviours and judgements. This analysis helps you to anticipate later difficulties in any system changes. In the example, the club might not welcome too much formalisation.
3. The *attributes that are needed* for a person to be powerful, for example, *formal authority, intellectual authority, skill, experience, charisma* and so on. These identify the local politics. This analysis tells you who has the power to ensure change and to make it happen. In the example, Ken has the most power to ensure change but he relies on the co-operation of others, while Mark's professional skills give him intellectual authority which others are reluctant to challenge.

Then draw a rich picture or informal diagram to show the important elements of the situation *but without defining the problem*. Rich pictures are unstructured and indicate the situation's many elements. Checkland and Winter (2006) suggest including as many as possible. You should include yourself in the rich picture but without drawing it from your own perspective. If you do, you risk ignoring other perspectives. In the rich picture in Figure 7.2, the problem-solver is depicted as an eye close to Ken, suggesting a perspective sympathetic to that of Ken, the problem owner. Roles may be quite easy to capture while values, norms and how power is expressed may be quite difficult. Nonetheless, they need to be borne in mind. The convention in SSM is to hand-draw diagrams but rich pictures are not essential: a few short descriptive statements can serve instead.

Understand the concepts that it's possible to extract from the rich picture. Here you move away from the real world to conceptual systems thinking. Using your rich picture, you try to understand the systems of interest that can be *derived from* it.

You identify some systems of interest and list these, beginning each with the phrase *A system to ...* You then identify the important elements of each one using what is called the CATWOE analysis. The key element, T, is a transformation in which an input is transformed into an output. The other element of importance is W, the reason for the transformation – what makes it worthwhile. This analysis, which provides a *root definition*, shows the perspective of the situation from a single standpoint.

Because you are in the conceptual world, you can trial different CATWOE identifications. For example, Joan does not have to be the 'actor' who manages the coaches if, ideally, another actor is better positioned and able to do it. However, the real-world situation inevitably informs your identifications although it should not dominate them.

Table 7.2 sets out the CATWOE elements to be identified. Note that the examples in column two are generic and unrelated to a particular system of interest.

Table 7.2 The CATWOE analysis

	What it stands for	Examples
C	**Customers**/clients who benefit (or are harmed) by the transformation	Primarily the youngsters from the deprived area; the community
A	**Actors** involved in the transformation of inputs to outputs; they can be actively involved or cause activities to happen	Ken, the committee members, the coaches
T	**Transformation** of inputs to outputs (what are changed, into what, and how)	Youngsters without life skills are transformed into those with life skills by using sport and club membership as a proxy
W	**World view** (the values and thinking that justify the transformation and make it worthwhile)	All youngsters deserve opportunities to learn life skills and realise their sporting potential
O	**Owners** of the problem who have power and could cause an activity to cease	Ken, primarily, but also the committee
E	**Environment** that might restrict or constrain activities; it is difficult to influence or change but exerts influence	Sponsors; parents who allow their children to attend the club; owners of the facilities the club uses; existence of the tennis academy

Table 7.3 Levels of *Why, What* and *How* for the coaches and their manager

Manager		Coaches	
R Why	To fulfil club's mission		
P What	Manage the coaches effectively	R Why	Belief in the club's mission
Q How	Tasks to ensure that coaches 'transform' youngsters	P What	Coach the youngsters
		Q How	Teach, demonstrate, encourage, guide, advise, etc.

The 'level' of the transformation in the system differs according to perspectives. In the tennis club example, the inputs for the manager are unmanaged coaches and the outputs are happy, well-managed ones who fulfil their roles in line with the club's mission. The coaches' inputs are youngsters with few skills and the outputs are youngsters with improved life skills. Checkland (2000) suggests a 'PQR' check that identifies: *what* to do (P); *how* to do it (Q) and *why* to do it (R), that is, do P by Q to achieve R. So when you conceptualise a system for doing P, you consider the system levels above and below P from a given perspective.

Table 7.3 shows the *Why, What* and *How* for the coaches and their manager. R, *why* the transformation is made, normally includes the problem owner who could stop the activity. Q, *how*, includes all the activities that transform the input into the output.

Together, the CATWOE and PQR identifications describe a system of interest, its subsystems and the wider perspective. Each system of interest is then studied in terms of three Es.

1. Efficacy (the power or capacity to do something).
2. Efficiency (how economically this is done in terms of resources).
3. Effectiveness (how well the objectives are achieved).

In a system to manage the coaches and their activities, a manager relying on informal power needs good leadership and 'people' skills. Managing the volunteers may be more costly in terms of time than other resources but time needs to be managed productively. Effectiveness depends on the coaches' skill and their management and requires some kind of measurement.

The three Es can suggest how you might test different CATWOE identifications to improve efficacy, efficiency and effectiveness.

You then use the root definitions that your CATWOE and PQR analyses have provided for each system of interest in the construction of your conceptual models, which comes next.

Compile a conceptual model. Draw one or more conceptual models using your root definitions as in Figure 7.3. Remember you are in the conceptual world so your diagram won't reflect what currently happens in the 'real-world' situation (but may be influenced by it). Your aim is to produce a diagram of a *conceptually* *ideal* system for doing something (*A system to ...*) regardless of what is *actually* done. As well as showing key components and their interconnections, your model should indicate resources, decisions, and performance assessment.

Checkland (2000) suggests that models are confined to 7±2 components and drawn quickly by hand. His method is:

- Identify all the activities that can be done at the same time and which aren't dependent on one another.
- Draw these in a line and label them using action verbs such as decide, carry out, use, identify and so on. The bottom row in Figure 7.3 shows this (although *Committee approval* could be included in this row, too, and labelled *Seek committee approval*).
- Above this line, draw in activities that depend on the ones below and draw arrows to indicate dependencies.
- Above *this* line, draw in any further activities – ones that depend on those in the row below and, again, draw arrows to indicate dependencies.
- Add more lines as necessary to indicate dependencies.
- Redraw the diagram so that, ideally, the arrows don't cross.
- Finally, draw a boundary around the components and, outside the boundary, add components to show how the activities are monitored and controlled.

Compare your model/s with the real-world situation – what exists – and consider what is desirable and feasible to change. Normally you use your conceptual model(s) for discussion with key actors in the real-world situation. These discussions reveal the way in which the real-world situation behaves, how it differs from the conceptual models and where real-world improvements could be made. The conceptual models are not 'correct' ones but vehicles for debate and insight among those who could, or could help to make improvements that are desired and culturally feasible.

Changes may not be confined to process changes but may include shifts in outlook or attitudes. An example of a change in attitude in the tennis club scenario would be Joan's realisation that the 'good intentions' of tennis coaches are the foundation for managing them effectively rather than justification for not managing them.

An alternative to discussion is to compare each component in your conceptual model with the real-world situation and ask: *Does the real-world situation behave like the conceptual model?*

To identify desirable and feasible changes, Checkland (2000) suggests a series of questions to ask:

- What combination of structural, process and attitudinal change is needed? Why?
- How can it be achieved?
- What enabling action is required?
- Who will take the actions? When?
- What criteria will judge success/lack of it and completion?

In the tennis club example, the real-world situation is that Mark's publicity campaigns are successful but are off-message because there is no oversight by the club's committee; the club's committee also appears to evaluate the effectiveness of campaigns purely on the number of new members. There is also no consensus among the coaches on the transformation they are trying to bring about with the youngsters and the lack of management exacerbates this problem. A fundamental issue is how the committee operates: poor management, lack of oversight and a lack of appropriate performance measurements are tolerated. *Ideally*, structural, processual and attitudinal changes are needed to bring about change here, led by Ken who might or might not agree. He might be persuaded if he can see that changes will have a positive impact on the youngsters the club tries to help. Alternatively, he might step aside to allow the election of another chairperson who can lead and enable improvements, perhaps with different actors taking responsibility for various actions. Thus, intervention can be a problem in itself, something soft systems practitioners take into account early on when considering roles, culture, power and local politics.

A graphic summary

The process of SSM is summarised in Figure 7.4 based on Checkland's latest four-phase methodology (2011).

Think in terms of systems

Using SSM is not easy but the more practice you have the easier it will be to 'think in terms of systems'.

> **ACTIVITY 7.4** Carry out this activity with a fellow student. *Individually*, choose a system of interest from the list in the tennis club example and carry out the CATWOE, PQR and three Cs analyses, making sensible assumptions where information is lacking. Then draw up an *ideal* system, devising suitable system components and interconnections.
>
> When you have done this, ask your companion to adopt the role of the problem owner in your ideal system and discuss it with him or her. Do the same for your companion. What modifications do you need to make to your ideal system following the discussion? You might need to change one or more of the CATWOE identifications along with some system components.
>
> The simplest system of interest to model is that of managing the coaches. Arguably the most important ideal system to devise is one to ensure a shared vision and values.

This activity is designed to help you to conceptualise an ideal system using a logical framework while realising that the process is not a rigid one. Don't spend too long drawing up your model because, like professional practitioners, you may need to redraw it a number of times, testing out different problem owners, actors and so

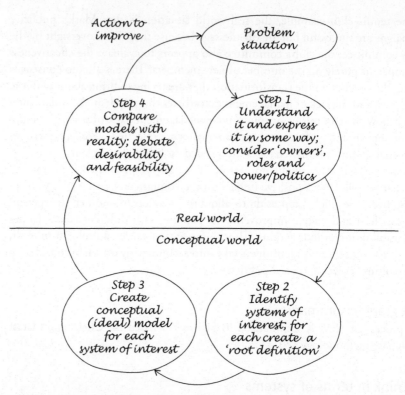

Figure 7.4 A graphic summary of SSM

on. There is always more than one way to sort out a muddle and the appropriate one in the real world depends on the people involved, the culture and the politics.

SSM is complex but offers a structured approach to soft systems improvement. Critics point to the difficulties of using it in situations where there are no clear goals. It can also be hard to agree on the nature of the problem, making it difficult to 'locate', and often one view or solution will ultimately prevail. This can leave some system participants or stakeholders unhappy. However, in the social care example at the beginning of the section, specific goals were probably not defined until the systems were studied in order to locate the problems. Further, some political stakeholders may not have been happy to find that targets were more a hindrance than a help.

SSM provides a way of looking at and understanding systems: a foundation for day-to-day systems thinking. When you are studying, take a systems view of activities you read about or are involved in. Getting into the *habit* of systems thinking prepares you for the workplace where it will be truly welcomed.

Creative thinking

It's 2050. The world population is 9.3 billion, 2.3 billion more than now; there has been rapid urbanisation and most people live in high-density cities where services are concentrated. Climate change has put pressure on resources: products and services that emit CO_2 and other greenhouse gases can't be used; competition for resources has led to conflict; parts of the world are uninhabitable because of desertification and rising sea levels. Further, the negative impact of the loss of biodiversity and fragility of water resources was acknowledged too late by national governments, changing ecosystems and the geo-political landscape.

Travel has been transformed: the passenger airline industry has survived with the development of electric aircraft; other forms of urban, national and international public transport are thriving but infrastructure costs are crippling.

Land use and food production have undergone significant change: meat is disappearing from diets and cities boast urban growing spaces run by co-operatives. Micro-production of both food and energy produces half of all needs. Sea fisheries have collapsed as a result of the acidification of oceans. Health services as we know them are unaffordable and are now often run by co-operatives, interest groups and volunteers. The emphasis is on keeping healthy, helped by wearable technology that indicates when medical intervention is needed.

Work has changed. 'Career' jobs are few, mostly in the technology and knowledge industries. Crowd-sourcing is a feature of the social and business landscape and many people have a variety of 'micro' jobs earning small amounts of money this way. Production systems have changed with the development of 3-D printing, which now uses recycled materials. Taxation is based on the resources used in products and services. The gap between rich and poor has grown but violence has given way to increased democratisation: technology allows ordinary people to participate in political decision-making. Technology has revolutionised education too; learning is tailored to individuals and, among adults, peer-to-peer learning is the norm for developing skills. Technology itself has benefited from the successes of science: the devices that have replaced your smart phone no longer contain finite resources such as tungsten and gold. 'Sustainability thinking' has become commonplace.

Many features of this scenario are predicted by the United Nations (Clark, 2012), climate scientists and technologists. Some but not all predictions will be correct. The point is not the accuracy of the predictions, however. It is that huge change is anticipated: what do we need to consider, plan or change *now* to meet the challenges? What if, currently, you produce and export mineral water, or import coffee? What if you are involved in healthcare, education or crowd-sourcing?

ACTIVITY 7.5 With a group of fellow students, consider three factual aspects of the scenario: climate change, population growth and the development of technology. How do you think these will affect at least two areas of life set out in Table 7.4? Key issues are affordability and environmental sustainability (using no more resources than can be easily replaced).

Table 7.4 Areas of life to consider

Lifestyle	Products	Transport
Health	Services	Energy
Social care	Housing	Communications
Education	Technology	Politics
Food production	Work	Social organisation

'Lifestyle' includes leisure/social time, domestic and family life. Social organisation refers to relationships between individuals and groups including levels of co-operation, networking and division of labour. Make your responses concrete and consider the impact of a change in one area of life on another, for example, changes in transport affect work, service provision and consumption. State

- your assumptions
- the changes you envisage
- the implications for organisations now.

An example is given for transport.

Example

Assumptions. Recycling and renewable energy have a resource cost so it is assumed that transport, for example, will be expensive. Infrastructure costs of high-tech alternative forms of travel will be unaffordable unless some existing infrastructure can be (re)used. People need to live as near to work and services as possible to reduce travel but the need and desire for travel won't disappear.

Changes. Most people live in cities; successful cities offer a good quality of life. Expensive air travel is complemented by ultra-high-speed rail-type travel powered by renewable energy, generated in the Sahara, for example, but it's not fully developed because of cost. Sea travel has a new lease of life. High-speed public transport in cities means that cars aren't needed; driverless cars take the place of taxis and are used communally or for car-sharing. Rural transport is a problem: more services need to be delivered using technology and by community groups.

Implications for organisations. Construction industry/politicians need to consider housing in conjunction with new forms of work, quality of life, including access to recreational space, services and food-production needs. Rail transport providers need to think about cheap, ultra-fast local, national and international transport and infrastructure. Companies that construct and maintain road infrastructure need to think about major changes to their business in the long term (10–20 years).

Car manufacturers need to consider what fewer cars will mean; perhaps manufacturers could be central to car-sharing or community-owned cars.

Governments need to develop international power grids and invest in social capacity-building so that rural communities are sustainable.

The airline industry needs to speed up research and development in order to survive; an additional business could be servicing 'production islands' – flying-in the necessary equipment for remote solar energy production, for example, to avoid the need to build road/rail infrastructure. Shipping and ferry companies need to prepare scenarios in which fewer goods and more people travel by sea.

There are no correct or incorrect responses for Activity 7.5, except that 'business as usual' is not an option. The point of the activity is to emphasise rapid change and the need to be innovative and flexible. The *same* goods and services may not be needed. Some changes will be evolutionary – incremental or bit-by-bit – while others will be revolutionary, that is, radical ones involving discontinuity. What kind of thinking is needed to produce these innovations and how will organisations ensure that they have the capacity to innovate? Creative thinking is a fundamental part of the answer.

Five steps

Different theories of creativity have placed emphasis on the characteristics of creative people, the process of creative thinking, the context in which it occurs (the climate and circumstances) and the product in terms of turning a creative idea into reality. While people are naturally creative, it helps if you can:

- tolerate ambiguity and complexity
- find new perspectives
- challenge assumptions and received wisdom
- take risks
- accept failure and mistakes as a normal part of being creative.

Being objective and thinking logically are important, too, because creative thinking is not just about dreaming up novel ideas. Other skills include presenting ideas and being able to mobilise resources, including other people. Implementing creative ideas demands knowledge and skill. Most writers on creative thinking incorporate some or all of these elements. Typically they emphasise these five steps.

Step 1: Gain as much knowledge as possible about the situation or issue. While new perspectives and novel ideas may arise through *absence* of knowledge, they are unlikely to proceed beyond being unfocused ideas. You need good understanding of a situation or issue to be able to recognise novel perspectives and why an idea might be useful. Make sense of any new information. Interpret, organise and combine it with your existing knowledge. It is important to be open and to retain information that doesn't 'fit', however. Use critical thinking and questioning to seek and explore information. What you are doing is preparing to pose *the right sorts* of questions, those that are most likely to produce creative answers.

Step 2: Consider the situation or issue. This is the step where creative thinking is concentrated. Different theorists have different ideas about what you might do and all of the ideas are useful. Try these methods for *generating* ideas. (Don't select or evaluate any ideas at this stage; simply generate and explore as many ideas as possible.) Make a note of them, resisting the temptation to dismiss those that challenge your existing knowledge or beliefs or that seem ridiculous. Don't stop when you generate a first 'good' idea. Be willing to 'play' with ideas.

Reframe the situation or issue to gain new perspectives on it

Examples from art show how this works. Consider painting a picture of a chair. You could simply paint the structural elements but, equally, you could paint the spaces between the elements or the scene around and through the chair's structure. You could consider just the colour or light. You might think about how the chair feels to sit on and try to capture subjective sensations in colour, or consider how a chair is moved and try to capture movements. Aspects of its 'cradle to grave' life cycle might be interesting to consider, too. Each perspective triggers a different way of thinking about 'depicting a chair'.

The idea of reframing is to consider as many perspectives as you can. James Dyson, who developed the first cyclone vacuum cleaner, could have viewed the problem of clogged dust filters as 'just' a problem with filters. Instead he viewed it as one of separating dust from air. Reframing can involve asking new questions. For example, if the problem is how to provide a service, you can ask how people could *avoid needing* the service.

Synthesis or combination

You can generate ideas by combining ones. Take a look at your smart phone. It probably does nothing more than you could do before with separate components such as a computer, satellite navigation, a camera and so on. The new idea was to bring various technologies together. Cash-free money transactions and parcel tracking by consumers were enabled by technology but relied on a synthesis of ideas. Try combining ideas that are not obviously related to see what possibilities arise. New ideas don't have to be big to make a difference: a small change can have a significant impact.

Reapplication

This involves taking an existing solution and reapplying it to a new problem. Dyson solved his problem of separating dust from air by using the idea of cyclones that separated sawdust from air in sawmills. Biologists realised that an algorithm created by forensic scientists to locate serial killers could be developed to locate endangered wildlife and assess population sizes. The world and organisations are full of existing solutions that can be applied to other contexts. Curiosity and knowledge are important here so that you are aware of how problems have been solved previously. You also need to be able to recognise the potential for reapplication.

Metaphor

We often emphasise the difference between things to help us to focus on what distinguishes one thing from another. A metaphor does the opposite: a word, phrase or image is used in place of what we mean, in a non-literal way, to emphasise similarity and offer insights. Everyday examples include *branch office*, using the metaphor of a tree to convey something of an organisation's structure. The usefulness of metaphors depends on what is identified as being of interest: your mind is prepared to see a link. Taiichi Ohno, a creator of the Toyota production system, saw supermarkets as a system in which customers take an item from a shelf and the item is immediately replaced. For him, this was a metaphor for ideal car production.

Step 3: Let go of the problem or issue. So far you have been using your conscious mind, even if in a free-ranging way. Now it's time to let your unconscious mind take over for a while. No one is sure why this helps. A useful analogy is trying to recall a person's name. When you stop thinking about it, the name springs unbidden to your mind. It has been found that being tired or slightly distracted or just lying down seems to help the unconscious mind take over. It may be that these 'loosen' attention so that the more peripheral aspects of a situation are not ignored. It can be useful to use this step after Step 1, too, as preparation for Step 2, if you find it hard to adopt the less-controlled thinking that ideas generation involves.

Step 4: Return to the problem and the ideas you generated. For this step you use critical thinking, including logic. Evaluate each idea for its usefulness, viability and feasibility in addressing the situation or issue. Work on the ideas that remain after this process: consider how they could work. Finally, select one. If none is viable, then return to Steps 1 and 2. Missing information is often more easily identified at this point and can help you to reframe the issue. Accept 'failure' and iteration as normal.

See *Logical reasoning* and *Critical thinking* in Chapter 6

Step 5: Plan and implement the idea; monitor the implementation. This is the innovation stage, where an idea is turned into reality. For small, incremental changes this step is the same as for problem-solving. For larger ones and radical innovations and changes, it is the major part in the creative process. Dyson, for example, needed to adapt his cyclone idea for vacuum cleaners to produce a commercially viable product. That involved a good deal more creative thinking and innovation. Radical innovation that is 'new to the world' is often undertaken by project teams.

See *Using critical thinking for investigations* in Chapter 6

Note how creative thinking cycles its way through being creative and being critical, evaluative and analytical. At times you need the highly focused attention involved in being analytical and critical. You avoid irrelevant information. At other times you need a wider focus of attention to embrace seemingly irrelevant information as you take a broader, less-controlled search for solutions. The cognitive flexibility needed to do this is a rare skill – and so a highly desirable one in workplaces.

Climate for creativity and innovation

Creative thinking occurs more readily and easily in some organisations than in others. This is because creativity and innovation require an appropriate environment in which to flourish. Hierarchical, 'command and control' organisations are least likely to possess this. Creative thinking and innovation are fostered in organisations where there is willingness and readiness to change; quality of work is valued; new ideas are welcomed and received in a non-judgemental way; staff are trusted; and there is practical support for developing and implementing ideas.

Organisations that rely on radical innovation to remain ahead of competitors do more than this and do it strategically: they aim to create and use knowledge (of markets and of their own operations and processes); they actively encourage staff to challenge what is currently done; they expect individuals to take initiative and responsibility; they guide and support the development of new ideas; they create momentum to push innovation and overcome resistance. Such organisations have 'innovation capability', which is difficult to create and even more difficult for competitors to copy.

While ideas are often produced by staff, highly creative, committed and persistent individuals may work alone to innovate, that is, to carry through creative ideas, securing the support and resources they need. Increasingly, however, project teams do this. The originator of an idea may or may not lead the team and may not even be a team member. Research by Kelley and colleagues (2011) shows that this is primarily because cross-functional knowledge about the organisation is needed, along with experience in bringing major innovation projects to fruition (and knowing when to 'kill them off'). Making an idea a reality demands more than the skills of an ideas generator. The innovator needs:

- drive, vision, passion and intrinsic motivation
- commitment to the organisation's overall objectives
- a diverse outlook
- a general aptitude for radical innovation, not just for a single project
- technical knowledge with an understanding of what's important to customers, users or clients
- cross-disciplinary knowledge
- the ability to draw from diverse sources.

Needless to say, innovators are in shorter supply than creative thinkers. Most of the necessary skills and knowledge, however, can be acquired provided you are committed, passionate and know how to use your curiosity to gain knowledge and 'see' opportunities.

ACTIVITY 7.6 Consider your work or study environment. Is it one in which creative thinking flourishes or not? To consider why this might be, see how many of these features apply to the environment you are considering:

- the quality of work is valued
- new ideas are welcomed
- people are non-judgemental about new ideas
- people are trusted
- there is practical support for developing and implementing ideas
- there is active encouragement to challenge
- people are expected to take initiatives and responsibility
- people receive guidance and support.

If many of these features apply then the environment is one in which creativity and innovation flourish. If few of them apply consider why they don't. If you considered your university environment, you probably found that some but not all applied: students can't normally develop and implement their innovative ideas about assessment, for example, but you might be able to suggest ideas.

Managing innovation team leaders

Innovators usually need support. This is because there can be tension between accountability to the organisation and the autonomy required to make progress with a project. This tension can be reduced by the skills of a good manager and, in professional life, you may find yourself in this role. Kelley and colleagues (2011) found that effective managers of innovation team leaders used a combination of 'hands off' and 'hands on' management, always allowing the innovator to make decisions but getting involved in detail. Other activities included:

- championing projects – supporting, protecting and defending them and acting as an informal sponsor while keeping failure quiet
- 'path clearing' to aid a project's progress
- giving legitimacy to projects
- using political leverage and control over resources
- providing advice and connections
- hand-holding – product innovators can feel lost because a market doesn't yet exist
- keeping team leaders focused
- guiding problem-solving and decision-making when necessary
- bringing oversight and discipline to the process of innovation
- monitoring progress against milestones
- evaluating with formal reviews.

Developing the skills and knowledge both of innovators and their managers while you are studying is difficult, but you can lay down foundational skills by practising when you are working on problems or scenarios. Whenever innovation is required, consider what innovators need and how the organisation and an innovator's manager can respond so that the innovation is successful. You may also need at least some elements of this when you work with other students on learning tasks when you want the group or team to be as innovative as possible. Working with others is the subject of the next chapter.

Chapter summary

❖ Complex thinking involves many other types. The chapter covers:
  • ethical thinking
  • systems thinking
  • creative thinking.

You can practise these types of thinking as you study, particularly when you are problem-solving or working on cases and scenarios.

❖ Ethical thinking is required in workplaces. Morality is different from etiquette, law and religion: moral principles have consequences to human welfare, animals and the environment. Philosophers are interested in how our moral values or standards are justified.

❖ Can organisations be 'moral' if they are driven by self-interest and the profit motive? CSR refers to the voluntary responsibility organisations take for the impact of their activities on society and the environment. But do they do this simply to avoid state regulation?

❖ The role of individual employees is important to business ethics. You take your own moral code to work with you. But it's easy not to use it: people can fail to question or become socialised into the way things are done in the organisation.

❖ Business ethics focuses on the 'three Cs' (compliance, contribution and consequences) but to fully apply them individuals need to recognise ethical issues, fact-find, weigh up alternative actions, decide, act and reflect on the outcome. You do this by asking questions systematically.

❖ Systems thinking is highly valued by organisations but rarely taught to business and management students. SSM is complex but worth mastering: who would not want to do more with less or to achieve it more sustainably and ethically?

❖ Systems have particular characteristics; the defining one is that they are not reducible to any one part. Systems often have many subsystems and 'layers'.

❖ System problems can lie in a system's components or in its interconnections. Without proper consideration, interventions can have unintended consequences elsewhere.

❖ When you analyse part of a 'soft' human activity system you identify the *who, what and why* and performance. Then you model one or more ideal systems to compare with what actually happens. It is an iterative process. Organisations need systems thinkers to help them solve problems and to improve or change activity systems.

❖ Creative thinking is vital not only in product and service innovation but in addressing pressing issues such climate change and population growth and in making use of technological developments. What sorts of changes do organisations need to make?

❖ Creative thinking involves more than dreaming up novel ideas using techniques such as reframing, synthesis of existing ideas or reapplication of an existing solution.

❖ Critical thinking and logic are essential in order to recognise when and why a novel perspective might be useful and to evaluate ideas.

❖ Innovation is the stage when the idea is turned into reality. For large and radical changes, this is the major part of the creative process. It requires further skills and knowledge.

❖ Organisations that rely on innovation encourage staff to challenge what is currently done. When you are solving problems or cases as part of your studies, it is useful to understand creative thinking.

❖ Creative thinkers and innovators are needed by organisations and in your professional life you might be required to manage them – or to develop the skills, knowledge and attributes to be one.

References

Checkland, P. (2000) 'Soft systems methodology: a thirty-year retrospective', *Systems Research and Behavioural Science*, vol.17, no. S1, pp. 11–58.

Checkland, P. (2011) 'Autobiographical retrospectives: learning your way to "action to improve" – the development of soft systems thinking and soft systems methodology', *International Journal of General Systems*, vol. 40, no. 5, pp. 487–512 [Online]. DOI: 10.1080/03081079.2011.571437 (Accessed 20 April 2016).

Checkland, P. and Winter, M. (2006) 'Process and content: two ways of using SSM', *Journal of Operational Research Society*, vol. 47, no. 12, pp. 1435–1441.

Clark, H. (2012) 'Our world in 2050: more equitable and sustainable – or less?' Address to the World Affairs Council of Northern California, 7 November 2012, San Francisco, California.

Dowie, M. (1977) *Pinto madness*, Mother Jones, September/October [Online]. Available at www.motherjones.com/politics/1977/09/pinto-madness (Accessed 20 April 2016).

Kelley D.J., O'Connor, G.C., Neck, H. and Peters L. (2011) 'Building an organizational capability for radical innovation: the direct managerial role', *Journal of Engineering and Technology Management – JET-M*, vol. 28, no. 4, pp. 249–267.

Reynolds, M. and Holwell, S. (2010) 'Introducing systems approaches', in Reynolds, M. and Holwell, S. (eds), *Systems approaches to managing change: a practical guide*, London, Springer, pp. 1–23.

Santa Clara University (2015) 'A framework for ethical decision making', Markkula Center for Applied Ethics. Primary contributors include Manuel Velasquez, Dennis Moberg, Michael J. Meyer, Thomas Shanks, Margaret R. McLean, David DeCosse, Claire André, and Kirk O. Hanson [Online]. Available at www.scu.edu/ethics/ethics-resources/ethical-decision-making/a-framework-for-ethical-decision-making/ (Accessed 20 April 2016).

Seddon, J. and Caulkin, S. (2007) 'Systems thinking, lean production and action learning', *Action Research Research and Practice*, vol. 4, no. 1, pp. 9–24 [Online]. DOI: 10.1080/14767330701231438 (Accessed 20 April 2016).

Smith, A. (1776/1904) *An inquiry into the nature and causes of the wealth of nations*. Cannan, E. (ed), 5th edn, London, Methuen and Co Ltd [Online]. Available at www.econlib.org/library/Smith/smWNCover.html (Accessed 20 April 2016).

CHAPTER EIGHT

Working with others

You may not consider yourself to be very knowledgeable right now but you are! Much of your knowledge is not academic and has not come from formal education: it has come from living in a socially and culturally organised world and your interactions with other people, your observations of them and from imitating or modelling their behaviour. Without realising it, you've acquired much know-how from these social learning processes.

> **ACTIVITY 8.1** Think of something you learned outside formal education, for example, how to use your first mobile phone, organising a gap year or volunteering. How much of your learning involved interaction with others? List the types of social interaction with other people – formal and informal – that it involved.

You are likely to have included talking and listening to other people, being shown or watching and then copying. Some research and reading may have been necessary but when, for example, people buy a new phone, reading the instructions is often the last thing they do. Reading is simply one-way interaction with others, of course.

In workplaces, most learning is done using social processes, informally and formally: you learn how an organisation works by talking to people and by observation. You find out the best way to do something by discussing it with others or being shown. You hone your leadership skills by modelling the behaviours of an effective leader. New staff may 'shadow' a more experienced person to learn how to do a job. You may be coached or mentored to develop knowledge and skills. Later, you may be expected to induct and develop new or less-experienced staff in these ways. Formal training and development is often reserved for teaching staff good practices (and ending the bad habits that staff have learned from each other). Even so, such courses are likely to involve role play and discussion. Thus, most organisations rely on social learning even when important knowledge needs to be transferred or exchanged.

Your learning progresses faster if you can work with other people effectively. Many universities recognise this and provide opportunities for collaborative work with your peers. To maximise your own learning (and that of others), however, you need communication and interpersonal skills and knowledge of techniques in order to make the best of collaboration. Peer-work can take many forms, formal and informal, and can involve just one other person right through to a large number, such as when you present your work to others and receive feedback. At undergraduate level, common causes of discontent in peer-work include questions and comments being expressed disrespectfully, people feeling ignored, unequal contribution, poor discipline and lack of preparation. Poor communication alone can result in poor-quality work outcomes. Communication isn't just talking about work; it *is* work.

Communication and interpersonal skills

Communication and interpersonal skills are essential for working with others. But, first, do you know how they work?

ACTIVITY 8.2

A group of colleagues meets informally to discuss an office move. Sam, the meeting organiser, has asked everyone to look at the plan and come to the meeting prepared with questions and comments. At the meeting Sam starts by asking people to call out their views and questions while he lists and organises them into topic groups on a white board.

The first topic to be discussed is the lack of information in the plan. Paula, Kaman and Artur remain silent for most of the meeting. Paula admits she hasn't seen the plan. Artur focuses on his smartphone. Marilena tries to explore the views of others but Sam prevents her, saying sharply that it's perfectly clear what people mean and the meeting must 'move on'. Several others contribute to the discussion only when 'their' questions come up.

At the end, Sam's attempts to summarise the discussion result in conflict: the summary doesn't reflect the views of participants and some of them protest. Kaman finally speaks and is highly critical of the issues people have raised, describing them as trivial. Most participants leave the meeting feeling that nothing has been achieved.

What kinds of communication and interpersonal problems can you identify in the scenario? How did Sam hinder the communication process? Can non-verbal behaviour send messages as clearly as verbal ones?

You probably identified the lack of opportunity for people to express their different views, gain feedback, listen to and understand the perspectives of others, ask questions of clarification and arrive at a consensus view. Sam hindered the process by limiting opportunities for exchanges and exploration of views. Artur's behaviour conveyed lack of interest.

This chapter covers the fundamental skills you need in order to work productively with others at university and at work.

Perspective-taking

When you say *That assignment was difficult* how do you know that another person understands your meaning? If the other person is a fellow student it's a safe assumption that they do, more or less. According to the widely accepted constructivist theory of communication, we individually make sense of our experiences, but we do so within a sociocultural context. Thus, our understandings are often similar to those of others in the same socio-ethnic culture.

There are always differences, however, because people don't have exactly the same experiences. Even apparent similarity is deceptive. You may enjoy alpine skiing in France while I enjoy white-water sports on the Noce River in the Italian Alps. Our experience and understanding of mountains is different but we might discuss our leisure activities without fully realising this. We both make assumptions; after all, aren't we talking about the same mountains? Now imagine you're an indigenous subsistence farmer in the Andes. I *know* your experience of mountains is different from mine but I don't know what your perspective is.

Understanding another's perspective involves empathy. It is different from sympathy, a predominantly emotional response (feelings of concern) rather than a largely cognitive one (involving understanding). The two are often confused, wrongly leading to warnings against having too much empathy.

Six steps to empathy

Frameworks for developing and using empathy are surprisingly few. The following is based on the work of Milton J. Bennett, a writer on intercultural sensitivity and communication over a number of decades.

1. **Assume everyone is different from you.** This sounds obvious but when we meet another person we often try to establish what we have in common. Differences emerge later, especially in romantic relationships! It helps to be curious about others: how does that elderly cyclist you see every day view car-owning? How do your fellow students from different cultures regard what you may take for granted, such as energy, food and water security, health care or education? What features of your own culture might other students find unusual? Is there any such thing as 'normal'?

2. **Know yourself.** Self-knowledge enables you to know your views and understand how you acquired them. Self-knowledge uncovers unfounded prejudices – fixed, incorrect views often based on untested assumptions about others – and prepares you to accept that there are perspectives other than your own. You may have assumed the elderly cyclist can't afford a car, for example. You may be intolerant of people without considering whether they had your opportunities or possess your capabilities.

See Recognising assumptions in Chapter 6

3. **Step into the other person's shoes.** When you talk to another person, focus on what the person says and means. Enter *his or her* world temporarily. To do this, put aside your own views, just as you may do when watching a film or reading a novel. Many people spend time in other cultures to do just this: they temporarily switch their frame of reference from their own culture to the new one.

4. **Check your understanding and be guided by correction.** Check your understanding of what the other person is saying. The usual way is to ask questions, such as: *So, am I right in thinking that your view is …?* Your questions are requests for feedback on your interpretation and you should be prepared to be corrected. In some cultures correcting others can be unacceptable so you may need to 'give permission'. You can add: *Please tell me if I've misunderstood; I won't be offended.*

5. **Construct the alternative view.** Use the information to construct the other person's view; it will be an approximation but it should be enough to develop understanding. If you and the other person have *exchanged* perspectives, you have a basis for shared understanding. This is often how reconciliation and peace-building programmes work to create tolerance between adversaries. The benefit of understanding an alternative perspective in both study and work situations is that you build trust and better relationships, gain knowledge and can more accurately predict a person's behaviour and responses.

6. **Step out of the other person's shoes.** Finally step back into your own shoes and 'unsuspend' your own perspective. Invariably, you find *something* has changed because being empathetic quickly extends your social, cultural, practical and self-knowledge. This happens when you reduce mental barriers to allow yourself to be receptive. You don't necessarily change your own perspective but you better understand those of others and can avoid or remedy misunderstandings that threaten your relationships with them.

Adapted from Bennett, 1986

Now try the six steps for yourself with a willing student or colleague who seems very different from you. A vital part of empathy is listening so you may want to read *Active listening* in this chapter before carrying out Activity 8.3.

ACTIVITY 8.3 Explain your aim to your fellow student or colleague and find an area of experience that is very different for you both. It could centre on conventions such as gift-giving or table manners at home. Individually, make a note of your own current perspective. Then use the six steps (you can do this in turn). At the end, review your initial perspective and whether it has changed. Consider, too, what you learned about the other person and whether you uncovered and overturned any assumptions you had.

The activity is invariably rewarding, provided you focus on differences rather than similarities (although it can be hard not to). The key to empathy is entering the other person's world and the essential component of this is active listening, covered later in this chapter.

Developing an international perspective

University is an ideal place to begin to develop a much-needed capability: the competence to work with people from other cultures. In doing so you develop a wider frame of reference than your own country, neighbourhood or workplace.

Organisations need employees who are able to work effectively across and within different cultures, but according to The British Council (2013) they often don't know how to describe their needs. They want employees who:

understand cultural differences	are aware of their own culture
accept cultural differences	are open to new ideas
are respectful	listen and observe
are multilingual	are flexible
adapt to different cultures	build trust
adjust their communication	tolerate ambiguity
can work in diverse teams	are continuous learners

The usual term to describe these attributes is *intercultural competence*. Governments, organisations and educational institutions require it because globalisation embraces more than international trade and investment: it also involves greater interdependence and integration and, with these, sociocultural transfers of knowledge and exchange of world views.

A major benefit that arises from interaction between people from different sociocultural, economic and political backgrounds is 'the potential for economic, social and personal development' according to Berggren and Nilsson (2015). At university, where you are likely to encounter students from many other cultures, you have the opportunity to work on the social and personal aspects of this development.

A developmental process

Intercultural competence is more than the possession of conventional knowledge. A widely accepted definition is 'the ability to effectively and appropriately interact in an intercultural situation or context' (Perry and Southwell, 2011). What is not so clear is how this competence is acquired. A developmental continuum – the idea of gradual, step-by-step acquisition by individuals – has been suggested by Wells (2000) based on a synthesis of the work of others. The steps are:

1. **Cultural incompetence** (the assumed starting point).
2. **Cultural knowledge** – understanding how culture shapes knowledge.
3. **Recognition** of the cultural implications of behaviours.
4. **Integration** of cultural knowledge and awareness into behaviours.
5. **Routine application** of culturally appropriate interventions and practices.
6. **Integration** of cultural competence into the culture of the organisation.

Progression is not automatic but requires conscious effort because of what's involved. Most researchers agree that intercultural competence is transformative, involving the whole of a person, including: *dispositional attributes* such as open-mindedness, tolerance of ambiguity and flexibility; *emotional components* such as motivation to understand and accept difference; curiosity, empathy and respect, as well as *cognitive and behaviour change*. All are needed in order to be interested in one's own and other cultures; how they differ; to be aware of assumptions, stereotypes, values and beliefs (one's own and those of other cultures); and to think and behave differently, appropriately and naturally.

Hammer (2012, 2011, 2009) and colleagues (2003; Bennett, 1993, 1987; Bennett and Bennett, 2004), developers of the Intercultural Development Inventory, set out the path that many individuals appear to take.

1. **Denial** – cultural differences are first overlooked, ignored or avoided; there is lack of interest in them and/or intentional separation to preserve the current world view.
2. **Polarisation** – people adopt a judgemental 'them and us' stance that can take
   i) a **defensive** form: an uncritical view of their own cultural values and practices and a critical view of the 'other' culture's values and practices ('them and us'); or
   ii) the **reversal** of this, whereby people are critical of their own culture and uncritical of the 'other' culture; this is sometimes called 'going native'.
3. **Minimisation** – people focus on similarity and universal values that may obscure fuller understanding and appreciation of cultural difference; there can

be an assumption that people's own world view and values are universally shared.

4. **Acceptance** of cultural differences (and commonalities). People realise their culture is just one of many different ones and that different world views exist within a context. There is respect and curiosity.

5. **Adaptation** – a perspective change that makes it possible for people to change their cultural perspective and behave in culturally appropriate ways – and do so with authenticity. There is empathy and the realisation that more than one world view can be held.

6. **Cultural disengagement** – here, people disengage or detach from their own primary cultural group in order to adopt a wider frame of reference. Bennett (1993) views disengagement as *integration* and the possession of a number of frames of reference from which to choose in a situation. Personal identity is not based on a single culture, giving people the freedom to construct their identity.

Thus, intercultural competence involves considerable gains.

The thinking required

Yershova and colleagues (2000) set out what they regard as three essential types of thinking required in the process.

1. **Culture-general knowledge** – gleaned from intercultural experience, to help people go beyond the cognitive, emotional and behavioural limits of their own culture.

2. **Critical thinking** and dispositions towards it, such as flexibility, persistence, willingness to self-correct and mindfulness. This is a broader view of critical thinking, beyond the purely intellectual. In addition, Yershova et al. embrace several types of reasoning that they say are essential for new meaning and knowledge to be constructed:

   • *Value reasoning* – considering justifications for personal and moral values, as in ethical reasoning. Value judgements are often made without thought when we encounter 'otherness' and don't question how our own culture shapes our values.

   • *Analogical reasoning* – concluding, by analogy or by using metaphor, that two things are similar because they have a common element. For this we generally use inductive reasoning (A is similar to B; A has features C and D; therefore B also has these features or similar ones). Assumptions of similarity need to be analysed and confirmed (or qualified or refuted).

   • *Systems thinking* – seeing interrelationships and patterns so we can see the bigger picture and how the parts relate to it. This helps us to see multiple perspectives and their context.

   • *Reflective thinking* – looking inwards and challenging our own thinking, judgements and assumptions and then evaluating them.

- *Metacognition* – applying strategies to monitor our attention, what we think, how we think and how we use our knowledge and thinking.

3. **Comparative thinking** – comparing one thing with another to establish difference, the size of the gap. Yershova et al. offer a 'composite' definition of comparative thinking as deliberately relating views and perspectives on familiar things to the unfamiliar in order to uncover our assumptions and discover new ideas. We use comparative thinking when we describe or explain to ourselves or others a country or a culture: we do so by making comparisons with what we know of our own country and culture and what is different about the other country or culture. Conscious and deliberate comparative thinking is used as a tool for discovering assumptions and habits and discovering new ideas.

All but comparative thinking are covered in this book, mainly in Chapter 6. Metacognition is covered in *Learning how to learn* in Chapter 3. Comparative thinking can be risky if done without care. For example, people make 'upward comparisons', comparing themselves with people who are richer, healthier or more successful and can feel worse for the comparison. Or they do the opposite; they make 'downward comparisons', comparing themselves with someone worse off, for example. Then they feel less bad about their own situation (or superior). Yershova and colleagues' view is that, properly done, comparative thinking can be used to deconstruct our frame of reference to reveal its limitations and the assumptions and stereotypes that inform it. Practise this now using Activity 8.4, which is designed to be fun as well as informative.

ACTIVITY 8.4 Gather a culturally diverse group of four students, explaining that you want to uncover cultural frames of reference, assumptions and stereotypes through comparative thinking. Before you start, you may want to read Box 8.1 ('What *is* culture?')

It is essential that the communication climate is an open one that promotes trust. Ensure that the group has a shared understanding of the meaning of stereotype (a widely held, fixed view); an assumption (something personally accepted as true without proof) and a frame of reference (the criteria by which a person judges something, for example, as being of interest or what is 'real' to the person. A frame of reference includes assumptions.

Pair up students from different cultures. Each student in the pair explains key aspects of his or her culture to the other. Each prepares five statements about the other student's culture or way of life at home, paying particular attention to differences. Leave up to 10 minutes for the exchange.

All students then sit together. Each student in turn reads out his or her five statements. As each statement is delivered, the rest of the group tries to determine features of the reporting student's culture from the statements – the choice about what to tell the group is significant because the statements are selected on the basis of cultural difference. The group should also try to identify the statement-giver's assumptions and stereotypes, without being too concerned about distinguishing between these. An example is given

See *Creating an open communication climate* in this chapter below. The group should avoid stating assumptions, stereotypes or frames of reference that might cause offence to the statement-giver.

At the end of the activity, the group should carry out Activity 8.5.

Example

Walter, a resident and native of a rural area of northern Italy, explains to Maggi, a resident and native of London, aspects of his home life and culture. Maggi compiles five statements for group members who then try to discern from each of her statements her frame of reference, assumptions and stereotypes. In the example, these follow each of Maggi's statements.

1. Maggi: Walter lives in a Protestant area of Italy. The Protestant church only recently achieved parity with the Catholic church, such as receiving a proportion of government tax revenue.

   Assumption: native Italians are traditionally Catholic.
   Frame of reference: the UK, where church and state are separate.

2. Maggi: Every province of Italy has its own language in addition to Italian and, in rural areas at least, these local languages are spoken in the home unless people marry someone from a different province. Other languages spoken, such as French, German, Slovene and Serbo-Croat, normally depend on proximity to bordering countries. Walter speaks his local language to his father, Italian to his mother and French to his grandmother.

   Stereotype: native Italians speak Italian.
   Frame of reference: the UK, where accents but not language (apart from varieties of Celtic) vary by region.

3. Maggi: Walter's home is a valley where 180 of his relatives live and where his ancestors have lived for centuries.

   Frame of reference: the UK/London, where families are often dispersed as a result of social mobility, work and cost of accommodation; a society in which the notion of the extended family living in proximity is diminishing.

4. Maggi: Walter lives in a dairy-farming area: people eat butter and cheese. They also eat a lot of potatoes; rice is grown not far away. Some older people didn't encounter olive oil until relatively recently.

   Stereotypes: Italy is a Mediterranean country full of olive trees; Italians eat pasta (not potatoes).
   Assumption: Italy is not a rice-growing region of the world.

5. Maggi: Walter says you can't buy a mobile phone without an insurance number and once, when buying a loaf of bread, he was stopped by 'fiscal

police' to check that the shop had given him a receipt – it's to stop tax evasion by retailers.

Frame of reference: the UK, an economic and political context that is relatively less bureaucratic.

At the end of the activity it's likely that you'll be interested to know more of each others' cultures: even apparently similar cultures can be remarkably different.

Key activities for intercultural working

Cultural diversity exists in all UK universities but little work on intercultural competence has been carried out in this context (Ramanau and Tyler, 2011). Rather, researchers have focused mainly on staff as a part of the endeavours towards one form of internationalisation of UK universities, the creation of 'off-shore' campuses. The University of Warwick (Spencer-Oatey and Stadler, 2009) has devised a framework for working in cross-cultural contexts, derived from its work with international partner institutions. Here, it is adapted to show you what the key activities are considered to be.

1. **Knowledge and ideas:** gather information; observe; be open to challenge; be interested in finding out.
2. **Communication:** establish communication; listen actively; notice non-verbal behaviour; clarify the meaning of what's said; interpret indirect signals; pay attention to different styles of communication (for example, formal or informal; expressive or restrained) and adapt your own to suit the context; disclose information as well as seeking it.
3. **Relationships:** be interested in people and actively engage with them; build rapport on both personal and professional levels and have genuine concern for people's welfare; be sensitive to power relations and how they influence people in different contexts; understand roles, rights and obligations and how decisions are made; be aware of people's personal sensitivities and avoid making them 'lose face'.
4. **Personal qualities and dispositions:** develop a spirit of adventure and be prepared to step outside your 'comfort zone'; be aware that your own behaviour may be strange or be difficult to accept while accepting behaviour and ideas that are different from your own; accept people, their views and values as they are and look for the best in others; be willing to learn a wide range of behaviours and communication styles – experiment; avoid judging; develop coping strategies to deal with stress and learn to be resilient so that you can take risks, avoid being embarrassed by social mistakes and bounce back after setbacks.

See *Beyond words: speech acts and saving face* and *Active listening* in this chapter; see *Managing stress* in Chapter 2

ACTIVITY 8.5 In the group you worked with for Activity 8.4, consider and reflect on the key activities for working cross-culturally. In which activities did the group and individuals engage?

It's likely that you identified some items in all four activity categories. The fact that you were willing to take a risk and carry out Activity 8.4 at all means you are at least willing to try to develop the necessary personal qualities and dispositions for intercultural competence. Congratulations! Keep making efforts: the competence takes time to develop. Regularly check your progress against the developmental models.

Box 8.1 What *is* culture?

In setting out the sophisticated thinking required for intercultural competence, Yershova et al. underline why studying in or travelling to other countries doesn't guarantee its acquisition. Study in another country may be motivated by aspirations other than gaining international competence: students gain sufficient cultural knowledge to get by, return home and think and behave much as they did before. Travel can amount to cultural voyeurism rather than a desire for life-changing cultural exchange. The nature of culture is difficult to define but most researchers include:

- meanings and values that have arisen historically and are the lens through which people see the world and act in it
- social organisation, rules, laws, rituals and customs
- language, symbols, artefacts including tools, ornamentation and works of art
- behaviours and how relationships are conducted.

Culture is 'lived' and embodied in the above. It is shared, taken for granted and learned by successive generations. It also provides a sense of identity (that is, your sense of belonging to one or more cultural groups, although cultural identity is fluid and subject to exploration). Culture is adaptive, constantly changing (consider the development of modern technology). Aspects of it can be maladaptive through practices that are non-sustainable, leading, for example, to depletion of resources and environmental degradation (consider desertification through overgrazing). Note that some aspects of culture are visible (such as artefacts and behaviours) while many are not (such as values and beliefs).

In your studies you will encounter the concept of organisational culture – culture not as a way of life but as a way of working. This is culture with a lowercase 'c'. The history of an organisation and its traditions inform shared values and beliefs (invisible features) that, in turn, inform artefacts, dress codes, behaviour and how people go about their work (visible features). Maladaptive aspects of culture include, for example, being overly risk-averse leading to lack of innovation and competitiveness.

Active listening

How well do you listen? Carry out Activity 8.6 to find out.

ACTIVITY 8.6 *Part 1* – Do this activity with a fellow student or colleague. Each choose a different point of view that you want the other to understand. Then, in turn, explain it in two minutes as clearly as possible. Give reasons for holding the viewpoint. You can make notes to use when speaking but don't take notes while listening. Then, in turn, recount what each other said. Give feedback to each other on what elements were missing or incorrect.

How did you fare? The chances are that your listening wasn't very accurate. This is a common problem when you are highly motivated to speak: you don't focus on what others are saying. It can happen, too, when you are distracted, bored or nervous about expressing yourself. In the activity, the second person to speak may have listened less accurately because he or she was busy planning what to say. (You probably noted, too, the importance of being precise about what you mean when speaking!)

Listening actively helps you to understand more and recall better. In the workplace it is a particularly important interpersonal skill because talking and listening to others is often the primary method of information-giving and knowledge exchange.

How to listen actively

1. **Pay attention – fully.** Face the speaker and look at him or her directly. You learn a lot from body language: does the speaker seem nervous and in need of reassurance, or angry, or distressed? Not looking or making little eye contact sends the message: *I'm not really interested* or *I don't have time*. If necessary, find a place where distractions and interruptions are few. Still the thoughts in your own head and listen with a clear and receptive mind. If you don't have time to listen just then, arrange a time when you do. However, the speaker's need may be more urgent than your own.
2. **Let the speaker know you're listening** *without* **interrupting.** Use body language to let the speaker know you're attending. The behaviours, known as back channelling, include gestures such as nodding your head, smiling, or short verbalisations such as *OK* or *I see*. The use of Yes or 'uh-huh' is common but it can be mistaken for agreement with what is being said: you are simply listening.
3. **Get feedback on your understanding.** At appropriate points, paraphrase what you've heard and ask whether you've understood correctly. Begin your questions with: *So you're saying … or Am I right in thinking …?* This signals that you're clarifying. If necessary ask questions such as: *When you say X, what do you mean exactly?* If the speaker hasn't provided enough information or seems reluctant, encourage with questions or just wait: saying nothing is effective because speakers quickly fill a silence.
4. **Refrain from making a judgement.** Let the speaker finish before you decide how to respond.

5. **Acknowledge.** Before responding (or sooner in the listening process) acknowledge the speaker's feelings. You can say, for example: *I can see you're interested/concerned/upset/angry/frustrated (with me).*
6. **Respond.** When you respond be open and honest. Speak respectfully, as you would like others to treat you. Ask for time if you have no ready response.

Active listening demands discipline. You allow a speaker space and you try hard to understand what the person is saying. What they say may upset you or you may disagree with it but you put your own thoughts aside until you have fully understood. Use the technique with your tutors and fellow students. Differences in status and authority affect communication and are a particular feature of workplaces, but the protocol is the same whether you are studying or at work. When practising active listening, regularly check your thoughts. If they have drifted away from what the other person is saying, you aren't listening actively.

> **ACTIVITY 8.6** *Part 2* – Now repeat the activity with a different point of view, using the active listening technique. Did you do better this time?

Beyond words: speech acts and saving face

People can try hard to use the 'right' words when communicating only to find they have upset their listeners. This can happen in workplaces when, for example, senior managers announce changes, closures or relocations. Staff 'read between the lines' and assume criticism of their productivity or that they are insufficiently valued to be consulted. How do these miscommunications happen?

While academics think of speech as a context-dependent tool and analyse conversation and discourse in complex ways, it's helpful to understand that we invariably say more than the words we utter. The philosopher John Austin had some intriguing things to say about this over half a century ago. Indeed, his classic approach underlies many current theories and remains useful.

According to Austin (1962) anything that is said or written can be thought of as a *speech act* with three components.

1. The literal meaning of the words spoken (known as locution) such as *This room is cold.*
2. The performance of the speech act (known as illocution). This itself has meaning and 'force' which depends on whether a speech act informs, promises, warns, challenges, orders and so on. *This room is cold* may be a request that the listener close a window.
3. The effect or consequence (known as perlocution). This depends not only on the words spoken, the speaker and the circumstances but also on the prior knowledge and expectations of the listener. *This room is cold* may offend a listener if the speaker is an office junior and the listener is the operations director in whose office they are meeting. The listener might have expected a

courteous request to close a window. In different circumstances *This room is cold* may draw an apology from a listener: *Sorry, the heating isn't working.*

These three components mean that no speech act consists of 'just the words': it is not reducible. Thus, it's easy to get communication wrong. Austin's theory is complex but, in short, to get communications right, consider what you say, how you say it, the circumstances and the likely effect or consequences. Think about what listeners already know and believe; what they might take a message to mean and what might result if they interpret a message in a way you didn't intend. Consider how a speaker can use the same words in two different contexts to different effect. *Jason is such a perfectionist!* may have a negative effect if Jason is taking too long or a positive one if Jason's attention to detail is an asset in the situation. Now test your understanding.

ACTIVITY 8.7

Karl is a manager in an organisation with a poor reputation for staff relations and a focus on pleasing shareholders. He has been told to announce a cost-cutting merger of two branch offices which means the loss of two jobs and a longer commute for some staff with young children. He decides to announce the merger in a way that emphasises opportunities for staff and obscures the need for redundancies. While some staff do see opportunities, most are left feeling shocked and insecure: they don't share Karl's optimism.

Why did staff react as they did? How might you have made the announcement?

You probably recognised that the negative effect of the announcement was exacerbated by staff feelings about their prior treatment by the organisation. The announcement reinforced their view that the organisation undervalued them. Your own version of the announcement probably took account of likely impact, not just what you would say, how and when. You might have said that the decision was not yours; why cost-cutting was believed to be necessary and (if this were the case) that it did not reflect staff performance but locations of the branches and their proximity. Consider how you can use Austin's theory when you are working with other students. *This meeting room is too small/ill-equipped/badly located* is likely to offend the student who booked the venue.

Saving face

Another classic and groundbreaking approach to communication that remains in current use is politeness theory, first put forward by Erving Goffman (1967). He said people have 'face' – self-respect, a sense of worth, dignity, social status and reputation – to which they are emotionally attached and need to maintain.

This 'face' is an impression people construct to present to the world, rather like a photo of themselves taken in a good light. It is made up of various socially approved attributes, such as being good at one's job, being conscientious and so on. People *maintain* 'face' when events are consistent with expectations and *gain* 'face' when expectations are exceeded. They *lose* 'face' when expectations are not fulfilled, feeling shame, embarrassment or humiliation. This happens when their failings or mistakes are noticed and they need to acknowledge them. 'Face' maintenance is a kind of game: to maintain our own 'face' we must be considerate and help others to maintain theirs, too (although without necessarily privately accepting their 'faces'). Goffman calls this a 'working acceptance' that serves social interaction.

To help to protect the self-respect of others and defend our own, we use social skills: we show respect, make gracious withdrawals, feign modesty, leave things unsaid or ignore what has been said, take 'hints' offered by others about ourselves, use humour and ambiguity, willingly admit fault (*I've always been terrible at drawing*), apologise and offer to make amends and so on.

What you actually say depends on the social distance between you and the listener, the power distance between you both and cultural differences. When you point out a wrong figure in a colleague's document at an informal meeting, you might say: *That late night was a mistake!* thus excusing the mistake and indicating that it wasn't consistent with usual behaviour. If a senior manager uses a wrong figure in a presentation, however, you'd be more likely to say: *Might there be a typographical error on the chart?* allowing him or her to save 'face' by agreeing that the error had a trivial cause.

In other words, we use tact or diplomacy to resolve a challenge to 'face' satisfactorily. It's a valid question whether tact amounts to lying but a rule of thumb is, be ethical: don't try to deceive in order to maliciously manipulate; give others an escape route and trust that they will give you one, too, when you need it.

Strategies to reduce threat to face

Goffman's theory was extended by Brown and Levinson (1987) who identified different types of 'face' strategies: those that *reduce* threat to another person's 'face'. These includes strategies that

- recognise another person's autonomy and, therefore, his or her right not to comply with requests; in such cases you soften impositions (such as *I understand the difficulties of finding time to complete the work but the deadline is in three weeks* rather than *You must meet the deadline*).
- allow the listener to infer the meaning; for example, when you say *Our meeting with John is an important one* what should be inferred by the listener is the need for attention to preparation and presentation.

Which strategy people choose depends on social distance, power distance and culture. Recognising the autonomy of others is important in situations in which social and power distance are small and others are not obliged to do as you ask. This is often the case in study situations and in organisations with a 'flat' hierarchy where teamwork is often the norm.

> **ACTIVITY 8.8** You are co-ordinating a student team at university. You have no formal power or authority and there is little social distance between team members. You realise that the work schedule leaves too little time to practise the team's final presentation. Which message would you circulate and why?
>
> 1. You all have to leave time to practise the final presentation.
> 2. It would be great if you could finish by Monday to allow time to practise the presentation.
> 3. I know you're all working hard but we're going to have to finish half a day early to allow us time to practise the final presentation. Could you do that?
> 4. The final presentation will need a few hours' practice and we didn't allow for that in the schedule.

You probably opted for Message 3. You're not likely to circulate Message 1, which doesn't recognise the autonomy of recipients and your lack of authority. Message 2 recognises that members have autonomy but doesn't allow them to exercise it even if they had no intention to do so. Message 3 recognises the onerousness or difficulty of what is being asked, members' autonomy and their right to exercise it. The use of *we* conveys inclusiveness here. Message 4 is an indirect request that leaves the recipients to infer meaning. In a multicultural team you would avoid messages like this because of the risk of misunderstandings.

Using politeness strategies helps to avoid major upsets; you are respected for your tact and others are more likely to be gracious, offering ways to save your own 'face' when necessary.

Giving and receiving feedback

Giving and receiving feedback are features of university and work life: you might be asked to give feedback on a meeting, a presentation, a proposal, or someone's performance and you will receive feedback on your own efforts.

Giving feedback

The best guide to giving feedback is to consider the manner and phrasing of the feedback you would like to receive yourself.

> **ACTIVITY 8.9** Imagine you have just completed a presentation of your project proposal to colleagues and several more senior personnel whom you want to impress. One colleague was critical of your proposal when he read it a few days ago to prepare his response. At the presentation you feel a sense of foreboding as you see him rise to his feet. How would you *like* him to provide feedback that expresses his views in a way that doesn't destroy your confidence in yourself and your work?

You are likely to have said that you would like the colleague's feedback to be intelligent, balanced, honest and, above all, constructive and respectful. It should reveal insightful thinking (yours and that of the speaker), what was good and what was not, together with constructive suggestions. Importantly, it should be delivered in a positive manner. Wholly negative, unconstructive feedback not only undermines the recipient but reflects poorly on the person who gives it.

In general, constructive feedback has three components.

- **What is praiseworthy.** State this first. You can say, for example: *What you're trying to achieve is impressive. I think the project will be valuable.* There is always something to identify as praiseworthy, even if it's simply the effort a person has made: *I appreciate the trouble you've gone to.*
- **What is lacking.** Select only those aspects that can be changed and suggest how. Introduce your criticisms in a supportive way. You can say, for example: *I'd like to query some aspects of the project. I think there might be a problem if you try to do X because [...] but I wondered if this might be avoided by doing Y or Z [...] What are your own thoughts on this?*
- **A positive conclusion.** An example is: *I'm looking forward to the next draft/ seeing the project move forward.* Even if a great deal more work is needed, you can say: *It's a positive start on which to build.* If the work has taken a misguided direction, it's still possible to say: *I think the work has been useful in showing just how important and difficult it is to establish an approach. Shall we give some thought to it?*

When your feedback is clear and direct the listener is more likely to be receptive than if you are blunt and harsh. Alternatively, give the author, designer or presenter the first opportunity for comment. Depending on how far the person's work has progressed you can ask: *What would you do differently if you were to do this again?* Or *Since drafting the proposal have you had any more thoughts on it?* The person is unlikely to consider his or her work perfect, particularly in retrospect, and there may be reasons why some aspect of it is less than ideal.

Receiving feedback

Receiving feedback can be as difficult as giving it. Put yourself in a positive frame of mind, managing your expectations and emotions. Instead of anticipating a hostile reaction, look forward to others engaging with your work and providing insights. Then do the following:

- listen actively and ask questions of clarification.
- don't react; rather, consider what is being said.
- acknowledge what you agree with; correct inaccuracies and counter what you think is not supported by evidence; explore interesting elements.
- consider what you will change in light of the feedback and say so if appropriate.

Correct misconceptions, show insight and take criticism graciously. Use charm. For example you might say: *I'm sure you're right and I would have done that with the luxury of time; I'd certainly adjust the process next time to allow for it.* You can also ask for suggestions for solutions. If you have already considered what you could improve or would do next time, then you can pre-empt criticism by including this in your report, presentation or proposal. It creates the appropriate climate for constructive feedback.

If feedback is delivered in a hostile and unconstructive way, you can say: *I think I understand what you are saying but I'm not sure what to make of it/do with it. Do you have some suggestions about X, Y and Z?* This encourages the speaker to be more helpful. Praise is always good to receive but constructive feedback always challenges *something* that you can use to improve your work. Welcome it, explore it and use it to advantage.

Communicating assertively

Assertiveness is needed in situations in which one person is causing difficulty or distress. But assertiveness is often misunderstood. Carry out Activity 8.10 to test your understanding.

> **ACTIVITY 8.10** Consider the following scenario.
>
> Jan, a formidable facilities manager, likes to micro-manage. Pietro, the head groundsman, seems to take far too long for lunch on some days. Pietro regularly inspects the habitats of protected flora and fauna and, unknown to Jan, he likes to combine this where possible with lunchtime tours of the grounds for staff as part of his remit to promote conservation awareness. Finally, Jan demands to know why Pietro isn't working his contractual hours but doesn't wait to hear his response, instead telling him to improve his time-keeping. Pietro can deal with the situation in one of several ways:
>
> 1. He can tell Jan angrily that her behaviour is appalling.
> 2. He can say nothing.
> 3. He can describe the behaviour he finds distressing, how it makes him feel and that he'd like it to end.
>
> Which response is assertive? Read on to check your answers.

Assertiveness is not simply standing up for yourself and expressing your feelings; it is about doing so in a way that respects others' rights. Aggression and evasion don't do this. Aggression infringes others' rights while evasion respects them but violates those of the evader. Assertiveness is needed in a variety of circumstances such as when you feel undermined, imposed upon or treated unfairly; or when you need to respond to unreasonable requests or criticisms or the way they are expressed. You may also need to be assertive when making requests and giving criticism. In the activity Response 1 is aggressive and Response 2 is evasive. Only Response 3 is assertive.

Practise assertiveness using the technique below. Note that the example statements use *I* rather than *you*. It's much harder for another person to argue that your feelings are wrong.

- **Describe the troublesome behaviour.** Think of specific examples of the problem behaviour and express them as observations, for example: *I see that my time-keeping is being scrutinised.* By doing this you are identifying the problem behaviour, not criticising the other person.
- **Say how the behaviour makes you feel or how it affects you.** Say, for example *It makes me feel I'm not trusted.*
- **Identify your needs.** Consider how to explain these to the person, for example: *I would like to be trusted to do my work efficiently.*
- **Identify what you want to happen.** This is the behaviour change you would like, for example: *I want to be able to organise my work including tasks such as checking on the X, Y and Z sites and conducting staff tours which need to be done at lunchtimes.*
- **Consider the consequences.** Think about the consequences of your wishes being complied with (*It'll be much easier for us both if you trust me*) or not being complied with (*If I'm not trusted, I'll take the matter further*). However, don't express negative consequences unless they are realistic and you can ensure they happen.

It's often easier to write down and rehearse what you want to say so that you can control your emotions. Your views will be better received if you acknowledge the other person's positive behaviours towards you at other times to show that he or she is valued and worthy of respect. If appropriate, include a request to help you to deal with the current problem to show that their help is valued. You are more likely to achieve what you want.

Remember, however, that the person may have justifiable criticisms of your behaviour or how you contributed to the problem: in the scenario perhaps Pietro was supposed to record such activities in his work log. Invariably it's best to explore with the other person the respective problems. However, the technique doesn't take great account of imbalances of power or authority. It can be hard to be assertive if the other person is far more senior than you are. One approach is to talk to the person from the perspective that he or she is unaware of the troublesome behaviour. Assertiveness can also be difficult if there are cultural differences. Assertiveness is a Western concept: in other cultures using tact and mutual deference may be preferable. It's best to assess issues of power difference and culture first and then consider what might be an appropriate approach.

ACTIVITY 8.11 Consider a current situation in which being assertive would be appropriate. It could be that a fellow student habitually dominates discussion at seminars. Work out what you will say at the next seminar bearing in mind any cultural differences.

It is an unfortunate reality that you need to become accustomed to dealing with poor behaviour: you'll find it in almost every workplace and among all categories of staff.

Creating an open communication climate

How can you define the quality of relationships among your friends and family and in the teams, groups and organisations to which you belong? The character or tone of relationships constitutes the communication climate and it can be 'open' or 'closed'.

In an open communication climate information flows freely and you feel able to speak without fear. You aren't criticised, your suggestions are welcome and mistakes are a matter for investigation, not blame. The climate is supportive, participative and trusting. The opposite is a 'closed' communication climate in which people don't share information freely; indeed, they may withhold it and use it as a source of power. As a result, information doesn't flow. People are judged and solutions that directly affect them may be imposed without discussion. Colleagues may be manipulative in order to gain personal benefit. Even 'niceness' can be a strategy for exercising power or control and for blocking constructive feedback.

Open and closed communications climates are illustrated in the following scenarios.

Erica's mistake

Erica and Nancy work for Erica's mistake different property letting companies. They meet one evening. Erica tells Nancy how she made a bad mistake, giving a potential major client wrong information about fees. The client called the branch manager who spoke to Erica and realised there was a problem with identifying the most up-to-date information source. The manager raised the issue at a group meeting to consider solutions. He asked Erica to speak first to explain how the mistake arose. Her solution wasn't the one the group chose but she was happy that it solved the problem. *Giving wrong information was the same mistake I made six months ago*, Nancy responds. *You were lucky: I was threatened with losing my job.*

Enzo's difficulty

Enzo has been assigned to a team that is designing a survey for a study assignment at university. His first task was to find out about survey development but he's found that it's far more complex than the team thought. He tries to explain this at the next meeting but Tina, the team leader, stops him. *So you haven't done the job. Will someone else do it?* The other team members say nothing and no one offers to take on the task: each is afraid of being humiliated by Tina.

ACTIVITY 8.12 Was what happened to Erica in the first scenario a matter of luck? What features of an open communication climate can you identify in the scenario? What features of a closed communication climate exist in the second scenario? How could the climate be improved? Read on to check your answer.

A communication climate can exist between as few as two people as well as in groups and teams and in organisations, where different parts of them can have different climates. Because individuals, are responsible for their behaviour and what they say, they can contribute to improving a communication climate by attending to key behaviours.

Value and respect other participants. Listen to them. You may disagree with what they say but you can still acknowledge suggestions, effort and so on. Be honest and genuine, however: patronising others causes offence.

Avoid blaming others. When mistakes are made, focus on putting things right and ensuring they don't recur. This helps to build trust between people.

Be well informed. This helps to avoid misunderstandings. But don't be afraid to admit you don't know something: people often take pleasure in explaining and helping others. It also provides an opportunity to check shared meanings.

Invite input. Information, views and opinions can't be exchanged if only one person does the talking. Barriers to participation include feeling unsupported, so welcome contributions. Rephrase unconstructive ones (*So you're suggesting a different approach?*) and explore (*What did you have in mind?*).

Give feedback. Feedback ranges from acknowledgement to constructive critique. People need to know they have been understood; feedback also inspires and motivates people and ensures that they don't repeat errors of thinking or judgement. The way you provide feedback is the key to its benefits. Ask for feedback to improve your own learning.

See *Giving and receiving feedback* in this chapter

Allow for self-correction. Allow people the opportunity to give their own views on their work before others comment. If further work is needed, the person whose work it is should also have the first opportunity to say how it could be improved.

Be open to dissent and creative thinking. Alternative views, dissent and conflict can be constructive – perhaps there *is* a better way to achieve a task. Explore views and keep discussion focused on task attributes rather than personal ones. Ensure that conflicts are resolved.

Handle conflict sensitively. Listen even if someone is finding fault with what you do or did and don't react defensively. Personal grievances need to be addressed in confidence outside a group or team.

In the first example, Erica's manager showed many of the above behaviours. In Nancy's case, there was too little information to assess but it's clear that her manager blamed her and did not allow self-correction.

Aim to make the communication climate in any group or team in which you work, or between you and someone else, as open as possible both when you are studying and when you are at work. Information flow through formal and informal channels is vital to organisations and you can facilitate this by making a difference to their communication climates.

Making peer-work effective

Peer-work, whether in an informal study group or in a team tasked to carry out a formal project, requires each member to participate fully.

> **ACTIVITY 8.13** Think of times when you have participated in group work. What did (or didn't) other people do that frustrated you? How did you contribute? How did your behaviour and that of others help the group to achieve its aims (or not)?

It is always easier to identify the frustrating behaviours of other people. You probably listed domination of discussions, not listening, not contributing to discussion, making irrelevant contributions, not making equal effort, lack of preparation for group work and not taking responsibility while benefiting from others' contributions. These are common complaints. The list of your own contributions probably included only positive ones!

To help a group achieve its aims, each member needs to:

- value other group members as individuals
- demonstrate this in communication and contributions
- understand and agree on the objectives of the group
- understand and agree on how these will be achieved
- prepare for each meeting
- listen actively
- contribute to discussion with views, comments, and questions
- be supportive
- give and receive feedback
- contribute to the planning of tasks
- take initiatives and, if appropriate, act on them
- take on equal responsibility for tasks
- be assertive when necessary, for example, if one member dominates
- be prepared to provide respectful, honest views on meetings or how the group is functioning.

See *Giving and receiving feedback, Communicating assertively* and *Creating an open communication climate* in this chapter

When participants fail to do one or more of these, however, don't automatically assume they don't want to. The communication climate may need attention. Other barriers to full participation include:

- lack of social confidence
- lack of confidence in abilities
- cultural differences
- communication difficulties
- genuine lack of time/life events.

A supportive group encourages people to express their fears, their lack of confidence or their perceived lack of ability. As a result the group reaps benefits: when you provide support you develop the capabilities of others and your own. People from other cultures may have different views about what to do and how to behave in a group. In Western cultures, for example, interruptions are tolerated to some extent while in other cultures they may be taboo. It may also be unacceptable to disagree. People may need reassurance.

See *Perspective-taking* in this chapter

Beyond this, diversity is a positive attribute because a group or team can benefit from the different skills, abilities and experience that people bring – provided you are willing to explore differences and use differences to advantage. A person's language or communication skills may mean that he or she misses opportunities to speak: allow space for contributions and communicate clearly.

An often-overlooked barrier to participation is lack of time as a result of unexpected life events or heavy commitments elsewhere. The latter problem is most common among part-time students who work full-time: family-care responsibilities and work can place sudden demands on them (for example, when a child is hospitalised or when cover for a colleague is needed). Ask how much time people are able to give and explore why a person's participation has suddenly fallen. People are often willing to do more at other times or work on different tasks. If you want to work in a high-performing group or team you have to help to develop it!

Organising and running groups

How do you go about working with others? If you wait to be told you will be ill-prepared for the workplace. Formal peer-work is normally required as part of your studies but many students gain substantial benefits from meeting informally for learning support or for revision. Setting up an informal study group – and keeping it going – is demanding but rewarding. It requires organisation and a structured approach to ensure everyone's needs are met, primarily because people choose to belong and can leave the group if they don't benefit.

A process for forming and running an informal study group is set out below. It includes most of what you need to know for organising any other kind of group. Adapt it to suit very informal groups or formal ones where the purpose of meetings, usually discussion of a topic, may already have been decided. Organising and structuring the work of teams tasked with producing an output are covered later in this chapter because more planning is involved. First, consider what you know about organising an informal group.

ACTIVITY 8.14

Faruq decides to set up an informal study group. He posts a message in a general student forum giving a day, time and venue and a general statement about mutual support for study. On the day, 23 people turn up, not all of them on his course. A number of them haven't met before but they soon form small 'chat' groups. Faruq tries to bring the gathering to some order. Almost all of the 23 people turn to look at him expecting him to take the lead, while he looks at them to guide him.

Write down some key organisational activities that Faruq should have undertaken. Check your list using the text that follows.

Starting an informal study group

An informal study group usually focuses on discussion of new course topics and associated reading, forthcoming assignments and/or exam revision. It meets regularly to provide mutual study support and endures to the end of a course. The amount of organisation required depends on your study circumstances: more will be needed if you study part-time or at a distance.

Adapt the guidance if you are working wholly online. Specific guidance for working asynchronously (online at different times) and synchronously (at the same time) is given later in this chapter. The guidance here assumes you can meet other students in person and be in touch via email, a student forum or social media. It also assumes you are taking the initiative for starting the group. The work can be shared later. Make sure all your communications are warm and welcoming; make suggestions rather than impose your own views.

Starting the group

1. Be bold. Ask who would like to join an informal study group and then exchange contact details. Don't be concerned if the number of people is larger than ideal (five to seven, although larger groups can be successful). Not all those who express an interest will attend and some may drop out later.
2. Find out in general what people want to discuss at group meetings and what they expect to gain.
3. Arrange a first meeting (agree on a date, time and place) and ask for suggestions for a first agenda including study topics. Choose an appropriate venue: meeting rooms are ideal while cafés and libraries are not.
4. Select one topic (or two smaller ones) based on the majority view and create an agenda (covered below). For a first meeting, there will be once-only agenda items that are important to include even if no one suggests them, so you will be able to discuss fewer topics. Beside each agenda item, estimate a time allowance. (A total meeting time of two hours is normally sufficient.)
5. Circulate the agenda.

6. If you are in regular contact with potential group members you can agree roles before the first meeting. A convenor of meetings and chairperson or facilitator who can move the group through the agenda are usually needed as a minimum.
7. If contact is frequent you can also agree group norms in advance, too. Important ones are that all participants prepare for meetings and contribute respectfully.
8. Organise any materials needed, such as a flip chart and pens, or use a venue with equipment.

Two or three days before the first meeting, remind participants and ask them to let you know if they are coming. If responses suggest numbers will be below the ideal, invite others. (If the meeting is to be held synchronously online and any set up or familiarisation is needed, send out reminders sooner. Online working is addressed later in this chapter.)

The first meeting

An agenda for a first meeting depends on the discussions that have already taken place. The following example assumes that there has been no discussion about roles or group norms.

1. Introductions
2. What we want from belonging to the group
3. How we want to organise discussions
4. Our group's norms (or ground rules)
5. Group roles
6. Topics for discussion
   Topic 1
   Topic 2
7. Do we want to continue the discussions between meetings and how?
8. Contact details and permission to circulate them in the group
9. Feedback on this meeting
10. Agenda items for the next meeting
11. Date, time and venue of the next meeting.

Adapt introductions according to how well participants know each other. An ice-breaking activity helps. For example, participants can find out as much as they can about the person to their left or right in one minute and then introduce each other. Other short ice-breakers include a self-description in five words or the title of your dream job. The point of ice-breakers is for people to reveal something authentic, interesting and positive about themselves.

A group survives only if participants have similar needs that the group meets, so establishing what these are is vital. If all needs cannot be accommodated then agree on several realistic ones. Consider how discussions or activities should be structured. Will one person present an interpretation of an assignment question or will all group members do this? Alternatively, the form of a discussion or activity can be decided when an agenda is set, depending on the subject matter.

A basic set of ground rules or norms ensures fairness and respect for others. Keep these to a minimum and be prepared to add further ones later. They should include preparation for meetings, shared effort and contributions at meetings, equity in speaking time and communicating respectfully. The importance of this last group norm will be evident when participants give and receive feedback or disagree.

See *Giving and receiving feedback* in this chapter

Group roles ensure that meetings run smoothly. Essential ones are a **convenor** who organises the meetings and a chairperson or **facilitator**. The facilitator's role is to guide the group through the agenda and keep order. It's useful to have a **timekeeper** to ensure the group keeps pace with the agenda timings. A **record keeper** can make and circulate notes on agreed group norms, roles, topics for the next meeting, the date/time/venue and who does what and by when if tasks need to be accomplished between meetings. A **task progressor** may also be needed. For an informal group this job may be as simple as checking that anyone who has promised to prepare something for the next meeting is doing so and arranging help if needed. Roles can be shared, combined and/or rotate.

If the group decides to continue its discussions online, agree on a medium. It should be inclusive so that each posting is seen by everyone. If online discussion becomes protracted and inconclusive it indicates the need for a more structured debate in a meeting. Note that personal contact details shouldn't be shared among members without their agreement.

Feedback on a meeting helps to shape the next one. Elicit feedback by asking each person in turn. Encourage participants to be specific. If necessary, ask questions such as whether people felt the atmosphere was supportive, if everyone felt they had sufficient opportunity to participate, what they would like more – or less – of and whether the format of the discussions was constructive. Ask for a suggestion from each person on how the next meeting can be improved.

It may take several meetings to arrive at the 'right' format. Be tolerant of any negative feedback you receive: it's easy to be offended if you have made all the effort to organise the first meeting but a successful study group is 'owned' by all its members, not just one person. Feedback can be put to immediate use when the agenda for the next meeting is set. Arrange the date, time and, if possible, the venue for the next meeting: co-ordinating diaries/calendars later is time-consuming.

An agenda introduces structure to a meeting. Importantly however, it reflects expectations and following it ensures these are met. Facilitation can be 'light-touch' to avoid unnecessary formality. Facilitation involves welcoming everyone and then introducing each agenda item (*Item 3 on the Agenda is about…*), opening the discussion (*Chaz said he would present his ideas for us to critique and add our own…*) and then closing it (*We'd better leave the discussion there. To summarise …* or *Perhaps Ali (or someone) can summarise the discussion for us.*)

The facilitator ensures that discussion time is shared, draws in people who have not spoken (*What do you think about that, Stef?*) and ends the meeting on time. If questions or secondary discussion points remain, the facilitator should ask for suggestions for continuing the discussion outside the meeting. It's quite common for one person to struggle with a concept that others seem to have grasped. One or more other members might offer help.

Subsequent meetings

Agendas for subsequent meetings are usually simpler and shorter, allowing more time for additional topics. The last three items of the first agenda are a feature of every agenda, however. Feedback and taking account of it when planning the next meeting help the group to work productively and meet individual needs. This, and a sense of belonging, helps a group to stay together.

Guidance for group members

The value of group work depends on what and how participants contribute. Even if you are not convening or facilitating a meeting, understanding what needs to be done and how to participate are important contributions to a successful one. A facilitator needs willing and positive contributors.

Before a meeting

Prepare to contribute. Carry out any reading or preparatory work.

Know what you want to achieve from a session. You may have questions arising from your preparatory work. You may want to be in a better position to prepare an assignment.

See *Active listening* in this chapter

During a meeting

Listen actively. Show you are listening.

Contribute your views. Make sure they are relevant to the discussion and don't dominate or speak for too long. Be respectful; use tact and diplomacy.

See *Giving and receiving feedback* and *Beyond words: speech acts and saving face* in this chapter

Ask questions and comment constructively. Make a note of questions and comments that occur to you while someone is speaking to avoid interruption. Some questions may be for clarification; some may explore and some comments may challenge the views of others. Frame challenges as questions, for example: *How does that follow from what you said earlier about X?* or *Is your understanding of X's theory that it covers all contexts?*

Be prepared to answer questions and have your own views challenged. Note constructive criticisms. Never be afraid to say *I don't understand; could you explain that to me?* Conversely, if you understand something well, helping others to understand deepens your comprehension and highlights what you know less well. Learn by teaching.

Be inclusive. Participants won't have equal confidence or ability on every topic. Avoid excluding those who are quiet. Ask what they think. When you speak, address everyone in the room.

Take initiative. If the session is designed to produce an output, make suggestions for tasks or activities (and be prepared to contribute equal time and effort).

Check your informational needs have been met. Have the questions that arose during your preparatory work been answered? If not, ask them.

Check how well the group work met your other needs (or exceeded them). If it didn't, provide constructive feedback. Say how you think your needs might be accommodated.

Make notes and a note of tasks. If any work was agreed on for the next meeting, know who you need to liaise with.

After a meeting:

Read your notes. Rewrite them as a summary of agenda items or discussion.

Carry out any tasks you agreed to do. If an online forum has been organised, visit it regularly. Use it to give and to get help and support.

See *Recognising plagiarism* and *Avoiding plagiarism* in Chapter 5

Don't forget that the outputs of group work should be your own individual work. The only exceptions are formal group or team assignments where a single mark is awarded.

Informal group work *sounds* formal but it isn't; rather, it is disciplined, organised and structured to meet needs. If needs are met, group members are happy. Fun arises from working together. Mutual social support occurs naturally as people come to know and trust each other. Members of such groups are likely to become part of your future personal and professional networks; individuals keep in touch and continue to provide support. Moreover, the organisational and interpersonal skills you develop can be carried directly into the workplace. There, your ability to work with others, participating, co-operating and making effective contributions – and ensuring that others are able to do the same – is fundamental.

Working in a formal team

A team tasked with producing a joint output demands more of its members than other types of peer-work. Use Activity 8.15 to assess your current understanding.

ACTIVITY 8.15

A team is asked to produce a business case designed to help a transport company reduce diesel emissions over a five-year period ahead of new regulations. There is a wealth of material available including financial information; there are options to be generated and decided on, the business case to be drawn up, a brochure to be designed and a presentation to be made.

What demands will be made of team members?

Your first thought may be that the task requires all team members to work in a highly co-ordinated way to achieve a collective output. There is *interdependency* between people and between tasks. This defines a team and distinguishes it from a group. Activities and responsibilities that flow from these interdependencies include:

- identifying and organising resources, usually in the form of people, their skills and knowledge
- sharing, scheduling, co-ordinating and monitoring activities and tasks
- taking collective responsibility for the output.

Planning and organisation are essential, with more needed than for informal group work. Read the section *Setting up and running an informal study group* in this chapter now if you have not already done so. Team members need to take the steps set out below.

1. Define and agree on the goal
2. Decide how to work as a team (norms)
3. Define roles and decision-making processes
4. Work out and agree on the necessary tasks and activities
5. Assess resources and allocate tasks
6. Schedule the tasks, sub-tasks and activities
7. Agree the standards to be achieved and a monitoring system
8. Decide on how to coalesce the task outputs into the team output.

The goal

The first task of the team at its inaugural meeting is to agree on the goal. This requires all members to understand it fully. The nature of the task may influence the ways in which the team works, how it makes decisions and how the tasks are to be achieved. Understanding and defining the goal may require a little research. If the output is to be assessed, study the guidance. The team may need a model to work from depending on the team task, which may be a business plan or a survey with a presentation attached. This helps to establish an overall standard for the team's output.

Team norms

Behavioural norms need to be agreed. They should include a combination of task, process and team norms such as:

- carry out agreed tasks to agreed standards
- adhere to the schedule
- communicate progress
- prepare for and participate in meetings and discussions
- make constructive contributions to discussions
- communicate respectfully
- support fellow team members.

Each person should take responsibility for achieving the team output. In addition to interpersonal skills to contribute to the smooth running of the team, members need to be able to change swiftly from information gatherer to analyst and from creative risk taker to overviewer, for example. Student teams – and workplace ones, too – are usually too small for people to be anything other than adaptable. Decide on the media to be used for the work but be adaptive when considering tasks: match the medium to the task, if possible. Also agree on how you continue discussions between meetings. Resources often dictate practical issues such as whether team members work together or alone on tasks.

Roles

Teams often rush to allocate roles. But, if you can, it's preferable to understand the team goal and ways of working first. Roles are then easier to allocate based on the goal and the team's preferences about how it wants to operate.

Roles need to be well-defined with no overlap of responsibilities. Usual requirements are a meetings convenor, a facilitator, a record keeper (who also takes minutes of meetings and keeps time) and a task progressor or co-ordinator. Some roles are much the same as for an informal group while others such as the task co-ordinator are more demanding. Role sharing and role mergers are possible.

What you do depends on the size of the team and its activities. Conceivably, one person could take on all the roles and the job of coalescing task outputs. The task co-ordinator's monitoring activities are easier if day-to-day work is done online in a forum or workspace, but team members should agree to be online daily.

Decision-making

Decision-making can be a source of conflict that often arises when one or two people change what's been agreed. When the team creates team roles and allocates tasks, it needs to consider the extent of individual decision-making powers. Minor decisions may need to be made by individuals to avoid interrupting workflow but judgements need to be made about what requires team approval. Decisions that affect the work of others should not be made by an individual. For team decisions consensus is generally preferable to a majority vote. Consensus is usually achieved if team members have an opportunity to express their thoughts: a solution emerges that everyone agrees upon. If there are disagreements, dissenters (if in a small minority) should go along with decisions nonetheless. This is part of the commitment to a team and its work.

Tasks and activities

It is not easy to break down a large task into smaller ones and, at the same time, overlook nothing. Think through the overall task in a practical way, drawing out the smaller tasks. How many steps are involved in the preparation of a survey?

Does the team need to gather information first? How many more steps are involved in conducting the survey, analysing and making sense of the data? What does a presentation involve? Haste in defining tasks and activities can lead to scheduling problems and conflict later. When all the smaller tasks are identified, consider whether further division is possible or necessary.

Assessing resources and allocating tasks

Resources in student teams are mainly human ones and normally exclude outsiders. Whether you have time to develop knowledge in a weak area or must take on work that plays to your strengths is a matter for the team – this is something that the time and skills of other members often dictates. Task allocation must be fair: all team members should undertake an equal workload. Some people take longer than others to achieve the same work but in a team you learn to work at a fairly common pace because of the interdependency of tasks and the need to meet deadlines.

Scheduling tasks

Use a chart or planner to schedule tasks. Scheduling can be complex: it's more than a matter of working out the order in which the tasks need to be done and how long each will take. Some can or must overlap or be done in parallel and some need to be completed before others can start. Leave contingency time at appropriate intervals. Your schedule is likely to need revisions before it's complete. Adjustments are needed if one team member has too much to do at one point and too little at another. Allow time for assembling all the smaller outputs to construct the team output and for comment and editing. Also allow contingency time for slippage – it's a fact of life, so it's wise to accommodate it.

Agree standards and a monitoring system

The task co-ordinator should have an overview of all the team members' work, know where each part fits and understand the schedule. The role involves monitoring tasks and activities to ensure they are done on time and to the required standard. This ensures that the standard of the overall output is achieved, too. Using a management tool such as the control loop, the task co-ordinator can help over-conscientious members to see that they have met the agreed standard, arrange support for a struggling member or alert the team if tasks need to be adjusted or objectives revised. Thus, an important team task is to agree on simple performance markers for each task. (The schedule and 'model' output are useful here.)

See *Monitoring your progress* in Chapter 2 and *Creating an open communication climate* in this chapter

The monitoring process depends on the medium used for the work, which may be visible to all if wikis are used. If it isn't, team members can report at agreed intervals on progress to the task co-ordinator who then decides what to communicate to whom. The co-ordination and monitoring process is one in which an open communication climate is essential; the role holder needs to be disciplined, efficient and diplomatic.

Combining outputs from individual tasks

Bringing all the outputs together to produce the overall team output can be difficult unless the team has agreed on what the output should 'look like' and who should do it. Discussion on the final, crafted form of the output is likely to continue as team members work on tasks but the team should avoid 'mission creep' away from the agreed goal. Artwork can add considerably to the workload, so allow time and keep it simple. Allow time, too, for comments and editing suggestions. If the output is to be assessed, it needs to be evaluated against the guidance provided.

Meeting agendas

An agenda for a first team meeting should include all the readily achievable team task items listed earlier together with introductions, exchange of contact details (by consent), feedback on the meeting and the date, time and venue of the next meeting. Agendas for subsequent meetings are best set just before a meeting: items will depend on task progress.

The importance of acquiring teamwork skills is hard to overemphasise. At first you may be uncomfortable with or self-conscious about the need to adopt a professional approach to your participation. As you gain experience, try taking on a role or different roles. Be a participative and productive team member so you can take the skills with you when you graduate.

Working with others online

Are you a 'digital native'? If so, you have grown up with computers. Email, texting, the internet and social media feature prominently in your life. But you may still be inexperienced in the art of working with others online to achieve an outcome. In many national, multinational and transnational organisations employees need to do this and to manage – and be managed – from a distance. These organisations may have sophisticated methods of working: collaborating online and virtual teams are now common. Learning the necessary skills now, while you are a student, means you can make the transition from knowing something of the digital landscape to shaping the way technologies can be used to advantage where you work.

So how do you make the transition? Imagine you're at work, perhaps giving a presentation, managing staff or in a meeting to discuss a project proposal. The odd thing is that your physical self is at home and the 'you' at work is a robot you are controlling. Your colleagues can see your face on the robot's screen-face and you can see them, you can talk to them and you can carry out many physical tasks thanks to the capabilities of the robot and the technology you have at home. This isn't science fiction – such robots exist. The point of the example is to demonstrate what robotics pioneer Marvin Minsky (1980) called *telepresence* to refer to technologies that enable people to feel as if they are present when they are somewhere else.

The robot example shows that where telepresence is high, not very many additional skills are needed for remote working: interactions with others are synchronous, facial expressions are visible and physical work with others can be done in the same location. It's not very different from being present.

This isn't yet the case in much of the online collaboration you do when you study, or in many workplaces, however. The media you use as a student is probably asynchronous, such as email and discussion forums, with the use of intranets and the internet for resources. Small groups may meet synchronously via social media apps or virtual learning environments (VLEs) with streaming audio and video, although not all participants may have the required broadband speed or bandwidth (capacity).

This doesn't mean there are fewer benefits from working online, only that it is a little more demanding than face-to-face interaction. This is because trust and mutual respect among group members take longer to establish, explicit protocols (or codes of conduct) are required and it takes good organisation and discipline to achieve a goal collaboratively.

In other respects, collaboration online is the same as working face-to-face: for example, members need a shared understanding of the goal and will need to plan and allocate tasks, work out responsibilities and then carry out the tasks according to an agreed process. As in face-to-face collaboration, take care to find out whether outputs are to be assessed individually: see Box 8.2 *Team or individual assessment?*

See *Organising and running groups* and *Working in a formal team* in this chapter

---

Box 8.2 Team or individual assessment?

An important consideration when you work collaboratively is how the output will be assessed. In workplaces, a team's *collective* output is usually important while, for students, it's often the *individual* output. Be sure to find out in order to avoid inadvertently plagiarising the work of others. Usually, when work is to be assessed individually, group work *informs* an individual assignment which is done after the collaboration.

See *Recognising plagiarism* and *Avoiding plagiarism* in Chapter 5

Asynchronous communication

Initially, many students feel nervous about working with others wholly online – that is, before they begin. As soon as they set to work, these anxieties are generally overcome. Students quickly appreciate that synchronous ('same time, same place') interaction requires knowledge of the technology used but is otherwise similar to face-to-face work.

Asynchronous ('different times, same place') working can be both more challenging and more rewarding. Its primary benefit is that people can contribute, read and review postings when they have had time to think and can reflect on their contributions and those of others. They have the opportunity to make considered, high-quality inputs. Educators who use a number of media with students often refer to the asynchronous one as *the reflectors' medium* when it's used well.

There are eight basic rules for effective asynchronous communication.

1. **Frequent log-on.** How often you log on depends on the nature of the group, the tasks to be achieved and the schedule. Once or twice daily is usual when collaborating on a task unless the team is working full-time on it but be prepared for more frequent log-on at critical times.
2. **Active participation.** Frequent log-on is insufficient alone. While it keeps you up to date with discussion and provides opportunities for contributions, you aren't participating if you are simply a passive reader of others' contributions. Passive reading is normally acceptable in fairly large, general forums but not when you are actively working in a group or team.
3. **Make and adhere to protocols for written postings.** Activity 8.16 is designed to help you recognise why protocols are needed.

ACTIVITY 8.16

Alex responds to a posting by Josh who has asked if anyone knows of a critical review of a particular theory. Alex's message asks Josh about his new smart phone. Josh posted something about it at the end of an earlier message that Alex can't be bothered to find.

Dora also responds to Josh with a message that reads: *Doh! You should know that … it's on the reading list!* The tone of Dora's message isn't new. Josh, exasperated with Dora, decides to email the team leader to ask if Dora can be persuaded at least to be polite.

Malaika responds to Josh's query, saying: *Item 3 on the reading list is the critique, Josh. I've attached a copy I downloaded along with a more recent one I found that suggests there are some flaws in the first one. I thought the most interesting points were […]. It would be good to hear your views.*

What kind of communication protocol would you draw up for the group? There are examples of good and poor behaviour in the scenario. Did your protocol encompass Items 5 to 9?

4. **Consider what you say, to whom and to what effect.** As with all communication, you should consider what you want to say to whom, how you phrase your message and what impact it might have. Re-read what you write.

5. **Be on best (communication) behaviour.** Be encouraging, helpful and supportive, constructive, courteous and respectful to ensure the full co-operation and participation of all. It takes very little effort to say: *That's a good point; wish I'd thought of that!* (encouragement); *Here's a copy of the article* (helpful and supportive); *When we create our resource by posting articles we've read why don't we provide a one paragraph description of each?* (constructive); *Thanks, Malaika, that's great!* (courteous).

   All the above messages convey respect for recipients but it's important to show respect when disagreeing with or challenging another person's view. In these circumstances, an example of a respectful message is: *I understand your point of view, Simon, and I liked your insights on A. My perspective focuses more on B so I came to a different conclusion [...] What do you think?*

6. **Deal with bad behaviour.** Ill-judged attempts to resolve conflict can exacerbate it. If you have established ground norms for online working, poor behaviour is easier to deal with diplomatically at group or team level. Alternatively, a one-to-one email message may halt the poor behaviour. If that fails to work, then email the person who needs to take action, for example the facilitator or forum moderator. But consider carefully anything that might be construed as 'going behind another person's back'; it may make matters worse.

   See Avoiding and dealing with conflict in this chapter

7. **Use subject-line discipline.** Subject-line discipline is needed for all online posting and messages: lack of it makes information difficult to find. Replies should be about the subject of the first posting. Don't mix different types of content. Postings with new content need descriptive subject-lines. Organise threads into separate discussion forums with titles such as Assignment 1. Alternatively, keep single-topic threads running and maintain content discipline.

8. **Keep social chat separate from work discussion.** If there is only one forum, create a thread with the subject heading 'Social chat' or 'The Café' that people can reply to. Morale-boosting social exchange is important, so make participation easy and be inclusive.

9. **Don't forget that, online, copyright rules apply in the same way as they do when you write. You need to acknowledge sources.** It is normally permissible for students to share a digital copy of an academic article or other study material in a 'closed' environment such as a student forum.

   See Plagiarism: recognising and avoiding it in Chapter 5; see Giving and receiving feedback in this chapter

When you are studying, following online protocols may feel out of character or a little formal at first. Familiarity comes with practice, however. Such behaviours are expected in workplaces where online work is commonplace; where it's less common, you'll be the model for good practice.

Vital factors for success

Effective communication is vital to successful collaboration but it takes more to achieve great results.

ACTIVITY 8.17 Think back to an occasion when you worked with others online to achieve a group or team task. Was your experience wholly positive or could it have been better? What kinds of factors (other than good communication) could have improved it? Check your responses using the text that follows the activity. If you have not worked in an online group or team, use the scenario below.

Members of a new virtual team have been briefed by email on a task and haven't yet met. Over two or three days, members log into an asynchronous work forum but there are no postings to read apart from one from Dani with a list of names, allocated tasks and an overall work schedule.

Mollie wonders if Dani knows what particular competences people have: Mollie's task is supposed to be working on costings but finance is her weakest subject. Fulvio, who has some experience of virtual team work, realises that the schedule takes no account of the additional time often necessary for asynchronous discussion and decision-making: the process can take several days. Amos sees that Dani has omitted anything about co-ordination of tasks.

No one posts anything to the forum for fear of challenging Dani. Finally, Mollie, posts a message introducing herself, her interests and what she thinks she can bring to the team task, and invites everyone to do the same. Suddenly the forum is busy.

Compare this scenario with what would happen at a first face-to-face meeting of a group or team. What features could be adapted for asynchronous work and how? Read on to check your responses.

A face-to-face meeting is likely to begin with introductions so that participants can get to know each other and their relevant skills and knowledge. One person might temporarily take responsibility for facilitating the meeting until the team goal has been discussed and tasks and roles allocated. Online, these activities should also happen but they take longer. Key activities for online groups and teams are set out below.

Build trust. Mutual trust and respect are essential to the effectiveness of a group or team. Allow time for members to reveal their interests, strengths and weaknesses, find out about one another and begin to develop an open communication climate. Ice-breaking activities are useful. Take the initiative if no one else does and ensure that each member participates.

See Communication climate in this chapter

Develop a shared understanding of the group's or team's goal. This is important *before* tasks are allocated and group or team roles are agreed. A good understanding of the work required avoids crises later. Explore what the goal involves and the tasks, activities, roles, responsibilities and co-ordination required. Each participant should do some individual fact-finding if necessary and contribute to the discussion. It's easy to identify that a task involves the development of survey questions, for example, but understanding what's involved may need research. Misunderstood tasks and goals consume time and may not be achieved.

Allocate roles with clear lines of responsibility. These are normally the same as for face-to-face groups and teams although a meeting convenor will be necessary only if synchronous meetings are planned. Online role-holders need to be highly disciplined to avoid delays that can seriously disrupt people's work. A benefit of online work is ease of access to and updating of digital calendars, schedules and progress charts. An additional task may be keeping the forum well organised; this can be combined with another role. Aim for organisation that supports the needs of members to work efficiently, not perfection.

See *Setting up and running an informal study group* and *Working in formal teams* in this chapter

Allocate tasks to individuals. When group or team members agree to do a task they must accept the responsibilities that go with it. In an open communication climate it's possible for people to ask for help. During task allocation people normally indicate those tasks to which they are most suited. Sometimes, however, more learning is achieved by people taking on tasks that involve skills they *want* to develop. The feasibility of this depends on what's at stake and whether resources are sufficient for some tasks to be done by two people with the more-skilled person helping the other.

Schedule the tasks, including decision-making. Stages and deadlines need to be set. Where group or team decisions need to be made, allow time: it takes much longer when you work asynchronously. The usual method is for the facilitator to start a discussion, invite contributions and set out the time frame. When participants log on once or twice daily, it can take up to five days to make important decisions: two days for discussion, one for the facilitator to summarise and propose a decision (or what the consensus appears to be), one for members to respond and one for the facilitator to announce the decision, its implications and so on. This is set out in Table 8.1.

All members contribute at least once during each stage and check the forum at least once a day. Decisions can be made by majority vote but consensus is preferable. Organise the overall schedule to accommodate the pattern of discussion/decision 'rounds' and run these in parallel with other activities. Allow contingency time. To save time, arrange synchronous meetings at appropriate points.

Decide on a process for getting the job done. The process will depend on the task to be achieved, the medium you use and the facilities it offers. A wiki, for example, allows written work to be jointly produced, commented on and edited. However, editing rules are necessary to maintain good relations and avoid constant changes. If work is posted in attached documents, ask people to insert comments *in turn* to avoid a number of annotated versions. Each person needs to label the document with a different version number to avoid confusion. Small details such as 'version control' can be important.

Table 8.1 Decision-making schedule for asynchronous work

Discussion	Summary and proposal	Responses to proposal	Decision result and implications
2 days	1 day	1 day	1 day

Agree group/team norms. The basic norms or rules are the same as for face-to-face groups; additional ones involve taking responsibility for regular contribution, timely responses and initiative-taking. Unplanned events may prevent a person from participating but he or she may be able to rectify this later or carry out offline work such as research. Explore any lack of participation or continual breaches of protocol by members. Sanctions such as being barred from the group or team are a last resort and may not be necessary if, for student group or team work, your university requires participants to contribute and imposes penalties if they don't.

See *Working in formal teams* in this chapter

Synchronous and asynchronous mixes

Using a mix of technologies saves time. Synchronous media are useful for meetings and decision-making and range from multi-user, text-based chatrooms to full virtual environments with presentation facilities, voting buttons and so on. Unless everyone is familiar with the chosen synchronous medium, one person should take responsibility for learning how it works and running a test session for the group before it is used for a live meeting. This person should seek outside help if necessary.

Your university may allow the team to use its VLE but a chatroom or hangout may need to be set up. Before any option is chosen, some basic checks need to be carried out to ascertain:

- whether participants need to share their screens
- how many people can use the facility at once
- whether registration is needed
- how to create a circle of users
- whether all group or team members have equipment such as a microphone and webcam
- what they need to do to join a virtual meeting.

Media with streaming video are preferable because discussion is more natural, but they need more bandwidth than audio or text-based ones: video and sound quality may suffer and cut-outs may occur. The team should have an alternative plan for the meeting if the technology fails on the day, but prepare for it in advance so that members can easily switch.

Preparing and organising asynchronous online meetings is the same as for face-to-face meetings set out earlier in this chapter. The facilitator or meeting convenor needs to ensure that any documents required are available before the meeting. Two hours are sufficient but the convenor or facilitator should be online at least 15 minutes before the start and be prepared to advise on technical difficulties, by phone if necessary.

Don't be concerned if it takes time to become accustomed to online work. Universities normally create a 'safe' learning environment in which students can make discoveries by making mistakes. Take the opportunities to learn and at the same time, keep up to date with media you can use for online work. Your employer may not just expect you to know but also to lead the way.

Avoiding and dealing with conflict

The effective way to avoid conflict is to create an open communication climate that promotes trust – and trust also helps you to deal with conflict through co-operation and collaboration. Kristin Behfar and colleagues (2008) found that high-performing student teams whose members also experienced satisfaction with working in the team used *pre-emptive strategies* based on equity for avoiding conflict. These included:

- assigning work based on skill
- scheduling work and forecasting workload difficulties
- shared understanding of the reasons for any compromises
- focusing on the content of members' verbal contributions rather than the manner of delivery.

In these teams, which were characterised by fairness, good use of resources and good working relationships, the norms included:

- attending meetings on time (and timing meetings)
- ensuring constructive criticism
- being open to ideas
- listening
- ensuring shared understanding
- being respectful.

Thus, how a team plans and prepares for working together successfully prevents many conflicts from arising later. When they do, however, common causes are:

- the task
- interpersonal relationships
- the process for achieving a task.

Tensions over any one of these can have a negative effect on performance and outcomes. Friction can be expressed in differences of opinion, personality clashes and arguments over how to accomplish tasks and share the work. Members can resort to destructive, unproductive or divisive behaviours such as attributing blame, excluding people from debate, withholding information, withdrawal from debate and other forms of manipulation. Responsibilities and effective actions for dealing with conflict lie with individual members of the group or team. This is the case in student teams in which the facilitator is not responsible for formal management, and in many workplace teams. Behfar et al.'s (2008) research among 57 student teams reveals what high-performing, high-satisfaction teams do when faced with conflict.

1. Task conflicts were addressed by:
   - open communication
   - discussion and debate
   - compromise and consensus.

2. Relationship conflicts were rare but when they occurred members:
   • ignored bad behaviour, listening but otherwise not reacting.
3. Process conflicts were prevented from escalating. Members were able to balance under-contribution with higher contribution at other times, for example. Teams did the following:
   • rotated responsibilities
   • discussed the views of all members and made compromises.

These strategies ensured that all members expressed their views, interpretations were analysed, arguments were evaluated and members engaged in problem-solving, while taking care to avoid taking matters personally or negatively. Compromise involved securing common understanding.

> **ACTIVITY 8.18:** Review the material in the section on *Working in a formal team* in this chapter. How important is planning and preparation to preventing conflicts arising during the team's work? Which aspects did you regard at first as being inessential or too time-consuming but now regard as vital?

Your choice of inessential aspects of planning and preparation will be personal to you, but you probably later regarded as vital all those aspects that involved the establishment of norms, open communication, discussion and agreement. Diving straight into teamwork without regard for these has a negative effect on the team's performance and output and on how members feel about working in the team. A good experience ensures that team members want to work together again. This is often essential in workplace teams.

The psychological contract

Conflict often arises from members' unstated expectations. In workplaces this is known as a psychological contract. It has nothing to do with formal contracts but concerns mutual expectations of inputs and outcomes: conflict arises when expectations differ. A person may believe his or her commitment will be rewarded in some way over and above the agreed salary, while an employer may expect commitment as a matter of course and instead reward behaviour such as knowledge sharing, for example. Another person may expect formal training and development while the employer expects employees to do it informally through such means as co-operative working. A mismatch of expectations can exist in teams, too.

> **ACTIVITY 8.19**
>
> Helen has done a good job on her individual team task but believes Keith made her work difficult.
>
> **Helen (upset):** You kept making suggestions but they just held me up. OK, some were helpful, but I just couldn't see the point of others.

> **Keith (defensively):** I was only trying to help.
>
> **Helen:** Well, it was my work and I didn't need help.
>
> **Gloria (trying to mediate):** We're all kind of responsible for all the tasks, Helen, and …
>
> **Helen (interrupting angrily):** No one seems to appreciate what individuals do in this team!
>
> What do you think Helen's and Keith's different expectations are?

Helen appears to have a strong sense of ownership of her work, whereas Keith – and Gloria – believe that ownership is shared, at least to a degree. They are likely to take individual responsibility for the team's final output. Helen also expects the team to reward individual effort.

In such situations it can be useful for a team and its members to review collective and individual expectations to reveal mismatches. Perhaps the team *does* assume that all inputs will be relevant and well-communicated. Perhaps it *does* regard individual acknowledgement and praise as unimportant. Perhaps a team member *does* expect 'over-giving' to be welcome. However, don't expect reasons for being over-helpful such as to be liked or to exercise control to be revealed. The point is for individuals to understand their own and collective expectations and to adjust behaviours.

An alternative and arguably better way to deal with mismatches – and changing expectations as the team and its members develop – is for individuals to practise stepping back and considering their own and the team's expectations in relation to a particular situation. Skill in switching perspectives, or frames of reference, from your own to that of others and back again is required in professional life to resolve conflicts and misunderstandings.

See Perspective-taking in this chapter

Collaborative negotiation

Negotiation is used to deal with conflicts in which opposing views are hard to reconcile. There are many negotiation styles, from adversarial, with winners and losers, to compromise, which may not result in the best outcomes for a group or team. A modern one is collaborative problem-solving, where parties work together on a fair and equitable solution to the conflict. It's hard for people to reject a solution they have helped to devise.

The collaborative approach can be used with a whole team even if the conflict involves only a minority of members. The aim is to restore and improve the team-working relationship and enhance productivity. The focus is on co-operation and collaboration to find a solution, not the positions adopted. Conflicting positions are reframed as one or more problems to be solved. Just as in problem-solving, criteria for a solution should be established. Good communication skills are needed. Team members should:

See Using critical thinking for investigations in Chapter 6

- be objective and keep control of their emotions
- identify the substantive problem
- offer alternative ways of viewing the problem

- offer or encourage solutions that acknowledge and recognise people's interests, efforts, skills and experience
- build on partial solutions
- explore solutions while keeping the whole picture in mind: solutions must help the group or team towards its desired outcomes
- be open – this encourages trust
- listen actively – it's important to people that their perspectives are heard and acknowledged
- ask questions that guide discussion towards constructive outcomes
- reframe negative inputs into positive, solution-oriented ones – this helps people to relinquish an unhelpful position and 'save face'
- summarise
- avoid solutions that compromise a team's desired outcomes but be open to creative thinking that might enhance them.

See *Creative thinking* in Chapter 8; see *Active listening* and *Beyond words: speech acts and saving face* in this chapter

If the attempts to resolve conflict fail, ask for outside help. Negotiation is a feature of everyday professional work, where it is needed in a variety of situations ranging from dealing with suppliers to how to handle a project.

Techniques for group and teamwork

Imagine you could clone enough instant copies of yourself to form a team: discussion would be pointless. A key benefit of group or teamwork is diversity: the mix of talents, knowledge, perspectives, experience and thinking skills. Diverse individuals each bring something different to a debate.

Techniques for group and teamwork take advantage of this diversity. They are very common in workplaces and can be used face-to-face and online.

Brainstorming

Brainstorming is a way of generating many ideas quickly, for example, to resolve a problem or decide on an advertising message. There are important rules, however.

ACTIVITY 8.20

You and your team need a theme for a fundraising event. At a meeting, members put forward suggestions but with each suggestion, someone says: *That won't work, it's too complicated* or *No, it's been done too many times before*. The meeting ends with no decision made.

What went wrong? List some suggestions that could have made the meeting more productive.

You are likely to have recognised that when ideas are being generated negative responses are often enough to stop people putting forward new ideas. The *assessment* of the ideas has got in the way of *generating* them.

Brainstorming involves these two separate processes: generating (and recording) ideas and assessing them. If you are working online you may need a web-based wall and sticky notes. Look online for free tools such as *Wallwisher* (Padlet) on educational technology and mobile learning websites. Also look for tutorials on *YouTube* to see how to use the tools.

The generation stage

In the generation stage, rules apply to ensure a good supply of ideas:

- no idea should be criticised verbally or non-verbally; criticism has an inhibiting effect
- any idea should be accepted whether seeming relevant or not (although decency and ethics apply)
- the more ideas put forward the better: like a lottery, your chances of winning increase with the number of tickets you buy
- work individually *and* together: don't let the ideas of others inhibit the flow of your own but allow the ideas of others to trigger more of your own.

It's usual practice to generate ideas in a group but sometimes the ideas of others inhibit the flow of diverse ones, producing a clustering effect around just a few. If so, then change the format. Participants can write down as many ideas as possible individually, share them and then, individually, write down more.

The assessment stage

In the assessment stage, ideas are 'clustered' around themes or courses of action to make them easier to assess. Participants themselves do the clustering, moving sticky notes to join others that share some features. When there is general agreement a consensus usually emerges.

Organising a brainstorming session

Five to seven people is an ideal number. To organise a session the facilitator contacts participants with a statement of the problem to be solved, the 'rules' of participation and the date, time and venue. If the session is run face-to-face, one person records the ideas on a flip chart as they are called out so that everyone can see them, also transferring them to paper sticky notes ready for the assessment stage. Online, the ideas can be written directly onto digital sticky notes provided all participants can see them.

Start the session with a 10-minute warm-up that involves generating and assessing humorous and unusual ideas for an unrelated issue such as *How to ensure dropped toast lands butter-side up*. This puts people at ease and allows them to practise the 'rules'. Then run the main session. Allow up to an hour overall. Ideas-generation can take as little as 10 minutes but allow it to run until ideas dry up. Take a break and change the format (to small-group or individual work) if necessary. Working in smaller groups is easier to do in face-to-face settings unless your online medium has break-out rooms.

For the assessment stage, the sticky notes are attached to a wall or flip chart sheets. Participants move the sticky notes around, clustering similar ideas together. Duplicate sticky notes can be created. Each cluster can be given a descriptive title. The process may lead to stable clusters and a consensus about an idea. Alternatively, participants debate and evaluate competing ideas or small groups can cluster ideas and compare their clusters with those of other groups. Choose the method that best fits the medium. Allow up to 30 minutes for the assessment stage; it may take longer online so allow additional time or have separate meetings for the generation and assessment.

While brainstorming can be useful for solving simple problems, its disadvantage is the risk of group conformity, which reduces creativity. An alternative is for individuals to make suggestions that others then build on. The technique focuses on what already works and how to build on it.

Buzz groups

Buzz groups are useful for engaging all participants prior to a discussion or when a discussion becomes 'stuck'. Small groups of two or three people are each given the same issue to debate. If the issue is complex, each group can be given a different aspect. Discussion can be limited to a few minutes. Groups appoint a spokesperson who records (or remembers) the main points discussed and then presents these to the other groups. If the discussion is online, for both synchronous and asynchronous media you will need break-out rooms. Sharing views within and between groups raises issues that might have been overlooked and generates further debate. For good quality discussion, the leader of the main group should ensure that participants have adequate information about the issue.

Giving presentations

The prospect of giving a presentation can be daunting. But consider the benefits.

ACTIVITY 8.21 What are the advantages of using presentations in the following situations and, in each case, who are the beneficiaries?

1. New recruits are being inducted into an organisation. They need important information right away.
2. Three student teams have been set a learning task: they must exchange information about the different business plans they have created using the same scenario.

3. A project team needs to outline its innovative proposal to senior managers to secure resources.
4. An organisation interviewing new graduates requires them to say, in 10 minutes, what contribution they could make to the company.
5. Funders have financed several social initiatives by European not-for-profit organisations. Now they want to know the outcomes. Funders think it will be beneficial for the organisations to share results with each other too.

Presentations are a memorable way of persuading, providing training, learning and teaching or simply informing. They are often used in the selection of job candidates and to assess students. The benefit for the audience is that they are time-efficient. In almost all the above cases, the beneficiaries are the audience but in Situations 2, 3, 4 and 5 the presenters stand to make considerable gains too.

Presenting your ideas, or those of your group or team online or face-to-face, is a feature of both study and work environments. Presentations can't be avoided so it's best to accept that university is an ideal place to develop this essential professional skill. Planning is the key to success whether your presentation involves giving information with the help of several PowerPoint slides or presenting a proposal to a large audience using a mix of media.

The preparation process

There are found main steps to follow in the preparation process.

1. **Plan**
2. **Prepare the presentation**
3. **Work on your delivery and timing**
4. **Check the room and equipment**

1. Plan

Ask and answer these questions:

What do I want to communicate?
Why does – and why should – the audience care?
What do I know about the audience?
What result do I want?
What are the *main* points I need to convey?
Do I have all the information I need?
For how long will I be speaking?

Answering these questions helps you to prioritise the points you include and keep your audience's needs to the fore. You know your audience's general interest, knowledge, status, expectations and decision-making powers. You know whether people expect to learn something new, be inspired to act, or be persuaded or convinced. If you are preparing a group presentation participants should answer these questions together.

2. Prepare the presentation

Key points memorably made capture the attention of the audience. Too much information is a common cause of dull presentations. You can give more detail in response to questions. The first rule of preparation is to know your topic, so do sufficient research. Then work on a logical narrative. One approach is to draw a 'road map' of points. Another is to list everything you think is relevant and then select the most important points from the list.

For a 15-minute presentation that includes two to three minutes for questions, about three main points are sufficient together with information to support or explain them. The exact number depends on the subject matter but people rarely recall more than seven points. (As a guide, if you wrote out your presentation *in full* it would amount to about five or six A4 pages of text.)

Writing the narrative

People often write the introduction and conclusion last. If you write them first, however, they set the tone and help you to structure the middle. Think of an 'opener' to capture audience attention. Stories and anecdotes or quoting a commonly accepted platitude and then challenging it are common among business presenters. However, openings like these by students or inexperienced professionals can seem pretentious. An effective one for business and management students is to ask a 'what if' question which takes the form: *What if we could (predict customers' next choice of car)? It won't happen but I want to convince you (that we can make predictions that are far better than chance …)* Business writers say the first 30 seconds of a presentation are the most important. Thirty seconds don't give you time to answer your audience's private questions (*What's this about? What's it got to do with me?*) but you can ensure that people want to listen.

In addition to allowing you to introduce yourself, introductions enable you to achieve several important tasks.

Capture listeners' attention with your 'opener'. Alternative openers to *What if…* appeal directly to the audience's interests: *Most of you know from experience that it's hard for an organisation to reduce its carbon footprint. Get it wrong and it costs you your reputation; get it right and it raises the bar on customers' expectations.*

Set out your message in brief. *This project aims to reduce or carbon footprint but it approaches the problem from a novel perspective, involving customers and potentially increasing their loyalty […].*

Tell listeners what they or the organisation will gain from the presentation. *An effective way of engaging customers will reduce costs and promote realistic expectations.*

Explain briefly the structure of your presentation. *First I'll ...; second, I'll ...; and lastly I'll ...*

Indicate when you will take questions and if there are handouts. Most presenters take questions at the end. The exceptions are for questions of clarification and when the audience needs to understand each point as it's delivered. This may be the case when presenting health and safety information or initial ideas for a project in order to encourage audience participation.

Conclusions normally do the following:

- Reiterate the main points.
- Summarise the presentation's 'message'.
- Pose a challenging or rhetorical question, urge action or a decision, such as *So, finally, do we try to keep pace with rising expectations or do we engage our customers and manage expectations?*
- End the presentation – the simplest way is to say *Thank you.*
- Open the floor to questions – alternatives to saying *Do you have any questions?* include *Do you have any thoughts?* and *I expect you have some thoughts on X, Y or Z* if you think that X, Y or Z may be controversial in some way.

Preparing and reducing your notes is rather like reducing your notes when you revise for an exam. You start with lots of detail but end up with a series of cards with a few words written on each as reminders. When you make your presentation you can keep the detailed notes beside you 'for safety'. By having just a few words and phrases, you avoid reading from your notes. This encourages you to face your audience, make eye contact and judge responses.

Slides and other visual aids

Decide on what visual aids such as diagrams, graphs, charts, pictures or video clips will help you, making sure they relate to what you want to say. Don't clutter your slides or visual aids: aim for elegant simplicity so that they are easy to comprehend quickly. Presenters who are unused to giving presentations often use too many slides, too many words and text conventions rather than more-visual ones. The use of standard templates is often to blame. Templates lead to many slides looking very much the same: a title and a list of bullet points. Slides need to be consistent in design (they should look as if they belong to the same set) but without being identical. Some professional presenters avoid templates simply to overcome the problem of endless bullet points and too much text; it is hard for audiences to read and listen at the same time.

Slides shouldn't be your notes or aide memoire. Instead, reserve them for the points that are vital to your message and use pictures and other visual aids where possible. Find professional examples online (try search terms such as *avoid bullet points on slides*). There is one caveat: always follow any guidance you are given both at university and at work. In many organisations, for example, you are required to use the company logo, particular colours, typefaces, sizes and so on so that your slides are consistent with 'corporate identity' – and to prevent design disasters.

Avoid difficult-to-distinguish colours for text and background, such as yellow, and others that colour-blind people find hard to see (red, green and blue). When using text, select a font size of no less than 24–30 points and larger for headings. The maximum content for a single slide is about six lines of text, or one or two diagrams, or one graphic image and up to ten words.

There is little consensus on the number of slides to use; suggestions vary between four and 25 for a 15-minute presentation that includes questions. It depends on the information on each slide. It may take a minute to discuss a graph but only a few seconds to show a photograph. Avoid jargon. Your first slide should give the title of your presentation and your name; the list slide can invite questions. The vexed question of whether to provide handouts of slides is discussed in Box 8.3.

Box 8.3 Should I provide handouts?

Handouts normally contain copies of slides. Some professional presenters say handouts should be avoided altogether or provided at the end of a presentation because audiences can be distracted by reading them while you are speaking. It is a matter of judgement, however. They can be useful at the outset *if* your slides are devoted mainly to diagrams or graphics and if you leave space for notes. They are useful, too, at the beginning or the end, to provide full references to your sources. In a paperless environment, digital handouts are best provided at the end to avoid people attending to their device screen rather than to you.

---

3. Work on your delivery and timing

In a 15-minute presentation that includes questions you talk for about 12–13 minutes. Add or remove material to fit the timing. Allow about one minute for your introduction, 10–11 minutes for the main parts and one minute for the conclusion. Practise speaking more slowly than you do normally and note how long you can spend on each main point in the presentation. Decide what detail you can leave out if you overrun. Practise at least once with an audience of selected friends who ask questions. Note whether their questions are mainly requests for clarification (some part of the presentation may not be clear) or for more details. Then consider answers to likely questions. Finally, work on the parts of the presentation that need clarification or that you find difficult to deliver. Use spoken language. Inexperienced presenters often try to memorise what they have written (or read their notes) and then stumble over their words: written language is hard to speak! Box 8.4 provides advice if your spoken language needs improvement.

> ### Box 8.4 Improving your verbal skills
>
> Speech punctuated with expressions such as *like* or *you know* sounds unprofessional and lacks authority. Overcoming habitual use of such words and phrases takes a little time, so start at least three weeks before a presentation (or any other public speaking event). First, notice when you use the expression. Then work out what it is you mean and find the appropriate, non-colloquial substitute. When you say *like*, you could mean *I thought*, *he reacted*, *is similar to*, *as if*, or *including*, for example. People often develop speech habits to fill a pause while they think of how to continue a sentence. Allow yourself to pause. The correct use of *like* and other words and phrases is covered in Appendix 2.

4. Check the room and equipment

Check that the IT equipment in the presentation room is in working order. You may need to take your own laptop or memory stick, connect to a local server or to your cloud storage. Check where you will stand (make sure you don't block the display screen) and where you will put your notes or laptop. Ask a friend to test that you can be heard at the back of the room, bearing in mind that sound carries less far with an audience present. You may need a microphone. Make sure the seating is suitably arranged. Seats in straight lines can convey too much formality especially for a small audience, while a café style arrangement of tables and chairs can be too informal unless you're an experienced and commanding presenter.

Delivering the presentation

ACTIVITY 8.22 List the characteristics of the experienced presenter you hope to be with practice. Try not to think in terms of 'performance' but of engaging and building a relationship with your audience. It helps to watch presentations online by people such as Bill Gates and Steve Jobs: what did they do? how? and what characteristics would you like to emulate? Truly great public speakers convey their authenticity to which an audience immediately responds. How do they convey this authenticity?

Keep your 'wish-list' in mind – and add to it – as you read about presenting. Then save it and refer to it each time you make a presentation to see if you have moved a little nearer to your ideal. The following guidance should help you.

1. **Put on a cloak of confidence.** It's normal to feel nervous before a presentation. Reassure yourself that you are well-prepared. Breathe deeply, tense and

---

Box 8.5 You don't have to be perfect

Take a look at the presentation *Unconscious Bias@Work* on YouTube by Brian Welle, Director of People Analytics at Google Ventures (2014). He hesitates, makes occasional speech errors, starts sentences then stops to rephrase them. The content and his authenticity and charm, however, produce a compelling presentation. The video shows that interesting content delivered intelligently in logical progression is more important than being word-perfect. If you need to develop your spoken communication skills, make this a personal project that you work on every day, not just before a presentation: it won't work!

---

un-tense your shoulders and smile to relax your face. Then adopt an expansive 'power pose' for two minutes (feet apart, chin up, chest forward, arms stretched outward and upward, or elbows out and hands on hips): they boost your endocrine levels and your performance, according to research by Amy Cuddy (Cuddy et al., 2012). (Watch her presentation on the internet: *Your body language shapes who you are.*) When you face the audience, deliver your introduction and opening line without notes. An audience that assumes you are confident helps you to be confident.

2. **Use your conversational voice.** It places emphasis on important words and uses different pitches and pace according to what you are saying. If you need to refer to your notes, look back at the audience as soon as you can and resume the 'right' voice. Don't worry about occasional hesitation. If your voice goes 'flat' re-energise it. Your body language should match your words: mismatches are disconcerting to listeners. However, trying to attend to too many things at once can make you feel very self-conscious. Relax and be your natural self on 'best behaviour'. Perfection is normally an unattainable goal (see Box 8.5).

3. **Watch the audience.** Be responsive to what you see. If you notice signs of confusion, stop and say: *I can see some puzzled expressions; did I explain that clearly enough?* Signs of boredom are trickier to deal with. A confident presenter might invite questions on the presentation so far or ask the audience about his or her line of argument. Presentation schedules can be a problem: people's energy levels dip after lunch for example.

4. **Keep to time.** Presentations have less impact if some parts are rushed. If you need to speed up, omit the detail you identified earlier and tell the audience you can expand on particular points during questions. Be sure not to hurry your conclusion.

5. **Handle questions skilfully.** Questions need not be feared if you have anticipated at least some and you know more than you included in your presentation. Listen to questions carefully and ask for clarification if necessary. Repeat people's questions so that the whole audience hears them. Some techniques for dealing with questions include:

Rephrasing. Reword questions before answering them to avoid yes/no answers. You can say: *Could I rephrase that so I can explain how X affects Y?*

Admitting you don't know. If you don't have a ready answer, say so. If you don't have important information to hand offer to provide it later. Alternatively, depending on the question asked (*Do you think that's the best way of doing Z?*), put it to the audience to answer.

Answering with a question. Questioners are not always explicit. Asking, for example, *How does your question relate to Y?* requires the questioner to be specific.

Inviting discussion later. This can be useful if a questioner focuses on details that don't interest others.

Any of these tactics can be used with hostile questioners. If the audience is engaged and interested, question-and-answer sessions can be lively and constructive. If there are no questions, introduce opportunities next time you prepare a presentation. You can say, for example: *I chose this way of conducting the survey for no other reason than that it was the least complex; it would be interesting to know your views during question time.* Highly productive discussions can result from a presenter revealing his or her thought processes. You can also suggest questions: *The question I'd ask is how could I discover the professional seniority of survey respondents? Do you have any ideas about this?* What you do depends on the topic of the presentation, the audience and the context. After the presentation, make notes on what went well and what didn't. Learn from every presentation.

Poster presentations

We may think of posters as marketing devices, but formal and informal ones abound in all areas of life. The key purpose of them all is to attract attention. Beyond that they may be designed to inform, persuade, motivate, inspire, warn or arouse curiosity. The objective of *academic* posters, whether part of your assessed work or at a student conference, is to give information about your work quickly and interestingly to a wider audience – and for longer than a presentation. What makes any poster a good one?

> **ACTIVITY 8.23** Find a student or workplace notice board. Choose the best poster and the worst one. What are the features of an effective poster and which features should be avoided?

An effective poster attracts your attention and conveys a clear message, helped by the design. A poor poster leaves you searching for what it means or the key message; you may even have overlooked it at first. Posters often fail because originators try to convey too much information. This is also the case among posters produced by students.

Preparatory work

Many people immediately set to work on a poster design, but this is premature. Planning your poster begins by answering these questions:

What do I want to communicate?
Why – and why should – the viewers care?
What do I know about the viewers?
What do I want the poster to do?
What are the main points I need to convey?
Do I have all the information I need?
What is the size of the poster?

Knowing the target audience for your poster is vital: a poster that introduces marketing to school-aged children differs from one that presents your survey results to assessors. The audience determines the type and level of information you provide and the language you use. It also influences what your poster is designed to *do*.

Decide on the content

A poster is a visual device: text is short and easy to assimilate. Think of it as a 'taster' that leaves viewers with a desire to know more. Poster sizes are often A1 (59.4 cm x 84.1 cm) or A0 (84.1cm x 119.9 cm). Even these sizes normally require only 300–500 words unless you are advised otherwise, so you need to limit content to key points and three or four graphs or charts. How you divide up your text depends on the subject matter. A research poster, for example, normally provides an introduction, which includes the rationale for the study, what you did and your hypothesis; a method section, which covers the sample, procedure and what was measured; followed by a results section, a conclusion and implications for practice and further research. A good deal of your poster space will be 'white space' for readability and visual impact.

Format the text

For headings choose a sans-serif typeface that's easy to read, such as Arial, and for the text a classic, serifed one such as Times New Roman. The poster needs to be readable from about two metres so use 72–84pt for the title, 36–48pt for headings and 24–36pt for the text. Separate short blocks of text with emboldened headings and side headings. Text is easier to read if it is aligned to the left and spaced at 1.5 lines. For informational posters, refine and edit the text when you have considered the poster design.

Prepare the images

Decide on the images to use and then prepare them but make sure the size can be adjusted. Use Excel or Word drawing canvases if you are creating your own

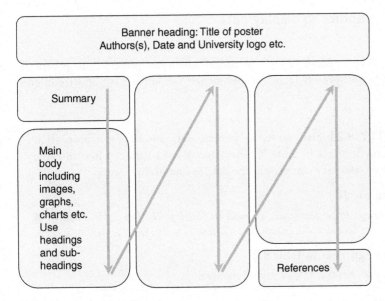

Figure 8.1 A common poster layout

figures. Introduce colour on graphs and charts to indicate different data groups and make data lines thicker than the axes. Make sure the axes and all elements are labelled so that the figure can be understood without reference to the text. Give each figure a border and title. For pictures, the definition should be no less than 300 pixels per inch (118 pixels per cm) or they will be blurred.

Design your poster

First sketch your poster design on paper. The most common layout has a banner heading and three columns. The columns can be divided into sections according to content as in Figure 8.1. The grey lines show the flow of text and images through the poster.

You can use PowerPoint to create a large-scale poster. Free templates are available online (try *Aesplancopy*). Insert your text and images into the template. Check and edit the text and resize images to fit. Choose colours carefully: in addition to black for text, use no more than two or three colours on which text can be read easily. Search for poster colour charts online and examples of colour combinations. Posters take considerable time to create, so keep designs simple. Many universities provide poster-printing facilities; otherwise look for economical print services locally or online (try *Pwauk* or *Studentprinting*) and preferably next-day delivery or allow time in your schedule. Check the poster before printing!

You can construct a large poster from individual A4 sheets mounted on poster card but it takes longer; banner headings will run across several sheets that need to be aligned. With care, they can look professional. Entirely hand-made posters are common in the creative industries and have a certain cachet.

Using graphics to display data

Aim to make your work easily understood when you present it to others. In presentations and posters (and in assignments) use visual tools and techniques where possible.

ACTIVITY 8.24 Sian wants to present data showing the proportion of sales on Sundays in Store X. The value of sales varies in line with the number of sales. She can present the data in one of three ways.

1. **Using words**

   On average, 10 per cent of sales are made on Mondays, Tuesdays and Wednesdays, 15 per cent on Thursdays and Fridays, 35 per cent on Saturdays and 5 per cent on Sundays.

2. **Using figures as in Table 8.2**

   Table 8.2 Average sales x days of the week

Day	Sales	%
Mondays	1,000	10
Tuesdays	1,000	10
Wednesdays	1,000	10
Thursdays	1,500	15
Fridays	1,500	15
Saturdays	3,500	35
Sundays	500	5
Total	10,000	100

3. **Using a pie chart as in Figure 8.2**

   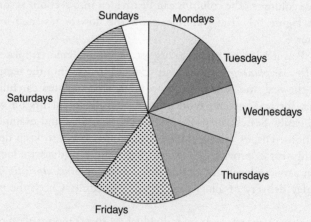

   Sales

   Figure 8.2 Proportion of sales

   Which method best expresses the message *Sundays are our poorest day for sales in Store X?*

Without doubt, you would choose the pie chart. You might present the total sales and proportions in a 'legend' by the side of the pie chart. Eye-catching, graphical representations capture people's attention far more than text or talk. Graphics give a useful focal point for what you say in verbal presentations. While it's usual to explain the content of tables or graphics in texts such as a conventional written assignment, for posters you can simply refer audiences to the figure or table by number and title. (*Sales on Saturdays exceeded those on all other days: see Table 1 Average sales x days of the week* is sufficient, or if the word count is very limited just give the table number.)

Graphical representations of data are easy to create in Word. Look for the tab and menu that allow you to insert a chart and then choose the type of chart you want. You then complete an Excel table of data from which the chart is automatically constructed.

Pie charts

Pie charts are instantly understandable. They show relative *proportions*. To create a pie chart you must know what the 'slices' *represent* – sales, categories of employees, costs and so on – and the *numbers* for each slice. Then you can work out the percentage of each slice. All the slices together should come to 100 per cent. A pie chart can have many slices but it's usual to combine the very small ones in the category *Other* to retain the visual impact of the main slices.

How to create a pie chart

1. Work out the number to be included in *each* slice.
2. Work out the percentage of *each* of these numbers in relation to 100 per cent.
3. Draw and label the pie chart accurately, with each slice showing its proportion of the whole.

You can use Word to create a pie chart. You label and list the number for each slice (you don't have to work out the percentages) and Word creates a pie chart with correctly proportioned slices. Customise the legend and create labels as necessary.

ACTIVITY 8.25 Make up some data or use the figures in Table 8.2 to create a pie chart in Word. Label it appropriately.

Bar charts

Bar charts show *frequency* rather than proportion. You can show the data given in Activity 8.24 in a bar chart. A bar chart has two axes: a vertical one and a horizontal one. In the case of the sales data, the vertical axis represents sales and the horizontal one represents the days of the week as in Figure 8.3.

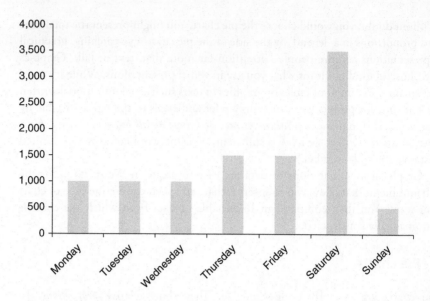

Figure 8.3 Simple bar chart

How to create a bar chart

1. Draw the vertical y-axis, using appropriate numerical units and marking it at suitable intervals (in this case the units are 500 sales).
2. Label the horizontal x-axis with the categories (in this case days).
3. Draw a bar for each category; make it the height of the numerical total for that category.

Again, Word can create bar charts automatically. You can create vertical or horizontal ones. It doesn't matter if the bars are adjacent or spaced. If you want to compare, for example, average sales x days for this year and last year, you can have two bar charts and show them side by side. You must use the same scales on the vertical axes, however: if one graph shows intervals of 500 up to 4,000, the other must too. If not, the data will not be easy to compare. This is clear from the charts in Figure 8.4. It's easy to mislead people into thinking *Last year doesn't look very different from this year.*

Alternatively, combine the two sets of data on one bar chart. Figure 8.5 shows a 3D version.

ACTIVITY 8.26 Use the figures in Table 8.2 or make up some data to create a bar chart in Word. Check that the labels are correct, including the title.

Line graphs

Line graphs are useful for showing relationships between two variables such as sales and time to show variation or patterns. The dependent variable (in this case, sales)

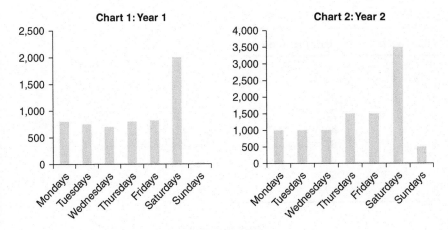

Figure 8.4 Simple bar charts used incorrectly for comparisons

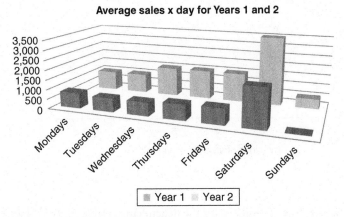

Figure 8.5 3D bar chart showing more than one set of data

is plotted on the vertical axis (known as the y-axis); the independent variable (time, a continuous variable) is drawn on the horizontal axis (the x-axis). Time is always plotted on this axis in *time series* graphs. For other line graphs, the x-axis represents any continuous variable (others include age or distance), while the y-axis indicates what was measured (normally by count, such as clients or website traffic).

The creator of the line graph in Figure 8.6, a tool manufacturer, recalled professional brush cutters assembled in one particular factory, because of a safety problem. To monitor progress, it used information from its authorised dealers to plot the percentage of affected machines returned for modification over a period of two months. The graph shows results.

How to create a line graph

1. Create a table of the variables you want to show the relationship between, as in Table 8.3.

Table 8.3 Time and machine recall

Time (weeks)	Recall response %
0	0
1	18
2	41
3	72
4	84
5	87
6	89
7	89
8	89

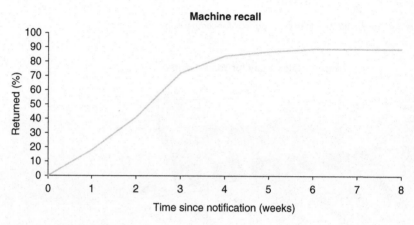

Figure 8.6 Simple line graph

2. Plot your graph, using the vertical axis for the dependent variable (the one that is dependent on the other variable, in this case, the cumulative percentage of machines returned for modification). Plot the independent variable (weeks) on the horizontal axis. Both axes should meet at zero (known as the origin of the graph). Your graph will look like the one in Figure 8.6.

The slopes of line graphs provide instant information. Figure 8.6 shows that, while the recall was successful (the sector average is 80%), reminders should be now be sent to the remaining owners. Explore what you can do with graphs.

ACTIVITY 8.27 Make up some data or use the figures in Table 8.3 to create a line graph in Word. Don't forget to give the graph a title. You may find that the axes don't join at 0 (zero). In Word, it is not obvious how to get them to. Here's how: right click on the x-axis; then select *Format Axis* and choose the option *Position axis on tick marks*. The axes should now meet at zero.

Scattergrams

Line graphs track changes in something over time or show how two related factors vary together. Not all factors behave like this: unlike *Sales* and *Cost of sales*, there may be no necessary linear relationship between them. In these cases a line graph is inappropriate. Sometimes you want to discover whether a relationship exists and reveal it (or the lack of one) graphically. You might want to show that sales are not related to weather, or to discover whether absenteeism could be related to weekend working or how strong a relationship there might be between study time and assignment grades. A scattergram cannot show *causal* effects without further investigation, of course.

Table 8.4 shows the average study time of 14 fictional students and their average assignment grades over one semester. The data were created by asking students how long, on average, they study each day and their average grade for the semester so far. From these numbers, the scattergram in Figure 8.7 was created using Word.

The scattergram shows a relationship but it is an imperfect one: while limited study time is associated with lower average grades, longer hours are not necessarily associated with high grades. Perhaps a third variable such as study skills is important.

How to create a scattergram

1. Use the same method as for a line graph, but choose *X Y Scatter* from the Word Charts menu. If the variables are assumed to be unrelated, one will not be dependent on another. Thus, you decide which variable is best shown on the horizontal (x) axis and which on the vertical (y) axis.

Table 8.4 Average study time and grades data

Study time (average hours per day)	Grade for semester (averaged per cent)
2	39
3	45
4	47
5	52
8	63
7	75
8	85
2	42
3	41
4	49
4	50
6	60
7	62
8	95

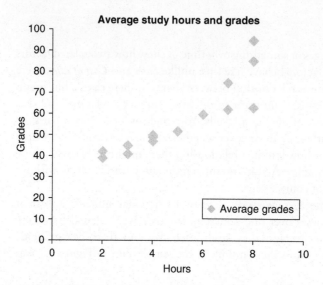

Figure 8.7 Simple scattergram of average study time and grades

If there is one variable that increases by regular increments, however, such as time in increments of one hour, then place that variable along the x-axis. If you believe one variable to be dependent on the other, put it on the vertical y-axis.

ACTIVITY 8.28 Quickly carry out a simple survey, for example, the distance 20 randomly selected students travel each day and their mode of transport (bus, train, bicycle, on foot, by car and so on). Then, using the data, plot a scattergram. You can give each mode of transport a number or letter and provide a key to the scattergram that says what the number or letters mean.

Pictograms

Pictograms are useful for presenting simple data in presentations using symbols that are understood at a glance. Say you collected the data on mode of travel and distance travelled daily in a survey of 20 students. Perhaps there was no meaningful relationship between modes of transport and distance. However, you now know how many students used each mode of transport, so you could show modes of transport by popularity. Some data are shown in Table 8.5.

How to create a pictogram

1. Decide on a maximum number of symbols you want to use in a line. Five is a common number.

Table 8.5 Modes of transport x number of users

Mode of travel	Number of users
Bus	10
Bicycle	5
On foot	4
By car	1

2. Decide on appropriate symbols (use Bing images and after using a search term, choose from the License menu *Free to modify, share and use*, or *Free to modify, share and use commercially*). When you select an image you can find out if you can use the image. Normally students can do so, but don't forget to cite and reference the image creator.
3. Work out how many 'events' each symbol represents (in this case students using each mode of transport). Do this by selecting the largest group in your data set and divide it by the maximum number of symbols you want to use in a single line, for example 10 ÷ 5 = 2. Thus each symbol will represent two 'events': you need five symbols to represent the largest group. Then do this for all the other groups to see how many symbols you need to use for those groups. In Figure 8.8 each symbol represents two student users. There can be fractions of symbols.
4. Copy and paste sufficient symbols for the data.
5. Then create your pictogram as in Figure 8.8. Create a legend or key saying how many 'events' each symbol represents. If you don't include your sample size in the key, provide this in your text or presentation talk, to save your audience having to calculate it.

ACTIVITY 8.29 Create a pictogram using the data you collected in Activity 8.28. Use easily recognised symbols or pictures.

Matrices

Matrices can be used to good effect to present data. They are arrangements of rows and columns to create cells. The simplest ones have four cells (called two-by-two matrices). They are useful when you want to reduce and present a mass of survey data on, for example, the cleanliness of the rooms, bathroom facilities, IT services, the friendliness of staff, whether they greeted guests, were available and helpful and so on.

To reduce the data, you group survey questions into independent categories, say, room quality and customer service as judged by guests as in Figure 8.9. The row and column data should be independent of each other – a hotel can have clean and good amenities but unfriendly staff and vice versa. You can see immediately from the values in the matrix whether the quality of rooms or staff

Figure 8.8 Pictogram of modes of student transport

		Customer service	
		Low	High
Room quality	**High**	100	25
	Low	70	17

Figure 8.9 A 2 x 2 matrix

training needs improving. In this case, a majority of guests thought the room quality was good (High) but that customer service was poor (Low).

To create a matrix

1. Consider your data. Which groups of variables are independent of one another?
2. Decide which of these variables can be grouped into two categories (for a two-by-two matrix). Give the categories a name.
3. Create your matrix using two groups of independent variables as the rows and columns as shown.
4. The final step depends on your data. If, for example, people have rated survey items on a scale of 1–10 then, for each variable, class scores of 1–5 as low and those of 6–10 as high. (The scale must be equally divided.) Then for each variable calculate the total number of low scores and the total number of high scores. Insert these figures into the matrix.

You are able to see and show clearly that staff training is needed in order to produce the highest score in the High/High cell. A matrix can convey an overall picture to senior managers if you are making a case for additional training resources, for example, but you might want to retain more detail for staff trainers or provide more finely-tuned charts. You can produce matrices with more than two columns and rows but the larger the matrix the less readily it is understood.

Evaluation matrices are covered in *Decision-making* in Chapter 6

ACTIVITY 8.30 In a group, conduct a simple two-question survey such as the importance to each person of, for example, the status of the organisation he or she would like to work for and the level of job satisfaction desired. For each question use answer choices such as (1) Not at all important, (2) Not very important, (3) Important, (4) Highly important. Then use the data to create an evaluation matrix.

For each question, calculate the respective number of responses falling in the ranges 1–2 and 3–4 (these will be 'low' and 'high' respectively). Then draw up a matrix like the one shown in Figure 8.9 and insert the totals of 'low' and 'high' responses into the correct cells.

Graphic representations of data are powerful – and they are vital in business and management because of the volume of data available and the need to understand what the data mean and set out its meaning unambiguously to allow decisions to be made at speed. Getting your message across becomes a vital part of the data-to-decision process. The practice of using graphic techniques is so important it now has its own name – data visualisation – and skill is expected by organisations. They need employees who can understand data and appropriate graphics and can use them in communication.

Become familiar with using tools and techniques to present information and try new methods to turn wordy explanations into immediately understandable charts, graphs, matrices and diagrams.

Chapter summary

- ❖ Social learning processes are important because much workplace knowledge is acquired this way. Working effectively with others requires communication and interpersonal skills that you can enhance as you study.
- ❖ A fundamental component of good communication is being able to understand the perspectives of others so that you avoid making wrong assumptions.
- ❖ A related skill demanded by employers is intercultural competence to enable you to work successfully with people from other cultures and internationally. It requires you to broaden your frame of reference. University is an ideal setting to begin to develop this competence.
- ❖ Talking and listening to others in the workplace is the primary method of giving, receiving and exchanging information on which activities and decisions depend. Active listening is essential, but how well do you do it?
- ❖ When you speak you communicate more than just the meaning of the words you use: understanding what else you are communicating is important to working harmoniously with other people.
- ❖ You build trust when you communicate in ways that allow people to save 'face', reduce threats to their self-respect and acknowledge their autonomy.

❖ Giving and receiving feedback is a feature of professional life, one which you begin to acquire as you study. There are techniques you can use and one to help you to be assertive when the situation requires it.

❖ Communication climates can be 'open' or 'closed'. In an open climate people trust one another. You can make positive contributions towards the creation of open climates.

❖ You are expected to work with peers when you study and in the workplace. Organising, running and participating in an informal group in a way that fulfils the expectations of members are important first steps.

❖ Work in a formal team places additional demands on participants because you must agree on tasks and activities, assess resources, allocate work, draw up schedule, monitor progress and produce an output.

❖ Working with others online requires more than knowledge of the digital landscape. Organisation and discipline are needed along with full participation. Online work can be synchronous or asynchronous or a mix of both.

❖ Unconstructive conflict in teams can be avoided or reduced when members engage in open discussion. Conflict sometimes arises through mismatched expectations. There are occasions when negotiation is necessary because views become entrenched.

❖ Brainstorming and buzz groups are useful techniques for groups and teams to generate ideas or to restart a 'stuck' discussion. Commonly used in workplaces, they can be done face-to-face or online.

❖ Presentations are useful for informing and persuading. Planning and preparation ensure that you deliver your material confidently. There are techniques to calm nerves and ways to monitor improvement each time you give a presentation.

❖ Poster presentations are a form of visual communication. It takes time and care to produce an effective message for a target audience in 300–500 words and several images.

❖ Bar charts, line graphs, scattergrams, pictograms and matrices are useful ways of conveying information visually in a way that is readily understood. It is simple to produce them when you know how.

References

Aesplancopy (n.d.) [Online]. Available at www.aesplancopy.co.uk/ (Accessed 11 April 2016).

Austin, J.L. (1962), *How to Do Things with Words*, Oxford, Clarendon Press.

Behfar, K.J., Peterson, R.S., Mannix, E.A. and Trochim, W.M.K. (2008) 'The critical role of conflict resolution in teams: a close look at the link between conflict type, conflict management strategies and team outcomes', *Journal of Applied Psychology*, vol. 93, no. 1, pp. 170–100 [Online]. DOI: 10.1037/0021-9010.1.170 (Accessed 11 May 2016).

Bennett, J.M. and Bennett, M.J. (2004) 'Developing intercultural sensitivity: an integrated approach to global and domestic diversity', in Landis, D., Bennett,

J. and Bennett, M. (eds), *Handbook of Intercultural Training*, 3rd edn, Thousand Oaks, CA, Sage, pp. 147–165.

Bennett, M. (1986) 'Towards ethnorelativism: a developmental model of intercultural sensitivity', in Paige, R. M. (ed), *Cross-cultural orientation: new conceptualizations and applications*, New York, University Press of America.

Bennett, M.J. (1993). 'Towards ethnorelativism: a developmental model of intercultural sensitivity', in Paige, R.M. (ed), *Education for the intercultural experience*, Yarmouth, ME, Intercultural Press, pp. 21–71.

Berggren, N. and Nilsson, T. (2015) 'Globalization and the transmission of social values: the case of tolerance', *Journal of Comparative Economics*, vol. 43, no. 2, pp. 371–389.

Brown, P. and Levinson, S.C. (1987) *Politeness: some universals in language usage*, Cambridge, Cambridge University Press.

Cuddy, A. (2012) 'Your body shapes who you are', filmed June 2012 at TEDGlobal 2012, TED Ideas worth spreading [Online]. Available at www.ted.com/talks/amy_cuddy_your_body_language_shapes_who_you_are/transcript?language=en (Accessed 9 April 2016).

Cuddy, A.J.C., Wilmuth, C.A. and Carney, D.R. (2012) '*The benefit of power posing before a high-stakes social evaluation*', Harvard Business School Working Paper, No. 13–027, September 2012 [Online]. Available at https://dash.harvard.edu/bitstream/handle/1/9547823/13–027.pdf?sequence=1%20 (Accessed 9 April 2016).

Goffman, E. (1967) *Interactional ritual: essays on face-to-face behavior*, Garden City, NY, Anchor Books.

Hammer, M.R. (2009) 'Solving problems and resolving conflict using the intercultural conflict style model and inventory', in Moodian, M.A. (ed), *Contemporary leadership and intercultural competence*, Thousand Oaks, CA, Sage, pp. 219–232.

Hammer, M.R. (2011) 'Additional cross-cultural validity testing of the Intercultural Development Inventory', *International Journal of Intercultural Relations*, vol. 25, no. 4, pp. 474–487 [Online]. DOI: 10.1016/j.ijintrel.2011.02.014 (Accessed 29 April 2016).

Hammer, M.R. (2012) 'The Intercultural Development Inventory: a new frontier in assessment and development of intercultural competence', in Vande Berg, M., Paige, R.M. and Lou, K.H. (eds), *Student learning abroad*, Sterling, VA, Stylus Publishing, pp. 115–136.

Hammer, M.R., Bennett, M.J. and Wiseman, R. (2003) 'Measuring intercultural sensitivity: the intercultural development inventory', *International Journal of Intercultural Relations*, vol. 27, no. 4, pp. 421–443.

Minsky, M. (1980), Telepresence. *OMNI*, June, pp. 44–51 [Online]. Available at https://omnireboot.com/?portfolio=omni-magazine-06-1980-june (Accessed 7 April 2016).

Perry, L.B. and Southwell, L. (2011) 'Developing intercultural understanding and skills: models and approaches', *Intercultural Education*, vol. 22, no. 6, pp. 453–466 [Online]. DOI: 10.1080/14675986.2011.644948 (Accessed 29 April 2016).

Pwauk (UK) Digital Displays (n.d.) [Online]. Available at www.pwauk.com/index.htm (Accessed 8 April 2016).

Ramanau, R. and Tyler, S. (2011) 'International management learning: comparative study of The Open University students', Conference paper presented at the European Humanities University, Vilnius, Lithuania, 14–16 June [Online]. Available at http://oro.open.ac.uk/id/eprint/31645 (Accessed 22 April 2016).

Spencer-Oatey, H. and Stadler, S. (2009) 'The global people competency framework: competencies for effective intercultural interaction', Warwick Occasional Papers in Applied Linguistics No. 3, The Centre for Applied Linguistics, University of Warwick.

Student Printing (n.d.) [Online]. Available at www.studentprinting.co.uk/ (Accessed 8 April 2016).

The British Council (2013) *Culture at work: the value of intercultural skills in the workplace* [Online]. Available at www.britishcouncil.org/sites/default/files/culture-at-work-report-v2.pdf (Accessed 22 April 2016).

Wallwisher (n.d.) [Online] Available at https://padlet.com/ (Accessed 8 April 2016).

Wallwisher in the classroom (2010), YouTube video, added by TechGeek83 [Online]. Available at www.youtube.com/watch?v=ATKt_4d-Uek (Accessed 22 April 2012).

Welle, B. (2014), Unconscious Bias @ Work, YouTube video, added by Google Ventures [Online]. Available at HYPERLINK "http://www.youtube.com/watch?v=nLjFTHTgEVU" www.youtube.com/watch?v=nLjFTHTgEVU (Accessed 16 September 2016).

Wells, M. (2000) 'Beyond cultural competence: a model for individual and institutional cultural development', *Journal of Community Health Nursing*, vol. 17, no. 4, pp. 189–199.

Yershova, Y., DeJaeghere, J. and Mestenhauser, J. (2000) 'Thinking not as usual: adding the intercultural perspective', *Journal of Studies in International Education*, vol. 4, no. 39, pp. 39–78 [Online]. DOI: 10.1177/102831530000400105 (Accessed 29 April 2016).

CHAPTER NINE

Your career in business and management

Where do you see yourself in five years' time? This standard job-interview question may seem premature if you've only just begun your business and management degree programme. But consider this scenario.

> You're about to graduate. You hunt hurriedly for jobs without fully researching potential career paths. Disappointingly, you find you can't meet all the essential and desirable criteria for attractive positions – but it's too late to use your time as an undergraduate to hone or gain the required skills and relevant work experience. You accept a less-than-ideal job, telling yourself you'll find the right career trajectory over time. Good jobs are difficult to get, after all. What you don't know is that you're already two to three years behind fellow students who prepared for this moment.

Will this be your situation or will you start preparing now? It's never too early to start, even if you're sure of your career aspirations (and if you're not, then your first step is to develop some).

This chapter covers how to choose and prepare yourself for fulfilling professional work while you study. Unlike most other chapters in this book it's designed to be read as a whole. It doesn't give detailed information on completing application forms or how to prepare for different types of selection processes such as interviews and assessment centre testing. You can find comprehensive guidance on many university, careers and jobs websites. Rather, unlike many of these websites, the chapter takes you through a more gradual process that prepares and positions you *as you study*, not just when you are about to graduate and haven't a clue where to begin. If you doubt this wisdom, read diaries or blogs of jobseekers on job websites such as *Monster*. This chapter will be useful, too, if you are a part-time student wanting to change jobs.

ACTIVITY 9.1

Aldi Stores' area management training programme for graduates is intensive and well paid. It wants its supermarkets' area managers to be resilient leaders who are confident, committed, hard-working and ambitious, with excellent skills in areas such as communication, team work, problem-solving and decision-making. It needs people who can take a high level of responsibility. Basic requirements are a 2.1 degree, at least three A levels and a preparedness to work a 50-hour week including weekends. If your application is accepted, you take a battery of tests, produce a video and attend group and individual interviews. During the process, you are expected to show an understanding of the aims and constraints of working in retail, knowledge of setting clear objectives, fairness, managing and rewarding performance, what affects motivation, when to allow others to make decisions (and when not to) and what makes you right for the job. You're also expected to be familiar with the company, its products, its distinctive selling points and business strategy. Activities in the interview process involve team work, problem-solving and leadership.

(Adapted from Aldi Stores, 2015)

Consider Aldi's requirements. Which ones could you prepare for immediately before the application and selection process and which ones require development and practice long before that? Which of those that require development and practice might you learn (directly or indirectly) from studying and which ones through non-study activities?

The only selection requirements you could prepare for immediately before the process are those that involve researching Aldi's business strategy, market, stores and products. You need to prepare for the remainder a long time before you graduate. Knowledge of, for example, the aims and constraints of working in retail and aspects of human resource and operations management you can gain directly from your business and management studies. You can also acquire skills such as the fundamentals of communication and team working during your studies. But how *do* you acquire confidence, commitment, leadership skills and the skills required to solve problems and make decisions *in action*?

You may not be considering a career in store management with Aldi or rivals such as Lidl (whose graduate scheme website helpfully allows applicants to write reviews). However, most of the skills you need are likely to be common to all business and management graduate jobs. Plan and act now to acquire and develop the skills, knowledge, experience and attributes you need to enter and succeed in professional life. It's possible to make yourself 'career-ready' even before you have chosen a particular career path.

Importantly, many of today's business and management students are likely to have what's known as *protean* careers. These are careers that change because of the changing nature of the business world, organisations and economic climates. The direct and indirect effects of global economics, mergers, take-overs, structural reorganisations, relocations and closures and political decisions are likely to affect you. A single-track career is unlikely: you change paths within or between organisations over the course of your working life. Common features of these path changes are likely to be job satisfaction and fulfilment. These important factors mean being in work situations that are in harmony with your personal values as much as your talents, knowledge, skills and experience. Protean careers also mean that you *must* take responsibility for your learning and development and for planning your next career move. Taking responsibility for your learning and development is, of course, something with which you should be familiar already!

See *Your journey to success* in Chapter 1

Who am I?

Your personal qualities, skills, knowledge

A first step towards a fulfilling professional career is self-awareness: knowing your skills, values, talents and interests to help you to identify work that matches your qualities.

> **ACTIVITY 9.2** This activity is set out as three steps in which you consider your important personal attributes and skills.
>
> 1. Interests and activities outside your studies
> 2. Formal education
> 3. Work experience including volunteering.
>
> As you carry out each step, identify your personal qualities, your skills and how you learned them. You'll need this information later to create an evidence-based CV. Attend, too, to any skills and experience gaps and list them separately.

Step 1

Use Table 9.1 to help you identify your non-study interests and activities. Mark those in which you are involved and add any interests that are not listed. The *motivations* for your particular interests are covered in a later activity.

Table 9.1 Common interests and activities

Social groups and clubs (scouts, computer clubs)
✓Voluntary groups (St John Ambulance/Red Cross, befriending)
✓Outdoor activities (trekking, skateboarding, cycling, survival skills,
   orienteering)
Indoor activities (art/craft, gaming, dancing, chess)
✓Sport activities (athletics, football, tennis, archery, gymnastics, fitness training)
Water sports (swimming, kayaking, sailing)
✓Music (playing an instrument; belonging to a group, choir or orchestra)
Care of children or others
Special interests (cinema, literature, technology, animals/wildlife, human rights)
Childminding/babysitting
Running a home
Amateur dramatics (performing, directing, staging, technical)
Environmental projects (footpath maintenance, habitat restoration)
Cooking
Gardening
DIY
Language-learning
Extra-curricular learning (evening classes)
Non-fiction reading (technology and computing, science, economics)
Social media participation (from Twitter to international diplomacy forums)

Look to Add ←

Get back on Spanish? ←

Now think carefully about each activity you have identified and consider your participation in it. Identify and list the personal qualities, skills, knowledge and experience you gained from each, with examples. Use Table 9.2 to help you identify important transferable skills – those you can transfer to the workplace – along with other attributes of employability. Some items overlap and there may be gaps as the table's authors, Mantz Yorke and Peter Knight, acknowledge. However, it remains the most comprehensive, student-focused list to date. It covers personal qualities as well as transferable skills. Use the list thoughtfully. In learning and speaking more than one language, for example, you may have experience of other cultures and developed awareness of cultural diversity, active listening and empathy. Cooking is creative, requiring planning, co-ordination and execution to a deadline. Running a home requires many skills including sustaining routine activity, budgeting, prioritising and dealing with competing demands under pressure. Many activities in Table 9.1 may require or involve teamwork.

See *Perspective-taking* and *Active listening* in Chapter 8

Step 2

Now use Table 9.2 again, this time to help you identify the personal qualities, skills, knowledge and experience you've gained from your *formal studies*. Beside each personal quality or skill you identify, give at least one example of how you developed it. At the same time, identify qualities, skills and experience you *don't* have or need to improve. Make a note of them. If discovering your skills is difficult, then try the online Skills Health Check Tools offered by the UK's National Careers Service.

Table 9.2 Aspects of employability

1	Malleable self-theory: belief that attributes (e.g. intelligence) are not fixed and can be developed.
2	Self-awareness: awareness of own strengths and weaknesses, aims and values.
3	Self-confidence: confidence in dealing with the challenges of employment and life.
4	Independence: ability to work without supervision.
5	Emotional intelligence: sensitivity to others' emotions and effects.
6	Adaptability: respond positively to changing circumstances and new challenges.
7	Stress tolerance: work effectively under pressure.
8	Initiative: ability to take action unprompted.
9	Willingness to learn: commitment to ongoing learning to meet the needs of employment and life.
10	Reflectiveness: the ability to reflect on and evaluate the performance of oneself and others.
11	Reading effectiveness: the recognition and retention of key points.
12	Numeracy: understand and use numbers and data appropriately.
13	Information literacy: ability to access and evaluate information from different sources.
14	Language skills: possession of more than a single language.
15	Self-management: ability to work in an efficient and structured manner.
16	Critical analysis: ability to 'deconstruct' a problem or situation.
17	Creativity: ability to be original or inventive and to apply lateral thinking.
18	Active listening/empathy: focused attention in which key points are recognised; perspective-taking.
19	Written communication: clear reports, letters etc., written specifically for target audience.
20	Oral presentations: clear, confident presentation of information to others [also 21, 35].
21	Explain: orally and in writing [also 20, 35].
22	Computer literacy: use a range of software.
23	Global awareness in terms of cultures and economics.
24	Commercial awareness: operate with understanding of business issues and priorities.
25	Political sensitivity: appreciate how organisations work; act accordingly.
26	Ability to work cross-culturally within and beyond the UK.
27	Ethical sensitivity: appreciate ethical aspects of employment; act accordingly.
28	Prioritise: ability to rank tasks according to importance.

Table 9.2 (cont.)

29	Plan: set achievable goals and structure action.
30	Apply understanding and knowledge from degree programme.
31	Act morally: have a moral code and act accordingly.
32	Cope with complexity: handle ambiguous and complex situations.
33	Solve problems: select and use appropriate methods to find solutions.
34	Influencing: convince others of the validity of one's point of view.
35	Argue for and/or justify a point of view or course of action [also 20, 21, 34].
36	Resolve conflict: intra-personally and in relationships with others.
37	Make decisions: select the best option from a range of alternatives.
38	Negotiate: discussion to achieve mutually satisfactory resolution of contentious issues.
39	Team work: work constructively with others on a common task.

Based on Yorke and Knight, 2006

Step 3

Next, identify personal qualities and skills you've acquired through any paid work. Include any voluntary work that you didn't consider in Step 1. Skills are likely to include work-specific ones such as dealing with customers or clients. Some are transferable but don't forget that having to acquire a set of work skills quickly can be confidence-building and that retail work, for example, can help you to be commercially aware. Examples of common work-specific skills are set out in Table 9.3. List your skills and examples of how you gained them.

Table 9.3 **Examples of work skills**

Meet / set performance standards / targets	Deal with customers / clients / consumers	Comply with policies / procedures
Supervise	Keep records	Delegate
Process payments	Create product displays	Assess risk
Budget	Interview / recruit	Use business software
Order / receive supplies	Operate equipment	Teach / train

By now you have compiled these items of information from many areas of your life:

- Lists of skills and employability attributes
- Examples of where you have acquired them
- Important skills and experiences that you don't yet have or require development.

Strengths	Weaknesses
Your skills	Gaps in your skills
Opportunities	**Threats**
Ways to fill gaps	Barriers and hindrances

Figure 9.1 SWOT analysis of skills

You need these when you carry out other activities in this chapter. Now you carry out a SWOT analysis, a useful tool used in business and management for strategic planning. A SWOT matrix for analysing skills is shown in Figure 9.1. It helps you to see what you need to do to make yourself career-ready.

ACTIVITY 9.3 Your SWOT analysis concisely reveals your strengths, weaknesses, opportunities and threats. Use your notes on your skills and skills gaps from the previous activity and consider opportunities and threats which are explained below. Use the matrix in Figure 9.1. When you have completed the activity, keep your SWOT analysis and notes for later.

Strengths are the areas in which you believe you have skills and competence.

Weaknesses are skills you lack or need to develop. Use Table 9.2 to guide you.

Opportunities are those you can take advantage of to remedy important weaknesses: there may be opportunities at university or during vacations. Filling skills gaps may simply involve a more focused approach to your studies and full engagement with study skills or perhaps choosing a course option that extends them. For example, project work and dissertations involve a number of vital skills including information literacy, self-management, initiative-taking, planning and decision-making.

Threats are circumstances or events that might prevent you from taking advantage of opportunities to remedy skills gaps. Barriers and hindrances include time and money but you may be able to overcome them with creative thinking, time management and planning. When you do overcome a barrier, you can use this as evidence of skills such as dealing with competing demands and challenges.

Your SWOT analysis provides you with a good idea of what you can, or could, offer any employer *at present* and the gaps you need to fill. Your most-developed skills probably reflect your interests but in professional work a range of skills is needed. Opportunities for gap-filling and threats need careful consideration.

Many skills can be honed – and deficits remedied – simply by being more curious and involved in what you already do. For example, if you work part-time or full-time, or undertake voluntary work, you can increase your business awareness by discovering how the organisation conducts its business and why. If you're a member of a club or society you could participate in the organisation of its activities.

If you do none of these, join a club or society that interests you or sign up to help other students. Volunteering and work experience ideas are covered in Box 9.1 *Catch up on volunteering* and Box 9.2 *Types of work experience*. Above all, be prepared to step outside your confidence boundaries (your 'comfort zone'): if you don't you'll miss many learning opportunities. Actions don't need to be large scale. Small adjustments can bring about big improvements.

Revise your SWOT analysis as you gain and hone skills. Your progress will be evident and you'll see which skills, knowledge and experience deficits are becoming more urgent to remedy. You will need your SWOT analysis later in this chapter together with your notes from earlier activities.

An up-to-date SWOT analysis is a good resource for preparing for an interview. If you can identify your weaknesses so, too, can potential employers. The weaknesses, opportunities and threats cells can be a way of anticipating awkward questions and show that you are able to be self-critical and to plan.

Box 9.1 Catch up on volunteering

No volunteering experience? Many voluntary activities can take just two or three hours a week of your time. Find out about volunteering opportunities locally and at your university. If you have commitments that restrict your time or your ability to participate regularly, you could try micro volunteering, that is, projects taking typically less than 30 minutes such as contributing data or studying data to aid research. It's also known as pyjama volunteering as most contributions can be made online from home. Pick organisations carefully and choose tasks that require you to learn and develop work-related skills. Look online for reputable micro-volunteering sites for information and advice. Consider, too, combining something you already do with volunteering: if you swim regularly, for example, why not teach others?

Your personal values

Work needs to be meaningful and enjoyable. But what fulfils one person may not fulfil another because of differences in personal values. Knowing yours helps you to identify areas of professional work that will be fulfilling to *you* and avoid those that will continually challenge them.

A research-based set of 19 human values has been developed by Shalom Schwartz and colleagues (2012). The values set out in Table 9.4 are not just beliefs: they motivate you to behave in ways you believe are desirable in any situation. So, for example, if you believe in honesty, you behave honestly in and outside the workplace and evaluate the behaviour of others using this value as a criterion. Actions often express more than a single value.

> **ACTIVITY 9.4** Consider each value in Table 9.4 and decide how important it is to you personally. Give each a score between minus 1 (–1) and 5 as set out.
>
> –1 In opposition to what you believe
> 1 Of no importance
> 2 Fairly unimportant
> 3 Neither unimportant or important
> 4 Fairly important
> 5 Extremely important
>
> It's important to understand that no individual value is 'good' or 'bad'; they are simply those held by people in many cultures. When you have your score for each value, write it into Figure 9.2.

Table 9.4 **Human values**

VALUES	YOUR SCORE
Self-direction – thought: freedom to cultivate one's own ideas and abilities. People valuing independence of thought are likely to care more about being able to take initiative than high income.	4
Self-direction – action: freedom to determine one's own actions. The difference between this and self-direction of thought is a greater emphasis on high income.	5
Stimulation: excitement, novelty, challenge and change. This can diminish depending on life-stage and circumstance.	4
Hedonism: pleasure and sensuous gratification for oneself. These values differ from stimulation values in that enjoyment and comfort are sought.	4
Achievement: success according to social/cultural standards. People with achievement values gain social approval by competent performance that generates resources for individuals to survive and for groups and institutions to reach their objectives.	5
Power – dominance: power through exercising control over others. There is not necessarily a desire to be admired for success. Power/dominance values appear to be more important to men than to women.	3
Power – resources: power through control of material and social resources. Wealth and high income are likely to be important when choosing a job.	3
Face: security and power through public image and avoidance of humiliation. Money is less important.	4
Security – personal: safety in one's immediate environment. Harmony, stability of relationships and a sense of belonging are important.	5
Security – societal: safety and stability in the wider society. People with these values are likely to take an interest in international affairs and politics.	4
Tradition: maintaining and preserving cultural, family or religious traditions that are not subject to change.	2

Table 9.4 (cont.)

VALUES	YOUR SCORE
Conformity – rules: compliance with rules, laws and formal obligations. There is no necessary involvement with family or religion in this kind of compliance.	4
Conformity – interpersonal: avoidance of upsetting or harming other people. Importance is attached to smooth interaction and group functioning. Schwartz (2012) points out that people who value conformity are aware of expectations and are responsive to changes in these.	3
Humility: recognising one's insignificance in the greater scheme of things. Self-promotion is avoided.	5
Benevolence – dependability: being a reliable and trustworthy member of an 'in-group' (the one with which a person identifies).	4
Benevolence – caring: devotion to the welfare of in-group members.	3
Benevolence – concern: commitment to equality, justice and protection for all people. This benevolence goes beyond the in-group.	4
Universalism – nature: preservation of the natural environment.	5
Universalism – tolerance: acceptance and understanding of people different from oneself. Universalism values in general stem from the survival needs of people and nature's provision of the necessary resources.	5

Adapted from Schwartz et al., 2012

Values are related to one another in a circular continuum shown in Figure 9.2. The further a value is from others, the more likely it is to conflict with them; closer values are more similar.

The 19 values are grouped into a higher order of description described by Schwartz and colleagues as *Self-transcendence, Openness to change, Self-enhancement* and *Conservation* (2014). *Self-transcendence* refers to transcending self-interest for the sake of others; *Openness to change* means readiness for new ideas and experience; *Self-enhancement* is the pursuit of one's own interests and *Conservation* refers to self-restriction, order and avoidance of change. Some values sit on the boundaries of these higher orders because of their similarity to adjacent values.

The outer two circles show even broader organising principles. *Personal focus* refers to protecting oneself against threat while *Social focus* refers to concern for others or established institutions. *Self-protection/Anxiety avoidance* refers to how much a person controls threats, maintains order, avoids conflict and deals with anxiety. *Growth/Anxiety-free* indicates self-expansion, grouping the values that are likely to motivate people when they are free of anxiety.

Your scores show which values are important to you. What did you find? It's likely you discovered there is a *pattern* to your values. You may be able to identify the higher-order groups that describe your values, but your individual values are useful in deciding on suitable types of work or a career path.

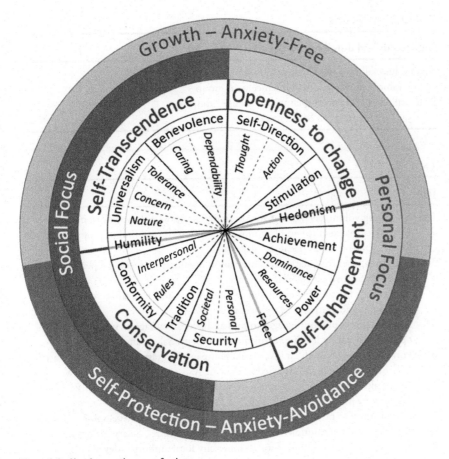

Figure 9.2 Circular continuum of values

Cieciuch et al., 2014

How to use your values in career and job choices

Now see how well your values fit a particular line of professional work. At this point you aren't choosing a career path or a first job but testing how the matching process works. Carry out the two parts of Activity 9.5 below. The first part is designed to provide some practice at matching values with job types.

ACTIVITY 9.5 *Part 1* – Quickly match each of the people in Table 9.5 to one of the jobs in Table 9.6. To simplify the task, assume that the individuals have the skills, knowledge and talents to do any of the jobs listed. The individuals' values have been simplified to a single, dominant group.

Table 9.5 Individuals

Individuals and dominant values group

Sara's values fall into the Conservation group
Marc's values fall into the Self-enhancement group
Josh's values fall into the Openness to change group
Petra's values fall into the Self-transcendence group

Table 9.6 Jobs

Jobs

---

1 Managing volunteers in a not-for-profit organisation. Salary: low to medium.
2 IT project manager for an IT company requiring the creation of project plans for new products and releases. Salary: high.
3 Brand manager for a national conservation organisation seeking a person with bold and creative ideas. Salary: average.
4 Corporate card administrator; ability to work fast and accurately, following procedures and systems. Salary: average.
5 Business development manager to find and take advantage of business opportunities for a leading recruitment company. Salary: medium to high.
6 Portfolio associate with an investment company in a fast-paced entrepreneurial environment. Financial knowledge, data analysis, team work, ability to work cross-culturally and on own initiative with little supervision are essential. Salary: very high.
7 Opportunity to be a partner in an entrepreneurial venture developing renewable energy solutions for sustainable communities. Salary: uncertain.
8 Business Intelligence Officer for an inner city local authority, developing evidence-based policies to meet strategic challenges; expected to lead and manage research projects. Salary: average.

You probably matched Sara to Job 1 or 4; Marc to Job 2 or 4; Josh to Job 5 or 7 and Petra to Job 3 or 8 on the basis of matching core personal values (such as conformity or achievement) to key job characteristics (such as following procedures, salary, entrepreneurship and so on).

Now do the same matching task for yourself in a more considered way.

ACTIVITY 9.5 *Part 2* – Find five *diverse* job advertisements and descriptions from different sectors including not-for-profit. Each job should require a business and management degree (or unspecified degree) and, for this activity, up to 10 years' experience. The jobs sections of online newspapers such as *The Guardian* and online job sites such as *Monster* are good sources of advertisements. Follow links to full job and person specifications (if available) and the employing organisation. Gain a good understanding of each job, the requirements and the employer.

Which job (and employer) appeals to you most and which least? Use your values results to consider why this is so, rather than your skills and capabilities. Perhaps your important values focus on caring and tolerance (Self-transcendence) and one or more of the jobs would be more suited to a person with high achievement aspirations who controls resources (Self-enhancement). It's wise to consider *all* your important values when considering job descriptions and employers, however, not just one or two.

The activity should convince you that your values are important when choosing a career path and a first job. If jobs are in short supply, your first job may not be ideal but your self-knowledge helps you to recognise more suitable opportunities when they arise.

Your talents and interests

Your interests and talents are important: indeed, important enough for some organisations to focus on these in their selection process. Your talents and interests usually reflect your values – what motivates and engages you – and tell organisations about situations in which you thrive and flourish. Consider this scenario.

Teamwork brings out the best in Eva; she's proud of her ability to get people to work together harmoniously and she's very persuasive. Her passion is horses but she isn't planning an equestrian career: she has higher aspirations than the full-time job she's been offered at the tack shop where she works during vacations. But, at her university careers office, she sees a number of career paths in the equine industry for people with business and management degrees.

She reads the profile of a person who is a Quality Assurance Manager for an animal pharmaceutics company. The company wants a strong team player and team mobiliser. The job is clearly for a person with experience and she doesn't have all the required skills. She's not even sure she'd like all the administrative work and data handling but it's helped to provide her with some ideas. A little more research reveals career possibilities in the retail and supply chain management of veterinary products, feedstuffs and equipment to equestrian businesses. Prospects for career progression are good.

Eva gains some ideas about a potential career direction from thinking about her interests and talents that bring out the best in her and her passion. Carry out Activity 9.6 to help you do the same.

ACTIVITY 9.6 Consider

- what you feel passionate about
- what you enjoy
- situations in which you flourish
- your successes and proudest achievements
- what gives you deep satisfaction
- when you feel most 'at home' with yourself, 'in the zone' or highly focused without much effort.

You may enjoy being creative or be passionate about your voluntary work. You may have felt a sense of achievement when you were chosen as captain of a sports team. You may flourish when working independently or in challenging situations – academic or otherwise. You may be most focused when working on case studies that stretch your thinking. Self-development may give you a deep sense of satisfaction so you seek out opportunities.

Your findings tell you in what kinds of situations you're likely to find success and fulfilment. They also tell you about your adaptive skills: those you possess because of your interests, talents, passions and personality. But you can probably identify many skills, too. Canoeing, for example, may reflect your love of water and involve highly specific skills and knowledge but it also develops your resilience, self-reliance and problem-solving abilities.

Putting it all together

Your SWOT and values analyses and your review of your talents, interests and passions have provided you with a profile of yourself and what you can offer an employee. In particular, your SWOT analysis has identified skills gaps to remedy in order to improve your employability. Keep all this information; review and add to it, preferably before the beginning of each semester, term or course. You also need it for other activities in the chapter: there are further steps to take, ones that careers advisors say are vital but are frequently omitted by students.

Careers research

Your next step is to visit your university's careers office or website. It's never too early to do this. Your aim is to research fields of work that are consistent with your SWOT analysis, values, your talents and interests *and* the skills and experience you aspire to at graduation and have planned to acquire by then. Your careers office may offer profiling to help you.

Be systematic in your research. Browse careers by categories such as administration, hotels and tourism, retail and manufacturing and supply chain management. Pay attention to emerging or growing fields such as the green economy ('green-collar jobs'), IT and health. Some career paths such as marketing can be followed in many sectors. Others such as those involving healthcare administration and management can be sector specific. However, the field of healthcare expands far beyond traditional boundaries if you include support industries ranging from catering and the supply of medical instruments to research and development. Good sources of careers information in the UK include the websites of *Prospects* and Durham University. *The Job Crowd* website lists sectors, samples of roles, job descriptions and jobs currently available.

When you have identified an industry or sector of interest, discover as much as you can about it:

How big is it?
Which organisations are key players?
Which are up and coming?
What are the external threats to the industry?
What are the opportunities and growth areas?
What kinds of roles or jobs exist for business and management graduates?
How many such roles or jobs are there?

Do this for renewables [handwritten margin note]

Professional positions that are limited in number or that command a high salary are usually highly competitive. For any job, however, you will always be competing against other candidates. Your credentials matter!

Find job advertisements and see what the desirable jobs involve: what skills and abilities are required? In this way you narrow the field and begin to match your skills, knowledge, experience, values and interests against specific roles. At the same time you identify skills gaps while there is time to remedy them. (Add these to your SWOT analysis.)

It's useful to look at trade journals and the careers websites of organisations and universities for profiles of people employed in particular jobs, to discover how they gained the experience they needed for their current role. This helps you to see how a career takes a particular direction. Some people may have started in an unrelated job and gained knowledge and experience with a series of job changes; others may have gained places on graduate schemes.

Then, without focusing too narrowly on *specific* roles, keep up with an industry or sector of interest by reading trade publications and broadsheet newspapers. Also set up free email alerts and RSS feeds for news on organisations and sectors of interest via websites such as *Breaking News*, Forbes and the BBC. (This helps you in your studies, too.) Use and develop your network of contacts to find out more. Seek information on opportunities for work experience, short-term placements and internships (see Box 9.2 for descriptions). Competition for these can be high, so treat any applications as if you were applying for a job (application forms, a cover letter and a CV are often required).

You don't have to wait for work experience opportunities to be advertised, however: some small and medium-sized organisations may not advertise, so contact them and follow up with an application if there is an opening. Also try asking to volunteer or to shadow a person in an appropriate role. When you take up an opportunity you gain more than work experience: you gain insight into the organisation, the sector and whether possible roles within it are for you. Know what you want to find out. A good organisation will welcome questions.

See *Networking* in this chapter

Box 9.2 Types of work experience

Work experience is a general term for any work you do. Opportunities for students include:

Short-term placements You work for an organisation on a temporary basis. Look for organisations offering short-term placements during vacations. Placements can be paid or unpaid.

Internships These are usually short periods of work experience carried out in vacations. Organisations offer supervised work in particular roles but competition is high because many internees are offered jobs after graduation. Choose organisations you want to work for.

Volunteering This is unpaid work, normally in not-for-profit organisations, that can be done in vacations or as a regular commitment. Volunteering outside the UK is possible.

Shadowing You observe a professional person such as a manager for a few days to see what they do and how. Shadowing is usually unpaid.

Effective networking can help you identify opportunities and gain introductions. Internships *can* be exploitative so gain as much information as you can beforehand. Make sure you benefit from your experience by making a daily list of what you want to know about the organisation or sector and ask questions.

All the types of opportunity set out in Box 9.2 allow you to remedy skills gaps, gain work experience and enlarge your network of contacts. Make sure you know what's involved and consider whether you can afford to be unpaid. Ask your careers office to help you look for opportunities. Useful UK websites include the *Graduate Recruitment Bureau, Milkround, NCVO* and *Volunteering England* (there are sites for Wales and Scotland, too). The UK Government's webpage *Volunteer placements, rights and expenses* is a good source of links and information. Careers fairs are also a valuable source of information about work experience opportunities. They are generally open to first and second year undergraduates and allow you to approach organisations directly to ask about internships, work experience, vacation work and so on. Also check the websites of *Prospects* and the *Association of Graduate Recruiters*.

Be creative

Finally, use your initiative. If you have a passion for steam trains, for example, combine it with a placement in tourism or hospitality. Try the Ffestiniog & Welsh Highland Railway and other steam railway operators. If your interest is canal restoration, the Waterways Recovery Group might train you to be part of a leadership team for its week-long work camps. Search creatively, back to front: start with an online search for information on your passion or interest, then look for organisations.

Researching a potential career from the beginning of your time as an undergraduate may seem premature but your efforts will be rewarded. You spend up to 45 years in work. Will you be a person who makes many untargeted applications and drifts from one unsatisfying job to another? Or will you be well-prepared, knowing which first jobs to apply for and possessing what's required to succeed?

Developing an evidence-based CV

A curriculum vitae, better known as a CV, is a brief account of a person's qualifications, skills, work experience and achievements. The last time you provided something like a CV was probably when you applied to study for a degree. If you still have a copy of your application form, read it. Consider who you wrote it for and why. Would you use your exam results and personal statement to apply for an internship or part-time work next week? No: it's already out of date and was written for a very different purpose.

It's never too soon to start compiling your CV in preparation for job seeking. It's easy to add to it as you gain further skills, experiences and knowledge, while the new, relevant content is fresh in your mind. It's then ready to be tailored to a particular job and employer when the need arises. Professional people usually update theirs every 6–12 months. A CV written 'from scratch' just before applying for your first graduate job won't be a carefully considered one and probably won't reveal your uniqueness and suitability for the position. You need to stand out from other candidates.

A good CV is evidence-based and concise: it tells a potential employer the aspects of yourself you want to be noticed. It should cover in one to two pages your education, work experience and achievements and your skills, including relevant work and adaptive skills. A short, personal profile is optional but it's an excellent way of summarising what you have to offer and your ambitions.

The recommended CV structure for new graduates seeking a first job is what's known as reverse chronology. You set out your most recent educational achievements and work experience starting with the most recent. The usual order is as follows:

1. Your name
2. Personal profile (optional)
3. Your educational qualifications and where you obtained them

4. Relevant courses/modules studied
5. Work experience including voluntary work with your role, responsibilities and skills used or gained
6. Skills, achievements and interests not previously mentioned, with evidence.

You weave your skills into this content in an evidence-based way, starting with your personal profile.

The personal profile

A personal profile should be tailored to a particular area of work or a specific job but you can write a generic one as a 'place holder' and customise it when you need to. It's your opportunity to show that your skills, achievements and ambitions are an ideal match for a job (and organisation). An example is:

> An adaptable and responsible graduate seeking an entry-level position in public relations that will utilise the organisational and communication skills developed through my involvement with Kent Rag and promotional work during vacations.
>
> During my degree I successfully combined my studies with work and other commitments, showing myself to be self-motivated, organised and capable of working under pressure. I have a clear, logical mind with a practical approach to problem-solving and a drive to see things through to completion. I enjoy working on my own initiative or in a team. In short, I am reliable, trustworthy, hard-working and eager to learn and have a genuine interest in PR.
>
> University of Kent, 2015

Note how this personal profile conveys management of competing demands, flexibility and tenacity, which may be otherwise difficult to demonstrate. Take care to ensure that your CV covers or implies all the important qualities you want to highlight.

The skills weave

The art of CV writing is to *weave* your knowledge and skills into your CV by showing examples and evidence of them wherever you can, without repetition. When you set out the courses you have studied you draw in the skills you gained and how. For example, when you mention a project course you can say how it helped you to develop your information literacy skills or to lead a team. For a *draft* CV, include all the transferable skills you gained (look again at Table 9.2 *Aspects of employability*). (When you *tailor* your CV, you select those skills that best match the job requirements.)

When you set out your work experience give examples of how you used your transferable skills and gained work-related ones. For each job, say what your main responsibilities were, the transferable skills you needed and how you used or developed them. For example, if you worked voluntarily as a gardener at a home for people with sight loss you might emphasise how your initiative-taking helped residents to take up gardening which, in turn, honed your communication and interpersonal skills. Work in a shop may have developed your customer-awareness and business knowledge.

When setting out skills not mentioned earlier in your CV, give examples of when you used them to good effect. Achievements can include publicly recognised ones such as winning a 'Young fundraiser of the year' award and personal ones that gave you great satisfaction, such as successfully handling a difficult challenge. Your achievements reveal your personal qualities and capabilities. When you set out your interests, select those that reveal skills, aptitudes and what motivates you. Being a regular steward for a youth orienteering group says far more about you than expressing a general interest in people, for example. A suitable layout for your CV is set out in Table 9.7. Note the asterisks and notes below the table.

There are many examples of CVs online. UK students should select a format from a UK website (North American conventions can be different). Select one that is easy to read at a glance. This will mean honing your CV content and structure to near perfection. If you are a part-time student already working professionally, you can use a *skills-based* or *functional* CV structure. You match your skills to those required in the job you are applying for. Examples of these are also available online. However, it doesn't matter which format you use.

CV writing tips

Be honest; avoid exaggeration. It's easy to elevate the level of your skills and previous responsibilities, but don't. At interview your CV may be used to introduce questions such as *I see you worked as part of a team when you [...]. Tell me more about that. How did you handle conflict?* You will be found out either at interview or when you start work. Treat any desire to exaggerate as inner dialogue or self-talk: you are communicating your development aspirations to yourself. Listen and act! Live up to your aspirations. This is one reason why preparing a CV in advance of need is so useful. You also see how providing evidence and emphasising your enthusiasm for learning and development obviate the need for exaggeration.

Avoid gaps and inconsistencies. There is a reason for avoiding gaps in your education or work record: they make it look as if you're covering something up even if you're not. If you do have gaps, say how you made positive use of them. If a gap was due to prolonged illness, rehabilitation or being gaoled for criminal activity, use a skills-based or functional CV format which places less emphasis on dates and more on matching your skills, knowledge and capabilities against those required for a particular job. Seek advice from your careers office.

Check your CV for inconsistencies. If work and study dates are identical or overlap substantially, you'll need to say why. What seems to be an inconsistency to a recruiter can often be avoided by the simple insertion of the term *part-time*.

Table 9.7 Suggested layout for reverse-chronology CV

YOUR NAME
* Address; email address and phone number
Personal Profile
Education and qualifications

20XX – 20XX	University of Z, country if outside the UK
	Degree name; degree class
	Academic awards, if any
	Courses/modules studied
20XX – 20XX	XYZ School / Sixth Form College; Town, County
	A Levels
20XX – 20XX	ABC Comprehensive, Town, County
	GCSEs

** *Work experience*

Month 20XX – Month 20XX	Organisation
	Your role, what you did, what you were responsible for; skills used or gained; any recognitions or awards
Month 20XX – Month 20XX	Organisation
	Your role, what you did, what you were responsible for; skills used or gained; any recognitions or awards
Month 20XX – Month 20XX	Organisation
	Your role, what you did, what you were responsible for; skills used or gained; any recognitions or awards

Other skills

Achievements

Interests

Notes

*If you intend to put your CV online, omit your address and phone number. In any case, don't include photos. Many careers advisors suggest omitting your date and place of birth; you don't have to state your gender, either. These omissions reduce the potential for discrimination.

**Including months is helpful if your work was temporary or done in vacations. For work in which you remain involved the convention is: *Month, 20XX – to date* or *present*.

Support your claims with evidence and examples. Set out *skills and experience* in the context in which they were used or gained. Rather than describing yourself as a goal-oriented person with drive, it's preferable to say *Demonstrated initiative and leadership skills in achieving the goal of sustainable membership of the university's Adventure Society*. Your evidence speaks for itself.

When you set out your *achievements and interests* avoid saying, for example, that you take a keen interest in technology or have a passion for problem-solving. It's better to say you have an interest in something *because* it involves these features or has helped you to develop these particular skills. You can draw out many transferable skills and personal qualities from activities such as building your own computer or a working engine from junk. These also show your sense of adventure and resourcefulness. When referring to achievements, mention any challenges or obstacles you faced, what you did and any positive consequences, such as being asked to help others to gain similar achievements.

In your personal statement or elsewhere in your CV, try to find a way of demonstrating flexibility and willingness to learn: employers want to know you can adapt and learn. Sometimes diversity of skills experience and interests alone show these attributes but give evidence if you can. Employers are looking for evidence of your potential as well as what you can do already.

Choose your words carefully. Use action verbs such as *achieved, developed, organised, initiated* and *demonstrated*. Avoid meaningless clichés such as *dynamic* and standard phrases such as *excellent communication skills* that lack evidence and any reference point against which excellence can be measured (see Box 9.3). It's better to say: *Developed effective communication skills during vacation retail work*. Avoid adjectives such as *vast* or *immense* when describing your skills and experience: it's probably not true and you won't be believed, casting doubt over the veracity of the rest of your CV.

Avoid using CV templates. Many free CV templates are available online but they may introduce length restrictions, unwanted sections, colour schemes and graphics. More importantly, their formatting may render your content inaccessible to applicant tracking systems (ATS) that many potential employers use to digitally screen information. Use Word and, when you customise your CV to apply for a job, optimise it for ATS by using key words from the job advertisement, description and the organisation's website.

Check your spelling and grammar. Poor spelling and grammar and a badly laid-out CV speak louder than your claims to communicate well in writing. Poor communication in business reduces efficiency and frustrates other employees. Ask your careers office or a senior colleague to check your CV and apprise you of errors.

Box 9.3 Avoiding clichés

A cliché is an overused word or phrase and often one that has lost its original meaning. A cliché-ridden CV may look professional to you, but consider the recruiters' perspective. One cliché-ridden CV (or cover letter or application form) looks much like another. When you use clichés you lose an opportunity to show your uniqueness. Clichés often refer to attributes that no person should be without. Just consider the opposite meaning. For example, the opposite of hard-working is lazy. Table 9.8 sets out clichés to replace or avoid. Organisations may use clichés in their advertisements but don't repeat them!

Table 9.8 Clichés to replace or avoid

Clichés to replace	Instead, give evidence / examples of	Meaningless clichés to avoid
Team player	Team work	Dynamic
Going the extra mile	Work and effort beyond the call of duty	Highly motivated
Initiative-taking	Assessing and acting before others did so; working independently; taking charge	Solution / results / detail-oriented
Problem-solver	Developing solutions to problems and working in challenging situations	Proactive
People person	Interpersonal skills such as communicating, persuading, negotiating, mentoring, handling conflict, active listening, leading, delegating	Dedicated
Entrepreneurial	Creative skill and effort to initiate and bring new ideas to fruition	Driven

ACTIVITY 9.7 Draft a CV using the results of Activities 9.2, 9.3 and 9.4, structured as in Table 9.7. Then compare it with some 'good' examples online. Revise and edit your CV until you are satisfied with it. If possible, ask your university careers service to check it and provide feedback. The activity provides you with a *generic* CV to update regularly. When you need to use your CV, you tailor it to suit your purpose.

Tailoring your CV for job applications

When you use your CV to apply for a job you customise it to show what makes you the best person to fill the role. You emphasise the skills and experiences that are relevant to the job – and to the organisation. First, consider the essential and desirable criteria on the person specification for the job.

Use your SWOT analysis systematically, this time matching your strengths to the essential and desirable skills. In this way you assess the relevant skills, knowledge and experience you can bring to the organisation and the role. Include interests and talents, too. Also match your values with those of the organisation: if, for example, your core values include self-transcendence ones and the organisation embeds sustainability in its business strategy, look on the organisation's website to find out how this works. Many organisations are now values-led and want employees who share the same values. But check that an organisation's values are not empty words in a mission statement: dig deep to see how the organisation measures how well it lives up to its values.

Then select and refine your findings to create positive statements. Select those strengths that match what's required with the most relevant examples from your notes. If the job requires being systematic, for example, emphasise work experience or interests that demonstrate this over those that involve risk-taking. Mention your shared values in your CV and, where possible, how you could contribute.

If you lack particular skills, consider training and development opportunities offered by the organisation. You can say in your personal statement which opportunities you welcome.

Use key words and phrases from the job description and the organisation's website but avoid reusing clichés (see Box 9.3 *Avoiding clichés*). Instead, give evidence of your possession of essential and desired qualities. If possible, show you can offer 'value' to an organisation by stating, for example, how much revenue you attracted or the cost savings you made in a previous job or your current one. Even if you are new to professional work you can make your CV 'speak' to an organisation's recruiters.

ACTIVITY 9.8 Find an advertisement and further particulars (job and person specifications) for a graduate job that's attractive to you – one you'd like to apply for now or later. Research the organisation and then tailor the CV you compiled in Activity 9.7 to suit the job and the employer.

Does your CV make you sound as if you're good match for the job and the organisation? The benefit of the activity is not just to practise customising a CV but to help to identify potential skills and work experience gaps.

Checking and improving your online profile

Take a look at your online social media profile. Are there messages, photos or links you'd prefer to forget? Does your profile suggest you have a partying lifestyle or that you look the part for a professional career? Anything that makes you appear irresponsible, however innocent – and anything concerning crime, sex, drugs, alcohol, discrimination and some forms of criticism – can damage your professional reputation. Many potential employers check candidates' profiles on the internet and social media so you may want to take action.

Follow the advice on the BBC's Newsbeat webpage *How to remove embarrassing Facebook and Twitter accounts*. There are many other sources of information but make sure that it's up to date. Even after you have gained your first professional job it's wise to take care: to maintain their reputation and brand images employers often check the social media profiles of those who work for them.

Follow this general advice.

1. **Search for yourself online.** Do this from someone else's laptop or device to see what information about you is in the public domain (your own device may be recognised and show all content). Search your name and your email address, using quotation marks around your name and, if possible, your location to avoid your search returning too many people with the same name as you. Alternatively search for yourself using *Pipl* or *Socialmention*. Search for pictures and images in addition to text, blogs and message boards. Indeed, look for all types of content: even your *Amazon* and other retail wish lists are likely to be in the public domain. Delete anything embarrassing or change privacy settings to make wish lists private. If you find something you cannot remove yourself, ask the person who posted the content or the site administrators or owners to remove it.

2. **Check and update your profiles.** Do this for *Facebook* and other social media accounts.

3. **Reset filters and privacy settings.** In *Facebook*, filter who can see your material and edit the privacy setting of past posts. Remove photo tags that identify you if the photo is one you wouldn't want potential employers to see.

4. **Check your *Twitter* account.** You will be able to delete some tweets. You can 'protect' your tweets so they are seen only by people you approve.

5. **Consider deleting your *Facebook* and other social media accounts altogether.** You can open a new account or operate two, one for personal use and one for professional use.

6. **Consider using 'self-destruct' apps.** These apps allow you to send messages and photos that self-destruct after a few days or as soon as they are seen.

Ways to improve your online profile

There are ways to improve your online profile. Try one or more of these methods.

1. **Own your own domain name.** You can do this for a small annual fee and create website content including your CV and what you want people to know about you.

2. **Use a single website for all your content.** Try *Tumblr* or *WordPress*. A single website means you can manage content more effectively. People using your domain name can be taken directly to your content on these sites once you have made the necessary link.

3. **Alternatively, create a number of profiles.** One way to improve your online presence is to create a number of profiles on websites such as *Google+*, *LinkedIn*, *YouTube* and *About.me* so that a Google search returns several sources of information about you. Use your full name and make links from one site to another. Multiple links move you up Google's search results. Then maintain your profiles.

4. **Join professional social networks such as *LinkedIn*.**

5. **Separate your personal and professional accounts and profiles.**
6. **Be active regularly online.** Your aim is to ensure that anything you don't want potential employees to see is not on the first page of a search engine's results. Making informed comments on blogs (or writing them) and posting interesting articles you find is an effective way of being active. Monthly contributions should be sufficient. You could also join a question-and-answer site such as *Quora* as a quick way of increasing your online presence, or sign up to some respected business discussion forums. Search online for business forums; this helps you to network, too.
7. **Join *LinkedIn* or *Twitter* groups that match your professional interests.** This also has the benefit of expanding your network.
8. **Keep up to date with changing privacy rules.** Social media sites such as *Facebook* update them, so keep pace.
9. **Set up a Google alert.** This notifies you every time content associated with you is put online so that you can monitor your online presence and profile.
10. **Be aware of responsible use of social media.** Employers may ask how you use these media.

Every time you post something online in the public domain remember you are building your own brand image. It should be authentic, however, or it won't be believed.

> **ACTIVITY 9.9** Carry out an internet search on yourself. Identify content that you wouldn't want a potential employer to see. Take steps to deal with it and start creating an improved profile. Join a professional social networking site and upload your CV (but don't forget to replace it each time you update it). It's a great way to start networking with people already working in the field you're interested in but follow the site's protocols about making invitations.

Finding your job

How hard do you think it will be to find the job you want? Your belief will be reflected in your motivation, focus and effort. Will you upload your CV to internet job sites and wait to be contacted by recruiters? Will you apply for every job advertised, whatever it is, and send off identical applications? Or will you plan your search, use multiple sources of information, select jobs that match your skills, interests and values and then tailor your applications? The latter is the most successful strategy.

Plan and prepare

Planning your search ensures that you are systematic and thorough. You should know by now the areas of work you're interested in and the main employers. This information should help to define where and how you search. It doesn't necessarily mean narrowing your sources of information but using them intelligently. Key resources for job hunters are set out below.

Careers fairs

Careers fairs are recruitment events where organisations 'set out their stalls' with personnel on hand to talk to you. They are ideal for graduates who are undecided about their career paths but are equally useful if you already know. You gain information directly about organisations of interest, graduate jobs, career paths, what is sought in an ideal candidate and any training programmes. Some organisations have recent recruits on hand to talk to you. Careers fairs allow you to extend your professional network to some of the people you meet. Find out if the organisations you'd like to work for are represented and at which fairs. Your own university may organise fairs; others are likely to be regional or national. Your careers office can provide information; another source is the *Prospects* website. Look up details as soon as possible, then select, plan and book if necessary. Separate fairs are held for some fields such as engineering, IT, law and the social sector. Prepare for careers fair and make the most of your time at them.

Before attending, do the following:

Before a fair

- **Research the employers** who will be represented so that you don't ask for unnecessary information.
- **Make a prioritised list** of employers you want to meet.
- **Prepare questions** to ask (and ask only those you couldn't find answered elsewhere).
- **Compile a brief introduction** that sets out what you are seeking.
- **Take an up-to-date CV** so that recruiters can glance through it while talking to you. You may need more than one version if you have more than one possible career path.
- **See what else is on offer** at the fair, such as professional CV checking and workshops on various aspects of recruitment and selection; plan your time.

At a fair

- **Create a good impression** by dressing as a professional or as if you were attending an interview.
- **Behave as a professional** by paying attention to your interpersonal and communication skills.
- **Organise the literature** and business cards you've been given and add notes on what people said to help you identify them later.
- **Be open to opportunities** or organisations you were unaware of.
- **Take time to learn** by making the most of professional careers advice and workshops.

Jobsites

Online jobsites bring organisations and jobseekers together. Not only are jobs advertised but normally you can upload your CV. Some recruitment agencies use jobsites to 'head hunt' suitable candidates and some organisations regularly scrutinise CVs (often using ATS). However, jobsites should be just one element of your search strategy. Choose your jobsites carefully, selecting those that are popular with recruiters and free of charge for jobseekers, such as *Monster*. This site allows you to create your own homepage, search jobs by sector and find out about companies advertising jobs.

Others that connect jobseekers and employers include *Indeed* where you can upload your CV and search the job advertisements using filters; recruiters can request email notification of newly uploaded ones that fit their needs. *The Guardian* newspaper's jobs website, *jobs.theguardian*, and *Jobsite* operate in much the same way. Good websites offer careers advice (*jobs.ac.uk* offers downloadable career action plans and toolkits) and some offer industry-specific advice. Most allow you to register free of charge for email alerts as does *NHS Jobs* which advertises jobs in the UK's public health care sector.

You can also use *LinkedIn* and other networking sites for job seeking. Set up your profile as one that makes it clear you are searching. The University of Oxford's website has a simple 10-step guide to creating a jobseeker's profile on *LinkedIn*.

Networking to create opportunities

Networking is recognised as an effective method of finding out about job opportunities. You need to know how to do it, however. Networking is about developing relationships. If you've already put effort into relationship-building then you're ready to use your network. If not, join *LinkedIn* and groups and professional associations related to your preferred career path. There are also special interest groups you can join via via *LinkedIn* and *Facebook*.

The key to building relationships is to be interested in people and what they do; as often as not you'll find common ground. Be polite and professional, never critical. Ask people with whom you've already developed relationships to suggest people you should meet. Look for alumni of your university who are working in your field of interest. Don't forget old school friends, former teachers and people you have met in other spheres of life. Rekindle relationships and ask if people can put you in touch with anyone working in your field of interest.

Send potential new contacts a short message, perhaps asking about their career path, their work, the skills required to do it, a typical day or more general questions about the advice they would give to a person planning to enter the organisation on graduation. Don't ask for a job; rather, seek information. Before asking questions, first research the organisation and the person's role so that your questions are specific. You should introduce yourself and your reasons briefly and what, *genuinely*, you'd like to know. Make your list of questions short, consisting of 'open' questions – those that can't be responded to with a Yes or No – and bear in mind that you'll probably have limited opportunity to ask follow-up questions.

You can also do this in person: choose a relatively senior person in an organisation, do your research, make contact and arrange a meeting. This is known as an *informational interview*, a well-developed practice in the USA that is becoming popular in the UK. The University of Oxford's website has a short guide while the USA's *Quint Careers* has a comprehensive one. Both give guidance on the preparation of questions. Dress as for an interview. Always thank people for their time and responses (and make use of what they tell you).

Recruitment and selection processes need to be fair to all candidates so don't expect to be offered a job by your network contacts. Rather, your network contacts provide suggestions, hints and information about opportunities that you need to follow up. You may be told about internal vacancies – those that are advertised only within an organisation. There is usually nothing to stop you applying for these. When you have already applied for a job, avoid approaching contacts in the organisation to better your chances of success: it will be unwelcome.

Once you have extended your network, find ways of keeping in touch. Networking sites make this easy. An effective network is measured by quality not size, however; a large network can be difficult to maintain and bring few benefits.

Other resources

Other useful resources include:

- **Online 'employer hubs'** that provide information direct from organisations and can be searched by career sector.
- **Professional associations, organisations' own websites and sector-specific websites** such as *Big Hospitality* for jobs in the hospitality sector.
- **Newspapers** such as *The Guardian* (jobs are also online).
- **Trade magazines** such as *The Grocer* (online) for jobs in the Fast-Moving Consumer Goods industry.
- **Job centres (UK)** Check *totaljobs* to find one near you (you'll need to visit in person).
- **Graduate recruitment agencies** which match you to an employer/job; the *Prospects* website has a list and advice.
- **Graduate schemes** Some organisations recruit only from their graduate schemes. Search organisations' websites for these.
- **International job sites** The UK's *Prospects* website gives popular job sites for many countries together with details of major sectors and whether you need a work permit.

You don't have to wait for employment opportunities to be advertised because many are not, as Box 9.4 reveals.

Box 9.4 Speculative approaches

A very large number of jobs are never advertised. Estimates vary upward from 60 per cent. This is reason enough to warrant making speculative approaches to organisations about job opportunities. First research an organisation and types of work. Send a covering letter and customised CV to a named person and then follow up by phone. You don't have to apply for a specific job but for work of interest to you that you believe you're qualified to do.

A systematic approach to job applications

So, you've seen a job advertisement or have been asked to make an application. What next? Your preparation can mean the difference between being offered the job you want and failing to be shortlisted. Be systematic.

1. Print off the advertisement, further particulars and application form (there will usually be one); know what information you need and any requirements such as a criminal record check (see Box 9.5).
2. Research the organisation thoroughly.
3. Customise your CV so that it emphasises and reflects the skills required for the job and those the organisation wants.
4. Contact potential people (references or referees) who can vouch for your skills, abilities and suitability for the job.
5. Complete the application form (this normally requires details of your referees).
6. Write a cover letter.
7. Contact the organisation for any details you need for your application.
8. Make sure your contact details are correct.
9. Spell- and grammar-check everything you intend to send.
10. Meet the closure deadline (no excuses!).
11. Check that your application arrives: if you send it by email make a delivery request; if you send it by post, phone to ask if it's been received.
12. Make sure you're available for interview.

See *Customising your CV for job applications* in this chapter

Your references

References (or referees) are people who can make authoritative, positive statements about you to support your job applications. Referees are people who know you well. Two referees are normally required and they need to be asked as soon as you begin your job search. A referee must at least be able to provide information about your abilities and suitability for the job. A personal or character reference is insufficient alone. When you apply for your first professional job, your referees are often your educators but it is useful to include a part-time employer, voluntary work supervisor or a person you worked with during an internship. For students already in full-time work, choose at least one referee from your workplace.

Approach referees as soon as you start job seeking. You can ask more than two people and choose the most appropriate ones for a particular job application. Having additional referees helps if an employer asks for more than two. Importantly, when you apply for a job, send your preferred referees a copy of the further particulars for the job you're applying for and your customised CV so that they can tailor their reference.

When you complete your application form for the position, make sure you know your referees' job title, the organisation they work for and full contact details including email address. Organisations may require a written statement; others ask referees a series of questions. However, referees are not always contacted by potential employers. Let your listed referees know the outcome of your job application and thank them even if you didn't get the job or they weren't called upon.

Box 9.5 Criminal record checks

In the UK, some fields of work require a Disclosure and Barring Service check on a person's criminal convictions, cautions, reprimands, warnings and fixed penalties. Be prepared for a potential employer to ask for one if the job entails working with children, vulnerable adults or in healthcare. You can refuse but you won't be offered a job. Full details are on the UK Government's *Disclosure and Barring Service* website.

Cover letters

A cover letter sent with a CV and a job application form can do much more than personalise and summarise your application for a job: it can sell you as an ideal candidate. Use it to make your case for being shortlisted for interview. Potential employers generally tell applicants if a cover letter is not required; in the absence of advice, write one. Most advice on cover letters suggests you include the these eight items.

1. The title of the job you're applying for, reference number and where you saw it advertised
2. What attracts you to this specific job (and the organisation)
3. What makes you suitable to do the job
4. If you are changing jobs, why (but don't state personal reasons)
5. Your hope or desire to be interviewed
6. If necessary, dates when you won't be available

7. When you could start work
8. Thanks to the employer in anticipation of a positive response to your application.

The aim is not to replicate what's in your CV and application form but to highlight your particular skills or attributes that the job requires. You might want to mention that the job provides the challenge and opportunities for further learning and development that you seek. If you are changing jobs, give positive reasons such as readiness for greater responsibility. Use action verbs as you did in your CV; adopt a professional style but sound approachable and enthusiastic. A cover letter may be a good way to mention a career gap (and how you used the opportunity). Think carefully about mentioning a disability. If you do, don't give details, simply emphasise that it will not affect your ability to do the job. You can discuss later any reasonable adjustments that the organisation will need to make (organisations have legal obligations). End your letter with some forward-looking statements.

Write no more than four or five short paragraphs that fit on one side of plain A4 paper. Set out the letter formally and address it to the employer, or preferably a named person. Letters addressed *To whom it may concern* suggest a lack of research and a generic approach to job applications. It you're not sure how to set out a formal letter, look for UK examples online (avoid Word templates). Print off an example and follow the conventions in detail: note the layout of addresses, date and so on and how to sign off the letter. Use *Yours sincerely* for a letter to a named person. Use paragraphs correctly and check the grammar and spelling. Don't forget to sign the letter. If you are emailing your application you can use the text of the letter, unsigned, as your message or attach a signed, scanned pdf file with your CV and application form (but make sure they arrive).

If you are making a speculative approach to an organisation, adjust the first paragraph so that it conveys your interest in a specific type of work. Match your skills and abilities to those generally required for the work. (Tailor your CV in this way, too.) You can still end the letter by welcoming the opportunity to be interviewed.

ACTIVITY 9.10 Draft a cover letter based on the material you used for Activity 9.8 (the advertisement, further particulars, results of your research into the employing organisation and your customised CV). Address the letter to the appropriate person in the organisation.

Writing formal letters is an art and it's more difficult when the stakes are high. Master the basics now.

Application forms

A job application form is a way for an organisation to ensure that each applicant supplies the same type of information in the same way. Typically this information includes your education, work experience, skills, abilities and qualities. Some require a personal statement and some may ask job-related questions. There may be considerable overlap between what is required and the contents of a customised CV, so organisations may not want a CV. Find out before you complete the application form. If no CV is needed, the content of your CV can be customised and used on the form. If a CV is required, customise it and use the application form to elaborate (but take care to answer the questions).

Approach application forms as you did your customised CV and cover letter in Activities 9.8 and 9.10: research the organisation and the person and job specifications so you fully understand what's wanted. The now-familiar process of matching your skills, abilities and qualities to the job allows you to emphasise and elaborate on your relevant education, work experience, achievements, interests and talents.

Aim to meet *all* of the essential and desirable skills and qualities listed on the person specification. Your work on activities earlier in this chapter is useful here. Use your work and other experiences as evidence of maintaining professional standards and customer-focus under pressure, for example, or your ability to plan, organise and divide your time effectively or taking responsibility and working with others. Your achievements may reveal something about your suitability for the job. When you think in this way, you make a case for your suitability and reveal your uniqueness.

If you lack an essential skill, such as holding a full driving licence, apply for a provisional licence and book lessons. On the application form you can then say *Provisional licence holder currently following a driving course*. If you lack a number of essential skills consider whether you should apply for the job.

Don't leave questions unanswered. You can answer ones that haven't been asked by skilfully including information in appropriate places. You may have general work-related competences such as being accustomed to public speaking, or fluency in several languages. These abilities help your application to stand out.

If a personal statement is required, use it to showcase skills, experience, abilities and talents that the job and the employer require. Say why you want the job and what you can offer. Mention, too, something positive about the employing organisation. It may not be the biggest or most successful in the sector but it may offer training and development, be small enough for individuals to make significant contributions towards its growth, offer unique and interesting products or services or have 'green' credentials or values that set it apart. Link at least one feature to your skills, aspirations, interests or values.

Use positive language with action verbs as you did when compiling your CV and cover letter. Also do the following:

- Copy the form and use the copy to make a draft of your application.
- Write simply and concisely so that all the information is easy to read quickly.
- Adhere to any word limits; write *to* the limit (no more, no less).

- Provide correct and full details of referees (make sure you have their permission and contact them with details of the job).
- Edit your text and check the grammar and spelling.
- Ask your careers office or trusted person to read the completed form and provide feedback.
- Complete the original application form when you are happy with your draft.
- Scan or copy the completed form and submit the original with your CV, if required, and cover letter as soon as possible.
- If you are invited for interview, take copies of the form, your CV and covering letter with you; they are likely to be used at the interview.

What not to put on the form

It sounds obvious, but avoid expressing doubts, shortcomings, lack of confidence in your abilities, the need for supervision or difficulty in working with others. It's easy to convey what you did not mean to when you say, for example, *I hope I can rise to the challenge of ...* rather than *I look forward to the challenge of ...* If you are asked about your weaknesses, say how you overcame obstacles, challenges and skills gaps and developed as a result. Avoid clichés and one-word responses to questions.

See Box 9.3 *Avoiding clichés* in this chapter

Forms may ask for your expected degree result. State it without qualification even if you have doubts: your degree class may not always be as important as you believe it will be (see Box 9.6). Forms shouldn't ask for personal information such as age, gender, religion, ethnicity and sexual orientation that are covered by the UK's Equality Act 2010. If they do, you need not answer. It's more usual for organisations to ask these questions on an equal opportunities form that is treated in confidence and is not available to selectors.

Box 9.6 Does my degree class matter?

If your degree result is not as expected or not anticipated to be as high as you hoped, don't be too concerned. Employers in many sectors accept graduates with degrees lower than a 2.1 and some well-known organisations don't specify. Focus on these organisations and what you can offer them. You may be able to improve your academic standing with a part-time MBA or specialist Master's degree later when you have more work experience. If your studies were interrupted or disturbed by circumstances such as bereavement, you can mention this in a positive light: it shows you had the tenacity to continue.

ACTIVITY 9.11 If the job you chose for the last two activities did not have an application form, search for a similar job that does – one that is attractive to you. Download the application form along with the further particulars. Research the organisation and study the job and person specifications. Then attempt to complete the application form. Look online for sample answers to standard questions if you need to, but use your own examples: you are selling *you*.

This is a particularly productive activity because it helps you to understand the usefulness of the previous activities in this chapter. Application forms take time and thought to complete but your preparatory work serves you well. Jobseekers sometimes resort to copying and pasting CV content into them to apply for numerous positions. But these applicants are the most likely to be rejected. Choose potential jobs with care and then put effort into your application. If your application is not successful you can ask for feedback (see Box 9.7).

Box 9.7 Ask for feedback

If you are not invited for interview, ask for feedback. While it's more usual to ask for feedback after an unsuccessful interview, there is no reason why you shouldn't ask for feedback on your application. Email the person to whom you sent your application, saying that it would be helpful to know why you didn't reach the shortlist. Organisations aren't obliged to provide feedback at any stage in the recruitment and selection process but they often do – and the worst answer you can receive is a polite *No*. Be brave. Feedback can improve your job applications if you can take a little criticism.

A selector's perspective

Senior staff in organisations are often called on to be involved in selection. Here is the experience of one such person in a traditional organisation.

We shortlist applicants according to essential and desirable criteria – the same as those on the person specification – and use identical criteria at interview. We devise interview questions based on them so every interviewee is asked the same ones, although follow-up questions can vary. We're very strict about following good practice and we undergo training before being on a selection panel. Newcomers to interview panels can be as nervous as the candidates!

When we look at applications, those we reject first are from people who aren't qualified for the job and those who appear to be applying for numerous jobs. The information they give is so general that you can't tell if they will be suitable or not. From the remainder we compile a shortlist of six applicants who appear to be the best fit for the job. These are from people who craft their applications: they show they're applying for the job advertised and that they meet the criteria. They give job-relevant examples that reveal what they can bring to the job and sometimes something extra you didn't quite expect. It can add value: you see, for example, that their technical skills could help them to innovate in an otherwise not very technical job.

At interview, we can better assess their interpersonal skills, which are essential in our team-working environment. The questions candidates ask show their knowledge and research – and interest. Often more than one candidate could do the job well, which is just as well if the candidate we choose lands a great job elsewhere the next day. Lack of success at this stage *can* be about the competition on the day. I've met really good candidates who don't get the job but whom we contact if there's a similar vacancy coming up.

Interviews and other types of selection

Interviews aren't necessarily what you think. It's best to think of an interview as part of a selection process and consider it from an employer's perspective. If *you* were choosing a person what would you do to be sure of identifying the most suitable candidate? Take this knowledge test.

ACTIVITY 9.12 Which of the following activities do you think might be required to do as part of an interview or selection process?

1. Asked a series of questions about your skills and experience
2. Presented with a case study with problems to solve
3. Interviewed by one person or a panel of selectors
4. Given reasoning and problem-solving tasks
5. Asked for examples of how you've used your skills and abilities
6. Put under pressure to see how you respond
7. Asked to make a presentation
8. Invited to an assessment centre instead of or in addition to an interview
9. Interviewed or asked to carry out tests by phone or video link
10. Invited to socialise with assessors, staff and other candidates
11. Interviewed in a group with other candidates
12. Asked to take psychometric tests
13. Given a written test, such as producing or reviewing a report

You should have ticked all the boxes: selection frequently involves several of these activities. It depends on the job advertised and the employer. Item 6 may be unusual but some jobs involve a good deal of pressure, such as many of those in the hospitality and retail sectors. Any timed task (most tasks are) is likely to put you under pressure, however. Interviews can be a traditional discussion or they can be a coverall for a variety of activities. It should be clear to you that when you apply for a job, you need to find out what's involved in selection and to prepare.

What to expect

Assessment centres

Typically, assessment centres involve a bundle of activities, exercises and interviews. Some may be combined as when a group of candidates is asked to solve a problem, resolve a case study or discuss a topical issue. In group work, your communication, listening and other interpersonal skills are usually being tested along with, in some cases, your leadership skills and ability to delegate. A common individual test is the In Tray, which aims to reveal how you prioritise and manage work under time pressure. Don't expect to be told the tasks an assessment centre will set; you are likely to receive only a schedule. Expect to attend an assessment centre if you are applying for a graduate scheme.

Case studies/scenarios

These are much like short, unseen case studies to review or resolve. They test your ability to analyse and think quickly and to communicate your findings or solution effectively. You may have to make a presentation or undertake written work afterwards. The case studies and scenarios may be typical situations you'd encounter in the job or they may cover an issue similar to one that the organisation faces. Thus, the more you know about the job, the organisation, its practices and culture, the better prepared you are. Case study work is often included in assessment centre activities and can be carried out in a group or individually.

Reasoning and problem-solving tasks

Like case studies and scenarios, reasoning and problem-solving exercises are often based on situations that you would encounter in the job. Do your research into the organisation and job.

Presentations

A common type of presentation is one in which you sell yourself. You may be asked to make a video of your presentation to upload online as part of the preliminary selection. If you attend an assessment centre you may be given a topic or a choice of topics for a presentation and you may or may not be given time to prepare in advance: if the latter, you prepare there and then. Presentations can be combined with other tasks such as case study work: you present the findings, solution or action plan. In any presentation an employer is looking for confidence and good communication and persuasion skills.

See *Giving
presentations* in
Chapter 8

Telephone interviews

Telephone interviews may be used as part of assessment centre activities or as a preliminary part of the selection process. If it's preliminary, prepare by finding out about the employing organisation and don't forget that you can ask questions, too. Organise a quiet environment for the call and treat it as formal.

Video interviews

A video interview can be preliminary or replace an in-person interview. If it's preliminary, you upload a video of yourself answering questions provided by the employer (but expect variations). If self-presentation skills are vital to the job you are evaluated on these, too. If the video interview replaces an in-person one, it is two-way and live, often taking place via *Skype*. Prepare as you would for an in-person interview. Both forms of video interview are cost-effective, have a low-carbon footprint and are increasingly popular. Once you know the medium to be used, practise using it.

Psychometric tests

Employers who use psychometric tests generally select those that measure one or more of the following: logic; inductive, abstract and critical reasoning; numeracy; aptitude; motivation; judgement; and personality. Many tests are timed and some are designed so that you can't convey a 'false' persona. Take a look at some at your university careers office so you know what to expect or look online at websites such as *TARGETjobs* (follow links). You can also take practice tests at *cebglobal SHL Talent Measurement, Linklaters* (Watson Glaser critical thinking test) and *Job Test Prep* (look for free examples).

You may encounter customised tests, such as those used by Proctor and Gamble, whose website allows you to practise. Prior to these tests, seek information about the organisation and how it operates because you may need this when you take the tests. Organisations may use online versions of tests, so online practice helps if you prefer paper and pen. Some organisations conduct personality tests by phone or video. USA-based, multinational companies are probably keener than others on psychometric tests. They believe tests are objective and remove selector bias. Tests are also used to screen large numbers of applicants. Organisations must take reasonable steps to accommodate disability that might disadvantage test-takers.

Social 'tests'

These are usually meetings that mix selectors, some employees and job candidates informally. You are being assessed on self-presentation, communication and interpersonal skills. Prepare for meetings by refreshing your research findings on the sector, the organisation and the external environment in which it operates so that you can ask questions about people's jobs, the organisation and its context.

Talk to a number of people and be professional and friendly to other candidates. At assessment centres, do the same during informal sessions or breaks when you may have the opportunity to talk to the employing organisation's recruiters and staff. (Assessment centre work may be outsourced to specialists; breaks may be the only time you meet those with whom you might work.) Assessment doesn't stop for refreshment or lunch.

Written tests

Written exercises are often included in assessment centre activities to ensure that candidates can communicate well in writing. Tests can include a written report on a case study you have just worked on, an action plan, a review of a document or a summary for a more senior person. Like other tests and activities, there is a time limit that is flexible only if you have a disability. You'll value the time and effort you spent writing assignments!

Interviews

Given all the activities that selection can involve, a straightforward interview probably seems inviting. There are now two types. The first involves the traditional focus on skills/competences such as those listed in Table 9.2 *Aspects of employability*. You are asked about your skills and to provide examples of how you have used them. If you carried out the activities in this chapter and their emphasis on providing evidence of skill you should have few difficulties. Researching the organisation and the job helps you to hone your evidence. This preparatory work allows you to focus on the interview itself, when you also demonstrate your communication and interpersonal skills.

The second type of interview is strengths-based. It explores your interests and what motivates you to perform at your best. Here, what you enjoyed most in your studies, your interests, talents and achievements are brought to the fore. Your work on Activity 9.6 is of particular value and worth carrying out again in conjunction with your research findings into the organisation and the job and person specifications.

For any interview, best behaviour is required along with formal dress. Make your travel arrangements in good time and, importantly, know the names of those who are interviewing you. Smile, shake hands, introduce yourself and quickly establish a relationship to help your interviewers to do their job of discovering your suitability. Your task is to show you are eminently suitable. Making their job easy and enjoyable helps you to do this.

Preparing for interviews

The most effective preparation for interviews is practice. Your university careers office should be able to help you. If not, try this:

- Study the job and person specification; know your 'fit'
- Be able to recall instantly the contents of your cover letter, CV, application form and key information from your research into the organisation
- Know why you want to work for the organisation, what you can offer and your aspirations for your development and your career
- Compile possible interview questions (try *TARGETjobs* and other websites for lists and advice on responses)
- Run through possible answers to questions, including difficult ones
- Make a list of questions about the job or the organisation that you want to ask your interviewer.

If you have prepared well there should be no question you can't answer. Practising and rehearsing responses helps you to have information at your fingertips. Even if many questions are never asked, you have material you can weave into other answers. Importantly, if you have spent time choosing an area of work and have some preferred organisations, you gain confidence from being sure of your aim to work in *this* field in *this* organisation for *these* reasons. Your motivation, enthusiasm and knowledge will show.

If you are unsuccessful at interview, ask for feedback and use it. If you like the organisation, show your determination by applying for a similar vacancy when it arises. If you do get the job: well done for making the effort needed. Once in the job, look for opportunities that will further your career.

Other options for graduates

Some graduates decide not to move directly into a job, some remain unclear about a career path, some decide to change direction, while others don't find immediate employment in their chosen field. What are the options? There are many: you can often take a break, seek wider experience, boost your skills and improve your employability simultaneously. You may find a new direction or, with some additional preparation and planning, a job in your chosen field or even a dream job you didn't know existed.

Travel. Think carefully: you need to ensure that it's purposeful and you gain international and work experience. Consider taking jobs that pay your way. Alternatively, work voluntarily for an organisation that pays living and travel expenses. Look online for opportunities and know the difference between informational websites and those offering placement for a fee.

Voluntary work. Think beyond charity shops. Choose organisations whose work you feel passionate about so you perform at your best. Ask for or negotiate a placement or internship. There may be opportunities for shadowing and, eventually, a job in the organisation. Some organisations pay expenses; they must pay you at least the minimum wage in some circumstances (see more information at the UK Government's *Volunteer placements, rights and expenses* webpage).

Further study at home or abroad. Whatever your study objective – an MBA, specialist Master's degree or a qualification such as accounting or marketing – consider funding first. UK Professional and Career Development Loans are low-interest bank loans available for any courses of up to two years (and they don't have to lead to a qualification). Before lending you 80 per cent of your tuition fees, however, banks will check your credit rating. Government-backed postgraduate loans are also available. Universities and charitable trusts may offer funds (ask your careers office). The *British Council* website provides information about funding for postgraduate study abroad.

A good alternative to full-time study is to work full- or part-time while studying part-time. Many UK universities offer part-time courses and The Open University offers only part-time courses that you can study anywhere, including abroad (an open entry route to its MBA is available to those who lack three years' professional experience). If you work full-time in a role relevant to a programme of study, your employer may fund or part-fund you.

If you decide to study law, a number of UK universities offer conversion courses (CPE and GDL) of one year (full-time) or two years (part-time). Student loans are available and law firms sponsor trainees. Some postgraduate studies, such as in healthcare and teaching, are part-funded by bursaries or student loans. The complexities of funding mean careful decision-making is required.

Be an apprentice. Many sectors offer apprenticeships, including law firms. Visit the *UK Government's Business, administration and law apprenticeships* webpage to check possibilities. Look for 'higher apprentices' in fields such as legal services, business innovation and growth, human resources, management and marketing. You don't need a degree for these but you are likely to have opportunities to study and develop a career path. Opportunities are advertised on *GetMyFirstJob* (look for *Current Business, Administration and Law vacancies*).

Set up your own business. It takes some special personal attributes to do this; if you have them you may already be a member of your university's entrepreneurship society or other group. Advice, mentoring and training schemes are available to help you. See *TARGETjobs How to become an entrepreneur when you graduate* for links to organisations providing these.

Find internships to gain work experience. Check the *Graduate Talent Pool* website, which advertises paid positions. You need to apply to organisations and go through a selection process. Internships are an excellent way of discovering whether you want to work in a particular field. You are supervised and you may be invited to apply for a position if your internship goes well.

Whatever you do, continue to network, attend careers fairs and keep in touch with your university careers office. Keep a log of your activities and update your CV regularly. Always have a goal, even if you change it.

Your journey

This book and this chapter have taken you on a journey. But it is just the start of a longer one for which you are now more prepared. If you have understood and practised the employability skills you need to enter the workplace, you do so with the capabilities to make a real contribution. By now you will have made the discovery that employability skills are, in fact, *life skills*: those that will serve you well throughout your career and in other areas of your life as you live, strive, learn and develop your full potential. Good luck on your journey to a fulfilling and successful career!

Chapter summary

❖ Your preparation for professional life begins long before you graduate: you don't suddenly become career-ready when you are awarded your degree. Discover the common attributes you need for graduate jobs to ensure that you acquire them as you study.

❖ A first step is self-assessment: identify your knowledge, skills, values, talents and interests. Values, interests and talents are important because some organisations are values-based and want to know what motivates you to perform at your best. Identify gaps in your knowledge, skills and experience and plan how you will fill them while you study.

❖ Begin your research into possible careers as soon as possible in order to understand what employers want and to begin the process of matching your strengths, values and interests with particular fields of work. You also identify further knowledge, skills and experience gaps you can fill at university and beyond through various types of work experience such as volunteering, vacation placements and internships.

❖ Writing an effective, evidence-based CV takes time and thought. Draft a generic one to update regularly and to customise later. Know what kind of format to use and how to craft it using examples and the inclusion of a personal statement. Learn to tailor it for job applications.

❖ Make your online profile one that you would be happy for employers to see. See what you need to change; know how to create and maintain an appropriate profile (future employers expect you to do this).

❖ There are many sources of information you can use for planning and preparing for your career. Careers fairs are useful to attend but there's a little work to be done before you go. Networking is effective if you understand how to do it.

❖ When you apply for a job, systematic preparation helps you to sell yourself as the ideal candidate. Speculative approaches to employers are worthwhile because many jobs are never advertised – but your approach needs to be targeted.

❖ 'The interview' often involves more than a meeting with an employer. Know what to expect: you may be asked to make a presentation or take psychometric tests online (resources are available for you to practise these). Assessment centres can involve many activities including problem-solving and writing.

❖ Not getting a job immediately you graduate isn't the end of the world. There are options that can enhance your knowledge and experience. Always have a goal, even if you change it later.

References

About.me (2016) [Online]. Available at https://about.me/ (Accessed 12 April 2016).

Aldi Recruitment (2015) [Online]. Available at www.aldirecruitment.co.uk/graduate/ (Accessed 19 November 2015).

BBC (2016) *News feed from the BBC.* [Online]. Available at http://news.bbc.co.uk/1/hi/help/rss/default.stm (Accessed 12 April 2016).

Big Hospitality (2016) [Online]. Available at www.bighospitality.co.uk/ (Accessed 12 April 2016).

Breaking News (n.d.) [Online]. Available at www.breakingnews.com/ (Accessed 12 April 2016).

British Council (2016) *Funding your studies* [Online]. Available at www.britishcouncil.org/study-work-create/practicalities/funding-studies (Accessed 12 April 2016).

CEB SHL Talent Management (2016) *Take practice tests to familiarise yourself with online testing experience* [Online]. Available at www.cebglobal.com/shldirect/en/practice-tests (Accessed 12 April 2016).

Cieciuch, J., Davidov, E., Vecchione, M., Beierlein, C., and Schwartz, S.H. (2014) 'The cross-national invariance properties of a new scale to measure 19 basic human values: a test across eight countries', *Journal of Cross Cultural Psychology*, vol. 45, no. 5, pp. 764–779 [Online]. DOI: 10.1177/0022022114527348 (Accessed 12 April 2016).

Durham University (2016) *Careers, employability and enterprise centre* [Online]. Available at www.dur.ac.uk/careers/ (Accessed 12 April 2016).

Facebook (2016) [Online]. Available at www.facebook.com/ (Accessed 12 April 2016).

Ffestiniog & Welsh Highland Railway (n.d.) [Online]. Available at www.festrail.co.uk/ (Accessed 13 May 2016).

Forbes (2016) [Online]. Available at www.forbes.com/ (Accessed 12 April 2016).

GetMyFirstJob (2016) [Online]. Available at www.getmyfirstjob.co.uk/ (Accessed 12 April 2016).

Google+ (2016) [Online]. Available at https://plus.google.com/ (Accessed 12 April 2016).

Gov.uk (n.d.) *Disclosure and Barring Service* [Online]. Available at www.gov.uk/government/organisations/disclosure-and-barring-service (Accessed 12 April 2016).

Gov.uk (2012) *Business, administration and law apprenticeships* [Online]. Available at www.gov.uk/government/collections/business-administration-and-law-apprenticeships (Accessed 12 April 2016).

Gov.uk (2015) *Volunteer placements, rights and expenses* [Online]. Available at www.gov.uk/volunteering/find-volunteer-placements (Accessed 12 April 2016).

Graduate Recruitment Bureau (n.d.) *Student jobs and internships* [Online]. Available at www.grb.uk.com/student-jobs (Accessed 12 April 2016).

Graduate Talent Pool (n.d.) *Gain essential work experience through a paid graduate internship* [Online]. Available at https://graduatetalentpoolsearch.direct.gov.uk/gtp/index (Accessed 12 April 2016).

Indeed (n.d.) [Online]. Available at www.indeed.co.uk/ (Accessed 12 April 2016).

Jobs.ac.uk (2016) [Online]. Available at www.jobs.ac.uk/ (Accessed 12 April 2016).

Jobsite (n.d.) [Online]. Available at www.jobsite.co.uk/ (Accessed 12 April 2016).

Job Test Prep (n.d.) *Setting standards in Psychometric test preparation* [Online]. Available at www.jobtestprep.co.uk/ (Accessed 12 April 2016).

Legislation.gov.uk (n.d.) *Equality Act 2010* [Online]. Available at www.legislation.gov.uk/ukpga/2010/15/contents (Accessed 12 April 2016).

Lidl (2016) *Glassdoor* [Online]. Available at www.glassdoor.co.uk/Interview/Lidl-Graduate-Area-Manager-Interview-Questions-EI_IE7428.0,4_KO5,26.htm (Accessed 12 April 2016).

LinkedIn (2016) [Online]. Available at https://gb.linkedin.com/ (Accessed 12 April 2016).

Linklaters Graduate Careers (n.d.) *Critical thinking test* [Online]. Available at www.linklatersgraduates.co.uk/application-process/critical-thinking-test (Accessed 12 April 2016).

Milkround (2014) *Internships and work experience for graduates* [Online]. Available at www.milkround.com/jobs/internships-and-work-experience/ (Accessed 12 April 2016).

Monster (2016) [Online]. Available at www.monster.co.uk/ (Accessed 12 April 2016).

National Careers Service (2016) [Online]. Available at https://nationalcareers service.direct.gov.uk/Pages/Home.aspx# (Accessed 1 May 2016).

NCVO (2016) *Volunteering* [Online]. Available at www.ncvo.org.uk/ncvo-volunteering (Accessed 12 April 2016).

NHS Jobs (2016) [Online]. Available at www.jobs.nhs.uk/ (Accessed 12 April 2016).

Pipl (n.d.) [Online]. Available at https://pipl.com/ (Accessed 12 April 2016).

Proctor and Gamble (2016) *Proctor and Gamble Assessments* [Online]. Available at www.practiceaptitudetests.com/top-employer-profiles/procter-gamble-assessments/ (Accessed 12 April 2016).

Prospects (n.d.) [Online]. Available at www.prospects.ac.uk/ (Accessed 12 April 2016).

Quint Careers (2015) *Informational interviewing tutorial: a key networking tool* [Online]. Available at www.quintcareers.com/informational-interviewing/ (Accessed 12 April 2016).

Quora (n.d.) *The best answer to any question* [Online]. Available at www.quora.com/ (Accessed 12 April 2016).

Schwartz, S.H. (2012) 'An overview of the Schwartz theory of basic values', *Online Readings in Psychology and Culture*, vol. 2, no. 1 [Online]. Available at DOI:10.9707/2307-0919.1116 (Accessed 25 November 2015).

Schwartz, S.H., Cieciuch, J., Vecchione, M., Davidov, E., Fischer, R., Beierlein, C., Ramos, A., Verkasalo, M., Lönnqvist, J.-E., Demirutku, K., Dirilen-Gumus,

O., Konty, M. (2012). 'Refining the theory of basic individual values', *Journal of Personality and Social Psychology*, vol. 103, no. 4, pp. 663–688.

Social Mention (n.d.) *Real-time social media search and analysis* [Online]. Available at www.socialmention.com/ (Accessed 12 April 2016).

Targetjobs (n.d.) *How to become an entrepreneur when you graduate* [Online]. Available at https://targetjobs.co.uk/careers-advice/choosing-an-employer/324809-how-to-become-an-entrepreneur-when-you-graduate (Accessed 12 April 2016).

Targetjobs (n.d.) *Psychometric tests* [Online]. Available at https://targetjobs.co.uk/careers-advice/psychometric-tests (Accessed 12 April 2016).

The Grocer (2016) [Online]. Available at www.thegrocer.co.uk/ (Accessed 12 April 2016).

The Guardian Jobs (2016) [Online]. Available at https://jobs.theguardian.com/ (Accessed 12 April 2016).

The Job Crowd (n.d.) *Graduate employer list* [Online]. Available at www.thejobcrowd.com/employer/ (Accessed 12 April 2016).

The Open University (2016) [Online]. Available at www.open.ac.uk/courses/ (Accessed 12 April 2016).

Totaljobs (2016) [Online]. Available at www.totaljobs.com/ (Accessed 12 April 2016).

Tumblr (n.d.) [Online]. Available at www.tumblr.com/ (Accessed 12 April 2016).

Twitter (n.d.) [Online]. Available at https://twitter.com/ (Accessed 12 April 2016).

University of Kent (2015) *How to write CV profiles, personal statements, career aims and objectives* [Online]. Available at www.kent.ac.uk/careers/cv/CVProfiles.htm (Accessed 19 December 2015).

University of Oxford (2013) *Building a great student profile* [Online]. Available at https://university.linkedin.com/content/dam/university/global/en_US/site/pdf/TipSheet_BuildingaGreatProfile.pdf (Accessed 12 April 2016).

University of Oxford (2016) *Informational interviewing* [Online]. Available at www.careers.ox.ac.uk/networking/ (Accessed 12 April 2016).

Volunteering England (2013) [Online]. Available at www.volunteeringengland.org.uk/ (Accessed 12 April 2016).

Waterways Recovery Group (2016) [Online]. Available at www.waterways.org.uk/wrg/ (Accessed 13 May 2016).

WordPress (n.d.) [Online]. Available at https://wordpress.com/ (Accessed 12 April 2016).

YouTube (2016) [Online]. Available at www.youtube.com/ (Accessed 12 April 2016).

Approaches to learning and studying inventory: self-score version

This inventory has been designed to allow you to describe, in a systematic way, how you go about learning and studying. The technique involves asking you to respond to 36 statements, which overlap to some extent, to provide good overall coverage of different ways of studying. Most items are based on comments made previously by other learners. Please give your **immediate** reaction to **every** comment in Table A1.1, indicating how you **generally** go about your studying and learning even if you are not currently following a formal programme. If you have not encountered a particular situation, try to imagine how you would react.

Table A1.1 Approaches to learning and studying inventory: self-score version

Put a tick in the appropriate box to indicate how strongly you agree with each of the following statements. Try not to use the UNSURE box unless you really have to, or unless the item cannot apply to you.	Agree	Agree	Unsure	Disagree	Disagree
1. I usually set out to understand for myself the meaning of what we have to learn.	☐	☐	☐	☐	☐
2. When I'm communicating ideas, I think over how well I've got my points across.	☐	☐	☐	☐	☐
3. I'm pretty good at getting down to work whenever I need to.	☐	☐	☐	☐	☐
4. Topics are presented in such complicated ways I often can't see what is meant.	☐	☐	☐	☐	☐
5. When I've finished a piece of work, I check to see if it really meets the requirements.	☐	☐	☐	☐	☐
6. I try to make sense of things by linking them to what I know already.	☐	☐	☐	☐	☐
7. I try really hard to do just as well as I possibly can.	☐	☐	☐	☐	☐
8. On the whole, I'm quite systematic and organised in my studying.	☐	☐	☐	☐	☐
9. Often I have to learn over and over things that don't really make much sense to me.	☐	☐	☐	☐	☐
10. I'm quite good at preparing for classes in advance.	☐	☐	☐	☐	☐
11. I tend to take what we are taught at face value without questioning it much.	☐	☐	☐	☐	☐
12. For an essay or report, I don't just focus on the topic, I try to improve my writing skill.	☐	☐	☐	☐	☐
13. Ideas I come across in my academic reading often set me off on long chains of thought.	☐	☐	☐	☐	☐
14. If I'm not understanding things well enough when I'm studying, I try a different approach.	☐	☐	☐	☐	☐
15. I try to relate ideas I come across to other topics or other courses whenever possible.	☐	☐	☐	☐	☐
16. I carefully prioritise my time to make sure I can fit everything in.	☐	☐	☐	☐	☐
17. I often have trouble in making sense of the things I have to remember.	☐	☐	☐	☐	☐
18. I generally keep working hard even when things aren't going all that well.	☐	☐	☐	☐	☐
19. I'm just going through the motions of studying without seeing where I'm going.	☐	☐	☐	☐	☐

Table A1.1 (cont.)

Put a tick in the appropriate box to indicate how strongly you agree with each of the following statements. Try not to use the UNSURE box unless you really have to, or unless the item cannot apply to you.	Agree	Agree	Unsure	Disagree	Disagree
20. Concentration is not usually a problem for me, unless I'm really tired.	☐	☐	☐	☐	☐
21. Much of what I've learned seems no more than lots of unrelated bits and pieces in my mind.	☐	☐	☐	☐	☐
22. I generally put a lot of effort into my studying.	☐	☐	☐	☐	☐
23. I think about what I want to get out of my studies so as to keep my work well focused.	☐	☐	☐	☐	☐
24. It's important for me to follow the argument, or to see the reason behind things.	☐	☐	☐	☐	☐
25. I organise my study time carefully to make the best use of it.	☐	☐	☐	☐	☐
26. I go over the work I've done to check my reasoning and see that it makes sense.	☐	☐	☐	☐	☐
27. In making sense of new ideas, I often relate them to practical or real-life contexts.	☐	☐	☐	☐	☐
28. Whatever I'm working on, I generally push myself to make a good job of it.	☐	☐	☐	☐	☐
29. I don't think through topics for myself, I just rely on what we're taught.	☐	☐	☐	☐	☐
30. When I find something boring, I can usually force myself to keep focused.	☐	☐	☐	☐	☐
31. I tend to just learn things without thinking about the best way to work.	☐	☐	☐	☐	☐
32. I work steadily during the course, rather than just leaving things until the last minute.	☐	☐	☐	☐	☐
33. When I'm reading for a course, I try to find out for myself exactly what the author means.	☐	☐	☐	☐	☐
34. I try to find better ways of tracking down relevant information in my subject.	☐	☐	☐	☐	☐
35. I look at evidence carefully to reach my own conclusion about what I'm studying.	☐	☐	☐	☐	☐
36. I pay careful attention to any advice or feedback I'm given, and try to improve my understanding.	☐	☐	☐	☐	☐

Have you responded to every statement? Please check before continuing.

Now score your responses and work out your learning profile.

How to work out your learning profile and interpret it

Step 1: Score the inventory

Score your ticks as shown in Table A1.2.

Table A1.2 How to score the inventory

Agree	5
Agree somewhat	4
Unsure	3
Disagree somewhat	2
Disagree	1

Step 2: Add the scores

In Table A1.3, write your score for EACH STATEMENT in the blank box next to that statement. Then follow the instruction in the table.

Table A1.3 Your scores

Aspect 1		Aspect 2		Aspect 3		Aspect 4		Aspect 5	
Statement	Your score	Statement	Your score	Statement	Your score	Statement	Your score	Statement	Your score
1		2		3		7		4	
6		5		8		18		9	
13		12		10		20		11	
15		14		16		22		17	
24		23		25		28		19	
27		26		32		30		21	
33		34						29	
35		36						31	

Write down your score total for EACH COLUMN in the corresponding box below.

Step 3: Convert the scores

Now turn your score for each aspect into a percentage. To do this, multiply your score for each column by the number in the corresponding box in Table A1.4 below. For example, if you scored a total of 20 for Aspect 2, multiply your score of 20 by 2.5, using a calculator if necessary: $20 \times 2.5 = 50$ per cent. Note that for Aspects 3 and 4, the multiplier is a different number.

Table A1.4 Score conversion

Aspect 1	Aspect 2	Aspect 3	Aspect 4	Aspect 5
2. 5	2. 5	3. 33	3. 33	2. 5

Write your percentage for each column in the boxes below.

Step 4: Create a bar chart

Now transfer your percentages on to bar chart A1.1. Look at the scale on the left of the chart and the labels on each column. Draw a line corresponding to your percentage for each aspect on the appropriate column.

When you have constructed your bar chart, the height of each bar will correspond to your percentage score for each aspect of learning and studying. This is the PROFILE of your overall approach to learning at the moment. Now you need to know what your profile means.

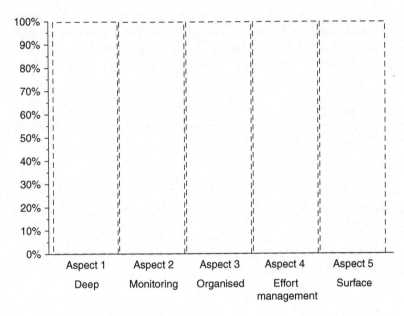

Bar chart A1.1 Blank chart

Step 5: Understand that your profile is not a perfect fit and can change

It is important to realise that standardised questionnaires like the one you have just completed will not reflect perfectly your individual perspectives and experiences. Your profile will be like an off-the-peg suit rather than one that has been made to fit *you* (and no one else). Your profile is a *guide* to your approach to learning and while it may not fit exactly, it will help you to identify what you need to work on to improve your approach to good effect. It is important to realise, too, that this profile describes how you see yourself learning *just now*. How you learn can change: it is up to you.

Step 6: Identify the five aspects of learning and studying

Within the *Approaches to Learning and Studying Inventory* there are sets of statements which cover **FIVE** different aspects of learning and studying. The bar chart you produced indicates your relative position on each of these aspects. These five aspects are explained in Table A1.5. Read this now to see what each bar on your chart refers to. You will need to refer to the table again later in Step 7.

An *ideal* pattern of scores would show high scores on the first four aspects of learning – *deep, monitoring study, organised studying and effort management*. Conversely, a high score on the *surface approach* alone indicates a pattern that requires serious attention. However, most people have rather mixed patterns; some of the most common are discussed below. Bear in mind that the aspects of learning that make up an overall approach have much more to do with *attitudes* than anything else. If you believe that learning is simply the intake of information, then this will be reflected in the way you go about your studies. If

Table A1.5 Five aspects of learning and studying

Five aspects of learning and studying
Aspect 1: Deep approach
This aspect of learning is called the deep approach, although it is one aspect of an overall approach to learning and studying of the same name. It covers the characteristics set out below.
Intention to understand for yourself:
• working out for yourself the meaning of what you have to learn
• finding out for yourself exactly what an author means.

Relating ideas:
• trying to make sense of things by linking them to knowledge you already have
• coming across ideas when reading that set you off on long chains of thought
• trying to relate ideas you come across to other topics or other courses whenever possible
• in making sense of new ideas, relating them to practical or real-life contexts.

Use of evidence:
• attaching importance to following an argument or seeing the reason behind things
• looking at evidence carefully to reach your own conclusions.

Aspect 2: Monitoring study
This aspect of learning – monitoring study – covers the three characteristics set out below.

Monitoring study effectiveness:
• checking a finished piece of work to see it meets requirements
• thinking about what you want to get out of your studies so as to keep your work well focused.

Monitoring understanding:
• trying a different approach if you find you're not understanding things well enough
• going over assignments to check your reasoning and see that it makes sense
• paying careful attention to any advice or feedback in order to improve your understanding.

Table A1.5 (cont.)

Monitoring generic skills:
- when communicating ideas, thinking over how well you've got your points across
- not just focusing on the topic of an essay or report, but also on trying to improve your writing skill
- trying to find better ways of tracking down relevant information in your subject.

Aspect 3: Organised studying
This aspect of learning – organised study – covers the two characteristics set out below.

Study organisation:
- being quite systematic and organised when you are studying
- preparing for classes in advance.

Time management:
- getting down to work when you need to
- prioritising your time to make sure you can fit everything in
- organising your study time carefully to make the best use of it
- working steadily during the course, rather than just leaving things until the last minute.

Aspect 4: Effort management
This aspect of learning – effort management – covers the characteristics set out below.

Effort:
- trying hard to do as well as possible
- working hard even when things aren't going very well
- putting a lot of effort into studying
- pushing yourself to do a good job.

Concentration:
- finding no difficulty in concentrating on the work you are doing
- keeping yourself focused even when something is boring.

Aspect 5: Surface approach
This aspect of learning and studying is called the surface approach, although it is one aspect of an overall approach to learning and studying of the same name. It covers the characteristics set out below.

Memorising without understanding:
- learning over and over things that don't really make much sense
- having trouble in making sense of the things you have to remember.

Unreflective studying:
- going through the motions of studying without really seeing where you're going
- learning things without thinking about the best way to work.

Fragmented knowledge:
- not seeing how the parts of a topic combine into a meaningful whole
- feeling that you've learned lots of unrelated bits and pieces.

Unthinking acceptance:
- tending to take what's taught at face value without questioning it much
- not thinking through topics for yourself and instead relying on what's taught.

you are studying because of personal interest in the subject and want to apply new concepts and ideas at work, this will be reflected in the way you approach learning tasks.

Modifying your approach, then, will involve placing your attitudes under scrutiny and, if necessary, adopting and practising new skills that are consistent with your new ways of thinking about learning. Skills and techniques need to be underpinned by attitudes that drive you to truly embrace them and use them because *that's the way you think now*. It is a self-sustaining system.

Step 7: Identifying your current profile

Study carefully bar charts A1.2 – A1.7. They are idealised to make each one easily distinguishable from the others. In most cases the chart you created will be less well-defined than these. Decide which of the charts shown is *most like* the one you created from your own scores on the inventory. Then look up the interpretation for that approach to studying and learning.

Active deep approach

If the lines on your graph are like those in bar chart A1.2 – high in the **deep approach** and **monitoring** columns, with average levels in the **organised study** and/or **effort management** columns – you have a 'good' approach to learning, that is, an *active deep approach*.

1. You learn with the intention of understanding.
2. You are interested in the content of a course and in learning for yourself, just as much as you are in grades or level of academic performance.
3. You are actively interested in what you are studying and engage personally with learning materials and resources.

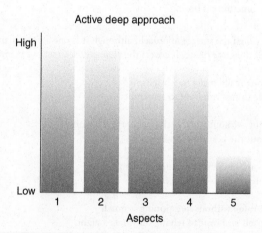

Bar chart A1.2 Active deep approach

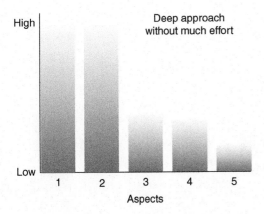

Bar chart A1.3 Deep approach without much effort

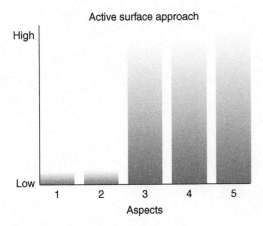

Bar chart A1.4 Active surface approach

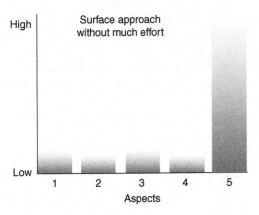

Bar chart A1.5 Surface approach without much effort

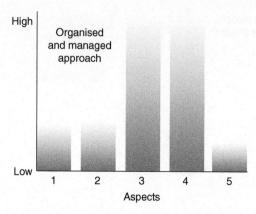

Bar chart A1.6 Organised and managed approach

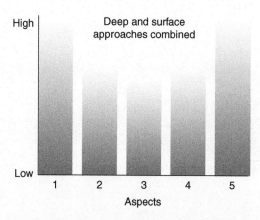

Bar chart A1.7 Deep and surface approaches combined

4. You use your prior knowledge when learning to help you understand new knowledge but you examine both the prior knowledge and the new knowledge with which you are being presented.
5. You question and use evidence critically; you seek out the main points and aim to gain an overview; you draw conclusions.
6. You see the purpose of a task or its use in a wider context than the study situation.
7. You monitor the effectiveness of your studies to ensure that your work meets your own requirements as well as assessment demands.
8. You monitor your understanding of the material you are studying, check your own reasoning and pay attention to feedback.
9. You also monitor general skills such as communication and finding learning resources.

Strength in the **organised study** column shows that you are:

- systematic, prepare for study sessions, organise your time, prioritise, and work steadily through a course.

Strength in the **effort management** column shows that you are:

- able to direct your efforts and to concentrate; you push yourself and keep going even when things aren't going too well; you don't seem to find concentration a problem and can force yourself to keep focused even when you are bored by what you are studying.

There is usually room for improvement, however! Is your 'surface approach' column too high? Could you improve on study organisation?

Suggested action plan

Look again at the descriptions in *Five aspects of learning and studying* to identify specific areas in which you could be stronger and then follow the action plan for *Deep approach without much effort*.

Deep approach without much effort

If you showed strength in the **deep approach** and **monitoring** columns, but little in the **organised study** or **effort management** columns, your profile is similar to that of learners who have adopted a deep approach but who are less well organised and do not manage their efforts as effectively as they could. You have a *deep approach without much effort*.

Suggested action plan

1. If your profile lacks strength in the area of **organised study** you are likely to improve your learning by working on this. Disorganised study wastes time while deep learning takes longer. You may need to adopt techniques to produce efficiencies to avoid overload. If you lack strength in **effort management**, getting down to work may be easier if you are more disciplined *and* more flexible. Setting aside study time is important. If you are finding it hard to 'get into' a study session, however, then be flexible and re-order your tasks so that you can start with a short or relatively easy one.
2. Look at the grouped statements under *Five aspects of learning and studying* and identify areas where you know you can make improvements. Use the relevant study skills advice in this book to develop good learning practices.
3. If the height of your **surface approach** column is too high, follow the suggested action plan for *Surface approach without much effort*.

Active surface approach

If your graph shows a high level in the **surface approach** column, with moderate or high levels in the **organised study** and **effort management** columns, you have the characteristics of a learner who has adopted an *active surface approach*.

1. You may approach study without much sense of purpose.
2. You may be concerned less with understanding learning material than with memorising information with a view to reproducing it when required, for example, in assignments and tests.
3. Your learning appears to be unreflective (you may accept information rather unthinkingly) and you may feel that your knowledge of a topic is fragmented.
4. You are not one to stray beyond the syllabus of a course.

However, the moderate levels of study organisation and effort management mean that you are fairly organised and may manage your efforts quite well. Learners with an active surface approach may not succeed in the way that they would like to and wonder why. Your study organisation and effort management are strengths to build on, placing you in an excellent position to spend time digging deeper into ideas, linking them to your own experience and applying them at work.

Suggested action plan

To improve how you go about your learning and to achieve more from it, follow the suggested action plan for *Surface approach without much effort*.

Surface approach without much effort

If your graph shows a high level in the surface approach column and rather low levels in all the others, you have adopted a *surface approach without much effort*. Your profile is similar to that of a learner who has adopted an active surface approach, but it differs in that you are less well organised and do not manage your efforts as effectively as you could.

Suggested action plan

1. Conduct an 'attitude check'. What are your beliefs and attitudes towards learning and studying? Are they consistent with the kind of learning that can change the way a person thinks and behaves? Seek support if necessary from teachers or peers.
2. Look at the descriptions under *Five aspects of learning and studying* and identify areas where you know you can make improvements. Pay particular attention

to the characteristics of the deep approach. You will need to work on trying to gain a deeper understanding of the material you study and learning to question. Read Chapter 6 *Thinking skills* and concentrate in particular on the topic of critical thinking.

3. Consider your motives for studying. These may be affecting your approach and your engagement. Did you enrol on your course because you wanted to develop knowledge and skills you can use in your career; to study business and management in depth; to develop yourself? Or did you enrol to prove yourself to others or because you want a business and management qualification (or were told you needed one), or because studying a business and management course would improve your CV? It will be hard to engage with learning if you are not very interested in the content of your course. Perhaps you can redefine your motives so that they are more constructive. For example, there is nothing wrong with wanting a business and management qualification but you would probably not want to gain the qualification without also gaining real knowledge.

4. It may be that you find it easier to learn using a highly practical approach. If so, you are particularly likely to benefit from opportunities to apply your learning. You can do this even if you work only part-time by relating what you are learning to practical situations. If you work full-time, then negotiate opportunities preferably in conjunction with a coach or mentor. When you 'see' how an idea can be used at work, you may find you engage more with course content and find it more interesting.

5. If you have not already enrolled on a particular course or course option, consider the type of learning situation that might best help you. In particular, if you are studying part-time and especially if you are studying at a distance, you might prefer a course that brings you into regular contact, face-to-face or online, with your teachers or peers. This can help with motivation and provide opportunities to discuss your work with others: conversations about learning material with other learners on the same course aid understanding. Whether you are a full-time student or studying part-time, starting or joining a study group or finding a study buddy is helpful.

See *Study buddies* in Chapter 2; see *Organising and running groups* in Chapter 8

6. Ensure that you have chosen a course that is at the appropriate level for you: the material you are studying needs to be sufficiently challenging to be engaging. Too little challenge can lead to boredom; too much challenge may result in the feeling that the effort needed to understand the learning material is not worth making.

Organised and managed approach

If the lines on your graph are high in the **organised study** and **effort management** columns, and are higher than those in the other three columns, your approach to learning is neither deep nor surface. Rather, you may be concerned to excel at your studies and be successful, but perhaps at the expense of thorough engagement with ideas, meaning and understanding. This can be thought of as an *organised and managed approach* to study and learning.

1. You are organised and systematic, prepare for study sessions, organise your time, prioritise, and work steadily through a course.
2. You direct and manage your efforts, channel your endeavours and push yourself.
3. You put effort into your studies and keep going even when things aren't going too well.
4. You don't seem to find concentration a problem and can force yourself to keep focused even when you are bored by what you are studying.

When the characteristics of organised studying and effort management *predominate*, however, you may be someone who is very keen to succeed in terms of course grades but whose understanding may not be equal to that of a deep learner.

These two aspects of studying – being organised and working hard – are excellent characteristics. But if they are the main characteristics, that is, if your line in the deep approach column is lower, you may not be making the most of your study organisation and effort management in terms of knowledge gain. Consider the difference between *efficient* and *effective*. A driver can be a thoroughly efficient driver, negotiating a difficult road with skill and precision. But the efficient performance will not be very effective if the person is driving down a road that doesn't go to the appropriate destination. You may get high assessment grades but will your understanding be sufficiently deep and comprehensive for you to be able to transfer your knowledge to the workplace – the place where it 'needs to go'?

Suggested action plan

Follow the suggested action plan for *Surface approach without much effort*.

Deep and surface approaches combined

You have an unusual but rather problematic approach to learning, with high levels in the deep and surface columns and moderate levels in the other three – monitoring, organised study and effort management. Your profile is that of *deep and surface approaches combined*. Learners possessing this approach seem to fare worse on courses. Because the profile seems contradictory and implausible, a good deal of research has been conducted into this pattern. The approach seems to be due to a misunderstanding of what is involved in learning and a lack of awareness of how to use the support and advice available, or that you sense a contradiction between the ways you want to learn and what you feel you have to do to get good marks.

Suggested action plan

1. See Items 1 and 2 under the Suggested action plan for *Surface approach without much effort*. Item 1 is of particular importance.
2. Explore what is involved in learning with the help of someone – your teacher or tutor, or even other learners. Read or re-read Chapter 3 *How you learn*. Explore, too, any personal conflicts or anxieties you may have about learning or the learning context.
3. Make a concerted effort to find out what study advice and support is available and then use it. You have everything to gain from adopting new and different study habits and practices.
4. Remember that you have strengths to draw on. You can use them as you discover what is involved in learning.

Other profiles

The most common learning profiles have been outlined together with one rather rare one, the combined approach. If your profile does not fit any of these, don't worry. Study the descriptions under *Five aspects of learning and studying* and try to identify your strengths and weaknesses. Discuss these with your teacher or tutor, and together work out some priorities for action. With good support you should be able to try out new strategies and tactics and abandon old ones.

© Tyler, S. and Entwistle, N.J.
Modified and reproduced with permission, The Open University (2015; Tyler and Entwistle, 2007)

References

Tyler, S. and Entwistle, N.J. (2007) Approaches to learning and studying inventory: self-score version, in Tyler, S. (ed), *The manager's good study guide*, 3rd edn, Milton Keynes, The Open University.

Effective writing

Formal writing should be concise, authoritative and credible. Poor construction, spelling errors and incorrect grammar and word choices detract from these qualities. They obscure meaning and create a negative impression of the work. This appendix shows you how to avoid common mistakes. For example, many students find the use of apostrophes confusing while those whose first language is not English experience a number of difficulties, in particular, with choosing appropriate prepositions (the troublesome little words such as *to, of, with, in* and *from*).

Scan this appendix and select what you need to improve your writing. No prior knowledge of grammatical terms is needed: where necessary, examples are given together with tips and tricks.

Basic rules

Use the 'active' voice. 'Active' and 'passive' voices describe how a subject and verb work together in a sentence. Compare the following sentences.

Sentence 1: SuperEkom employed 1,000 additional staff last year following sustained sales growth. (11 words)

Sentence 2: Last year 1,000 additional staff were employed by SuperEkom following sustained sales growth. (13 words)

Sentence 1 uses the active voice. The subject, SuperEkom, performed the verb 'action' of employing. Sentence 2 uses the passive voice. The subject is '1,000 additional staff' who were 'acted upon' by the verb. Using the active voice aids clarity and often reduces word count. It's advisable to use one verb tense predominantly and consistently, employing other tenses as circumstances dictate (past – *it was*; present – *it is*; future – *it will be*; or conditional – *it would be*).

Avoid jargon words and phrases. Jargon is used by people in the same line of work who know what they mean but the words are often inaccessible to 'outsiders' (think of medical and legal jargon). A second meaning is the language characteristic of a group: it doesn't have to be technical or specialised. Its use can be an attempt to appear informed (think of psychobabble). Some business examples are: to *disincent*; to *componentise*; to *disintermediate*; to *descope*; to *fail forward*; *long tail*, *disruptive innovation*; *ladder up*. Say what you really mean in plain language.

Repetition should normally be avoided. It often arises through poor structure. When written work contains a number of repetitions the writer has probably not developed a logical structure for a message, case or argument. Write something once, clearly.

Use paragraphs, headings and side headings. They break up a text into shorter, reader-friendly chunks. Headings and side headings indicate what the following text is (mainly) about and guide the reader. If you find it hard to create appropriate headings it may because too many different points are included.

> **ACTIVITY A2.1** Read again the messages shown in Chapter 5, Activity 5.1. In the first one, identify examples of the passive voice, jargon and repetition. Then identify where the second message uses the active voice and how the writer has overcome jargon. Count the number of repetitions in Message 2 and how many paragraphs each message uses.

You probably identified the examples shown in Table A2.1.

Sort your material into categories. Consider what your readers 'must know', 'should know' and what might be 'nice to know'. Be prepared to abandon everything except 'must know' if your text needs to be very concise.

Use a logical structure. Your points will flow more naturally. Put the main points first in a text or each section of text.

Be specific. Don't write *One major project was delivered a little later than we expected* but, instead, *One five-year project missed the deadline by two months*. The same number of words or fewer can deliver more precise information (and

Table A2.1 Voice, jargon and repetition

	Message 1		Message 2	
Feature	**Example**		**Feature**	**Example**
Passive voice	'has been completed and indicates that'		Active voice	'is'
Jargon	'net outturn position'		Non-jargon	'profit'
Repetition	Sentence 1: 'adverse variance of £3.2m' Sentence 3: '£3.2m shortfall'		Repetition	None
Paragraphs	1		Paragraphs	3

precision aids authority). Take care, however, to place words correctly. In the sentence *The manager was told about the accident yesterday* it is not clear whether the accident happened yesterday or the manager was told yesterday. Reword sentences to convey the precise meaning, for example: *The manager was told about the accident that happened yesterday* or *The manager was told yesterday about the accident*. Delete modifiers such as *very, really, totally, vast* and *soon*. If necessary, replace them with more precise wording to specify time, quantity and so on. Also avoid or delete expressions that convey nothing, such as *at this point in time* or *going forward*. Use *'now'* or *'in future'* (or better still, say *when* in future).

Avoid tautology. *Future plans, in addition,* and *also, unfilled vacancy,* and *new innovation* all say the same thing twice.

Be concise but not too concise. Your text should be concise but over-conciseness can lead to ambiguity. The sentence *We coated the products with welding marks* would be better expressed as *We coated the products because the manufacturing process left welding marks*. A memorable way of thinking about over-conciseness is to consider the sign frequently found in metro stations: *Dogs must be carried on escalators* and the cartoons it has spawned showing people searching for dogs to carry!

Use diagrams, tables and graphs where appropriate. Although you need to describe them in your text, they express information concisely. You can say: *Graph 1.1 shows the three-fold increase in turnover between 2010 and 2017 from €X to €XX.* The graph gives the detail.

Using apostrophes

Misunderstandings about the use of the apostrophe are all too evident. It is not unusual to see advertisements such as *The product comes complete with it's own carrying case*. Some writers seem to assume that almost every *s* on the end of a word should have an apostrophe before or after it, or that no word needs an apostrophe.

The first barrier to overcoming problems with using the apostrophe is knowing that you have a problem with it. Here is a quick diagnostic test.

ACTIVITY A2.2 Read the ten sentences below. By each apostrophe in each sentence put a tick or a cross to indicate whether you think the apostrophe has been used correctly or not.

1. It's stark exterior looked forbidding.
2. The womens' cloakroom is over there.
3. The red coat is her's.
4. My organisations' logo is a black and white shield.
5. The manager's were furious about the change's.
6. There was a long queue for the lady's changing rooms in the clothes shop.
7. I always think of accountancy primarily as a mens' profession.
8. This building was designed in the 1820's.
9. I have lots of CD's at home.
10. Consultancy firm Joop Coopes has relocated. Coope's old office block is for sale.

There are 11 apostrophes in the 10 sentences. For each tick you made score one mark and for each cross score zero. Add up your total score. If your total score was one or more, you need to read the following section.

All 11 apostrophes were wrongly used. Here's what you need to know in order to use apostrophes correctly.

1. The apostrophe signals missing letters.

The apostrophe is used to show where letters have been missed out from a word. It signifies the shortened form of *it is* or *it has*, as in *It's plain to see that …* or *It's been months since I last heard from you.*

Other examples are: *who's* (who is), *they're* (they are), *there's* (there is), *I'll* (I will), *wouldn't* (would not), *don't* (do not), *you're* (you are), *she's* (she is), *we're* (we are), *I'm* (I am), and so on.

2. The apostrophe signals possession.

The apostrophe is used as a possessive, denoting *of* or *belonging to*, as in the examples below.

1. John's new car was red. (The new car *belonging to* John was red.)
2. The purchaser's complaint was upheld. (The complaint *of* the purchaser was upheld.)
3. Purchasers' statutory rights are not affected. (The statutory rights *of* purchasers are not affected.)

Note the two different positions of the apostrophe. In Sentences 1 and 2 there is just one John and just one purchaser, so the apostrophe goes before the *s*. In Sentence 3 there are two or more purchasers, so the apostrophe goes after the *s* (purchasers is plural: putting the apostrophe before the *s* would make it singular).

Note two special cases. The first is when a word is singular but ends with an s. This often happens with surnames. Suppose you had a colleague called Jones, then his desk would be Jones's desk (Jones' desk is also acceptable). It would never be written as Jone's desk. The second special case is that of plurals which do not end in an *s*. Some examples are *women, men, people, children* and *staff*. Here, an apostrophe and an *s* are added, as in *the men's cloakroom* (the cloakroom of the men).

You may have wondered why *its* doesn't follow the possessive apostrophe rule, as in *After the merger with SuperEkom, we adopted its systems for staff recruitment*. The answer is that, like *hers, ours, yours* and *theirs, its* without an apostrophe is a possessive pronoun. Possessive pronouns are already possessive and there is no need to indicate possession. You must write *hers, ours, yours, theirs* and *its* without an apostrophe. The remaining possessive pronouns – *mine* and *his* – do not cause a problem.

ACTIVITY A2.3 Revisit Activity A2.2 and correct each apostrophe applying what you have understood from the explanations above.

Adapted and used with permission, The Open University
(Tyler 2007)

Using punctuation

Lack of punctuation or its inappropriate use can lead to text being misunderstood or, at least, readers having to re-read a sentence more than once.

Commas, colons and semicolons

Consider these sentences.

The new manager told staff he enjoyed cooking his family and his pet animals.
Jane worried about the cost of her purchases caught the bus home.

Commas avoid ambiguity and unintended comedy. Often you will need to reword a sentence to make the meaning clear.

ACTIVITY A2.4 Correct the sentences about the manager and Jane to make the meaning clear.

You probably introduced commas and perhaps rearranged the words to make the meanings clear:

The new manager told staff he enjoyed cooking, his family and his pet animals.
Worried about her purchases, Jane caught the bus home.

Colons act much like an equals sign and are used like this:

The new office is well-located: it is near the railway station and close to amenities.

Colons show a connection between two points in a sentence.

ACTIVITY A2.5 In the following two sentences which one uses a colon correctly and which incorrectly?
1. The new office is well-located: it has a lift.
2. The new office is well-located: it is two minutes from the railway station.

The colon is wrongly used in Sentence 1 because the office location has nothing to do with the lift. The colon is correctly used in Sentence 2.

Semicolons are used to connect two closely related sentences when, for example, separate sentences would be too abrupt. A semicolon creates a longer separation than a comma. It is useful when setting out complicated lists. Using semicolons creates appropriate separations between items.

ACTIVITY A2.6 To demonstrate to yourself how semicolons disambiguate a sentence, replace all the semicolons with commas in this sentence:

For sale: padded high chair that can be made into a table; potty; rocking horse; refrigerator; spring coat; size 8; dog collar.

What can the padded high chair be made into?

Hyphens help readers to extract meaning. In Pennsylvania, USA, drivers are banned from texting on mobile phones while driving. When the law came into effect, billboards announced confusingly:

No texting law is in effect.

ACTIVITY A2.7 Consider these three sentences.
1. The two year long projects are progressing well.
2. The small aircraft carrier will be ready in 2021.
3. The product is made in a carbon steel plastic extruder.

In Sentence 1 how many projects are running and for how long? In Sentence 2 is the aircraft carrier small or is it designed for small aircraft? In Sentence 3 what is the extruder made of? Now place a hyphen in the correct place in each sentence.

If you found the activity hard, it is. Only the authors of Sentences 1 and 2 know where the hyphen should go: *two-year* or *year-long, small-aircraft* or *aircraft-carrier*. In Sentence 3 it's possible to guess that the author is talking about a device made of *carbon-steel* to extrude plastic and so place the hyphen where it belongs. Conventions have a purpose: to avoid ambiguity.

The 'rule' for hyphens is that they are needed when two or more adjectives (descriptive words) or nouns (names of things) cannot be separated without resulting in ambiguity. One trick is to use each adjective or noun in the combination on its own: *The two projects ... The year projects ... The long projects ...* If none of these conveys what is meant, one or more hyphens are needed, for example: *The two-year-long projects ...* or *The two year-long projects ...* depending on the meaning.

Take particular care with compound adjectives containing the words *free, best, least, worst, most* and *least*. Without a hyphen – or a comma – you may convey what you did not intend. *There is a need for more careful analysis of data* can mean a demand for more care in analysing data (implying a lack of care hitherto) or a call for more analysis. Consider the meaning of the sentence with the insertion of, first, a comma and then a hyphen:

> There is a need for more, careful analysis of data.
> There is a need for more-careful analysis of data.

Misplaced modifiers

Misplaced modifiers are confusing to readers. A modifier is a word or phrase that provides a description or adds information in a sentence. An example favoured by teachers of grammar is a joke by the comedian Groucho Marx in the 1930 film Animal Crackers.

> The other day, I shot an elephant in my pyjamas. How he got into my pyjamas, I'll never know.

Modifiers such as *in my pyjamas* need to be placed directly beside the thing that is being modified, in this case, *I*. This usually means rewriting the sentence: *I shot an elephant the other day while I was in my pyjamas.*

Arguably the commonest misplaced modifier is 'only'.

ACTIVITY A2.8 Consider the following sentences and indicate what 'only' is modifying in each case and what each of the sentences mean as a result.

1. Only the patients were told to expose their faces to UV light for five minutes.
2. The patients were only told to expose their faces to UV light for five minutes.

3. The patients were told only to expose their faces to UV light for five minutes.
4. The patients were told to expose only their faces to UV light for five minutes.
5. The patients were told to expose their faces to UV light for only five minutes.
6. The patients were told to expose their faces to UV light for five minutes, only.

In Sentence 1, *only* modifies *patients*, implying that there were other categories of people who could be told. In Sentence 2, *only* modifies *told* implies that the patients could have received more information. It's best not to place *only* in a verb phrase. In Sentence 3 *only* could be modifying *told* or *to expose*. In Sentence 4, *only* modifies *faces* implying that no other part of the body should be exposed. In Sentence 5 *only* modifies *five* specifying the exposure time. In Sentence 6, placing *only* after *five minutes* provides emphasis. Which meaning do you think the writer intended in each case? Place *only* carefully in your sentences.

Other cases of misplaced modifiers involve putting whole parts of a sentence in the wrong place, as in this example:

Between their induction and the first three-month performance review, line managers should meet new hires weekly.

Between their induction and the first three-month performance review should refer to the new hires. A correct version of the sentence is:

Line managers should meet new hires weekly during the period between induction and the first three-month performance review.

... dangling modifiers

Modifiers *modify something*. Dangling modifiers are left by writers who have forgotten to include the *something* – usually the subject – in the sentence. An example is:

Arriving at the new offices, it was clear the builders had not finished their work.

It is the subject that is (wrongly) modified, rather than the person (omitted by the writer) who arrived at the new offices. The sentence needs a human subject who arrives and to whom it is evident that the builders have not finished work:

When the project manager arrived at the new offices, she saw that the builders had not finished work.

Using modifiers ending in – ly

Modifiers ending in *ly* such as *slowly, quickly, immediately* need to be placed correctly (just like the placement of only) to avoid ambiguity.

> **ACTIVITY A2.9** Consider the two sentences below and decide what each means, based on the position of the adverb *immediately*:
>
> 1. It was decided immediately to end production.
> 2. It was decided to end production immediately.

The meaning of Sentence 1 is that the decision was made immediately but there is no indication of when production ended or will end. Sentence 2 states when production stopped (immediately) but not when the decision was made. Place the modifying word so that the sentence conveys what you mean.

Making comparisons

Adverbs modify the meaning of other words and can be used to compare things. When used in this way, some (but not all) take the endings *-er* and *-est*, as in few, fewer and fewest. The three forms have names: *positive* (even if the adverb is negative, such as *poor*); *comparative* (poorer) and *superlative* (poorest). There are a number of irregular forms such as:

Positive	Comparative	Superlative
well	better	best
much	more	most
little	less	least
badly	worse	worst

The general rule for regular and irregular adverbs is that you use the comparative form when comparing *two* things and superlative form when *more than two things* are involved. Thus:

Claudia works hard. Giuseppe works harder. Patricia works hardest.

Comparative and superlative adverbs should not normally be used in conjunction with words that quantify: *more, most, less* and *least*. It is incorrect to write or say *more better* or *most fastest*. *Less fast* may sound right but *slower* is the correct comparative form. Use *few* or *fewer* when referring to anything that can be counted and *less* when referring to amounts.

Fewer than one in 20 customers leaves without making a purchase.
We now add less salt to sauces to comply with World Health Organisation guidelines.

Don't lose sight of the subject!

Nothing detracts from clarity more than a writer losing track of the subject of a sentence. (*I* is the subject in *I go* and *go* is the verb.) A typical example is:

> If customer records are lost by administration staff they will have to set up new accounts.

Here, the subject is *customer records*. The verb, *will*, should refer to the subject but does not. It is easy to see this if you remove all the words in the sentence except for the subject and the verb phrase (called a verb clause):

> Customer records will have to set up new accounts.

The writer meant either:

> If customer records are lost by administration staff, customers will have to set up new accounts

> OR

> If customer records are lost by administration staff, staff will have to set up new accounts.

ACTIVITY A2.10 Reword these three sentences which have similar problems.

1. Due to increasing problems with litter louts and vandals we must ask anyone with relatives buried in the graveyard to do their best to keep them in order.
2. To encourage the recruits to learn from experienced employees, managers let them work on the marketing project.
3. Made to work for pitifully low wages and live in squalor, gang bosses are found guilty of subjecting migrant workers to servitude.

In the first, often-quoted sentence from an unknown source and the second one the writers have lost track of what *them* refers to. In the third, one whole chunk (clause) of the sentence – *Made to work for pitifully low wages and live in squalor* – has been placed so that it wrongly refers to the subject of the sentence (*gang bosses*), rather than the migrant workers to whom it *does* refer. You probably reworded the sentences like this:

1. Due to increasing problems with litter louts and vandals we must ask anyone with relatives buried in the graveyard to do their best to keep the graves in order.

2. The managers let the recruits work on the marketing project to encourage them to learn from experienced employees.
3. Gang bosses of migrant workers made to work for pitifully low wages and live in squalor are found guilty of subjecting migrant workers to servitude.

Word choices

Choosing grammatically correct words helps your work sound more professional.

Who and that

That has become one of the most overused words of the twenty-first century so far, not only replacing *who* and *which* but used repetitively in sentences as a linking device.

> It was found that the people that shopped in the store and that complained that the advertising misled them were all over 50. (23 words)

It's clearer and more concise to write:

> Shoppers who complained about misleading advertisements were all over 50. (10 words).

The word *who* should be used whenever a person or people are referred to. It is acceptable to use *who* for anything with human-like qualities or characteristics, for example, a pet animal, a team or group of people, or an organisation when you implicitly refer to the staff.

That and which

The conventions for using *which* and *that* are simple: if you can remove the phrase following *which* or *that* from the sentence and it still makes sense, then you should use *which*. If you cannot, then you should use *that*. Here's an example:

> The company, which advertised its product as having health benefits, was forced to withdraw its claims when customers complained that the product did not improve their health.

Note that the phrase *which advertised its products as having health benefits* can be removed. The use of *that* in the sentence ('…that the product did not improve their health') is a little more tricky to assess. You *could* remove that part of the sentence and it would still make sense. So try another trick. Replace *that* with *which* and see if it still makes sense. In the above example, it doesn't.

ACTIVITY A2.11 Using the tricks, correctly place *that* or *which* in the gaps in the following sentences:

1. The customers complained __ the advertisement misled them.
2. The wording __ attracted numerous complaints was changed.
3. The company, __ had been not been profitable for a year, closed at the end of September.

The answers are 1) *that*; 2) *which* (although *that* might not be thought incorrect); 3) *which*.

Like, such as, as if

Like is also an overused word often wrongly used. *Like* is often used instead of *such as*. The choice of *such as* or *like* depends on whether you want to *compare* (like) or *include* (such as). *As if* should be used for hypothetical statements, as in: *It's as if the customers missed the in-store advertisement.*

ACTIVITY A2.12 Consider the following sentences and decide whether *like, such as* or *as if* is correct in each case.

1. Customers like Brand X cereals <u>like</u> we sell.
2. The company produces quality items <u>like</u> Footcladder boots and shoes.
3. The company manufactures products <u>like</u> snow tyres.
4. It's <u>like</u> the advertising campaign was a waste of time.
5. We stock eco-friendly building products <u>like</u> limecrete and wool for insulation.
6. We care about greenhouse gas emissions <u>like</u> CO_2.

Like is wrongly used in Sentences 1, 2, 3, 5 and 6 because the writers of the sentences do not mean to make a comparison. Rather, they are trying to give examples. *Such as* is the correct term to use where you want to *include*. If you use *like* you mean that something is *similar to* what mentioned, but not the actual thing. What is referred to as *being like* in these sentences is not the cereals, Footcladder boots and shoes, snow tyres, limecrete and wool and CO_2, but something similar. This is not what the writers meant.

In Sentence 4, *as if* should be used instead of *like* because no comparison is being made. Consider using other words and phrases instead of *like*, depending on whether you want to compare or include, such as:

including	similar to	for example
in addition to	compared with	in particular
along with	in contrast to	in this case
among	resembling	such as

Who and whom

Writers and speakers are often confused about when to use 'who' and 'whom'. Always use 'whom' after prepositions (such as *to, with, by, near, in* and *on*):

> This is the person to whom I gave the instructions.

It may sound very formal to say or write 'to whom' but it avoids the problem of placing the preposition *to* at the end of the sentence. It's wise to glue together 'whom' with words such as *to, with, from* and *beside*, and think of them as a unit.

I, me, myself, ourselves

Writers (and speakers) often get into a muddle about when to use the pronouns *I, me* and *myself* (and *you, your, yourself; s/he, her/his, herself/himself;* and *they, them, themselves*).

> **ACTIVITY A2.13** Consider the following sentences and replace any wrong pronouns with the correct ones. Can you devise a trick for assessing the right ones to use?
>
> 1. Marco and myself considered the report.
> 2. The director gave his comments to Marco and I.
> 3. Marco and me gave our response the following day.

In Sentence 1, Marco and myself are the subject of the sentence (we did the considering – the verb). Remove *Marco and,* and see if the sentence still makes sense: *Myself considered the report.* It should be clear that the correct word to use is *I,* so the sentence should be written as: *Marco and I considered the report.*

In Sentence 2, again remove *Marco and.* It no longer makes sense: *The director gave his comments to I.* Using *myself* would be incorrect too. The sentence should be written as: *The director gave his comments to Marco and me.*

In Sentence 3, again remove *Marco and.* The result *Me gave our response the following day* is wrong because you cannot use *me* as the subject of the sentence. The sentence should be written as: *Marco and I gave our response the following day.*

The singular they

A further problem with pronouns occurs when you are referring to one person, who must be a he or a she (English has no gender-neutral, third-person singular pronoun). It's relatively common to refer to one person as *they* but it can lead to confusion.

> **ACTIVITY A2.14** Consider the following sentences and say who *their, they, themselves* and *them* might refer to in each case.

> When a manager helps make a case for their direct reports, they can then get promoted and they receive a bonus themselves. It helps them rise in the organisation.
>
> How might you rewrite the sentence?

It's hard to decipher the meaning of the sentences and adjust the pronouns. You have to make the assumption that *their* refers to the manager; the first *they* refers to the direct reports; the second *they* refers to the manager and *themselves* also refers to the manager. You need to assume, too, that *it* refers to the system of giving managers bonuses for helping direct reports to move up the career ladder. Then the sentence can be reworded to make more sense.

> When a manager helps to make a case for his or her direct reports, the manager receives a bonus if a direct report is promoted. The bonus system for managers helps direct reports rise through the organisation.

If you want to avoid the use of *he* or *she*, then the following form is appropriate:

> When managers help to make a case for their direct reports, the managers receive a bonus when a direct report is promoted. The bonus system for managers helps direct reports rise through the organisation.

The use of *they* with a single subject (in this case *manager*) can generally be avoided by making the subject plural (*managers*) or by referring to a known manager who is a he or she (*My manager receives a bonus when she …*). There is usually a reasonable way to avoid the use of *they*. If you use it, then make sure it's clear to whom you are referring.

Practice and practise

Practice and practise are easily confused. In British English *practice* is a noun (a thing) while *to practise* is a verb. The correct uses are:

> I practised management at the medical practice.
> I am trying to improve my management practices.

If you mean you are becoming more accomplished at something, use *practise* to make your meaning clear: *I'm practising for the race/my presentation tomorrow.*

Effect and affect

These words are similar to practice and practise: *effect* is a noun and *to affect* is a verb. An effect is the consequence or outcome of something; 'to affect' means to have an impact on something:

> The effect of the change was to increase productivity.
> The change affected productivity.

'Effect' can be used as a verb, too. *To effect* means to bring about a consequence or outcome:

The change was effected swiftly.

To choose the right word, first decide on your meaning – to have a consequence, to bring about or to have an impact.

Lie and lay

Grammatical word choices can be difficult when verbs that mean quite different things take the same form in some tenses. Common errors are made with the verbs *to lie* and *to lay*. *To lie* can mean to tell an untruth as well as to position a thing in a horizontal position (there are also related meanings). *To lay* means to put something down. The meaning is somewhat similar to *to lie* but there is an important difference. When you use the verb *to lie* it is *not* followed by an object – a *something*. When you use the verb *to lay* it *must be* followed by an object – a *something*. Here, both verbs are shown in their present, simple past and past perfect tenses.

The report lies on file.
The report lay on file till yesterday.
The report had lain on file for years.
The secretary lays the papers on the desk.
The secretary laid the book on the chair.
The secretary had laid out her case for a pay rise.

Remember: *lie* – no object follows; *lay* – an object always follows.

Lead and led

The words *lead* and *led* cause confusion. Lead, as well as being the name of a metal (when the pronunciation rhymes with *fed*) is a verb – *to lead*, meaning to guide or direct (when the pronunciation rhymes with *bead*). You can lead a team. But when you want to write about leading a team in the past, you need to use *led*: *I led a team*. A useful mnemonic is:

You led me to your leader; now I'll lead you all to mine.

Right, sounds wrong; wrong, sounds right

Writers (and speakers) sometimes use incorrect grammar because it sounds right and avoid correct grammar because it sounds wrong. In the *right, but sounds wrong* category are sentences in which a <u>singular subject</u> is followed by a <u>plural modifier</u>, such as *a <u>list</u> of <u>items</u> is provided*, or *a <u>majority</u> of <u>people</u> likes*. The rule is that the verb used (*is* and *likes* in the examples) must agree with the subject, not the modifier. This produces sentences that are grammatically correct but may sound wrong, such as these:

> A <u>majority</u> of people in Europe <u>lives</u> in cities.
> A large <u>quantity</u> of products <u>is</u> awaiting shipping.
> There <u>is</u> a <u>number</u> of different treatments available.
> A small <u>number</u> of projects <u>presents</u> problems.

Many writers and speakers match the verb to the modifier because it *sounds right* (but is grammatically wrong):

> A <u>majority</u> of people in Europe <u>live</u> in cities.
> A large <u>quantity</u> of products <u>are</u> awaiting shipping.
> There <u>are</u> a <u>number</u> of different treatments available.
> A small <u>number</u> of projects <u>present</u> problems.

Careful writers who want to avoid the problem change the <u>subject</u> of the sentence to match the <u>verb</u> or change the *modifier* to match the subject (or both):

> *Most* <u>people</u> in Europe <u>live</u> in cities.
> *Large* <u>quantities</u> of products <u>are</u> awaiting shipping.
> *Many* <u>products</u> <u>are</u> awaiting shipping.
> *Different* <u>treatments</u> <u>are</u> available.
> *Few* (or *some*, depending on meaning) projects <u>present</u> problems.

A problem writers (and speakers) often have is deciding whether the subject of a sentence is plural or singular. *None*, for example, means *not one*, and is singular; *one* is always singular so *more than one* is also singular, so the following sentences are correct:

> None of the managers is qualified for the task.
> More than one of the managers is qualified for the task.

You might want to write these as:

> No manager is qualified for the task.
> Two or more managers are qualified for the task.

Subject–verb agreement is often poorly handled in sentences beginning with *there*. Many writers (and speakers) follow *there* with a verb in the singular form and then introduce a plural subject, for example:

> There <u>is</u> lots of empty <u>premises</u> in the area.

Overcome such problems by changing sentences so that the subject comes before the verb, for example:

Lots of empty <u>premises</u> <u>exist</u> in the area.

Many subject–verb disagreements arise from the use of contractions of words: it is probably easier to say *there's* than *there're* (these are the contracted forms of *there is* or *there has*, and *there are*). The use of contractions – usually in speech – often leads to completely aberrant grammar. The use of *should've* and *could've* (contractions of *should have* and *could have*) seems to have led to the deviant written forms *should of* and *could of*. English may be flexible, but correct use of verb and tenses remains necessary.

Troublesome prepositions

Prepositions – words such as *of, to, in, at, from* – are words that are 'positioned before' a noun (a thing) and show the noun's relationship to another word in the sentence, as in: The <u>receptionist</u> is *at* the <u>desk</u> *in* the <u>foyer</u>. Common errors are made by non-native speakers of English. But even native English speakers make errors when using prepositional verbs (a verb used with a preposition) that must be followed by an object – a *something* – as in *to compare with* (something).

It is easy to choose the wrong preposition, or the wrong form of a prepositional verb. Table A2.2 shows incorrect examples in common use and their correct forms.

Comprise, consist and compose

The verbs *to comprise* and *consist of* cause problems for unaccomplished writers. Some words already 'contain' the word *of*, as does *comprise*. *Of* can be added *to*

Table A2.2 Examples of incorrect and correct use of prepositions

Incorrect	Correct	Incorrect	Correct
Motivation behind	Motivation *for*	Opposite from	Opposite *to*
Motivated about	Motivated *to*	Contrary with	Contrary *to*
Focus around	Focus *on*	Bored of	Bored *with / by*
Centre around	Centre *on*	Compare to	Compare *with*
Adjacent with	Adjacent *to*	Regardless with	Regardless *of*
Different to/than	Different *from*	In regards with	*With* regard *to*
Similar with	Similar *to*	Based around	Based *on*
Except if	Except *for*	Preparatory for	Preparatory *to*
Sympathise for	Sympathise *with*	Fed up of	Fed up *with*
Discussed about	Discussed	Study about	Study

compose, provided it is used in the construction *is/are/were (etc.) composed of*. The correct uses of *comprise, consist of* and *compose* are:

> The marketing literature is limited: it comprises one A5 leaflet.
> Our limecrete consists of hydraulic lime, sand, aggregate and water.
> Erik composed the text of the advertising material the same day.
> The Federal Republic of Germany is composed of 16 Länder.

It would be incorrect to say:

> The marketing literature comprises of one A5 leaflet.

The verbs *to comprise* and *to consist of* are *inclusive*. When you use them you mean all the items that a thing is made of, composed of or consists of. Thus it would be incorrect to write:

> The countries that make up the UK include England, Scotland, Wales and Northern Ireland.

This would mean there were other countries not mentioned. Use the verb *to include* when you are providing a partial list, for example:

> Our limecrete mix includes sand and aggregate.

The superfluous for and of

The word *for* is often incorrectly added to words and phrases: *for sale* is correct; *for free* is not but is in common use. If you want to qualify *free* you can say what the thing is free of, as in *free of charge, free from conditions, free of tax*. Similarly the words *off, outside, half* do not need to be followed by the word *of*. The sentence *The scaffolding came off of the building in time for the opening* sounds awkward and *of* is unnecessary.

Trouble with numbers

Using numbers in writing can be tricky. This sentence breaks a writing rule:

> €350bn. That's how much the annual cost of natural disasters has risen in three decades.

The rule is simple: never begin a sentence with numbers written as numerals. If you want to begin a sentence with a number, you have to write the number in words. Dates are a particular problem in British English because of the convention of placing the day before the month, such as 16 July. Reconstruct sentences to

Table A2.3 Avoiding number problems

Original sentence	Reworded sentence
€350bn. That's how much the annual cost of natural disasters has risen in three decades.	The annual cost of natural disasters has risen by €350bn in three decades.
Two hundred and eighty seven more workers will be employed.	The company will employ another 287 workers.
16 July is the date set for the meeting.	The date set for the meeting is 16 July.
47 workers have been issued with redundancy notices.	Redundancy notices have been issued to 47 workers.

avoid starting with numerals or writing the number in words. Table A2.3 shows examples of substitutes. Note that in most cases fewer words are used and the meaning is clearer.

Need more help?

If you need more help with English grammar, there are easy-to-follow books. Tips and tricks may differ from those given in this appendix. One book that will make you laugh as you learn is this one:

Parody, A. (2007) Eats, Shites & Leaves: Crap English and How to Use it, London, Michael O'Mara Books. (A 2014 electronic edition is available from commercial sellers such as Amazon and Google Books.)

For punctuation try:

Truss, L. (2009) Eats, Shoots and Leaves: The Zero Tolerance Approach to Punctuation. London, Fourth Estate.

For comprehensive but accessible coverage of English grammar try:

Murphy, R. (2012) English Grammar in Use: A Self-Study Reference and Practice Book for Intermediate Learners of English, 4th edn, Cambridge, Cambridge University Press.
Tyler, S. ed, (2007) *The Manager's Good Study Guide*, 3rd edn, Milton Keynes, The Open University.

124–5; critical writing 190; guidance and checklists 129–31, 163; initial outlines 135–8; interpreting questions 131–3; knowledge gaps 135; process 133–8; structures 138–47; tasks 134; tips 143; understanding requirements 128–31; word counts 145, 147–8; *see also* assignments; argument; assumptions,

plagiarism; citing and referencing
writing: apostrophes 374–6; audience 124–5; clarity 124–7; further reading 390; grammar and word choices 381–8; making comparisons 380; modifiers 378–80; numbers 389–90; prepositions 388–9; punctuation 376–8; rules, principles and conventions

126–7, 372–4; *see also* writing assignments

Yershova, Y., DeJaeghere, J. and Mestenhauser, J. 253, 254, 257, 312
Yorke, M. 3, 8
Yorke, M. and Knight, P.T. 3, 4, 8, 316, 318

Zimmerman, B.J. 69, 70, 81